18850

THE THEOLOGIAN
AND HIS UNIVERSE

N. MAX WILDIERS

THE THEOLOGIAN AND HIS UNIVERSE

Theology and Cosmology
from the Middle Ages
to the Present

THE SEABURY PRESS / NEW YORK

1982
The Seabury Press
815 Second Avenue
New York, N.Y. 10017

Published originally as *Wereldbeeld en Teologie van de Middeleeuwen
tot vandaag* in 1977. Translated from the Dutch by Paul Dunphy. English
translation copyright © by Max Wildiers.

Printed in the United States of America

Library of Congress Cataloging in Publication Data
Wildiers, N.M., 1904-
  The theologian and his universe.

  Translation of: Werelbeeld en teologie.
  Includes bibliographical references and index.
  1. Cosmology—History. 2. Theology—History.
3. Religion and science—History of controversy.
4. Philosophy of nature—History.
I Title.
BD518.D8W5413   261.5'5   82-3257
ISBN 0-8164-0533-6   AACR2

CONTENTS

PREFACE

Our initial reaction on opening this book might well be that theology and cosmology have nothing in common. On closer examination, however, it soon becomes evident that our confrontation with the universe constitutes one of the principal sources of religious consciousness. Moreover, the Bible itself begins with a narrative concerning the world, and theology has from its origin been explicitly concerned with cosmological questions.

This age-old dialogue between the believer and his mysterious surroundings has sometimes led to a harmonious synthesis and sometimes to conflict and alienation. Owing to the rise of the natural sciences and the resulting change in our vision of the universe, the problem of the relation between cosmology and Christian thought has once more aroused considerable interest and can be said to form one of the most fascinating chapters of contemporary intellectual life.

In his profound essay *Religion in the Making*, Alfred North Whitehead argues that "religion is world-loyalty." It seems to me that the great Christian thinkers were always aware of this truth. A theology which ignores this theme soon loses all contact with reality and is reduced to a completely other-worldly affair. What is more, it cuts itself off from the sources of religious consciousness from which it derives its deepest inspiration when it confronts the mysterious depths of the world around us.

The story which is narrated here is by no means that of "The Warfare of Science with Theology." Our intention is more or less the reverse of A. D. White's in his celebrated book. The purpose of the present work is to examine to what extent cosmological views and changes in the generally accepted world picture have influenced the development of Christian theology, particularly in the period from the Middle Ages to the present day. It is my belief that this subject merits the attention not only of the theologian and the historian of religion but also of all who are interested in the history of ideas in the context of the Western tradition.

Finally, I should like to take this opportunity to express my gratitude to all those who assisted me in one way or another in writing this book. In particular I wish to thank Albert J. Zabala, S.J., chairman of the department of Theology at the University of San Francisco for giving me the honor of lecturing for so many years at this University. My thanks also go to William J. Monihan, S.J., whose outstanding knowledge of books was of great help to me. A very special word of thanks has to be given to my friend and colleague, Professor Jan Van der Veken at the University of Louvain, who very kindly read the entire manuscript with a critical eye and made many useful suggestions.

Max Wildiers
Louvain/San Francisco

INTRODUCTION

All human reflection on the deeper meaning of life ultimately revolves round three concepts, or the metaphysical trinity as they have been called: God, man, and world.[1] Each world picture can thus be said to derive its particular character from the manner in which these three concepts are conceived and connected with each other, even when, as in the case of contemporary atheism, one of the three is deleted and the problem is reduced to the relation of man and the cosmos. Philosophy has continually been directed towards reconciling these three concepts and exposing their mutual relations. Each of the three has in turn become the focus of attention. The ancient Greeks, for example, undoubtedly assigned a central position to the concept of cosmos, and for the later Greeks especially, the cosmos was a perfectly ordered whole, a supreme and sacred datum, looked upon with profound respect and endless admiration. Their thought was preeminently cosmocentric and their sensibility preeminently cosmic. For the Pre-Socratics as well as for Plato and Aristole, for the Stoics as well as for the Neo-Platonists, the feeling of being united with the cosmos assumed a predominant position.

According to Karl Löwith, a fundamental change was brought about by Christianity. In the eyes of the Christian the universe acquired a completely different outlook. Cosmic sensibility was totally alien to one desiring to know about union with God and not with the cosmos. Insofar as the Bible spoke about the world, it taught Christians to see the cosmos as God's creation for the benefit and service of man. It was man alone, and not the cosmos, that was created in God's image and likeness, and therefore only man could be significant in God's eyes. Man was the central datum, the object of God's concern. In this

1

way, there was a gradual shift in human sensibility away from the cosmocentric to the anthropocentric. Such a change is clearly to be found in Augustine.

In his *Soliloquia* Augustine affirms his desire to know but two things: God and his soul. For the pagan glorification of the cosmos he has nothing but a dislike: "Christ has freed the world from the world." What fills him with admiration and respect is not the motion of the planets, not the boundless starry sky, but rather the unfathomable depth of human consciousness. Augustine's main endeavor is to direct our attention away from external things towards the "internal": "Noli foras ire, in te redi, in interiore homine habitat veritas." This call to interiority resulted in Western man's increasing devotion to the study of the subject. Instead of being aware of himself as part of an eternal, all-embracing and predominant world order, man fell back upon his own resources and self-consciousness became the principal theme of his reflections.[2] There is clear evidence of this focus on self-consciousness in Descartes' Cogito, Kant's Transcendental Ego, Hüserl's Ego-concept, Heidegger's concept of Dasein, and Jasper's theory of existence. None of these philosophers remained completely outside the Judeo-Christian tradition. Thus under the impact of the Bible, western thought ceased to be cosmocentric and became anthropocentric.[3]

There is undoubtedly a kernel of truth in Löwith's notion. It cannot be denied that the Bible is more concerned with man's relation to God than with his relation to the cosmos. Similarly one can hardly doubt that Christianity has contributed to the discovery of human dignity and the awakening of self-consciousness. To this extent we can readily endorse Löwith's position. Nevertheless certain objections can be raised that are not to be taken lightly.

The first question to be raised is whether the influence of Christianity has been the only or even the principal cause of the turn to interiority such as is found in Augustine. Is it not possible that the influence of Plato and especially Plotinus could have been just as powerful, if not more powerful, in prompting him in this direction? Recent research confirms our supposition and provides a more nuanced interpretation of the matter.[4] It appears there was also a current in Greek thought that resulted in accentuating self-consciousness and interiority: "It was Socrates who by urging his listeners to self-knowledge shifted the emphasis in Greek thought definitively away from the 'external' towards the 'internal.' Socrates thus stood at the beginning of the road which, by way of Platonism and especially Plotinus and the entire Platonic tradition, would reach Augustine and was particularly disposed to being integrated into a Christian pattern of thought that is naturally spiritualistic."[5] Clearly, then, one cannot simply ascribe the turn to the subject and interiority to Christianity alone, even though it did play an important part in this change.

A second remark is in order here. Is it correct to say that Christianity has turned away entirely from consideration of the cosmos to pay exclusive attention to the "inner man"? It will indeed be seen that ancient and medieval Christian thought was much more interested in cosmological questions than one could conclude from Löwith's thesis. To support his view Löwith refers to several biblical texts and then to Augustine. Concerning his biblical quotations, it seems to us that once these passages are set in their cultural milieu, they are also open to a less extreme interpretation. The word cosmos appears with various meanings that need to be distinguished precisely. It was certainly not always used in a pejorative sense, as can be seen from the well-known text: "For God so loved the world [*Ton Kosmon*] that he gave his only son" (Jn. 3:16).[6] Of Christian writers only Augustine is mentioned. The question arises, however, to what extent he can be regarded as representative in this matter.

It is true that Augustine did not have much interest in astronomy and the natural sciences in general, but was he then not more of an exception? As will be seen in the course of this study, there was no lack of Christian writers who did have an interest in such topics. During the Middle Ages especially, but even much earlier, Christian writers focused their attention on cosmological questions. What is remarkable is that Löwith completely ignores the Middle Ages, when Christianity had an immense influence, by jumping from Augustine to Descartes—a leap of about one thousand years! The point which Löwith fails entirely to take into account is that the scholastics of the thirteenth century were concerned precisely with cosmological problems, making as accurate a study as was possible at that time. This was just the period when the metaphysical trinity—God, world, and man—was maintained in full.

In the meantime it is also true—and on this point we endorse Löwith's position—that the Christian attitude towards the cosmos was quite different from that of the ancient Greeks and that the doctrine concerning creation played a decisive role in this. Under the impact of the Bible the cosmos acquired new meaning and perspective. For the Greeks, the cosmos was adorned with a sacred and almost absolute character, a supreme reality to which men and often even the gods were subject. To be aware of being one with the cosmos, to join in harmoniously in its motions, to resign oneself humbly to its decisions, to look up to its majestic and undying beauty with respect and veneration—these constituted the highest wisdom and purest expression of religious feeling.

For Christians, on the other hand, the cosmos was a creation just as man knew himself to be a creation, and not a kind of divinity that could lay claim to our adoration. Christians recalled the exhortation of the mother of Maccabees, "I implore you, my child, observe heaven and earth, consider all that is in them, and acknowledge that God made them out of what did not exist, and that mankind comes into being in the same way" (2 Macc. 7: 28). Insofar as both are created, man and the cosmos are here placed on the same level. And if there exists a difference in merit between them, then precedence is given to man and not to the cosmos, since only of man was it said that he is created in God's image and likeness. The cosmos, however, is also the work of God, and as such it is admirable and a manifestation of supreme wisdom and omnipotence. It was, moreover, Augustine who declared that God has put two books at man's disposal, two books in which God revealed himself to us: the book of nature and the book of books, the sacred Scriptures. In both books the word came to us from God. In this way, the cosmos was also a "sacrament of God," a visible sign of his grace and of his love for man. As creation and as God's self-revelation, it deserved our attention, respect, and admiration. What Christians rejected was not the cosmos as such but a cosmos conceived as the ultimate, absolute, and sacred reality.

This, however, does not exhaust the relation between Christianity and cosmology. There has in fact been a remarkable evolution in theological thinking on this matter. Initially the attitude of Christian writers was rather negative. They not only had to wage war against every deification of the cosmos, or certain cosmic phenomena, but they also had to defend the Christian faith against its opponents who invoked cosmological arguments to attack it. In this context two points of Christian faith were under discussion: Providence and the doctrine of free will. Though Christianity as such had no cosmological doctrine to offer, one was nevertheless very soon compelled to meet opponents on their own terms and to treat questions concerning Providence and free will within the framework of the prevailing cosmological conceptions.

With the progress of time and the increasing reflection on faith, these questions were approached from a more positive standpoint. The problem was no longer what one ought to reject in the Greek cosmological conceptions but quite the reverse, namely, how can the latter contribute to the realization of a Christian view of the world?

Even though Christians were never actually preoccupied with the study of the cosmos, they nevertheless did not want to neglect it. It was precisely by virtue of their faith in God's creation of the world that they were compelled to pay full attention to this self-manifestation of the Creator.

By the end of the patristic era and at the start of the Middle Ages there was already a substantial increase in the number of texts dealing with cosmological questions. In the twelfth century when the works of Plato, Aristotle, Ptolemy, and other Greek writers once again came into the West, there was a conscious endeavor to integrate the old world picture as completely as possible into theological thought, an aim that reached its climax and most perfect realization in the work of the thirteenth-century scholastics. In this way a system of thought was designed whereby the three fundamental concepts—God, world, and man—were brought into harmony with each other. This resulted in a synthesis which for centuries remained a guiding influence in Catholic theology, even when the underlying world picture was assigned to the realm of myth by the work of men such as Copernicus, Galileo, Kepler, and Newton.

The phenomenon confronting us here greatly deserves our attention not only from a theological point of view but from the standpoint of sociology of religion. The point has already been made by Albert Schweitzer that Christians have continually attempted to make Christianity into a doctrine whereby the work of the ethical God and the natural course of the world could be brought into harmony, but that this endeavor has always failed.[7] Karl Barth on his part has argued extensively that there is such a thing as a Christian anthropology, but that a Christian cosmology is completely unthinkable, and consequently cosmological considerations are out of place in theology.[8] It is nevertheless a fact that medieval scholastic theology strove after a synthesis between the Ptolemaic conception of the cosmos and biblical doctrine, and it was only with reluctance, under the pressure of circumstances, that this attempt was abandoned. With this in mind, the American sociologist of religion Peter L. Berger has also contended that Catholicism presents itself as a "gigantic synthesis of biblical religion with extra-biblical cosmological conceptions."[9] To this day some Catholic authors have advocated belief in a predominating cosmic order as the foundation of every true culture.[10]

This presents us with a remarkable sociological phenomenon which has received little attention thus far. To explain this desire for a sacred world order, Peter Berger has propounded a theory in *The Sacred Canopy* that constitutes a fascinating contribution to the clarification of the problem. In Berger's view the origin of the appeal to a sacred cosmic order is found in man's desire to provide the culture he has established with a firm and unassailable foundation. In contrast to the animal, which in biological respect comes into the world entirely complete and has in its inborn instinct a line of action for its behavior, man is left entirely to his own resources. He has to build up his own world by searching and groping. The first task of each community is to create a world for man to live in. But the order that has been achieved at the expense of much labor and exertion remains extremely unstable and is constantly exposed to all kinds of threats, from within as well as from without. To give a firm foundation to this order which they have built up laboriously, human beings compare it to the order they think is to be discerned in the cosmos. Before long they discover a certain connection and continuity between the order they perceive in the cosmos and that which they have brought about in society: the order they have created appears to them as the continuation of the cosmic order. Because the latter is the work of the Creator, the order created by human beings immediately acquires a sacred meaning and is snatched from human arbitrariness. Henceforth the laws and institutions they have toiled to establish obtain a deep and unassailable foundation: they are the expression of the Creator's will and the reflection of the order he has imposed on all things. To rebel against this order is therefore to rebel against God himself.[11] It is especially in religious ritual that this fusion of ethos and worldview receives its symbolic expression,[12] and conversely, one can also say that cosmization implies the identification of this humanly meaningful world with the world as such."[13]

This, however, is not the end of the process. The consequence of identifying the order created by humans with the cosmic order is that they no longer remain lord of their own creation: *opus proprium* becomes *opus alienum,* a situation that can rightly be described as alienation. The humanly developed sociocultural order loses its fortuitous and transitory character, and acquires the shape of an order that is willed by God and is unchangeable, to which humanity owes absolute respect and submissiveness. Cosmization thus implies alienation. But alienation in its turn calls for dealienation. If human socio-cultural activity is not to become fossilized and to languish definitively, it must regain control of its own work in one way or another. It is characteristic of humanity never to be content with the world it has itself created. Whereas animals appear to be content with the world in which they are born, man is characterized by an invincible unrest, by a continually flickering discontent with the world in which he lives. In the words of Marsilio Ficino, "Homo solus in praesenti hoc vivendi habitu quiescit numquam, solus hoc non est contentus."

Man will never be satisfied with a particular order of sociocultural life, and will always be looking out for renewal and progress. This, however, demands that he once again become conscious of the creative freedom characteristic of his being, and conscious also of the relativity and transience of all he has hitherto accomplished. The dealienation process can be launched from two different directions. On the one hand, religious considerations can open the way to such a liberation. By teaching him to see things *sub specie aeternitatis*, religion teaches man the fickleness of all human creations, urging him on to detachment and self-perfection. On the other hand, the progress of the natural sciences and the growing knowledge of the cosmos make him see that his previous conceptions were groundless, thereby taking away every foundation to the prevailing indentification between the sociocultural order and the cosmic order. When ecclesiastical institutions nevertheless continue to associate themselves inseparably with this identification, there inevitably appears a secularization process that naturally turns against traditional religion. These three aspects of sociocultural life—cosmization, alienation, and dealienation—are not always clearly distinguished and can appear simultaneously.[14]

Such an appeal to the cosmos to justify sociocultural structures undoubtedly constitutes a typical pattern of thought, many examples of which are to be found in history. To illustrate the theory presented by Berger, reference is made to the semantic development of the Greek term cosmos that has gone into the usage of the whole of Western culture. As is commonly known, the term cosmos was initially employed to denote order, organization, regulation and can refer to all areas of life. To act, *Kata Kosmon*, means to act in the right way, to behave properly. When refering to things or objects it means that these be designed correctly and be useful and efficient. In reference to people, however, it means that they live in an orderly manner such as is the case in an army or in the Greek city-state. In this way the word cosmos initially belongs entirely and exclusively to the human social world and has as its counterpart the word *akosmia*, meaning disorder or chaos.

The term cosmos was gradually used to designate the universe, thereby acquiring a technical meaning it did not previously have. This shift in meaning clearly dates from the fourth century b.c., as can be seen from texts of Plato. It was only later in his life that the term cosmos was continuously used to denote the universe. In his earlier works the term appears twice only and from the way in which it is used one can plainly feel its meaning hovering slightly. The following quotation is a good example:

> The wise men, Callicles, tell us that heaven and earth, gods and men are held together by communion and friendship, orderliness, self-control, and justice, and that this is the reason why this whole world is called by the name of order (cosmos), not disorder.[15]

It is to be noted here that Plato explicitly attributes this expression to the sages, the philosophers, immediately insinuating that this was not the customary manner of speaking. Xenophon also makes the same remark when he uses the term cosmos to denote the universe.[16] In this case it concerns an expression peculiar to the Sophists. What is especially remarkable about Plato's statement is the fact that he describes the universe with the aid of concepts and properties derived from the human community. The universe is a *koinonia*, a community of heaven and earth, of gods and men, a community moreover that is characterized as a perfect society governed by love, sober-mindedness, and justice. In such a manner of conduct one can readily perceive the original meaning of the word cosmos.[17] Only in Plato's later works, and mainly in the *Timaeus*, do we find a more concrete description of the cosmos and its physical properties. As to the adjective *kosmikos* derived from *kosmos*, it first appears in Aristotle.[18]

From what we have seen so far, it is evident how the Greek concept of cosmos has to be considered as a sort of projection of the order that had been striven after in the city-states. What the Greeks saw in the world about them was order and beauty and for this reason the order of the earthly community and the perfect order of the universe were united harmoniously with each other. This perfect order of the universe became more and more the object of attention and admiration. Nothing was superior to, nor more beautiful than, the cosmos, the perfectly ordered universe. Before long it assumed a sacred character, so that Greek religiosity became entirely directed towards veneration of the cosmic divinity.[19] Pliny the Elder (A.D. 23–79) provides a beautiful description of this respect for the cosmos in the following text:

> The world is sacred, eternal and immeasurable; all and everything, indeed totality itself; infinite and yet related to the finite; the certainty of all things and yet related to the uncertain; it includes everything that is hidden or visibly present; the work of the nature of things, nay the nature of things itself.[20]

Once this stage had been reached, it was not surprising that the cosmos became the paradigm or the model for all human activity. The same view had already been expressed by Plato and it is repeatedly to be found in later authors, notably the Stoics, from whom it received systematic treatment. To act according to nature, to submit oneself consciously to the cosmic order, became the highest norm for moral activity. Ptolemy was also convinced that the study of the universe constituted the best school for one desiring to pursue an eminently moral life.[21]

What we find, then, in the development of the Greek conception of the cosmos confirms the theory presented by Berger. A striking illustration of the same theory is moreover to be found in medieval intellectual life where, as we shall see, an important role was played by the interaction of culture and cosmology. It was especially after the discovery of part of Plato's *Timaeus* that cosmological considerations gained significance and became increasingly influential. One cannot really understand the medieval mind, characterized by its pursuit of a perfect hierarchical order, if one does not take into account the underlying cosmology. This is particularly evident in theology, the keystone and summit of medieval intellectual life, governing the entire culture. In the Middle Ages the idea of hierarchical order, deemed to be present in the cosmos and deduced from the consideration of an imaginary cosmology, became the key concept for explaining Christian doctrine and at the same time the supreme norm for moral and political activity.

Such was the origin of a very typical interpretation of Christianity whereby, to use Berger's words, a gigantic synthesis was established between biblical religion and extra-biblical cosmological conceptions. It was precisely from this synthesis that medieval Christianity derived its particular character and this at the same time explains why, with the disappearance of the ancient world picture a process of dealienation or secularization became inevitable, leading to a tragic crisis within Christianity.

The fact that cosmological conceptions exerted such a powerful influence on the medieval interpretation of Christian doctrine and that ecclesiastical authorities so emphatically abided by this interpretation had far-reaching consequences not only for the situation of theological thinking within the Catholic Church but equally so for the position of Christianity in today's world. The situation of Catholic theology can be outlined as follows: medieval theologians applied themselves to the construction of an all-embracing Christian view of the world by the harmonious fusion of world picture and doctrine. This endeavor gave vitality to their work and inspired an impressive system in which cosmology, anthropology, and theology formed an admirable unity.

The foundations of this synthesis were shaken, however, by the revolution in cosmology ushered in by Copernicus. In spite of the fact that the old notions concerning the universe gradually lost all credibility, theologians, mainly under pressure from the central ecclesiastical authority, clung to the former synthesis. Initially the new way of thinking was completely rejected. When this no longer seemed possible, however, all allusions to the old world picture are seen to disappear gradually from theological treatises, on the understanding, nevertheless, that the spirit of these treatises was left intact and that the underlying interpretation of faith remained unchanged. From that time on until well into the twentieth century, a mutilated scholastic theology was thus maintained, which no longer provided any true inspiration, but merely functioned as a kind of ideology for the benefit of an ecclesiastical institution that felt supported by it. In the meantime, however, powerful opposition has arisen to this antiquated theology that has become estranged from the world. Conscious of the potential danger of such a situation, certain independent and often isolated thinkers have set themselves the task of laying the foundations for a renewed theology that does justice to the contemporary worldview and image of man.

Theology has thus entered a new period where it is confronted with a twofold task. What matters first is that the message of Christ be freed from fossilized conceptions in which it has been confined and that it be expressed as purely and perfectly as possible. There ought to be a clear line of demarcation between what actually belongs to revelation and the interpretations given to this in the past under the influence of the prevailing world picture. Such a demarcation line can really only be drawn if one is clearly aware of the influence this demolished world picture has exercised on formulations of faith. When Christians of former ages attempted to express their faith-experience, they were naturally dependent on the language and expressions of their surroundings. This evidently involved conceptions and ideas derived from the contemporary cultural climate and inherited from both the Jewish and the Hellenistic world of thought. One of the most important tasks for contemporary theology is to carry out an ineluctable process of demythologizing without allowing any of the original vision to be lost. Today's Christians also have the right to express their faith in a language which is their own and which differs largely from that of former ages.

The second task confronting contemporary theology is closely linked to the first. How can we distinguish the teaching of Revelation in all its wealth and perfection from our view of the world and of man? What role should the contemporary world picture (however difficult to describe) play in constructing a systematic theology? As we shall see in due course, the medieval doctrinal systems were mainly formulated with the help of a conception of order that was clearly derived from the prevailing world picture. This conception of order, however, has practically no role in contemporary thought.

Is it not for us to look out for another key concept that is more closely linked to our contemporary view of reality? This question is not easy to answer and can certainly not be disposed of with a simple negative or affirmative. It will elude no one that this also has bearing on questions closely connected with the position of Christianity in today's world.

The fundamental problem religious institutions have to contend with is, says Berger, "how to keep going in a milieu that no longer takes for granted their definitions of reality."[22] Since the rise of the modern natural sciences, the gulf between Christianity and the modern world has become increasingly wider. What is clear is that no end will come to the division as long as the Christian faith is interpreted in terms of concepts and ideas that no longer correspond to our contemporary experience of reality. It is precisely this situation which compels us to pay careful attention to the problem discussed in this book and to accept the eventual consequences. Perhaps the views expressed here will help to explain not only the renewal taking place in contemporary theology and in the life of the Church but also the present crisis of Western civilization.

Part One

THE COSMOLOGICAL BACKGROUND TO MEDIEVAL THEOLOGY

In vision I re-travelled, sphere by sphere,
the seven heavens, and saw this globe of ours
such, that I smiled, so mean did it appear.
Dante

In *De vanitate mundi*, the celebrated teacher Hugh of St. Victor provides us with a concise description of the curriculum of an abbey school in the first half of the twelfth century. Among the various sciences and arts that were studied in such a school, he includes grammar, mathematics, philosophy, physics, music, the arts of copying and of miniature, and finally he explicitly mentions the study of astronomy. There are those, he writes, who study the course and position of the stars, applying themselves to the description of the heavens with the aid of all sorts of instruments.[1] Astronomy in fact belonged to the liberal arts such as were later taught in the medieval universities. There are many other sources confirming the great deal of interest in cosmological questions that is to be found early in the twelfth century.[2] The world, envisaged as a harmonious whole, became the object of renewed study and reflection. It involved the study of the structure and coherence of the universe in its entirety: it was like a new discovery of nature.[3] William of Conches describes the world as an ordered collection of creatures.[4] To understand the world we must not only add up the sum of all the creatures we find in it, but we must especially trace the order into which they have been received by God's wisdom. The ordered connection of all things thus became the principal theme of sustained reflection, particular attention being paid to the ancients who had described this topic with so much knowledge and wisdom. Part of Plato's *Timaeus*, including commentaries by Chalcidius and Proclus, was closely examined and consulted almost with reverence. Also held in high esteem was Macrobius's *The Dream of Scipio*, the wonderful story with which Cicero concluded the sixth book of the *Republic*.[5] There were, moreover, many other writings sketching the picture of the world, so that the first features of a coherent view of the world began to stand out in relief.

The decisive breakthrough occurred then at the end of the twelfth century, when the works of Aristotle, Ptolemy, and many other Greek thinkers and scholars entered once again into the West, enriched, moreover, by the commentaries of Jewish and Arabian scholars. There were those, it is true, who were apprehensive of and even hostile towards the new insights coming to light at that time, but there were others who applied themselves wholeheartedly to the study of these works which appeared to them to be heaven-sent. The first requirement was to have a thorough grasp of what the ancients had taught. Then one had to bowdlerize the latter, expurgating the mistakes and errors objectionable to Christians. And finally one had to integrate the newly acquired insights into a Christian view on the world. This vast undertaking that was started in the twelfth century reached its climax in the thirteenth century, notably with the work of Bonaventure and Aquinas, having achieved a previously unequalled synthesis of faith and science.

In order to appreciate this interest in cosmological questions one has to bear in mind that the medieval theologian approached these questions from a standpoint entirely different from that of today's scientist. He was not primarily concerned with studying the cosmos as such but was more inclined to consider the universe in a theological context. What he had in view was a Christian interpretation of the cosmos as God's creation and revelation, as a pathway to the knowledge of God and as a partner in salvation. It is only from this perspective that one can appreciate the medieval interest in cosmological questions. Here we must remember the golden rule as outlined by A. C. Crombie, the distinguished historian of science: to understand the value of a particular scientific theory it is not sufficient to ask ourselves what this theory meant in itself and to what extent it compares with our contemporary scientific views. What are important are not so much the answers as the questions that gave rise to these answers. To make a proper evaluation of the work of earlier generations we must first ask ourselves what questions these theories were designed to answer.[6]

The question confronting the medieval theologian was not so much how to interpret the origin and structure of the cosmos on purely scientific grounds but rather what was primarily a theological question: How must Christians view the world? How can they see in creation a manifestation of God's wisdom and omnipotence? Clearly, then, the medieval theologian was principally concerned with theology and not with natural science.

In seeking to answer these questions he did not possess a scientific arsenal such as we now have at our disposal. Of all the available cosmological systems, Plato's was the most suited to serve as a starting point for a Christian interpretation of the world in that he acknowledged the existence of a Creator who had arranged the world in supreme wisdom. The name of Plato was highly respected ever since his teaching had been interpreted in a Christian spirit by Augustine.[7] With the emergence of Aristotle, Ptolemy, and Jewish-Arabian science at the end of the twelfth century, little change had to be made in Platonic theory. As far as the main features are concerned, Aristotle would subscribe to Plato's picture of the universe. There was, therefore, a world picture on hand and one, moreover, that had been patronized by the greatest authorities of the ancient world, so that a better choice was simply unthinkable at the time. Once the choice had been made, it was a matter of testing the newly acquired world picture by the data of Scripture and the teaching of the Church Fathers. This, however, gave rise to all sorts of problems. Certain statements were to be found in Scripture at one time apparently bearing out the Greek world picture, at another time seemingly deviating from it, or in any case not immediately reconcilable with such a world picture.

The question, then, was whether the Greek world picture ought to be altered in the light of the biblical statements or whether the latter ought to be interpreted in the light of Greek science? How, for instance, was one to understand Moses' statement about "the waters which were above the firmament" (Gen.1:7)? No mention of this was to be found among the Greeks. Furthermore, what was one to think of the heavenly spheres recorded by the Greeks but not in the Bible?. It was supposed that though the ancient scholars had an outstanding science at their disposal, they nevertheless lacked the light of Revelation. This accounted for the fact that, besides many admirable points, their work also contained great lacunae and even glaring errors.

The Christian thinker was therefore confronted by a vast and arduous field of action. In response to this challenge medieval scholars produced a large number of Hexaëmeron commentaries, whereby an attempt was made to reconcile the Greek world picture with biblical data and especially with the creation story in the book of Genesis.[8] From the very beginning of the scholastic era a lot of attention was paid to this problem, notably by the school of Chartres, renowned for its endeavor to bring Plato's *Timaeus* into line with the creation story to be found in Genesis.[9]

The medieval theologians, however, did not pioneer this venture. Long before they embarked on this task, others had already been involved in a similar enterprise. In fact, many ancient Christian writers, and by no means the least among them, had tried to reconcile Greek science with the Mosaic creation story. Though their statements were not always of the same tenor, they nevertheless indicated how one had to go about solving these problems. The writings of the Church Fathers had also therefore to be closely examined on this matter.

From what we have seen, then, there were three sources from which the medieval theologian could construct a Christian view of the cosmos:

1. the scientific conceptions of the ancient Greeks, supplemented by the works of Jewish and Arabian scholars;
2. the data of sacred Scriptures;
3. the teaching of the Church Fathers.

We shall now take a closer look at each of these sources.

Chapter One

SOURCES OF THE MEDIEVAL WORLD PICTURE

The Bible was undoubtedly the primary source from which the medieval theologian drew to resolve any problems confronting him. He continuously examined sacred Scriptures, employing the methods at his disposal. It was, moreover, precisely in order to reach a better understanding of Scripture that he appealed to ancient philosophy and science which thus became an aid to his theological work. Seen in this way, it would have been perfectly normal to have considered the Bible as the principal source of the medieval world picture.

However, after scrutinizing the medieval theologian's world picture more carefully, it soon becomes evident that most elements to be found in it and most questions to which it gave rise are in fact derived not so much from the Bible as from the Platonic-Aristotelian view of the cosmos. What is more, it is entirely inconceivable that a similar picture of the universe could have been attained on the basis of the Bible alone. For these reasons we must point to Greek cosmology as the principal source of the medieval world picture.

The Legacy of the Greeks.

When the medieval theologian started to form a picture of the universe, his thoughts inevitably turned to the writings of the ancients. For him Greece had bequeathed an unsurpassable wealth in the natural sciences, so that the authority of the old masters deserved to be trusted more than one's own experience. It appeared to the medieval theologian that the ancient Greeks had inquired into the heavenly bodies and the earth such as no one had done before or after them. Where, then, could one find better advice on how to picture the universe? It is generally known that the study of the cosmos constituted a significant part of the Greek *Paideia*[1]. Like all nations on the Mediterranean, the Greeks took great delight in contemplating the clear starry heavens, and were simply enthralled by the mysterious and fascinating spectacle of the sky at night. From the earliest times Greek thought was governed by cosmological considerations,[2] giving rise to various systems concerning the origin, structure, and composition of the universe, which in turn led to lively discussions.[3] But only one of them was of vital importance to medieval theology, the theme that concerns us here: this was the system originating from Plato's *Timaeus* and further developed in the work of Aristotle, Ptolemy, and the Jewish and Arabian scholars.[4]

Plato's *Timaeus* deals with two major themes of Greek thought: cosmology and anthropology. Only the first part of the dialogue was known in the theology schools of the twelfth century, thanks to the commentaries of Chalcidius and Proclus. This, then, was the text consulted by the early scholastics in constructing a picture of the universe. The starting point of the *Timaeus* was the problem of organizing the state and developing the best form of government.[5] When Plato sat down to write this dialogue he had just returned to Athens from his third stay in Sicily. Though his plans to realize an ideal state had once again been wrecked, he nevertheless continued to be occupied with the problem of how the ideal state of his dreams could be realized in practice. To give concrete shape to his dream he considered that we must carefully study the nature of man first and foremost, and that this is only possible if we include the cosmos in our study. Cosmology and anthropology cannot be separated from each other. Macrocosm and microcosm are complementary: both are designed according to the same basic plan and must therefore be studied together. For medieval theology this view also remained valid as an indisputable axiom.

This is the theme of the *Timaeus*. The world picture further developed by Plato and indeed repeatedly to be found in his writings (*Phaedrus, Epinomis, Laws*) presented many difficulties for the Christian thinker, but on the other hand was in many respects amenable to a Christian interpretation. According to Plato, the cosmos was made from a model previously present in the mind of the Creator. And precisely for this reason the cosmos was a perfect creation, at least insofar as the imitation of a perfect archetype can be perfect. The eternity of God's model is expressed by the introduction of time, the most perfect possible imitation of eternity. All things here on earth were formed out of four elements: earth, water, air, and fire. The earth is situated in the center of the universe, and around it are the seven spheres, which carry the planets, and an eighth sphere in which the fixed stars are found. Everything here on earth is transitory and unsettled, whereas the heavenly bodies are imperishable and always act consistently. The latter are moved in a circular orbit, from which one must conclude that they are animate and guided by reason.

> Wherefore, using the language of probability, we may say that the world became a living creature truly endowed with soul and intelligence by the providence of God. . . . For the Deity intending to make this world like the fairest and most perfect of intelligible beings, framed one visible animal comprehending within itself all other animals of kindred nature.[6]

Plato is aware of the inadequacy of his description of the universe, but human reason is simply not able to penetrate further into the wonder of God's creation. We must rejoice about that which we are permitted to discover and question no further, and admire the order and beauty of creation. We must especially fix our eyes upon the realm of eternal stars: by our body we belong to the earthly realm of instability and transience, but our soul, which can cherish eternal thoughts, does not belong on earth. The realm of eternal stars is the soul's home: for man is "a plant that is rooted not in earth but in heaven."[7] This double antithesis earth-heaven, body-soul forms the background to Plato's religiosity and is decisive for the entire Hellenistic period.[8]

A number of elements included in the Platonic picture of the universe appeared very attractive to the medieval theologian, thereby allowing for the possibility of an easy transposition into a Christian understanding. In the first place, Plato had attributed creation, or at any rate the ordering of the cosmos, to divine Providence, just as the biblical creation story had done. The universe appeared to him as a perfect order, worthy of supreme wisdom. All things were arranged hierarchically according to their inner dignity and perfection. There were certainly difficulties with Plato's theory concerning a world-soul, giving rise to many disputes, but on the other hand his doctrine of man as a microcosm received great approbation and was generally accepted. This was also the case concerning the number of heavenly spheres with their accompanying planets. Thus the entire cosmos appeared to form a magnificently ordered whole, constructed with a sense of proportion, testifying in its entirety and its parts to the wisdom, goodness, and power of its Creator. In this world picture not only were cosmology and anthropology closely connected with each other, but there was at the same time an implicit theodicy. The whole cosmos bore witness to God's existence and his concern for his creation. The cosmos was a way to God. In the *Laws* Plato gives us to understand that we are brought to believe in divinity by two things:

> What we have said about the soul and everything connected with the regularity in the course of the stars and of all other heavenly bodies ruled by the intellect, which has made everything into an ordered universe.[9]

The repercussions of the Platonic view were particularly strongly felt during the Hellenistic period: at this time the sight of the sky at night was a source of religious emotion, so that one can rightly speak of a cosmic religiosity.[10] This is strikingly expressed in Ptolemy's epigram:

> Mortal though I be, yea ephemeral, if but a moment
> I gaze up to the night's starry domain of heaven,
> Then no longer on earth I stand; I touch the Creator,
> And my lively spirit drinketh immortality.[11]

Plato's cosmology was thus laden with religious values to which medieval Christians were particularly sensitive. Nor is it any wonder that they felt especially attracted to it.

To the study of the cosmos Plato also attached a deep ethical significance that in point of fact underlies the whole dialogue. According to Plato, man's soul is connected with the world-soul, and precisely because the movements of the world-soul are perfect and orderly, the movements of the human soul will also share in the same beauty and perfection, when it knows its connection with the world soul. Cornford has rightly pointed out that the parallelism between macrocosm and microcosm governs the entire *Timaeus*.[12] Morality has to be founded on the order in the cosmos, and this is the conclusion which the whole work aims at.

In his much-read *Almagest*, Ptolemy later emphasized this ethical aspect of cosmology that for a long time belonged to Greek tradition and goes back at least to the school of Pythagoras:[13]

> This science of stars can . . . better than any other, render an excellent service in connection with our concern for an eminently moral life. For from the example of the similarity, precise order, symmetry, and simplicity which we experience with divine beings

(the heavenly bodies) it imparts to its practitioners love for divine beauty. What is more, through habit such an attitude of mind becomes second nature.[14]

Cosmology and morality were also closely connected in Stoicism,[15] where ethical life has not only to be founded on the movement of the planets but is actually caused by this movement. The ordered motion of the cosmos is thus the source of all morality. It will be seen that the medieval philosopher did not fail to notice this link between cosmology and morality. All in all, the Platonic world picture thus formed a splendid starting point for constructing a Christian view of the cosmos such as was striven after by the scholastics.

In Aristotle's cosmology,[16] the main features of the Platonic world picture were preserved, though on various points important changes were made and other points supplemented. Aristotle also accepted the earth as the center of the universe, and according to him, the four elements—earth, water, air, and fire—in their unmixed state form four earthly spheres. The celestial spheres and the stars are made from a fifth ethereal element: quintessence or ether. Between the celestial sphere with the fixed stars and the spheres of the earth, there are seven planets moving around the center in a perfect, circular orbit. The rotation of the circle is the perfect motion in that it has neither beginning nor end and constantly returns to its origin. It is the task of mathematics to demonstrate how, in spite of the contrary impression sometimes given, the planets in point of fact move in regular and concentric circles, observing, moreover, the same velocity. To make this result possible, Aristotle accepted the existence of fifty-five intermediary spheres rotating in opposite directions, thereby performing a counterbalancing and regulating function.

Aristotle arranged the planets in the same order as Plato had done. Starting at the bottom we find the Moon, the Sun, Mercury, Venus, Mars, Jupiter, and Saturn. These consecutive spheres do not all possess the same "dignity" and perfection, divinity and imperishableness. The closer they are situated to earth they are, as it were, contaminated and consequently lose something of their purity. The concept "dignity" thus plays a significant role in this cosmology and accounts for the hierarchical order to be found in the cosmos.

In contrast to the celestial spheres which, corresponding to their dignity, always move in a circle, the earthly elements continually move in a straight line, in the direction of the center of the earth and of the cosmos. The four elements thus have their natural place and propensity and find expression in properties such as weight and lightness. Weight is the inclination of the heavy elements (earth and water) towards the center of the cosmos, whereas lightness is the tendency of the other elements (air and fire) to move away from the center. Earth and fire are respectively absolutely heavy and light, while water and air are respectively relatively heavy and light.

But how is the motion of the celestial spheres to be accounted for in Aristotle's cosmology? Do the spheres of the planets receive their motion exclusively from the most external celestial sphere, or is the latter in its turn set in motion by a higher power? Since the appearance of Werner Jaeger's book *Aristotle: Fundamentals of the History of His Development*, this question has given rise to important differences of opinion, whereby, it is claimed, one has to take into account an evolution in Aristotle's views.[17] Irrespective of his standpoint in *De caelo*, there is no doubt in his other works, notably in his *Metaphysics*, that Aristotle ultimately ascribes motion in the universe to an "unmoved Mover," essentially distinct from the highest celestial sphere of the fixed stars. On the other hand, it appeared to him that the stars and planets ought to be considered as animate beings to which one had to attribute a certain intelligence.

With the medieval rediscovery of the work of Aristotle, theologians naturally focused attention on the theological aspect of this cosmology. For instance, Aristotle had deduced the existence of a first cause from the motion and order in the cosmos. On the other hand, his teaching on the intelligence of heavenly bodies was presumed to be an allusion to the existence of the angels. It goes without saying that Plato and Aristotle were not the only sources for the medieval world picture. Many other Greek scholars contributed directly or indirectly to this world picture (through the work of the Fathers of the Church and other Christian writers). Their writings and the commentaries to which they had given rise were studied very carefully. It seemed to escape their attention, however, that Greek scholars had also developed other cosmologies containing a heliocentric view of the universe and even defending the existence of an infinite number of worlds. For medieval theology it was only the geocentric world picture of Plato-Aristotle-Ptolemy and the later Jewish and Arabian commentators that was considered as essentially important.

Sacred Scriptures

In constructing a picture of the universe, medieval theologians first consulted Plato and Aristotle, where they felt they had found a completely elaborate and indisputable description of the cosmos. Naturally this world picture could not simply be adopted in its entirety without further ado. For, no matter how gifted the eminent scholars of antiquity were, they nevertheless had had no share in the light of revelation. This, then, accounted for the errors and lacunae that were to be found in their work. Their view of the world had therefore to be purged of any pagan elements it contained before being supplemented by the data Christians possessed by virtue of revelation. For this purpose one first had to examine the Scriptures to consider their teaching on the construction of the universe and on the true significance of God's creation.

Two questions came to the fore here. In the first place one had to examine the picture of the universe found in Scripture. Then one had to confront the biblical world picture with that of the Greek philosophers for the purpose of establishing a harmonious synthesis. It was with much diligence that medieval theologians devoted themselves to this twofold task.

To what extent can we speak of a biblical world picture?[18] Contemporary exegetes are unanimously negative on this point. Though the Bible undoubtedly contains a number of allusions to cosmological topics such as the construction of the universe and the motion of the planets, there is no question of a truly coherent and dogmatic description of the universe as such. In point of fact the Bible does not contain an explicit cosmology. As far as the New Testament is concerned (though the same can be said of the Old Testament) one can summarize the Bible's teaching in the following manner:

1. Cosmology is incidental to the New Testament. It is never the object of proclamation as in other ancient religions or even in Jewish Apocalyptic. In some ancient primitive religions a particular picture of the universe is not infrequently an essential part of the religious teaching. This is never the case in the new Testament.

2. There is no distinctive New Testament cosmology. What we find are no more than casual allusions to the cosmological conceptions of its contemporary world.

3. If one wanted to integrate all these allusions and sporadic pieces into a consistent whole, it would soon become clear that such a task is impossible. For this reason it would be meaningless to speak of a biblical worldview.

4. Cosmology does not belong to the message of the Gospel. The cosmos is an object of proclamation and consequently of Christian theology only insofar as it is related to God as its Creator, Lord, Judge, and Redeemer. This is the only sense in which the early Church spoke of the world.[19]

What is said here about the New Testament to a great extent also holds good for the Old Testament, though allusions to the world picture of the cultural milieu are somewhat more pronounced in the Old Testament than in the New Testament. This is especially the case in the first chapter of Genesis. In this creation story there is no doubt that emphasis is mainly given to the oneness of Yahweh and to the law of the sabbath. Such religious teaching, however, is expressed against the background of a cosmological view, derived from mythological ideas circulating throughout the Near East at that time. What is remarkable is that Israel made use of these ideas to express its own concept of God, after first having removed everything which was at variance with this concept.[20]

It is also to be noted that the Bible appealed to cosmological ideas of its surroundings to express religious truths. At one time Scripture urges us to admire the glory of Creation and to praise the Creator, at another time it warns us against a wrong interpretation of the forces of nature. In the Book of Psalms we are told that the heavens proclaim the glory of God (Ps. 19) and in the Book of Maccabees we find the mother of these militant Israelites urging her sons to recognize the power of the Creator in the beauty of the cosmos (2 Macc. 7:28). The Book of Wisdom, on the other hand, warns us not to idolize the forces of nature:

> Yes, naturally stupid are all men who have not known God and who from the good things that are seen, have not been able to discover Him who is, or by studying the works, have failed to recognize the Artificer. Fire, however, or wind, or the swift air, the sphere of the stars, impetuous water, heaven's lamps are what they have held to be the gods who govern the world. (Wisd. 13:1–5).

Taking into account the insights that we now possess, we can submit the following conclusions: 1. cosmology proper can never constitute the theme of the Christian message: investigation into the structure and development of the universe belongs exclusively to the realm of the natural sciences; the Bible cannot provide any information on this matter; 2. insofar as the preaching of the Gospel requires it, there is nothing wrong in appealing to prevailing cosmological conceptions, on the condition that this takes place with the necessary caution, never creating the impression that the Gospel is linked to one particular cosmology; 3. an appeal to the prevailing cosmology can at times be more, at other times less required according to the circumstances of the case. It is quite conceivable that occasions arise when a confrontation with prevailing cosmological conceptions fulfills an urgent need precisely with a view to proclaiming and safeguarding Christian doctrine.

All this can now be considered as common knowledge among theologians. We should bear in mind, however, that this interpretation represents a recent conquest for biblical scholarship and that a different explanation was held by most until late in the nineteenth century and into the beginning of the twentieth century, as is evident, for example, from the conflict concerning Concordism. Medieval theologians read the Bible with different eyes than we now do. For them there was no doubt that Scripture really did hold a particular picture of the universe and that the latter was basically in agreement with the view presented by Greek philosophers and scholars.

The main question with which they were preoccupied and to which they devoted numerous writings, was precisely how a harmonious fusion of biblical data and Greek science could lead to a completely satisfactory and irrefutable picture of the universe. Countless texts were devoted to this venture, whether in the form of commentaries on *Hexaëmeron* or commentaries on Peter Lombard's *Sentences*, which had dealt with this problem, or even in popular writings and collections of sermons. All these writings displayed wonders of subtlety, offering the author an exceptional opportunity to give evidence of his knowledge not only of Scripture but at the same time of earlier authors and their teaching on the structure of the cosmos. Writers were glad to make use of this opportunity and we shall later have to examine the outcome of all this.

It is to be noted, however, that there is no question here of an exception, as if such a view were only characteristic of the scholastics. It will presently be seen how the Fathers of the Church were already sensitive to this problem, making numerous attempts to reconcile Greek and biblical cosmology. On the other hand, even centuries after the heyday of scholasticism—one need only think of the conflict concerning Galileo—the prevalent conviction was that the Bible held a geocentric picture of the universe and that Christians were not allowed to deviate from this view.

The Patristic Era

When medieval theologians embarked on the task of constructing a Christian view of the world on the basis of a synthesis between Greek and biblical cosmology, they were by no means under the impression that they were pioneering a new venture or that they were introducing an innovation into theology. They were, on the contrary, very much aware of the fact that they were carrying on a task that had been started long before them and that had led to admirable results. As was the case in so many other areas, their main desire in this field was to follow the example of Christian writers from earlier centuries and to continue their work as best they could. Was it not true that the greatest among the Fathers of the Church had often appealed to the Platonic world picture and that they had very skillfully interwoven this view with their interpretations of Scripture? Clearly, then, the medieval theologian felt he had inherited a long and rich tradition, the wealth of a thousand years of Christian thinking. This spiritual wealth had of course to be developed further, with particular attention paid to the careful sifting of insights that had been reached, molding them into a harmonious whole.

The encounter between Greek culture and the Bible started very early, certainly before the rise of Christianity. The Jewish world, both in Palestine and in the diaspora, was also confronted with the omnipresence of Hellenism, which later pervaded the entire Roman empire. Plato penetrated the rabbinic schools of Palestine where there was much lively discussion on his view concerning the creation of the world according to a divine model.[21] It was, however, especially in the diaspora, notably in Alexandria, the spiritual center of the Hellenistic period, that the educated Jew entered into dialogue with the culture of his surroundings. The Bible was here translated into Greek by seventy scholars (Septuagint), while Philo of Alexandria purposefully endeavored to reconcile biblical teaching with that of Greek philosophy. Except for several infelicitous expressions, it can be assumed that in striving after this goal Philo remained loyal to the fundamental notion of Judaism concerning the oneness of God, and that he continually rejected the Platonic idea according to which the world had been created from a preexistent and eternal matter. There is no question, then, of interpreting his identification of the biblical Wisdom and Tora concept with the Stoic Logos concept as a forsaking of Jewish orthodoxy in the matter of the oneness of God.[22]

The first Christians were also soon confronted with Hellenism. Traces of this are already to be found in the New Testament: what is remarkable is that the apostles and evangelists very quickly used Greek to proclaim to the world of that time the message of Jesus that had been preached in Aramaic. Despite the many points of contact and similarities, it is here that we find a radical distinction with the Essene sect, a group whose beliefs and lifestyle are recounted in the Dead Sea Scrolls of Qumran. Whereas the Essenes shut themselves

up in cloisters or communities to practice prayer and penance in se-
clusion and solitude, the disciples of Jesus immediately directed themselves to the whole world of that time in the conviction that the
religion proclaimed by Jesus had to become the religion of the whole
world.[23] For this reason they chose Greek, the international language
at that time. With the language also came numerous concepts so that
the Hellenistic world of thought penetrated the original Christian
data, thereby commencing the struggle to keep the Christian message
pure, and to protect it against contamination.[24]

In the Hellenistic worldview, however, a central position was assigned to cosmological considerations. Prepared as they were by
Plato's *Timaeus* and probably even more so by Aristotle's dialogue *On
Philosophy*,[25] the Greeks regarded contemplation of the cosmos as the
religious theme par excellence. It was a question here of a religious
current without dogma, institution, or even a well-defined cult in
which the predominant mood would fluctuate from one of optimism
to one of pessimism. For some the cosmos offered the spectacle of a
splendidly ordered whole. It is not only the heavens which display
an admirable regularity, for in the sublunary world one also finds a
wonderful balance between the four elements. On earth plants are
subordinate to animals, which are in turn subordinate to humans. By
a careful consideration of the order and beauty of the cosmos one thus
comes to acknowledge a creative wisdom that can only be admired
and adored. Others, on the contrary, emphasized the chaos to be
found in the cosmos in spite of everything: the world is governed by
so much evil and chaos that these could be attributed to God and
evoke worship of the Creator. Whereas the first group argued that the
order in the cosmos actually presupposes the existence of less perfect
things, but that these imperfections are absorbed in the perfection of
the whole, the second group preferred to place between God and the
world a number of intermediary demiurges to whom the imperfection
of the cosmos can be ascribed. It is only by traversing and relinquish-
ing all this that one can approach the true God.[26]

It is hardly surprising, then, that Christianity, having emerged in
this cultural climate, very soon considered itself compelled to pay
attention to such views which were obviously laden with cosmological
elements, in spite of the fact that cosmology proper was not within
its sphere of interest and that it was more concerned with purely
theological and soteriological considerations. In the earliest datable
writing of the post-apostolic age, the letter of Clement of Rome to the
Christians at Corinth, written about thirty years after the death of the
Apostle Paul, we find striking considerations on the cosmic order

established by the will of the Creator as a model for an ordered and harmonious life.

This hymn of creation runs as follows:

> The heavens revolve by His arrangement and are subject to Him in peace. Day and night complete the revolution ordained by Him, and neither interferes in the least with the other. Sun and moon and starry choirs, obedient to His arrangement, roll on in harmony, without any deviation, through their appointed orbits. The earth bears fruit according to His will in its proper seasons, and yields the full amount of food required for men and beasts and all the living things on it, neither wavering nor altering any of His decrees. The unsearchable decisions that govern the abysses and the inscrutable decisions that govern the deeps are maintained by the same decrees. The basis of the boundless sea, firmly built by His creative act for the collecting of the waters, does not burst the barriers set up all around it, and does precisely what has been assigned to it. For He said: Thus far shalt thou come, and thy billows shall be turned to spray within thee. The ocean, impassable for men, and the worlds beyond it are governed by the same decrees of the Master. The seasons—spring, summer, autumn, and winter— make room for one another in peaceful succession. The stations of the winds at the proper time render their service without disturbance. Ever-flowing springs, created for enjoyment and for health, without fail offer to men their life-sustaining breasts. The smallest of the animals meet in peaceful harmony. All these creatures the mighty Creator and Master of the universe ordained to act in peace and concord, thus benefitting the universe, but most abundantly ourselves who have taken refuge under His mercies through our Lord Jesus Christ: to whom be the glory and majesty forever and evermore. Amen.[27]

In the writings of the apostolic Fathers we already find numerous allusions to cosmological conceptions of the period.[28] With the apologists this topic came up for discussion more often because criticism by pagan philosophers of the Christian teaching concerning creation, Providence, and free will was not infrequently inspired by the cosmology of the time. To invalidate the arguments of these philosophers, one could not avoid cosmological problems. In this context we refer especially to Justin Martyr.[29]

Even though the interest of Christian writers in cosmological considerations was initially more negative and only evoked by the necessity to defend true Christian teaching against its opponents, in the course of time it assumed a more positive character. The cosmos, it was said, is the work of the Creator and as such it deserves our respectful attention and admiration. It is precisely out of love and respect for the Creator that we must direct our attention to his work, thereby making the study of nature a religious concern. There can be no doubt, then, that Christian self-knowledge also implies a Christian view of the cosmos.

The first to strive after a synthesis between Christian doctrine and Greek philosophy and to carry out this program in an impressive manner was Origen (185–247?), next to Augustine, the most brilliant theologian of the patristic era. Not only was he the first to treat Christian doctrine in a methodical manner as a coherent system, but he can moreover be considered a teacher in the sphere of spiritual life and the founder of Christian biblical scholarship. It is precisely in his theological system that cosmological considerations assume a prominent position. More than any other theologian before Aquinas, he envisaged the world as a unified whole and attempted to situate Christian revelation in a world picture mainly derived from Plato.[30] Without this cosmological background, his thought is largely unintelligible, as is the case with his eminent contemporary Plotinus (204–270).[31] The work of Origen was given much credence and remained a guiding influence for many centuries, despite the objections to which it gave rise.

It was, however, not so much these earlier writers whom the medieval theologian consulted in his attempt to reconcile the Greek and biblical pictures of the universe and to resolve any difficulties he encountered in the process. There were other, and according to him, more authoritative writers to assist him in his task. There was in the first place Pseudo-Dionysius, the Areopagite, who was considered to be a direct disciple of St. Paul and to whom one assigned the highest authority after sacred Scriptures. What we find in the writings of the Pseudo-Dionysius is the broad outline of the Platonic world picture and the fundamental principles which governed the entire medieval conception of the cosmos: the whole cosmos is a perfect hierarchical order, in which the lower is governed and guided by the higher.[32] It will later be seen just how significant this principle of hierarchy was for medieval theology. In the work of the Areopagite considerable attention was also given to the place of the angels in the whole of God's creation.

There were, moreover, many other Christian writers in the heyday of the patristic era who contributed to the construction of medieval cosmology. The following have to be especially mentioned: Ambrose, Augustine, Basil, Gregory of Nyssa, John Chrysostom, Maximus the

Confessor, Isidore of Seville, John Damascene, Bede the Venerable, and of course, Boethius.[33]

The name of Boethius perhaps belongs more to the history of philosophy than to that of theology. It is well known, however, how much he was esteemed by medieval theologians and how gladly they adopted his well-formulated definitions. Following Plato, he also taught that man had to model his conduct on the example of the heavenly bodies. Addressing himself to Divine Philosophy, who comes to visit him in prison, he recalls the happy times when he used to sit in his library and was free to discuss with her the secrets of nature, and when she pointed out the course of the heavenly bodies with a ray of light, teaching him to regulate his deeds and his whole life according to the example of the heavenly order.[34] Boethius also gives a detailed account of the influence of the heavenly bodies on the sublunary world as instruments of Providence.[35]

Christian teaching on creation, Providence, and human freedom repeatedly provided the Fathers of the Church with an opportunity to subject the cosmological conceptions of their contemporaries to critical examination. They endorsed the broad outline of the world picture held by Plato and his followers, never doubting for a moment the correctness of this view. All of them without exception regarded the earth as the center of the universe, with the celestial spheres moving around the earth, exercising an influence on all material things which are composed of the four elements.

Unlike Plato, who taught that the world was made out of a preexistent matter, they considered the world to have been called up from nothingness by God's omnipotence. Evil in the world must not be attributed to God but to the sin of the first man. It is important to note that the Fathers of the Church saw the world as governed by God's Providence and not by fate. What is more, it was precisely in the motion of the planets that this found expression, for the planets were considered to be the instruments God used to direct events according to his will. There could therefore be no question of fate. But man's freedom was fully safeguarded. Since the influence of the planets only extended to material things and not to spiritual beings, it was wrong to think that human conduct was determined by the course of the planets. To the celestial spheres of Plato and Aristotle they added a still higher sphere, namely, the Empyrean, the abode of the angels and saints. According to Augustine this term was inspired by Porphyry, the disciple of Plotinus.[36] All these points were later to be found in medieval theology.

A striking example of this confrontation between the cosmological religion of the Greeks and the emergence of Christian theology in the patristic era is to be found in the *Hexaëmeron* of St. Ambrose, which begins as follows:

> What degree of infatuation have men not reached! There are those (Plato and his disciples) who accept three principles in the beginning: God, the original pattern, and matter. It is claimed that these three principles are imperishable, uncreated, without beginning. On this view God is not the Creator of matter, but a craftsman who, attentive to his model (the idea), has made the world with the help of matter. This matter is presented as that from which all things were made; the world, then, is also conceived as imperishable, uncreated, without cause.
>
> Others, such as Aristotle, who found it necessary to discuss this theory with his friends, accept two principles: matter and form, and besides this an efficient cause, whose right it was to realize in a competent manner whatever it considered worthwhile.
>
> What is more improper than to put the eternity of the work and the eternity of the almighty Creator on an equal footing? It is even more improper to pass the work itself off as God and in this way to render divine honor to the heavens, the earth and the sea. As a consequence of this, even parts of the world are considered to be divine, even though there are important differences of opinion concerning the world itself. Pythagoras claims there is but one world, while others say there are countless worlds. Hence we think of Democritus who in virtue of his antiquity enjoys considerable authority in the field of natural science. According to Aristotle the world itself has always existed and will always continue to exist. Plato, on the other hand, holds the view that the world has not always existed, but that it will always exist in the future. Then there are those who claim that the world did not always exist and will not remain in existence.
>
> How can we possibly discover the truth amidst all these differences of opinion? Some say the world itself is God, because, as they believe, it possesses a divine intellect; others claim parts of the world are divine; for others still the world and its parts are divine. How are we to imagine these gods? How many are there? Where do they abide? How do they live? With what are they concerned? Look how difficult this is to comprehend. For if we ascribe divine dignity to the world we are then compelled to conceive it as a god spinning round, spherical in shape, with fire inside, driven forward in a definite direction, deprived of all feeling and carried along not by its own strength but by an alien power.[37]

One can readily see how Ambrose, safeguarding the Christian concepts of God and of creation, wanted to settle accounts with all these cosmological theories of the Greek philosophers, with whom he was familiar either from a firsthand knowledge of their writings or, as is more probable, from his reading of Cicero, Porphyry, and others. In his commentary on the biblical creation story, he applied himself to clearing the Greek world picture of any theological errors and in this way to forming a Christian view of the cosmos.

The same concern, though to a lesser extent, is also to be found in Augustine. It is well known that Augustine had very little interest in the natural sciences. In actual fact, however, his attitude was somewhat ambivalent in this respect. On the one hand he never ceased to admire and extol the beauty and wonderful harmony of creation, in which he saw proof of God's existence.[38] On the other hand, in opposition to the prevalent fashion, he declared that one could be a good Christian even though one knew nothing about the structure of the world and the nature of plants and animals.[39]

At the same time, however, he proclaimed the doctrine of the "two books"[40] — a doctrine later cherished by medieval theologians. According to this doctrine there are two books from which we can come to know God: the book of nature and the book of sacred Scriptures. Although God has revealed himself in both books, the first appeared to Augustine to be of value only insofar as it refers to the second. One has to realize, however, that he was only moderately interested in reading the first book, which in any case never seems to have held any real fascination for him.

There were three parts to Augustine's world: on the upper level, God; on the lower level, material things; and in the middle, souls. Since material things were the least significant to him, he preferred to focus his attention on God and on the soul, especially in its relation to God. It is true, nevertheless, that one can find evidence of him endeavoring to give a Christian interpretation to the world picture which was then current. In his commentary on Genesis as well as in his sermons and major works (*Confessions, City of God, The Trinity*) we find important considerations that helped to establish a Christian cosmology such as was striven after in the Middle Ages. Of utmost significance in this context was Augustine's concept of order, which he greatly emphasized. His commentary on the passage from the Book of Wisdom (11:21) "You ordered all things by measure, number, weight" has never been forgotten.[41] It is also in Augustine that we once again find the notion of the cosmic order having to be reflected in man's soul and moral conduct. Macrocosm and microcosm are thus attuned to each other.[42]

Among the Greek Fathers, special mention must be given to Gregory of Nyssa for his very original integration of Platonic heritage into his theology. He also regarded the universe as a "perfect order," an ancient Greek notion which he felt was confirmed in sacred Scriptures. The world is considered to be entirely directed towards man, having been created for him. Like Basil the Great and Gregory Nazianzen, he held that man is a microcosm, reflecting the harmony of the universe. He did, however, have his own particular understanding of this idea. Following Aller's distinction of the various forms of microcosm, we should have to characterize his notion of the microcosm as symbolistic.[43] For Gregory of Nyssa, then, man is a reflection of the cosmos because he is in the first place an image of God, who is also reflected by the cosmos. It is precisely for this reason that we find the same order and harmony in man as is to be found in the world. Man's greatness is due not so much to the fact that he is a reflection of the cosmos but that he is a reflection of God. The image of God in the soul and the image of God in the cosmos must then display the same qualities and characteristics.[44]

Of particular interest in this context is the work of Maximus the Confessor (580–662) who greatly elaborated on the theme of man as microcosm and as mediator between the material and spiritual world,[45] so that his world of thought has been characterized as a "cosmic liturgy." There are many other Christian writers of the patristic era who ought to be mentioned for their influence on the medieval theologian's world picture. Irenaeus (d. 202),[46] for example, developed a Christology displaying important cosmological aspects and comparing the seven gifts mentioned in Isaiah to the seven celestial spheres. Lactantius (d. 340) deserves mention for the way he included cosmology in his defense of the doctrine of divine Providence. Isidore of Seville (d. 636) wrote what can be considered as encyclopaedias of the sciences of his day. Both his *Etymologiarium libri XX* and his *De rerum natura* were often imitated in the Middle Ages. In this context, particular attention has to be given to Bede the Venerable (d. 735) whose *De rerum natura*[47] was very much consulted for its general description of the cosmos and the main phenomena of nature. This work was in fact largely inspired by the *Historia naturalis* of Pliny the Elder. From Bede's detailed commentary on the *Hexaëmeron*,[48] we have a clear idea of how he viewed the cosmos and how he found this view confirmed in Scripture. Finally, we should also mention John Damascene (d. 749) whose *Institutiones de fide orthodoxa* only became known in the West during the pontificate of Pope Eugene III (1145–1153) and from that time on was held in great respect.

Chapter Two

THE WORLD PICTURE
OF MEDIEVAL THEOLOGY

In each age of the world distinguished by high activity
there will be found at its culmination some profound
cosmological outlook, implicitly accepted, impressing
its own type upon the current springs of action. This
ultimate cosmology is only partly expressed, and the
details of such expression issue into derivative special-
ized questions of violent controversy.[1]

These words of Alfred North Whitehead are particularly applicable to
the Middle Ages. The more one becomes absorbed in the study of
medieval culture, the more one is compelled to realize that the intellectual life of the period was indeed entirely governed by a unanimously accepted view concerning the general structure of the universe
and the place of man in this world. The main features of this cosmological outlook were never in dispute, even if there was often fierce
discussion on questions of minor importance. What is clear is that the
great spiritual unity and harmony manifested by medieval culture was
predominantly derived from this "ultimate cosmology" leaving its
mark not only on the current philosophy and theology but just as
much on the literature, plastic arts, and even on the sociopolitical life
of the period.

In this chapter we shall attempt to trace the main features of the
world picture invoked by the medieval theologian which form the
framework within which he interpreted Christian doctrine. In a later
chapter we shall have to examine to what extent this view of the

cosmos influenced Christian doctrine as such. It is generally known that the medieval picture of the universe was geocentric. The question is, however, how much importance medieval man attached to this picture of the universe, to what extent it was present in his consciousness, what place it occupied in the whole of his spiritual concerns, and finally to what extent it can be considered a "system-forming element" of the medieval mind. It is not easy for us today to enter into the spirit of this province of medieval life, partly because we need to ignore all that contemporary natural sciences have to teach us concerning the world and its constituent parts, and partly because we must take into account the fact that cosmography occupied a much larger place in the medieval world of thought than it does nowadays. Despite the progress of the sciences or, rather, precisely because of this progress, we are no longer able to form a picture of the universe in any way as clear, simple, or convincing as that held during the Middle Ages. We have become aware of the extreme complexity of reality and at the same of the relativity and limitations of our knowledge. With regard to the main issues concerning the structure of the universe, we mostly have to content ourselves with more or less plausible hypotheses, without being able to test their accuracy and value.

The situation was of course entirely different for medieval man who lived in the quiet certainty that his picture of the universe, as far as its general outline was concerned, corresponded completely with reality. The main features of the "world machine" were clearly present to his mind. It was, moreover, simply inconceivable that one would doubt the correctness of this picture which was, as he believed, presented to him by the infallible authority of sacred Scriptures and confirmed by the great minds of antiquity. Except for several writers who were dismissed as insignificant or simply as erring spirits, the whole of antiquity, pagan as well as Christian, appeared to proclaim the same unshakable doctrine. All those who possessed any authority in the eyes of men of that time had presented the same picture. Under such circumstances, who could harbor the slightest doubt as to the credibility of a doctrine warranted by such eminent authorities, human as well as divine? Medieval man thus lived in the quiet conviction that his view of the cosmos was the only correct one. It was especially during the twelfth and thirteenth centuries, the heyday of scholasticism, characterized by the renewed discovery of Greek science, that this conviction was prevalent. Just as today there are those who see a landscape through the eyes of an artist's interpretation of this same landscape, so medieval man saw the cosmos through the eyes of the authoritative scholars of antiquity.[2]

Countless descriptions of this world picture are to be found in the writings of philosophers and theologians, in literature and in art. The following titles are fairly indicative of the topics discussed, especially by theologians: On the nature of things, On the universe, On the world, On the picture of the world, On the philosophy of the world, On the division of nature. All, without exception, appeal to the geocentric picture of the universe as point of reference. What is most striking about these writings is the quiet self-certainty with which data are supplied. In the eyes of the writer these data are so clear and self-evident that there seems to be no need to advance even the semblance of an argument. Everyone knows that things are just as they are presented here: that the earth is surrounded by seven spheres carrying the planets which greatly influence birth, death, and all phenomena in the sublunary world; that the earth stands immovable in the center of the cosmos; that above the spheres of planets there is a higher sphere still or, rather, three spheres, the lowest of which carries the fixed stars; that the whole cosmos is completely round; that the planets move in a circular orbit; that macrocosm and microcosm are perfectly attuned to each other and constructed according to the same basic plan; that there are four elements—earth, water, air, and fire— each of which strives after its due place; that, in a word, the whole cosmos has been perfectly arranged by the Creator.

On every occasion this pattern was firmly adhered to. All facets of life were connected with it and all opinions and theories were tested by it. In short, it formed the background to a complete world picture without which medieval man is simply inconceivable. The spirit of the Middle Ages is on the whole the spirit expressed in this picture of the universe. It is clearly noticeable that medieval theology was from the beginning interested in cosmology and that this interest steadily increased over the years, reaching its climax in the thirteenth century. In the centuries which followed a particular view of the cosmos was likewise maintained as a natural and self-evident part of theological thought.

Of the so-called prescholastics, mention should be given to Rhabanus Maurus, archbishop of Mainz (d. 806), for his book *On the Universe* in which theology and the profane sciences were placed together.[3] More important still was John Scotus Eriugena (810–880), an amazing and exceptional figure who, according to M. D. Chenu, "rose as a monolith at the gateway to the Middle Ages." It is true that his principal work, *On the Division of Nature*, never had any real impact on account of its condemnation by Pope Honorius III, but for a considerable time it was a much-read book, despite some obscure passages.[4] It was nevertheless a remarkable book in which there is clear evidence of the influence of Augustine, Maximus the Confessor, and the Pseudo-Dionysius (whose writings were for that matter translated by Eriugena). The second and third part of the book contains a detailed commentary assimilated in the spirit of the Platonic world picture. Eriugena also considered man a microcosm for whom the macrocosm has been created. Through the microcosm redeemed by Christ the macrocosm is also brought to its destiny in God.

In the course of time there was a steady increase in the number of works with a cosmological strain. It has already been pointed out how the twelfth century was characterized by a considerable interest in the world envisaged as a single whole and how this concern was evoked by the desire to construct a Christian outlook on the cosmos, an all-embracing Christian world picture. There are many texts to be found bearing witness to this endeavor but only a few can be mentioned here. Of particular importance was the school of Chartres, which flourished in the first half of the twelfth century and was characterized by its humanistic tendency, namely, the endeavor to reconcile theology and profane science. There were three prominent figures at this school. In the first place there was Magister Theodoricus (also known as Thierry of Chartres, Carnotensis, Brito [d.1151]), highly respected by his contemporaries for his erudition, and author of a commentary on the *Hexaëmeron*, in which Plato's *Timaeus* and the Mosaic creation story come together.[5] More important still for what concerns us here was William of Conches, whose *Philosophia Mundi* was widely known and for a long time was attributed to various other authors such as Bede the Venerable, Boethius, William of Hirschau, Honorius of Autun, and Hugh of St. Victor.[6] William of Conches had much veneration for Plato and especially for the *Timaeus*, which he knew from the translation and commentary by Chalcidius. Besides the work we have already mentioned he also wrote glosses on the *Timaeus*.[7]

In his view, Plato was the greatest philosopher of all time, especially in the field of cosmology. He consulted Plato to the extent that he could reconcile the latter's teaching with Christian doctrine. What we find in his writings, then, is the traditional view concerning the four elements, seven planets, microcosm and macrocosm, etc. He dismissed the biblical claim that there were "waters above the firmament" (Gen. 1:7) as quite impossible and attempted to offer a different explanation of this text. According to him, Adam's body was formed out of clay, in which we find the four elements, and though Eve's body was likewise formed, the mixture was different.

Finally, we have to mention the work of Bernardus Silvestris, even though his relation to the School of Chartres is not entirely clear.[8] His *De mundi universitate* is, according to Etienne Gilson, of Christian inspiration, although besides biblical texts it also contains certain mythological and allegorical elements derived from pagan poets. The cause of this dogmatic ambiguity seems to be his exaggerated concern with literary style.

The School of Chartres was not the only school, however, to be interested in cosmological questions at this time. In practically all the schools and abbeys of the time we find evidence of this fascination with cosmological problems, always inspired by the same spirit: to construct a Christian view of the cosmos. The following are a few examples: Hugh of St. Victor (d. 1141), *Didascalion, De sacramentis, Adnot. Elucid. in Pentateuchon;*[9] Godfrey of St. Victor (d. 1194), *Microcosmos;*[10] Andrew of St. Victor;[11] Honorius of Autun (d. ca. 1130), *Elucidarium, Liber XII quaest;*[12] Gerhoh of Reichersberg (d. 1169), *De aedificio dei;*[13] Arnold of Bonneval (d. after 1156), *In operibus sex dierum;*[14] Alan of Lille (d. 1102), *De insulis, De planctu naturae, Distinctiones dictionum, Art. mundus;*[15] Adelard of Bath (d. after 1130) *Astrolabium, Quaestiones naturales;*[16] Abelard (d. 1142), *Expos. in hexaemeron.*[17] A particular mention should be given here to Peter Lombard. It is a well-known fact that his *Sentences* greatly influenced the development of theology, for a long time serving as a textbook in all faculties of theology, where each new "master of theology" had to write a commentary on this work. What is important here is that this book succeeded in introducing the discussion of the world picture into academic theology, making it an integral part of theological systematization (*Lib. secundus:* d. 12–15, on the creation of material things). There appears to be no doubt that during the early period of scholasticism theologians had a lively interest in the picture of the universe, the general outline of which can be considered to have been fixed.

Far from waning in the following period, this interest in cosmological questions actually increased in theological circles, under the influence of new translations of Greek and Arabic texts which appeared at that time. To be convinced of this one need only consult the repertory of the thirteenth-century masters of theology in Paris to determine the number of works devoted to the description of the universe, the motion and influence of the planets, and other phenomena of nature. Some of these works were in the form of commentaries on authentic or spurious writings of Aristotle or commentaries on the *Hexaëmeron* or on the second book of Peter Lombard's *Sentences*, while others appeared as individual tracts or *Quaestiones disputatae.*[18]

The same phenomenon is to be found in other universities of the time. In Oxford, Bologna, Montpellier, Salamanca, and Cologne cosmological questions were as hotly debated as in Paris. Oxford was particularly renowned in this respect, with names such as Robert Grosseteste and Roger Bacon. It was the latter who insisted that theologians should concern themselves more with the natural sciences, alchemy, and especially astrology, because human behavior could not be explained without these sciences.[19] Throughout western Europe astronomy and astrology were highly esteemed.[20] In this context one cannot rate high enough the work of Albert the Great who taught at Paris and Cologne, making considerable contribution to the spread of Aristotelian science. His influence on medieval intellectual life is sufficiently well known. Not only were his books on astronomy, alchemy, astrology, and physics widely distributed, but even his theological writings often dealt with these matters.[21]

Though no one doubted the general world picture, there was much lively discussion on subordinate questions such as: Is the empyrean both moved and moving or only moving and not moved? Why is the crystalline heaven necessary for the proper functioning of the world machine? Is an eternal creation conceivable? How far does the influence of the planets extend? Can a sinner attribute his faults to the planets? What are we to make of the practice of astrology and alchemy? What specific influences ought to be attributed to each of the seven planets individually? Any theologian worthy of the name had to be able to give a decisive answer to all these questions. The various opinions were carefully compared, the one authority confronted with the other, as a completely harmonious answer was striven after in a most subtle manner. There were copious writings on all these matters, whether in the form of more technical works or popular texts intended to urge the believer to devotion and guard him from superstition. Neither can there be any doubt that the same topics were not infrequently dealt with in sermons or at least that the sermons referred to a general world picture.[22]

Let us now, however, focus attention on the greatest of the medieval theologians, Bonaventure and Aquinas, with whom scholasticism reached its pinnacle. They too reflected quite consciously on the great cosmic order, giving detailed account of this in their writings. If we consider these authors at some length, it is by no means because they constituted an exception but, on the contrary, because they exemplify the spirit of the time. Related views and ideas are to be found in all of their contemporaries. It was, however, through the work of Bonaventure and Aquinas that the medieval world picture, in its relevance to theology, achieved its well-balanced completion. Here we find the most pure and perfect realization of the dream of a Christian view of the cosmos that had been striven after from the beginning of the scholastic period.

Saint Bonaventure

Unlike Aquinas and other medieval theologians, Bonaventure never wrote commentaries on Aristotle's works concerning natural science. It can generally be said that his writings are neither purely philosophical nor purely scientific. This is to be explained by the fact that he considered philosophy, natural science, and theology as a single whole, which we could label as a Christian view of the world. It is precisely this straining after a harmonious Christian outlook on man and the world that forms one of the principal characteristics of his thought. Until the end of his academic career, that is, until his final uncompleted work, *Collationes in hexaëmeron*, he opposed every attempt to destroy this unity in Christian thought.[23]

If we pay particular attention to the world picture forming the background to this whole view of the world, it soon becomes evident that Bonaventure had a clearly defined and resolute opinion on this world picture, which was moreover closely allied to his philosophical and theological thought. It could never be said that this is simply a matter of incidentals that have to be attributed to circumstances, being essentially unrelated to the rest (the indispensable part) of his work. From a careful reading of his work it is quite clear that his cosmology constituted an essential part of his religious view of life, and that he was always concerned to situate Christianity in the concrete world as it appeared to him under the influence of the prevalent picture of the time. What we find in his work, then, is a clearly defined world picture closely aligned to his philosophy, theology, and mysticism. The mark of his genius is precisely the fact that he united all these elements in a well-balanced whole, in no way detrimental to their individual character. There is no evidence in his work that he had any doubts about the validity of his world picture. Like most thinkers of his day, Bonaventure was firmly convinced that the Platonic-Aristotelian picture of the universe was unassailable as far as its main features were concerned and that it was, moreover, indirectly confirmed by Scripture. As we hope to point out presently, he unreservedly accepted in his philosophical and theological thinking the demands placed upon him by this picture of the universe.

How then did Bonaventure picture the cosmos? The answer to this question is made easy by the countless references in his writings to his view on the construction of the universe. One of the most explicit statements is to be found in his *Breviloquium:*

Concerning the existence of material nature the following points are to be held: the entire material world machine comprises a heavenly and an elementary nature. The heavenly nature is mainly divided into three heavens: the empyrean, the crystalline heaven, and the firmament. Within the firmament (the starry heaven) there are seven planets: Saturn, Jupiter, Mars, the Sun, Venus, Mercury, and the Moon. The elementary nature is divided into four spheres: fire, air, water, and earth. From the highest point in heaven to the center of the earth there are in all ten celestial and four elementary spheres. Thus the whole material world machine is constructed in a distinct, perfect, and ordered manner."[24]

What strikes one about this text is the quiet certainty with which Bonaventure announces his picture of the universe: "the following points are to be held." There is no sign at all of any hesitancy or reserve. Neither is there any question whatsoever of this being a poetic description or symbolic interpretation of reality; it is, rather, a completely matter-of-fact enumeration of the fundamental elements which in his view go to make up the universe. This holds good not only for the four elementary spheres and seven spheres of planets— something that was an absolute fact for medieval man—but also for the three highest heavens. The starry heaven (the Latin *caelum stellatum* or *firmamentum* conveys a sense of solidity) had already been considered by the Greeks and all later scholars as the all-encompassing sphere. As to the empyrean,[25] its existence was confirmed by various Fathers of the Church and appeared to correspond so well with the biblical teaching on heaven that any further argumentation was superfluous.[26] Concerning the crystalline heaven, things were not so easy. This heaven is made out of the element water, but then a water quite unlike the water we know on earth.[27] That at any rate is the most probable explanation. To prove the existence of the crystalline heaven, Bonaventure appeals to the analogy between macrocosm and microcosm. In the microcosm, man, the head is higher than the heart. Whereas the heart is by nature warm and fiery, the brains are cool and moist. And because the various parts of the macrocosm are arranged in the same manner as in the microcosm, it is logical to assume that there must be water to be found somewhere above the sun and the heavenly bodies which radiate heat.[28] The existence of the three heavens not only reminds us of the mystery of the Blessed Trinity, traces of which are to be found everywhere in creation, but also corresponds very well with the words of St. Paul, who by his own testimony was raised to the third heaven.[29] It is the task of the crystalline heaven to connect the empyrean with the starry heaven. All three of these heavens were understood to be perfectly circular.[30]

Below the three heavens we find the seven spheres of planets, among which we must count the sun and the moon. For Bonaventure, the number seven had a mysterious meaning. It is to be found in all areas, in the "mundus archetypus" as well as in the arrangement of earthly things. Besides the seven planets, there are seven days in the week. The candelabra in the temple has seven branches and there are also seven sacraments. There are, moreover, seven gifts of the Holy Spirit; seven virtues, three divine and four cardinal; seven works of mercy and seven deadly sins; and in music, seven notes or tones. What is more, there are seven pillars of wisdom (Prov. 9:1). On the day of God's wrath seven women will fight over one man (Is. 4:1). Christ multiplied seven loaves (Mt. 15:34–36; Macc. 6:38–41; 8:5–6). In the Book of Revelation, John addresses the seven churches of Asia Minor (Rev. 1:11) and sees seven golden candlesticks between which Christ appears (Rev. 1:12) and a closed book with seven seals (Rev. 5:1). The seven angels standing before God are given seven trumpets. The number seven is also to be found in the microcosm, man: his body consists of four elements and his soul of three faculties, intelligence, memory, and will. In all, then, man has seven powers. Neither is it by coincidence that Bonaventure divided his theological synthesis, the *Breviloquium* into seven chapters. The number seven appears to be designated to signify the totality of things.[31]

Beneath the three heavens and the seven planets we find the earth, made up of four spheres: fire, air, earth, and water. The mixture of these elements results in the mixed bodies, minerals, plants, animals, and humans. Another function of the planets that must be included is that they make it possible for various elements with contradictory properties (cold, hot, wet, dry) to exist together in the same body.

This, then, gives us a survey of the general structure that Bonaventure attributed to the cosmos in the spirit of the age. However, several important points have still to be added. The first concerns the matter of which the universe is made. Were heavenly and earthly things formed out of the same matter? Strictly speaking, both involve matter, though taken in its real state the matter actually differs in each case. On earth matter is transient and imperfect, while in the heavens it is imperishable and perfect.[32] This brings us to an important aspect of Bonaventure's picture of the universe. Like Plato and Aristotle he too considered the celestial spheres to be imperishable and perfect. The earth, however, was the realm of imperfection and transience. From the point of view of perfection, matter already displays a certain gradation: there is lower and higher matter. This gave rise to a problem: if we assume that the heavenly bodies are imperishable and perfect, may we not then conclude that they are eternal? Bonaventure never failed to oppose this belief most strongly. He regarded the cosmos as having been created in time—with a beginning—and even the possibility of a creation from all eternity ought, in his opinion, to be completely rejected.[33] It is well known that Aquinas held a different opinion on this question. The imperishableness and perfection of the heavenly bodies are created attributes, so that there is no question of them having existed from all eternity. The heavens are therefore made of a more perfect matter than the earth and for this reason also the heavens were placed above and the earth below.[34] The existence of two kinds of matter gave rise to another question: was the human body formed out of heavenly or earthly matter? According to Scripture man was made out of the dust of the earth (Gen. 2:7). But was it not more fitting that the human body should have been formed out of heavenly matter, seeing that it had to be joined to an imperishable soul? For surely there had to be a certain proportion between matter and form. Bonaventure solved the difficulty by appealing to Aristotle's teaching that the soul can extend to all things, and thus also to earthly matter, but more especially by appealing to the divine world order: what would perfect and imperishable matter be doing in the realm of imperfection and transience?[35] It is clearly a requirement of the world order that man be united with all things, the lower as well as the higher: through the soul man is united with the higher and through the body he is united with the lower.

It is of interest to note how Bonaventure considered the position that must be assigned to the earthly paradise in the totality of the world order. On this question Peter Lombard had claimed that paradise had to be in a very high place, extending to the sphere of the moon.[36] Many objections can be raised to this idea. Between the sphere of the moon and the sphere of air, there is the sphere of fire, in which it is impossible for man to live. Next one must wonder whether there is enough air above. According to Augustine the upper layer of air is extremely thin, so that even birds cannot live there. If paradise were to be found in such a high place, then man with his animal body would not be able to survive. What is more, at such a height man would be too close to the sun with its unbearable heat. In response, Bonaventure argued that paradise was to be found in a high place, where the air is always pure and healthy, suitable for beings destined for eternal life, and where the earth's unhealthful evaporations could not reach. And yet it was not quite so high that it would extend to the sphere of the moon. This last remark was only to indicate that paradise was to be found in an exceptionally beautiful, quiet, and well-lit place.[37]

A second question that still has to be discussed here concerns motion in the universe. Bonaventure considered the cosmos a gigantic mechanism, which he repeatedly referred to as the "world machine."[38] The question then arises as to how this huge mechanism is set in motion. This takes place, in the first instance, through God who, though he moves the world, is himself immovable.[39] The empyrean must also be considered to be immovable, by virtue of its perfection and nearness to God. Just as God causes motion in the starry heaven, he creates calm in the empyrean.[40] The starry heaven, the firmament, is set in motion by God, by means of a created force with which he cooperates directly.[41] This created force may not, however, be conceived as a kind of world-soul—the starry heaven is not an animate being—but rather as a property of the heavenly bodies, the inadequacy of which is supplemented by God, or better still, by God's influence by means of an angel.[42] For Bonaventure there was no doubt whatsoever that the angels have an important part to play in the motion of the celestial spheres.[43] To account for the motion of the planets Aristotle had appealed to the intervention of intelligent beings, separate "intelligences." It was not long, then, before the question arose whether these "intelligences" should be identified with the angels mentioned in Scripture. Despite some protest[44] this identification was soon adopted into medieval theology. Bonaventure had absolutely no objection to this, and considered the terms "intelligences" and angels as synonymous.[45] But to conclude from this that there are only ten angels, as Avicenna and others had done, was a gross error that had to be completely repudiated. But it is reasonable to accept that the heavenly bodies are moved by intelligent beings.[46] We should not conclude from this, however, that moving the heavenly spheres would be the most important activity of the angels and that they were created only for this task. The angels were created in the first place to behold God, and, in subordinate order, to set the planets in motion. This task is for that matter only temporary, because at the end of time all motion of the planets will finally cease.[47] Just as it is fitting that angels are sent by God for the benefit of man, it is no less appropriate that they are instructed to set the celestial spheres in motion and to direct them.[48]

The angels are thus seen to determine the motion of the spheres. But this gave rise to the question of the use of these motions. Why do the planets actually exist and what function do they have in the cosmos as a whole? How far does their power and influence extend?

Bonaventure was able to give a clear answer to all these questions. The planets were shown to be necessary for making the cosmos into a harmonious whole, forming a link between the three heavens and the four earthly elements which, by virtue of their nature, are so far apart that a gradual transition is needed.[49] In this way the cosmos was seen to form a splendidly ordered and well-balanced whole, a worthy reflection of God's wisdom and omnipotence.[50] The planets are thus necessary for the completion and adornment of the universe.[51] Besides bringing about the cohesion between the three highest heavens and the four lower spheres, they also accomplish all sorts of useful tasks. The first concerns the division of time. It is by means of the planets that we are able to distinguish days, months, and years.[52] Next, they exert influence on the coming-to-be and passing-away of all compound bodies on earth, namely, minerals, plants, animals, and the human body.[53] It is clear, then, that the planets have a decisive part to play in the coming-to-be and passing-away of all earthly beings. Without their influence there would be neither birth nor death. When, therefore, at the end of time the motion of the planets ceases, it will not only result in there being no days, months, and years, but it will also mean that no new beings can be born and no existing beings will be able to die. For this reason Bonaventure did not fail to connect the immortality of the risen body with the immobility of the celestial spheres.[54]

All physical occurrences on earth can, therefore, always be reduced to the influence of the heavenly bodies. The latter are the instruments, the secondary causes, God employs to call up all material phenomena. At the same time, however, Bonaventure emphasized that the instrumental causality of the heavenly bodies is restricted to material things. They can exercise no influence on spiritual beings, seeing that material instruments are entirely unsuitable for calling up spiritual phenomena. There is, therefore, no way whatsoever in which man's free decisions may be attributed to the influence of the planets. Such a view would destroy man's freedom and lead to fatalism.[55]

The human soul is directly subject to God alone. This means that the influence of the heavenly bodies is restricted to the delimitation of time and the control of material phenomena. Free actions in the future cannot, therefore, be read from the planets.[56] Concerning all the rest, however, the influence of the heavenly bodies is indispensable and decisive, and in this regard an important role is played by the zodiac.[57] Though Bonaventure wrote extensively on all these matters, it is necessary for us, in view of our theme, to confine ourselves to sketching the main features of his picture of the universe. From

what we have seen so far it is clear that there are very many cosmological elements to be found in his work, forming an important theme
of his thought.

Such a cosmology, however, also implies a view on man. For
Bonaventure the universe was a wonderful work of art, characterized
by perfect order and unfailing beauty and hence man's first task was
to praise the Creator, thanking him for the work of his hand and
recognizing the trace of the creative God in all created things. The
whole cosmos thus became a magnificent hymn of praise to the wisdom, power, and goodness of him who made this world for the benefit
of man:

> He who is not enlightened by the radiant beauty of created things,
> is blind; he who is not aroused by the noise of their voice, is deaf:
> he who does not praise God for all he has made, is mute; he who
> after so many indications does not know how to ascend to the First
> Principle, is a fool.[58]

God not only made the world in which man lives but he continuously guides and directs it. For this reason God's wisdom and power
are revealed in all events as well as in all things. Confronted with all
this man stands in awe and in contemplation of God's deeds. It cannot
be man's task to change anything in the order God has willed, for the
world is good and beautiful in all respects,[59] a source of joy and happiness for all who behold it. Bonaventure's attitude to life is thoroughly optimistic: there is no sign of any indulgence on his part in
the tragic element in human existence. With an almost childlike na-
iveté he rejoiced at the beauty of all creation. In his view man's task
is reduced to self-perfection or the attempt to realize in himself that
perfect, hierarchical order exemplified in the "mundus archetypus."
Microcosm and macrocosm are, moreover, perfectly attuned to each
other,[60] so that the cosmos undergoes man's fate and man in his turn
has to take his cue from the cosmos. In contemplating the world man
must focus his attention on the splendid hierarchical order prevalent
in the cosmos, while attempting to achieve the same order and harmony in his inner life.[61] There must also be a balance in his inner life
between the four emotions, corresponding to the four elements: fear,
sorrow, joy, and trust.[62] Just as physical health is only possible if the
four primary elements are to be found in the right proportion, so
mental health can only be attained when these four emotions are
evenly balanced.

In the moral field we find the four cardinal virtues which create
order in human life and correspond in the "mental hemisphere" to

the four points of the compass in the "earthly hemisphere."[63] The same basic structure is displayed, as it were, by the material and the moral world. By adding the three theological virtues to the four cardinal virtues we have seven virtues, all of which are to be found permeating the soul that has been arranged in hierarchy.[64] It is clear from the detailed descriptions we find in his writings that Bonaventure had a particular liking for this hierarchical conception of the soul, which refers not only to the order considered to be present in our inner life, but to the hierarchy among the souls themselves. Like the angels, the souls are grouped into nine choirs according to aptitude, effort, and the amount of grace received.[65] It is, moreover, a joy for the soul to be permitted to behold its own hierarchical order.[66]

God's creation is thus characterised in every respect by a hierarchical order so that whatever does not belong to this order must be considered as nonexistent.[67] Both the world outside us and the world within form a bright mirror from which we can read God's wisdom.[68] It is precisely this presence of order and beauty in the whole creation that Bonaventure considered to be the most obvious proof of God's existence. The world was therefore seen as a perfect order, leading us by the hand, as it were, on our way to God.[69]

Saint Thomas Aquinas

In Thomas Aquinas, perhaps even more so than in Bonaventure, there is clear evidence of a constant concern to integrate the Graeco-Arabian world picture into his philosophical and theological thought. It has sometimes been suggested that Aquinas considered this geocentric picture of the universe to be a mere hypothesis to which he attached little or no importance. In this view his philosophical and theological system is essentially independent of his cosmological conceptions, the latter being simply ascribed to circumstances. The fact, therefore, that these cosmological ideas are now quite obsolete by no means detracts from the intrinsic value of his philosophy and theology. We shall later have to examine how these conceptions were arrived at. In the meantime, however, recent studies have irrefutably shown that such a view is completely untenable.[70] There was never the slightest doubt in Aquinas's mind as to the validity of the world picture of the time, which he moreover described with considerable accuracy, giving clear indication that it certainly belonged to his thought. For Aquinas, as for most scholastics, cosmology, anthropolgy, metaphysics, and theology formed a well-balanced and harmonious whole.

From his detailed commentaries on the scientific works of Aristotle (except for those dealing with biology) we have clear proof[71] of the well-known fact that Aquinas was very much interested in the natural sciences. There are also other writings bearing testimony to his interest in cosmological questions.[72] In all these writings he took into account not only the scientific works of Greek antiquity but also the more recent writings of Jewish and Arabian scholars, in the conviction that a theologian ought quite consciously to include a consideration of nature in his theological work. This is most evident in the first chapters of the second book of the *Summa contra gentiles,* where Aquinas discusses the usefulness and necessity of directing our attention to nature with a view to a sound comprehension of doctrine. To have a perfect knowledge of anything we have to consider its workings, for this reveals its strength and quality,[73] indeed, its deepest nature. To know God, therefore, we must also focus our attention on his creation. The second chapter is entitled: "That the consideration of creatures is useful for building sure faith." Here consideration of nature is only commended as *useful* for a good understanding of faith, but in the next line this qualification is made more forceful and we read of the necessity of considering nature for reaching a knowledge of God.[74] To prove this thesis four arguments are advanced. God's wisdom is first revealed to us whenever we consider all created things, just as a work of art lets us see the artist's skill.[75] Such a contemplation of creation further allows us to admire God's supreme power, evoking in us a feeling of respect and veneration.[76] What is more, it teaches us to discover God's goodness: all that is found to be good, perfect, and beautiful in creatures must be referred back to God and fill us with love and gratitude.[77] In this way the contemplation of created things is seen to foster the love of God as well as knowledge and reverence. An even greater effect of this contemplation is that it grants us a certain similarity with God, imparting to us his supreme wisdom and perfection.[78]

Of course, one can ask oneself just precisely what Aquinas meant by this consideration of created things. Is it a question of a mere abstract, metaphysical, or even poetic contemplation of created reality? Does it also include what we nowadays term the natural sciences? It will be seen that Aquinas did not draw a boundary between these two forms of knowledge. In his view the more perfect our knowledge of nature, the more we share in God's supreme wisdom and the more we shall admire his power and goodness. For this reason our knowledge can never be great enough, and, irrespective of where it comes from, it is for the Christian a way to the true knowledge of God, to a better comprehension of faith. And conversely, just as a correct knowledge of created things leads to the true God, so a wrong conception of created things affects our image of God: errors concerning creatures result in errors concerning God.[79] Clearly, then, a sound knowledge and careful study of created things will guard us against mistaken notions about God.[80] He who does not know the true nature of things is also incapable of discerning the true order in creation. A consequence of this situation is that man begins to imagine he is subject to things which actually have no power over him, as for example, the heavenly bodies in relation to the free decisions of the will.[81] One cannot, therefore, have a proper understanding of the world order without a correct knowledge of created things. All this, then, is of paramount importance for a good comprehension of Christian doctrine.

If we consider, as we shall later show in more detail, how Aquinas defended God's working in creation not in the abstract but by situating it very concretely in the world picture of the time, the conclusion would appear to be justified that a concrete knowledge of nature is useful and even necessary for the theologian.[82] Does this mean that the theologian must study nature as the philosopher does? Not at all![83] Aquinas made a clear distinction between the task of the theologian and that of the philosopher (the natural sciences being assigned in the Middle Ages to the province of philosophy). The philosopher and scientist look at things on their own merit, whereas the theologian views things insofar as they are connected with God and reveal knowledge about God. The philosopher derives his knowledge from observation alone, while the theologian draws upon revelation, even though they have much in common concerning the knowledge of nature.[84] According to Aquinas, the natural sciences can in this way also lead to the revelation of God's wisdom,[85] just as revelation can prove useful to the philosopher. It would be absurd, therefore, for the theologian to be quite indifferent to natural science.[86]

How, then, did Aquinas put this view to practical use? To begin with, he gave clear indication in his theological writings that a certain picture of the universe, and notably of the order in this universe, is indispensable to the theologian. There is no doubt as to how Aquinas pictured the universe. In this matter, as in many others, he adopted the teaching of Aristotle and his followers.[87] This world picture was for the most part the same as that held by Bonaventure and other contemporaries of Aquinas: four earthly elements from which compound bodies are formed, seven celestial spheres with seven planets, and finally the three heavens.[88]

Aquinas was not very clear as to the number of celestial spheres, at times recording nine (*De. pot.*, 4, 1 ad 5; *S. th.* I, 68, 1 ad 1), at other times ten (II Sent. 14, 1, L. C), irrespective of the empyrean which occupies a separate place. This, however, is of little importance. What was beyond all doubt in his mind was that there were seven spheres and seven planets, and besides these, two or three heavens with their stars. On the question whether the celestial spheres were homocentric to the earth, as Aristotle had taught, or heterocentric, as Ptolemy had held, whether or not there were epicycles to be found in the motion of the planets and whether or not this motion was uniform, Aquinas assumed an attitude of reserve.[89] As to the first point, he nevertheless showed a certain inclination to side with Aristotle, appealing here to the theory of three simple motions.[90] Just as there are simple and compound bodies (*corpora elementaria et corpora mixta*) so there are also three simple and compound motions. Only the motion of the sphere can be considered the perfect, or rather, the least imperfect motion, and thus appears to fit better into the perfect order of God's creation.[91]

Sharing the presuppositions of the time,[92] Aquinas had no doubt as to the existence of the spheres and planets. This world picture formed the backdrop to his entire philosophy and theology and was a central theme of his reflections. What matter are the heavenly bodies made of? How do they differ from things on earth? Why are there seven planets and what influence do they have on the sublunary world? By what forces are they propelled and directed? Will they ever stop revolving? In answer to all these questions Aquinas constructed a coherent metaphysical system, intended as a fundamental explanation of the cosmos we live in and in no way dependent on the astronomical hypotheses which were then in dispute.

There is, as he believed, a fundamental difference between earthly and heavenly bodies. On earth everything is imperfect and transitory, whereas the heavenly bodies are in their kind perfect and imperishable. A clear indication of this perfection is the fact that the motion of the heavenly bodies is circular. Things on earth, on the other hand, move in opposite directions: from the top downward (earth and water) and from the bottom upward (air and fire). Heavenly and earthly things thus have a different nature.[93] We should bear in mind that for Aristotle and Aquinas perfection is synonymous with immobility. Of all motions, therefore, circular motion is the least imperfect in that one always returns to the same spot.

All created things are nevertheless composed of matter and form. It is to be noted that the concept of matter is here employed analogically,[94] for the heavenly bodies are made of a different, more perfect matter than that of earthly things. In this respect the cosmos already displays a hierarchical order, with the more perfect above and the less perfect below. Moreover, although the form of the heavenly bodies cannot be considered to be a soul, it is infinitely more perfect than the form of transitory things, because it fully exhausts the potential of matter.[95] For this reason the heavenly bodies are said to be nobler than all earthly things. Whereas the latter are transitory and can always lay aside their perfections, the former can never lose their perfection. Like the angels, the heavenly bodies are unique of their kind.[96] It is only on earth that we find many individuals of the same kind.

But how are we to account for this motion of the seven planets and the celestial spheres? Two solutions seemed to be possible: either they are living beings or they are moved by living beings (angels). Although Aquinas never made a clear pronouncement on the first hypothesis,[97] he nevertheless repeatedly affirmed that the heavenly bodies are guided by created spirits.[98] In contrast to his initial reserve,[99] he explicitly maintained that these separate intelligences, already discussed by Aristotle, may be identified with the angels.[100] An essential component of Aquinas's view of the world is that the heavenly bodies are moved by the angels, who fulfill this task in perfect submission to God's active guidance.[101] This was all the more necessary because the motion of the celestial spheres was considered to be aimed at man's well-being. Man, then, is the goal of creation but his well-being can only be looked after by higher beings.[102] From the fact that there are various motions to be found in the celestial spheres, Aquinas concluded that there must be various "intellectual substances."[103] Their number is, for that matter, much greater than the number of motions that are observed in the celestial spheres, for the order in the universe demands that the noblest things be the most numerous in God's creation.[104] Aquinas, therefore, rejected the opinion of Maimonides, according to whom there are as many "intellectual substances" as motions or spheres in the heavens.[105]

The heavenly bodies were thus seen to be God's instruments which are set in motion and directed with the help of the angels. However, this state of affairs repeatedly gave rise to the question as to how far such instrumental causality extends.[106] To summarize Aquinas's rather detailed answer, we can say that he regarded this causality as extending to all material things, particularly asserting itself in the coming-to-be and passing-away of all compound bodies. Thus there is not a single being on earth that escapes the influence of the heavenly bodies. If the latter were to cease moving, all motion on earth would come to a stop.[107] No material body can move of its own accord. If, then, God wanted there to be plants and animals, he was also obliged to create heavenly bodies.[108]

But the influence of the heavenly bodies extends in the first place to all changes that occur in the sublunary material world, insofar as these cannot be reduced to natural properties and propensities. The natural properties are the cold and hot, and the wet and dry. The fact, therefore, that water is wet and cool must not be attributed to the influence of the planets. Natural propensity means that each of the four elements strive after their due place in the world order. The influence of the heavenly bodies is not necessary, then, to account for the fact that flames reach upward. All other changes in compound bodies must, however, be ascribed to the heavenly bodies. To begin with, there is the origin of living beings. This can take place in two ways: living beings such as worms or small insects can be directly called up by the heavenly bodies, especially in places where a process of putrefaction has started. In this case the heavenly bodies first bring about the process of putrefaction and then make smaller living beings appear in this milieu. It is also possible that the heavenly bodies in their turn make use of an instrument[109] to let living beings come into existence. Dying is also to be ascribed to the planets. The same applies to man, for in procreation parents are only the instruments of the heavenly bodies. The sun has an especially important part in this: *homo generat hominem et sol.* For Aquinas this formula, which he derived from Aristotle, means that after God, the sun is the first cause of a child's coming into existence.[110] The sun, then, has each person as such in view, while parents come only second as instruments of the heavenly bodies. The natural fertility in parents and all living beings is assumed, on the understanding that it can be active only by virtue of the influence of the heavenly bodies.[111]

All coming-to-be and passing-away is thus to be attributed to the heavenly bodies, which determine almost all material events. Everything that happens in the world can therefore be reduced to the following scheme:

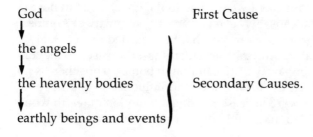

This view can clearly be characterized as a metaphysics of universal finality. Everything has an aim to be striven after, whether it be an end or an instrument for this end. In all events we must therefore see the will of the Creator. As everything has been created for man and for the salvation of the elect, it follows that everything has its foundation and starting point in the divine will.

There is, however, a double restriction to be imposed on this universal causality of the heavenly bodies. To begin with, they have no influence on our thinking or free will. The following reasons are given for this: material bodies, even if made of a nobler matter, can never exercise a direct influence on spiritual beings such as the human soul.[112] Even if the heavenly bodies were animate beings, such an influence on man's soul would still have to be excluded.[113] In this way Aquinas vigorously maintained human freedom and responsibility. Without his body, man cannot carry out his decisions. Moving one's hand, for example, is formally a free act but only possible with the cooperation of the heavenly bodies as a *conditio sine qua non*.[114] Man's free actions are not the only exception to the universal causality of the heavenly bodies, for according to Aquinas, certain fortuitous events in a sense escape the influence of the heavenly bodies. Such accidental occurrences can be accounted for either by the meeting of two causes in no way inferior to each other, or by a flagging of the efficient cause while performing its task, or by an unfavorable condition of the matter on which this influence is exercised. This explains how monsters can come into existence.[115]

The admission of the universal influence of the heavenly bodies automatically leads to a justification of astrology. Though he accepted this, Aquinas was nevertheless careful to point out that the precise interpretation of the motions of the heavenly bodies is beyond human understanding. Astrology, moreover, can never relate to events that depend on man's free will.[116]

As to the influence of the heavenly bodies, one has to bear in mind that each planet has a specific effect. This explains why there had to be various heavenly bodies, the conjunction of which also has its influence on the sublunary world.[117] Aquinas shared the view of his contemporaries that the motion of the heavenly bodies would cease at the end of the world. Only those actions that can be carried out without movement would be continued. The sun, for example, would continue to shine but would no longer move. The reason for this is clear: once the motion of the heavenly bodies has secured its object— the salvation of the elect—this motion no longer has any meaning.[118] According to this view, the end of time is represented as an everlasting

spring day. The cosmos was thus seen to form a harmoniously ordered whole where all things have their precise place in a universal
system of cause and effect. God—the first cause—is an unmoved
Mover in the full sense of the word, and the things he sets in motion—
the celestial spheres—are the instruments (secondary causes) he employs to achieve his will and execute his plans on earth. Ultimately,
everything depends on the divine pleasure. It is, as Dante concludes,
"love that moves the sun and the other stars,"[120] and in this way has
control of all events in the world.

Very little was added to the world picture of scholastic theology
after Bonaventure and Aquinas, from whom it received its definitive
form. Until the crisis caused by the Copernican revolution several
centuries later, this picture and interpretation of the world order retained its general validity, continuing to serve as a framework and
background to theologial thought. In the scientific field there was a
continuous stream of cosmological treatises, but these were of little
significance to theology and possibly only deserve to be mentioned in
a history of the natural sciences.[121]

Of the many writings that might have been mentioned here, we
confine ourselves to two texts in particular. In the first place, there is
the *Compendium theologicae veritatis*[122] of Hugo Ripelin,[123] a disciple of
Albert the Great. It is important not because it contains new ideas but
precisely because it is a classic example of the way in which Christian
teaching was interpreted within the framework of the prevailing
world picture. This compendium was very much read and had a profound influence on Christian life in the late scholastic period, not least
on account of the fact that for many preachers, such as Bernard of
Sienna, it was a source of theological knowledge. What is especially
remarkable here is that the interpretation of revelation is seen to harmonize so well with the prevailing cosmological conceptions.

Very much in the same strain, even though it was written three
centuries later, is Robert Bellarmine's *Ascensus mentis ad deum per sca-
lam Creaturarum*. Bellarmine played an important role in the first condemnation of Galileo (1616). In this work, as in his earlier writings,
he still held the medieval conception of the cosmos, intending moreover that his consideration of creatures would provide us with a ladder
by means of which we could in a sense climb up to God. This involved,
among other things, the four elements—earth, water, air, and fire—
and then, the sun, moon, and stars, which were seen to reflect the
heavenly hierarchy. In adherence to the medieval tradition, everything acquired a symbolic meaning.

From these and many other authors whom we are not able to consider here,[124] we can conclude that the medieval theologian contin-

ually worked within the framework of a very concrete and generally accepted world picture which was always present to his mind and which he studied as closely as possible. It would be fair to assume from his attitude and line of conduct that he felt compelled as a theologian to integrate the study of the cosmos into a Christian view of the world as God's creation. A Christian anthropology was plainly only part of the theologian's task, for a Christian cosmology was seen to be just as necessary.[125] In the light of the correspondence between macrocosm and microcosm,[126] it was evident that theological interpretation of man implied a theological interpretation of the cosmos. A Christian interpretation of the cosmos must, therefore be considered intrinsic to the medieval world of thought and not merely incidental to it.

At this point we might recall the main features of the world picture that governed the entire Middle Ages. It is well known that our perception tends to be selective. That is to say, we usually see only what we want to see or what interests us for one reason or another. The same was also true of medieval man. In his experience of reality the only aspects to be shown to full advantage were those that met his desire for order. For the medieval theologian, then, the world was a perfectly ordered whole. Moreover, God's wisdom required that he create order in everything he did. Had St. Paul not said "Quae autem sunt, a Deo ordinatae sunt?"[127] ("All that exists has been ordained by God"). The world was also defined as an ordered collection of creatures.[128] To doubt the reality of a perfect world order approached blasphemy. If ever there was any uncertainty whether a particular being actually existed, it was the criterion of world order that settled the issue. Thus wisdom compelled God to create the angels, without whom the world order would not have been complete.[129] What greater joy or perfection can there be than to assimilate this perfect world order and to have a thorough knowledge of it?[130] There was no doubt that this order is immutable: it dates from the creation of the world and will hold good until the end of time and beyond this unto eternity. Does not Scripture say that God never regrets what he has given? Divine wisdom has once and for all clearly distingushed one thing from another, assigning everything its proper place in the whole.[131] It is by looking at the stars that we have a foretaste of the imperishableness of God's creation and of the permanence of his world order. What is clear from such a picture is that there is no question of there being a gradual construction of order in the course of history.

Besides being perfect and immutable, this world order was also considered hierarchical. What is at the top is naturally nobler, and what is nobler is better and more powerful, and whatever is better and more powerful exercises the greatest influence.[132] The Pseudo-Dionysius, the Areopagite, had also taught that it was a law of divinity to connect the lower with the higher by means of intermediaries.[133] The principle of hierarchy is therefore to be found everywhere—not only in the Church, but in the choirs of angels and even in God.[134] Moreover, it is precisely because everything has been arranged in hierarchical order that theology can erect a ladder from earth to heaven by using philosophy and adopting from nature all that is necessary to form an image of the supernatural.[135] With considerable care and attention the medieval theologian described this perfect hierarchy of the cosmos created by God, realizing that it is an inexhaustible source of admiration and it teaches us to discover, more than anything else, God's wisdom and omnipotence.[136] Order and hierarchy were thus regarded as inseparably connected, the one concept evoking the other in the natural as well as in the supernatural order.[137]

Finally, this world order was also seen to be anthropocentric. For the medieval theologian there was not the slightest doubt that all things were created for man and that the entire cosmic order was aimed at him. This seemed so self-evident and so closely connected with his notion of order that there was no need for him to look for proof. It appeared to him that everything pointed in this direction: man was created last of all, with everything subject to him, and for this reason he has the right to kill animals and employ them for his use. In this way the whole cosmos can be said to be attuned to man.[138]

The medieval philosopher and theologian were plainly resolute in their conclusion that the universe is a perfect, immutable, hierarchical, and anthropocentric order. Having adopted this as a definite principle, they were continually influenced by it in the rest of their thinking. They looked upon this splendid world order with admiration and respect, while attempting to reach a better understanding of it and to assimilate it completely.[139]

Chapter Three

FROM WORLD PICTURE
TO THEOLOGY

With his intense interest in cosmological problems, the medieval theologian assigned himself the task of constructing a coherent picture of the cosmos on the basis of data he had gleaned from the Bible, Greek science, and the Fathers of the Church. Evidence of this interest and concern is to be found not only in separate treatises but also in biblical commentaries or more systematic theological writings. As we have seen, the world picture that originated in this manner formed the background to medieval theological conceptions. Thus to neglect this cosmological background is of necessity to blur our image of medieval theology and to lose sight of its fundamental purpose.

The question now arises, however, as to what extent this explicitly professed world picture also influenced the medieval interpretation of Christianity. It is in any case quite obvious that a theology conceived as "faith seeking understanding" never develops in a vacuum but only within the limits of a particular cultural climate. That is to say, a theological system is always the result of the way in which the thinking Christian of a particular period and cultural milieu has understood and interpreted his faith. For this reason a perennial theology is just as impossible as a perennial philosophy. Man's thought is plainly one more instance of the historicity of human existence.

It may be taken for granted, then, that a particular view of the world belongs to the most important components of a culture. But one has to bear in mind that a world picture can influence a particular culture in a variety of ways, according to the importance attached to this picture and the degree of unanimity with which it is received. Even the absence of a coherent and generally accepted worldview can in a way act as a "world picture" Now that we have established that the medieval theologian appealed to a clearly defined and unanimously accepted picture of the universe, it seems justified to ask how far this view of the cosmos has influenced the medieval interpretation of Christianity, or, to put it differently, to what extent cosmology and theology were in harmony during the Middle Ages.

One can expect a priori that traces of the prevailing picture of the universe are to be found in medieval theology. All sorts of problems arise, however, when it comes to indicating in particular the actual extent of this influence and the doctrines that have to be seen entirely or partly in this perspective. The influence of a particular world picture can make itself felt in various ways. We may consciously think from within a certain world picture and attempt to trace its implications for the rest of our thinking. But it is equally possible—and in most cases more obvious—that we are influenced unconsciously or by way of the general thought-patterns we have derived from our world picture. It also happens that an author who is conscious of working within a particular view of the world does not for that reason always feel compelled to point out this context in his treatment of special problems. What we find in those periods when the same world picture is held by almost all is that repeated reference to it is considered superfluous. This explains why it is not always practicable to show with the help of explicit texts and quotations that a particular author sets out from certain cosmological premises. The general tone of his work often provides more convincing proof of this connection than would scraping together sporadic references.

In order to answer our question it will therefore not be sufficient to trace whether there are statements to be found in medieval theological literature in which an author explicitly appeals to the world picture to substantiate his views. We shall also have to take into account the possibility that the author was not always aware of this influence or, if he was, that he considered it superfluous to explain this explicitly each time. It will be especially important to examine the extent to which the general tone of his world picture is to be found in his work and how far the general thought-patterns occasioned by this world picture have molded his interpretation of doctrine.

Concretely, this comes down to the question to what extent medieval theology bears the hallmark of the notion, derived from Plato's *Timaeus*, of a perfect, static, hierarchical and anthropocentric world order. It is within such a framework that we have to consider a host of problems discussed by the medieval theologian: God, creation, Providence, the angels, the first man, the Fall, the Incarnation, Redemption, grace, the sacraments, the meaning of prayer, the Church, morality, civil society, and the four last things. Only in this way can we measure the impact on the medieval theologian of the general thought-patterns predominantly derived from his world picture. Instead of a more scholarly analysis of a number of medieval theologians one by one, it would be more profitable, in view of our present purpose, to provide a general picture of medieval theology, paying particular attention to the points of contact with the prevailing world picture. It is to be noted here that not all views were explicitly shared by all authors, even though the same cosmological background is to be found in them all.

Let us first look at the general character of medieval theology. On the whole, medieval culture can be characterized by its pursuit of order, balance, and synthesis.[1] After the confusion and general disorder resulting from the migration of peoples and the collapse of the Roman Empire, medieval man seemed to be seized with a deep desire for order and tranquillity. One by one, new social and political structures were set up, gradually creating the possibility of an orderly and peaceful existence. In all areas of cultural life, theology included, we find evidence of this same urge for order and harmony.

One of the first things that strikes us about medieval theological literature is the highly structured and systematic character of these writings. In the major works of the period there was a desire to bring the entire Christian doctrine together in a perfectly ordered whole that was already apparent from the external structure and form. Such a synthesis was the result of long and sustained effort beginning in the patristic era but actually finding complete expression and reaching its climax only in the work of the scholastics.

But order and balance characterized the inner spirit of scholasticism as well as its external form. In the depths of its being it appeared to be an attempt to make a set of unsystematic doctrines into a harmonious and systematic whole. The medieval theologian never questioned the possibility of systematizing the whole of Christian doctrine. This, however, presupposed a guiding principle to order the material and disclose its logical coherence. Though various approaches were taken,[2] we mostly find the same scheme in the systematic writings of medieval theology: God, the angels, the cosmos, man—a descending order corresponding to the hierarchical structure of the medieval world picture. In his *Summa theologica* Aquinas further appealed to the neo-Platonic idea of the "procession and return of creatures." What is clear, then, is that the world order was highlighted, while Christology and eschatology became less prominent.[3] Thus Redemption was interpreted as a return to an original world order, and eschatology was considered to be a definite confirmation of this. The principle of order suggested by the world picture plainly made its influence felt here and in the constant endeavor to describe the teaching of the Gospel as a sacred order that is in harmony with the cosmic order.

Besides its external form and general structure there were many special areas in the medieval interpretation of Christianity that corresponded to the prevailing cosmology. St. Paul had taught that we know God and his attributes through created things. It follows, then, that our view of created things must necessarily influence our conception of God. For this reason the medieval theologian placed considerable emphasis on the revelatory character of created things. From the time of Augustine nature was regarded as a book through which we could learn to know God.[4] As Hugh of St. Victor pointed out, however, we can never understand a book simply by looking at the beautiful form of the characters in the way that an illiterate person would do. Since we must understand the meaning of the characters, we must also discover the spiritual meaning of created things. But because we are often blind to what God is expressing in created things, we need a second book to teach us to see the truth.[5] Just as there is a distinction between the literal and spiritual meaning of sacred Scriptures, so we must distinguish the outward appearance of things from their hidden, spiritual meaning.

In this way the medieval Christian set upon reading nature with "spiritual" eyes, thereby discovering without difficulty not only the existence of God but also his divine attributes: his power, wisdom, and goodness. It is common to note that all the main medieval writers believed nature to reveal a God characterized by power, wisdom, and goodness.[6] God's wisdom was disclosed in the order and beauty of nature, a perfect order that could not be doubted. The cosmos was seen to form a perfectly ordered single unit in which all beings have their proper place according to the part they play in the whole. It is characteristic of wisdom to create order. But the reverse is also true: wherever there is order, wisdom is disclosed. Nature further reveals God's power and goodness in the dimensions and forces we find in the cosmos and in the abundance granted. to man. This characteristically medieval conception is to be found in Dante's *Divina Commedia*:

All things whatso'er have order among themselves, and this indeed
is form, which makes the World God's image bear. Herein do the
higher beings the impress read of that eternal Worth, which is the
end whereto the aforesaid rule had been decreed. In this same
order ranked, all natures bend their several ways, through divers
lots, as near and farther from the source whence all decent . . .[7]

For Augustine[8] and for medieval theologians such as Alexander of
Hales, Bonaventure, and Albert the Great, this order and beauty of
the universe formed the principal proof of God's existence. Aquinas,
however, held a somewhat different view. In his *Summa contra gentiles*,
which he started in 1258, Aquinas, following Aristotle, argued especially from the motion of the planets to arrive at the existence of an
"Unmoved Prime Mover."

In his *Summa theologica*, started in 1266, Aquinas indicated five ways
that lead to the recognition of God's existence. Here also the argument
from the motion of the planets comes first, while the argument from
the order in the cosmos is last of all. No particular significance should
be attributed to this classification of the five arguments, which should
rather be seen as determined by historical circumstances. There is no
doubt that these five ways fitted exceptionally well into the framework
of the medieval world picture, even though they can also be trans-
posed to a more general scheme.[9]

The God revered by the medieval Christian man was not the God
of a vague and abstract world but the God of a concrete and clearly
defined world in which medieval man lived and of which he had a
distinct picture. It was, moreover, a God who loved order, and for
this reason had created the world in perfect order, expressing in it his
will for man. Thus to love God also implied that one love the order
he in his supreme wisdom had realized in his creation, and in comparison to which all human wisdom is but foolishness and nonsense.

We shall confine ourselves to only two examples of this respect and
admiration for the order and beauty of the world that was central to
medieval devotion. In his Hymn to the Sun St. Francis (d. 1226)
praised God, thanking him for all creatures and mentioning in turn
the sun, moon, and stars, air, water, fire and earth. No explicit mention was given of the animals which, according to his biographers, he
dearly loved, but since animals were made of the same four elements
as all earthly things, it was superfluous, in the medieval view, to
mention them separately. To describe the whole of creation it was
sufficient, therefore, to include the heavenly bodies and the four elements. Both Thomas of Celano and Bonaventure placed much emphasis on Francis's love of nature.[10]

Another example is to be found in the *Life of Blessed Ida of Nivella*, written in 1233:

> When she reflected, as she often did, on the works of God and looked at the flowers, trees, water or any other thing he had created, she could scarcely stop shedding tears, but starting from created things, she considered the goodness and wisdom of the Creator and with admirable joy she gave rein to her unutterable feelings of gratitude, expressing praise in the Creator of all these things.[11]

Evidence of this optimistic view of nature as an unfailing spectacle and reflection of God's supreme wisdom is to be found throughout the Middle Ages and there is no doubt that this view did much to promote the feeling for nature characteristic of the Renaissance.[12] For many centuries the beauty and order in nature was a recurrent theme in religious literature.[13]

As a whole, this picture of the world, so plainly and forcefully present in his imagination, was for the medieval Christian an impressive piece of theodicy. It appeared to him that the cosmos was like Veronica's veil on which he beheld the face of the Creator. In this way his picture of the universe corresponded with his conception of God.

But God not only created and ordered this perfect world, a transparent revelation of his wisdom, power, and goodness, he also governs and guides every part of it, taking care of it in his Providence and directing events according to his wise decree. The medieval theologian by no means restricted himself to formulating this general principle of God's universal causality; he also raised the question of how we are to form a concrete picture of God's control over the world. It was maintained that in order to carry out his decisions, God makes use of intermediate or secondary causes, whether spiritual or material. To enlighten man's understanding and will God employs spiritual instruments—namely, the higher spirits whom we call angels—while to govern material things he uses the heavenly bodies. An example of this conception of Providence, which was common in medieval theology, is to be found in Aquinas, who gave a detailed account of it.[14] On numerous occasions he described in particular the influence of the heavenly bodies on the entire material world, the coming-to-be and passing-away of things, never failing to connect this influence with God's Providence.[15]

Looked at in this light, all events in the material world acquired a particular significance. For medieval man they were the immediate expression of God's decisions and as such were infinitely venerable.

As all these events were linked to the position and motion of the planets, it was obvious that considerable attention was paid to astrology. The medieval theologians, led by Aquinas, defended the principle of astrology: that future events are determined by the position of the planets. On the other hand, they never ceased to warn against the way astrology was practiced at that time. It was argued that human freedom is not influenced by the position of the stars, at least not directly, and that it is not always easy to understand the exact meaning of the motions of the planets, with the result that we often make gross errors in our interpretation. We should not, therefore, place too much trust in the predictions of those who study the heavenly bodies. Although the theologians observed much caution on this question, they nevertheless continued to think along the lines of the prevailing world picture.

The main objection to this picture of the world was of course the problem of evil. If the world is created perfectly by God, how can one account for the existence of evil, suffering, and disorder in the world? However conscious the medieval theologian was of the existence of evil in the world, it never detracted from his fundamental optimism concerning the order in the world and the sheer perfection of God's creation. One sooner has the impression that his treatment of the problem of evil was indirectly intended as an attempt to defend his optimistic view of the world against any possible attack.

The following arguments were mainly put forward to explain the existence of evil. The first point to be granted was, as Augustine had pointed out, that evil as such has no reality of its own but must only be seen as the absence of something good. In declaring evil to be a negative concept, Augustine opposed the Manichean view whereby the same degree of reality was ascribed to good and evil. Next it was admitted that the order in the world actually presupposes a certain inequality among its component parts. For how could the world be made into a perfect order if all the elements in it were equally perfect and possessed the same dignity? A true hierarchical order can only be built up out of unequal parts, each of which makes its own contribution to the construction of a perfectly ordered world.[16] A final point that was taken into account was original sin, which upset the world order and brought all sorts of evil into the world. For this man alone was responsible. Here one can add that God is able to make evil extend to the good and thus let it contribute to the order in the world.[17]

The existence of evil did not make medieval man entertain the slightest doubt concerning the perfection and order of the world. This belief in the perfect world order was not the result of induction, but mainly had its origin in an a priori form of reasoning derived from Plato. It was argued that a perfect God can only create a perfect world,[18] a position moreover which corresponds with certain statements in Genesis. One then had merely to apply oneself to the interpretation of this world as a perfect order. Once this had been discovered, one could go back, and from the existence of the world order, conclude the existence of a God characterized by wisdom, power, and goodness. The medieval world picture and conception of God were thus seen to be completely analogous.

The angels assumed a prominent place in the faith and imagination of medieval man. In theology particular attention was also paid to the heavenly spirits, and a detailed investigation was instituted concerning the questions raised by the existence of such beings. There was in any case no doubt as to their existence. Not only the empyrean but the whole cosmos appeared to be inhabited by angels, without whom the cosmos itself was inconceivable. In the medieval view, the existence of pure spirits was not only justified by the testimony of sacred Scriptures, but was actually postulated by the very structure of the cosmos. The hierarchical order would evidently not be complete if, above the material beings and those composed of matter and spirit, there were no purely spiritual beings to serve as intermediaries between these lower beings and God, the infinitely pure spirit. It is precisely because these pure spirits have their place in the general world order that we can confirm their existence.[19]

It was a generally accepted conviction in the Middle Ages that the heavenly bodies were set in motion by the angels, who were instructed and empowered by God to that end. This is another instance of the indispensable role of the angels in the whole world order. Among the many issues that arose in this connection, there was the intriguing question as to whether the angels of sacred Scriptures could be identified with Aristotle's separate intelligences. The Greeks had already asked whether the planets moved by their own power or by an external force. It was assumed that behind the motion of the planets there had to be an intellect guiding their direction. Questions such as, "Were the planets endowed with understanding?" or "Were they animate beings?" had long been discussed by the ancient Greek philosophers. In the *Timaeus* Plato spoke of the world-soul: the universe was an animate being, like a large animal, that requires no food because it is immortal.[20]

On the analogy of the microcosm, the macrocosm was also believed to consist of body and soul. Throughout the twelfth and thirteenth centuries there were lengthy discussions on the existence of a world-soul,[21] and even in later centuries this question regularly arose. Although the medieval theologians rejected the existence of a separate world-soul, many of them nevertheless posed the question whether God could not in a sense be considered the soul of the world.[22] In reply to this it was said that while God is undoubtedly the unmoved Mover of the universe, on no account can he be understood as the soul or the form of the world.[23] Could the planets not then be pictured as animate beings? On this issue Aquinas did not commit himself, consoling himself with the thought that it was after all of no real consequence. The same reserve on this matter is also found in Augustine.[24] Aristotle, on the contrary, did consider the heavenly bodies as animate beings and during the Hellenistic period they were even held to be gods.[25]

But if the planets were not animate beings, at the very least they had to be guided by spiritual beings which have an intellect. On this point most theologians agreed. One had, therefore, to take into account the existence of separate intelligences or substances, just as many Greek philosophers had taught. Aquinas and the medieval theologians in general discussed in detail the nature, properties, and force of these separate intelligences. Despite the fact that we observe their effects, we can, said Aquinas, know little or nothing about them. We can certainly perceive their influence on earthly phenomena but this is not sufficient to give us an understanding of what they actually are, because their real force far exceeds the visible effect.[26] Their existence was never in dispute and it is understandable, then, that the question should arise whether these separate intelligences could be identified with the angels mentioned in Scripture. Was it not conceivable that, as in many other matters, the pagan philosophers had conjectured a truth that was only fully disclosed in Revelation? In commentaries on Aristotle and Ptolemy various Arabian and Jewish scholars had already identified the separate intelligences as angels. Though this question was hotly debated among theologians, no unanimous solution was arrived at. There were those, like William of Auvergne and Albert the Great,[27] who vehemently opposed this identification, while others, such as Bonaventure and Aquinas, had no objection to it, but on the express condition that the number of angels was not to be reduced to that of the heavenly spheres, as Averroes had done. If this were the case, there would only be seven or eight angels, whereas God had created a great many more of them to fill the heavenly Jerusalem.[28]

In keeping with the much-acclaimed *De Hierarchia Caelesti* of the Pseudo-Dionysius, the nine choirs of angels were also conceived as a perfect hierarchy. This clearly involves the idea of a hierarchical order, as is also the case when it concerns the way in which the angels are enlightened by God. Knowledge is first imparted to the highest choir of angels and gradually descends to the lowest. One of the most beautiful and typical accounts is to be found in the writings of Petrus Olivi.[29] Just as God sends his angels to the planets, he also sends them to human beings, to whom, Scripture tells us, they are sometimes made visible. But how can purely spiritual beings be visibly present to man? Albert the Great claimed that this was possible through the condensation of "quintessence," said to be of a very subtle matter which in its normal state is invisible but through heavy condensation can have a visible form. When the angels disappear, this means that the fifth substance assumes its natural state once again.[30] As man is destined to live with the angels, it was considered good that he should already become accustomed to their company.[31]

God was thus seen as the Creator of the heavenly spheres, the stars and the plants, and of the four elements, out of which the plants and animals are formed. But why did God create all these things? Medieval theology's answer to this question was invariable and clear: the whole world is created for man, or rather, for the elect. All things exist for man[32] and are subject to him.[33] The celestial spheres in particular revolve on his account,[34] for without their influence on earth man would not be able to exist. At the same time, however, we have the impression that some things are of little use and are even harmful and dangerous. But the medieval worldview held that, although many things have no direct use, they nevertheless serve to adorn the world and to delight man, as many stars do. Moreover, certain plants which appear useless have been found to contain a healing power for bodily disease, while dangerous animals provide us with an occasion to exercise our strength and bravery. There is, therefore, a reason for everything to exist: all work of nature is the work of intelligence.[35]

In answer to the question of why man was called into existence, most medieval theologians maintained that he had to take the place of the fallen angels. It was God's will that after a period of probation on earth man should fill the empty places in heaven and share the life of the loyal angels. Such a view implied that God had not originally intended to create man but merely assigned him a role as substitute. Some were discouraged by this view and immediately set themselves the task of picturing the intrinsic value of man as a being that deserved to be created by God on account of his inner grandeur and dignity.[36] And yet this never detracted from the notion that man was destined to be united with the angels in one way or another and to occupy the place of the fallen angels.[37] There was, moreover, much lively discussion as to how many would be saved. Hugo Ripelin summed up the views of the time by stating that the fall of the angels would be made good by the elect. Whereas Augustine claimed that the number saved would be equal to that of the fallen angels, Gregory the Great held the view that there would be as many saved as there were angels remaining. According to some, there would be two groups in heaven: on the one side, man, and on the other side, the angels, with the fall of the angels being made good by the virgins. According to this view there would therefore be as many elect as there were angels and virgins together.[38]

Man was thus created to join the blessed angels in adoring and glorifying God. There was an important distinction to be made here in that angels are pure spirits while man is composed of soul and body. The soul contains the three faculties of understanding, memory, and will, and the body comprises the four elements: earth, water, fire, and air. In man we thus distinguish seven layers, comparable to the number seven in the construction of the cosmos. Microcosm and macrocosm can readily be seen to display the same basic structure insofar as God has regulated the various forces in man on the anology of the order in the universe.[39]

Concerning the origin of each person there were two problems for medieval theologians: the coming into being of the body and of the soul. The origin of the body could easily be accounted for: parents give existence to the human body, though they themselves are the instrument of the planets and, chiefly, the sun.[40] Thus four elements making up the human body are brought together in the right proportion through the influence of the heavenly bodies and the agency of the parents.

There was at the same time intense discussion on the question of whether it would not be better for the human soul to have a body composed of quintessence. Both Bonaventure[41] and Aquinas[42] pointed out that the present situation is in accordance with God's world order and thus completely rational. Quintessence is, moreover, indivisible and therefore unable to be "connected" with the four elements, even though it can exercise some influence on them. For this reason a mixture of the five elements is also excluded.

But how does the human soul come into being? Owing to its spiritual nature it cannot be produced by material factors. The spiritual transcends the force of matter,[43] because the lower can never produce the higher. We must therefore distinguish two kinds of generation as far as the body and the soul are concerned. The body is composed of already existing matter, the four elements and the cooperation of the secondary causes, namely, the heavenly bodies[44] and the *virtus seminis.*[45] The soul, on the other hand, is not composed of any previously existing thing, for there is nothing eligible for this.[46] Neither is there any question of there being secondary causes; even the angels can be of no service here. It was concluded, therefore, that whereas the body is produced mediately, the soul comes into being through an immediate creation. All this seemed to fit very well into the framework of the medieval world picture.

Man was also said to have been created in a state of original justice. For the medieval theologian this meant much more than possessing sanctifying grace. Original justice was primarily seen as the perfect ordering of our being, a state in which conscience was completely subject to God, the will to conscience, the body and its passions to the will, and even the plants and animals to man. Order and original justice were thus considered to be synonymous. The first man was created in a state of order that displayed a perfect hierarchy in which the lower was governed by the higher.[48] In such a state of paradise, it was man's duty to respect and maintain this beautiful order established by God, and provided man did this, there would be no end to his happiness.

Through his unwillingness to obey God man destroyed the entire world order. Because his understanding and will rebelled against God, his body also opposed his will and even the plants and animals revolted against him. In this way the concept of sin was closely related to the concept of order: sin became the conscious negation of the order established by God. It is precisely because sin is a lack of appreciation of this order willed by God, that it is at the same time an offence against the Creator and a violation of his command.[49] The sin of the first man was thus seen to affect not only man but the whole cosmos. Everything was brought into disorder, with all beings becoming corrupt in themselves and unruly towards man.[50] The world therefore lost a great deal of its beauty and harmony until God in his goodness decided to restore the world order through the Incarnation of the Word.

The coming-to-be and passing-away of all beings must first be attributed to the heavenly bodies. Each person was thought to have been born under the influence of the planets, and mainly of the sun. But can the same be said of Christ? According to Albert the Great, Christ was never subject to the motions of the heavenly bodies, for he was born by the power of the Holy Spirit. Only in incidental matters such as cold and warmth did he undergo the influence of the heavenly bodies, and he was even freed from this after the Resurrection;[51] glorified bodies are no longer under the influence of the planets.

Christ came down from the empyrean to restore the world order, to cancel by his obedience the disobedience of the first man. Through his teaching and sacrifice he restores order, first in man and then through man in the whole cosmos, insofar as it was shattered by sin. The concept of order was thus also closely allied to the mystery of Redemption. While original sin formally consisted of a breakdown of order, Redemption consists of restoring this order. This is expressed in the first place in the person of Christ himself,[52] who is a living example of restored order: his soul was entirely subject to God, his body obedient to his soul, and all lower forces of nature were, as we can see from the miracles he performed, completely subject to him. Since perfect order was realized in him, there was no place in him for sin. Moreover, seeing that he had to put the world in order once again, he also had to have a perfect knowledge of it.[53] Aquinas further maintained that whenever Christ looked at the heavenly bodies, he knew immediately how far their influence reached and what effect they had on earth.[54] In his commentary on the *Summa Theologica*, Cajetan went further still, claiming that if need be the angels brought all things into Christ's view, so that he had an experiential knowledge of everything.[55]

By his life and death Christ restores order in man and in the world in a way that respects the divine order in everything.[56] Through the grace he had obtained, man is restored in his original justice: conscience once again becomes subject to God, the will to conscience, the body to the soul, and even the plants, animals, and all material elements become obedient to man again. This Redemption or restoration of original justice is already present in principle and will be completed at the end of time. It is, however, already revealed in the lives of the saints who have not only regained perfect inner order but even have the lower beings subject to them. The medieval hagiographer took great delight in showing how nature was again subject to man, how the animals once more listened to his voice, and how fire and water no longer presented a threat to him. Many examples of this are to be found, for instance, in biographies of Saint Francis of Assisi. The birds listened to him, bowing their head in agreement, while the dangerous wolf lay at his feet like a lamb, and even fire caused him no pain. His biographer Thomas of Celano writes: "I believe that this man, for whom these frightening things became affable again, had returned to original justice."[57] For medieval man the work of Redemption essentially consisted of restoring order in the cosmos, and in this sense Redemption was also seen to have a cosmic dimension.

In this context the doctrine of grace and the sacraments acquired a particular significance. It is generally known that the number of sacraments was fixed in the Middle Ages[58] and that, as if by chance, there were as many sacraments as planets. Both were considered to be God's instruments operating in a particular field, whether natural or supernatural. All material events on earth were under the influence of the heavenly bodies. Albert the Great explicitly compared this influence of the planets to the influence of God's grace in the human soul,[59] while Aquinas applied the same doctrine concerning instrumental causality to the heavenly bodies and to the sacraments.[60] Both these instruments of God were thought to operate by means of a fluid property or *virtus fluens*[61] and in reference to the sacraments this fluid property was called grace.

As to God's influence on man, we have to consider the human body, will, and understanding. To influence the body God uses the planets and the angels, to enlighten the understanding he also uses the angels; while to affect our decisions and movements of the will he operates directly. God's help is indispensable to the use of our will and it is rightly called grace.[62] It precedes every human act, just as the influence of the heavenly bodies precedes all material change.[63] God thus takes the initiative in every domain. He is the unmoved Mover in the natural as well as in the supernatural order. On that account, both Pelagianism and semi-Pelagianism had to be rejected, because they did not fit into the prevailing world picture with its strict hierarchical structure in which man was completely guided by higher powers.

Besides being the instruments of God to sanctify the individual, the sacraments were also conceived as the means God employed to order the religious life of the community. Without such order the community would not be worthy of the Creator who strives after the highest order in all he does. Only a perfectly hierarchical Church could fit into this perfect world order. In keeping with the Pseudo-Dionysius and his *De hierarchia ecclesiastica* there was increasingly more emphasis in the Middle Ages on the hierarchical character of the Church, both in external structures and in inner life.

A first distinction is carried out here by three sacraments which, according to Augustine, imprint a sign on the soul. Baptism introduces the separation between believers and unbelievers, while confirmation separates spiritual adults from children, and holy orders distinguishes the clergy from the laity. Holy orders is preeminently the sacrament of "order" because it gives to the Church its perfect hierarchical structure. It comprises seven stages, four minor and three major orders, which once again remind us of the seven planets. The consecration of a bishop and the coronation of a pope are not separate sacraments, for a bishop has the fullness of the priesthood and therefore belongs to the third of the major orders, while the pope is the first among the bishops.[64]

The Church as a whole thus displays a perfect, firm, solid, and irrefutable order.[65] At the very top stands Christ, our hierarch,[66] from whom all wisdom and grace flow. Next there is the pope who occupies the highest place in the hierarchy and has the fullness of authority on all matters in the Church,[67] and then come the bishops, clergy, monks, and finally the ordinary faithful. This means that besides the supercelestial and celestial hierarchy, there is also a subcelestial or ecclesiastical hierarchy.[68] Just as in the cosmos all motion comes from above and is gradually passed on to the lower spheres, so in the Church all direction comes from the top and is gradually spread over the lower sections. Everything in the Church is thus perfectly arranged[69] and in this way the Church fits into the perfect world order. Popes have not infrequently appealed to this order God has willed.[70]

Some medieval theologians further extended the notion of hierarchy to the world of souls, claiming that once man has been redeemed he must realize a perfect order in himself. This inner order has its origin in Christ, for there is but one monarch or hierarch from whom we obtain all order and hierarchy.[71] Bonaventure gave a detailed description of the soul that Christ arranges in hierarchy, pointing out how such hierarchy is the result of natural talent, personal effort, and supernatural grace.[72] As to their natural talents, the souls are divided into nine choirs like the angels, and hence we speak of the Doctor Angelicus (Aquinas) and the Doctor Seraphicus (Bonaventure).[73] By its own effort and with the help of grace the soul is completely arranged hierarchially in its knowledge and contemplation, just as in its virtues. The soul delights in being allowed to see how we obtain this hierarchical order.[74] What is remarkable about Bonaventure's description of the hierarchical order of souls is the number of times he refers to the hierarchy in the cosmos, which serves here as an analogy.[75] Though similar views are to be found in other medieval theologians and mystics, it was only in Bonaventure that this notion of hierarchy was of such paramount importance and was consistently maintained. The theme itself certainly belonged to the medieval world of thought. It is striking that the principle of hierarchical order came into force in the monastic institutions at the same time as the use of scholasticism. The great religious "orders" were gradually established, characterized by monasteries, abbeys, and priories of the same institution uniting to form an impressive whole governed by one abbot with the help of various superiors.[76] The same principle of hierarchy is, moreover, to be found in civil society, where the feudal system can be considered as a transposition of the cosmic order to the structure of the state. At the top there was the emperor or king, followed by the feudal lord and then the vassals—dukes, counts, barons, knights, etc.[77]—and finally the common people, who were entirely subject to the decisions of the upper circles. Thus all power was at the top, as unconditional allegiance and obedience were due to the feudal lord who set the various spheres in motion and granted them limited powers. Not infrequently an appeal was made to the order in nature to justify the feudal system as a form of polity.[78] This practice persisted for many centuries. In his celebrated letter on obedience Saint Ignatius of Loyola employs a similar theory: just as God directs the material world by means of the planets, so he governs the human society with the assistance of those in authority. Just as God's commands are gradually passed on from sphere to sphere, so too the divine decrees are made known to the subjects by way of the hierarchy of superiors.[79] Much the same line of thought is also to be found in many spiritual writers of later centuries.[80]

The same concern is prevalent in the medieval view on morality. As a science, morality teaches us how we must order our conduct to reach our human destiny. Many questions can be raised in this context: What is the basis of the distinction between good and evil? What criteria do we have to distinguish the one from the other? What is the foundation of the obligation to do good and avoid evil? The medieval answer to these questions was closely related to the prevailing concept of order: an action was considered good when it agreed with the order God willed and was considered sinful when it was contrary to this order. This general world order exists first and foremost in God; it is the eternal law, defined by Augustine as "the divine reason or will commanding that God's natural order be preserved and in no way disturbed."[81] This view is based on two theses: first, that there is an immutable order established by God and that this order can be known by man; second, that God wills us to respect this order by doing what it prescribes and avoiding whatever is contrary to it. Both these theses are consequently to be found in medieval thought.

As we have repeatedly shown, the medieval theologian never doubted that God had arranged the world in perfect order. Order was the essence of the world itself[82] and could be discovered simply by looking at the world, where even the smallest thing was seen to be ordained by God's Providence.[83] Just as he ordered the cosmos, God also saw to the order within man.[84] It was thus man's duty to carefully study this world order which appeared so evident to the medieval mind. In this way the medieval conception of morality acquired a cosmological background.[85] The order in the very nature of things had to be described as a natural law.[86]

Neither was there any doubt in the medieval mind that man had to respect the world order. How could God allow man to disturb the order that he in his supreme wisdom had devised?[87] Each person was obliged to bring his will into line with God's will, which was revealed in the order he had imposed on things.[88] Who could possibly want to change or improve this order? Morality was thus considered to be a transposition of the order in the cosmos to human conduct. This was another instance of the analogy between macrocosm and microcosm. There was a difference, however, in that the order God willed in material things was realized naturally and of necessity, while man did this freely. Just as early Christian writers had done before them, the medieval theologians vigorously opposed the teaching of those who claimed that man was subject to the same law as material things. To repudiate this view they maintained that the heavenly bodies had no hold on the human will, which could only be moved by God and then only with respect for its nature, that is, its freedom.

This contrast between the "obedience" of nature and the "disobedience" of man to divine laws is a theme that is frequently found in medieval literature. With Alan of Lille, for instance, nature was seen to reproach man with his disloyalty, suggesting that he take her as his model.[89] In many other writers we find the same idea of the moral lesson that is contained in the contemplation of nature.

There were, moreover, many analogies between the four elements and the four virtures. Just as the four elements had to be in good order for bodily health, so spiritual health was possible only with the four virtues, namely, fear of God, sorrow for sin, joy in God's gifts, and trust in his goodness.[90] Elsewhere the four elements were compared to the four cardinal virtues.[91] Such analogies were commonplace in medieval religious literature and were also reflected in medieval iconography.[92]

Further evidence of the influence of the world picture is to be found in the medieval conception of eschatology. It was believed that the world would come to an end as soon as the number of elect was complete, at which time there would no longer be a need for anyone else to be born or even for any new plants and animals. As the motion of the planets was aimed at the coming-to-be and passing-away of earthly things, it followed that this motion would cease to have meaning once the number of elect had been reached. The medieval theologians therefore declared unanimously that the motion of the heavenly bodies would be brought to a standstill at the end of the world.[93] The sun, the moon, and the stars would then be assigned their rightful place, with their working being restricted to those influences that can be exercised without motion, such as radiating light and warmth. Thus the last judgment would involve both the purification of nature and the resurrection of the body. According to Bonaventure and many others, the earth as such would not be completely destroyed, but everything that is combustible, such as plants and animals, would be consumed by fire. The four elements, especially air and earth, would be purified and renewed. In this view the just would also be purified and the damned tormented for all eternity.[94]

As to the bodies of the elect, Bonaventure held that they would acquire the four properties whereby they would become similar to the heavenly bodies: clarity, subtlety, agility, and impassibility.[95] The human body was thought to be composed of the four elements, but once granted these four properties the body would be freed of its imperfections and made worthy to dwell among the angels in the empyrean.[96] Since there must be a certain conformity between the house and its occupants, the bodies of the elect would naturally have to be adapted to this heavenly abode. Among the blessed there would continue to be a hierarchical order.

Instead of indicating where medieval theologians held divergent views, we have attempted in the preceding pages to focus attention on what was common to them all. As far as its main features were concerned, all accepted a clearly defined picture of the universe, endeavoring to integrate Christian doctrine as perfectly as possible into it, or rather, endeavoring to assimilate this world picture into the Christian world of thought. This resulted in a harmonious unity of cosmology, anthropology, and theology that is unique in the entire history of Western thought.

Central to this whole venture was the Platonic concept of order whereby the cosmos was seen to be a perfect, immutable, hierarchical, and anthropocentric order. Applying this concept to all aspects of Christian doctrine, the medieval theologian pictured God as the God of order who is known from the order in the world. Creation was especially considered to be the work of order, while sin was interpreted as a disturbance of the order God had willed, and Redemption as the restoration of the same. At the end of time this order would be brought to its final perfection and consolidated for all eternity. Medieval theology as a whole can thus be characterized as an all-embracing Christian interpretation of the world, but at the same time, as an interpretation of Christianity from a geocentric cosmology. The Platonic picture of the universe was, therefore, so thoroughly interpenetrated with Christian doctrine that it became extremely difficult to clearly distinguish the one from the other.

Here we have the greatness and the weakness of medieval theology. Its greatness and exceptional merit for its time consists in the harmonious unity it achieved between the concepts of God, man, and world. For medieval man the world had two essential properties: it was, on the one hand, characterized by rationality because it displayed a perfect order, and, on the other hand, by love, because it formed the object of God's constant concern and was an expression of his concern for man. In this way the world picture referred medieval man to a God characterized by wisdom and love, in complete harmony with the image of God that became visible in the person of Christ. Cosmology and Revelation were therefore seen to speak the same language and proclaim the same God.

This also resulted in a concrete and perfect realization of the fundamental principle of Catholic theology, namely, the harmony between nature and grace. The nature in question was, in the medieval view, the concrete world of creation, of which Greek science had given an indisputable picture. The events of salvation fitted into the framework of this world picture so that the world order was perfectly analoguous to the sacred order, both being aimed at man's salvation. Nature and grace, creation and Redemption were ultimately the same act of God to realize a glorified world. For medieval man the harmony between nature and grace was not simply an arbitrary alignment of abstract concepts but pointed to a real interpenetration of the cosmic and the supernatural order. Both worlds were seen to display the same basic structure and were attuned to each other, the one illuminating the other just as two mirrors which reflect each other's rays. By contemplating the world one could, therefore, ascend to faith and from the viewpoint of faith the whole world obtained symbolic value, giving rise to the wealth of medieval symbolism that is to be found in the miniatures, drawings, statues, and paintings and in the architecture, liturgy, and poetry of the time.[98]

It is, however, in the alliance between theology and cosmology that we also find the weakness of scholasticism. All too soon it became apparent just how unreliable the foundation of this synthesis was, when it was pointed out that the old world picture did not correspond to reality at all. Was it not then inevitable that the collapse of medieval cosmology should also carry medieval theology along with it?

From a sociological standpoint one can rightly consider the thirteenth century as a perfect example of what Peter Berger and others have called the cosmization of culture. The cultural ideal that was pursued in all fields had found its model in a perfect cosmic order to which man had to submit himself and direct all his endeavors. In this way the culture was seen to acquire a sacred character and the underlying model was withdrawn from human arabitrariness, resulting in an alienation that became all the more complete as it was confirmed by the prevailing theological system and found its theoretical justification in the work of the scholastics.

Sooner or later, however, such alienation seeks to remove itself to make way for a new sociocultural order. For no single system is powerful enough to check the progress of history or restrain human energy. Before long there was clear evidence of a striving after dealienation, as a reaction to the thirteenth-century cosmization of culture. This dealienation process started with Petrarch (1304–1374) and other Italian humanists who were inclined to emphasize the dignity and creative freedom of man, undoubtedly within the framework of Christian doctrine, but nonetheless, free from its scholastic interpretation. Cosmological considerations were thus consciously or unconsciously pushed into the background, while attention was focused on the greatness of man as God's image and likeness.

In theology, therefore, there was a definite shift of emphasis from contemplation of the cosmos to a growing awareness of the place of man. In his *De Hominis Dignitate* and *Heptaplus*, Pico della Mirandola (1463–1494) argued quite forcibly that man was exalted above the stars and planets and that more dignity was due to him than to the entire material cosmos. These and many other writings of the period clearly betray an endeavor to free man from the constraint of the medieval world picture, returning to him the mastery of his own creation.[99] From this time on the cosmological standard gradually lost its normative value, though it was only finally defeated when the old world picture itself was shown to be false by the progress of the natural sciences and was consequently abandoned.

Part Two

DECLINE OF
THE MEDIEVAL
WORLD PICTURE

Since Copernicus man seems to have come to a
slippery slope—henceforward he rolls faster
and faster away from the centre—where?
To nothingness?

Friedrich Nietzsche

In the preceding chapters we have seen how, in its heyday, scholasticism succeeded in achieving an almost perfect synthesis of world picture and theology. The dream of the first Christian writers thus seemed finally to have been realized: the cosmos had become a Christian cosmos, an integral part of an all-embracing sacred order. The cosmos and the Bible spoke the same language and referred to the same God in whom both had their origin. The world picture appeared to warrant the truth of Christianity, just as Christianity seemed to guarantee the correctness of the world picture. And just as Revelation had contributed to a better understanding of the cosmos, so the cosmos had helped to bring about a better understanding of Christianity, providing the theologian with the general framework he required to express revealed doctrine in a systematic manner. Cosmology and theology were clearly seen to be close allies, opening the way for man to know himself and the cosmos. For the theologian of that time it must, therefore, have been quite inconceivable that such an ideal harmony would ever come to an end.

Man, however, is destined always to be expelled from the paradise he has built for himself. The period we are about to study signified in fact the end of the medieval dream. Bit by bit the medieval world picture was demolished, and theology gradually became more estranged from the world as cosmology and theology ceased to be allies and went their separate ways. In this context we are reminded of the statement of E.J. Dijksterhuis:

> In the eighteenth century nothing contributed so much to the mutual estrangement of faith and science as the development of the mechanics of the heavenly bodies, which is the finest fruit of the science founded by Newton and intended as a support for faith[1]

In the course of time the separation of science and religion appeared to signify emancipation on both sides. Cosmology freed itself from the grip of theology, while theology was compelled—initially with some reluctance—to wrest itself from the power of an obliterated world picture. Owing to this division, cosmology could find its own method of applying itself to the study of its object as an autonomous science, and theology in turn could purify itself of foreign elements that had nothing to do with the original message of the Gospel. Despite the obvious and by no means insignificant gain on both sides, there were undoubtedly also certain disadvantages, which in the short term did not always appear to counterbalance the advantages. Through this separation of cosmology and theology Christians found themselves in a division of consciousness that necessarily gave rise to unbearable tensions: the Book of Nature and the Book of Scripture, which were once seen to proclaim the same wisdom, now appeared to speak a different language and could in any case not readily be reconciled with each other. For many this gave rise to the question whether the God of modern cosmology and the God of the Bible were one and the same God. As the answer to this question was no longer clear, it is understandable that this dilemma was not resolved by all in the same manner. This immediately accounts for the diversity of European intellectual life.

Historians have often labeled this period[1] as the crisis of European consciousness,[2] which reached its climax at the end of the eighteenth century. Paul Hazard has typified this intellectual revolution in the following manner:

> Never was there a greater contrast, never a more sudden transition than this! An hierarchiacal system ensured by authority; life firmly based on dogmatic principle—such were the things held dear by the people of the seventeenth century; but these—controls, authority, dogmas, and the like—were the very things that their immediate successors of the eighteenth held in cordial detestation. The former were upholders of Christianity; the later were its foes. The former believed in the laws of God; the latter in the laws of Nature; the former lived contentedly enough in a world composed of unequal social grades; of the latter the one absorbing dream was Equality.
>
> Of course the younger generation are always critical of their elders. They always imagine that the world has only been awaiting their arrival and intervention to become a better and happier place. But it needs a great deal more than that, a great deal more than such a mild troubling of the waters, to account for the change so abrupt and so decisive as that we are now considering. One day,

the French people, almost to a man, were thinking like Bossuet.
The day after, they were thinking like Voltaire. No ordinary swing
of the pendulum, that. It was a revolution.[3]

Various explanations have been sought for this sudden change in
European intellectual life. It would seem that Alexandre Koyré comes
closest to the truth when he attributes the primary cause of the revolution of the seventeenth century to the great change that occurred
in the world picture during this period.[4] By the end of the seventeenth
century the view of Galileo and Newton gained the day and the medieval picture of the universe was completely abolished. All certainties
that were founded on or supported by this medieval world picture
lost all force of conviction. Having lost his central position in the
cosmos, man was no longer able to situate himself in the totality of
things, because the entire framework of his existence had collapsed
without there being any evidence of a new coherent view of the universe. What was required was no less than a complete rethinking of
his views on the world, himself, society, and God.
In the words of Nietzsche:

> Since Copernicus man seems to have come to a slippery slope—
> henceforward he rolls faster and faster away from the centre—
> where? To nothingness?[5]

Before long an impression of uncertainty and disorganization destroyed the earlier feeling of security in a harmonious world order.
We shall now consider this important period in the history of Western
thought and examine how the old world picture was gradually demolished, what consequences this had, and how theology reacted to
this new situation.

Chapter Four

FROM COPERNICUS
TO DARWIN

The downfall of the medieval world picture did not take place in a day nor was it the work of one person. It was only very gradually and through the work of many scholars that it became clear to all just how untenable the earlier picture was. Since historians of science have repeatedly given a detailed analysis of this rather complex history,[1] it is sufficient for us to recall the principal changes involved.

No one would dispute the fact that the first impulse to review the world picture was given by Copernicus. It is undoubtedly true that among the ancient Greeks there were those who defended a heliocentric picture of the universe, but this was soon abandoned because it was never developed into a workable astronomical theory and because there seemed to be no answer to the objections against the motion of the earth.[2] There was, therefore, no real threat to the geocentric picture of the universe that continued to dominate Western thought from Plato until Copernicus.[3]

The first doubts as to the validity of this world picture began to arise at the end of the Middle Ages in the writings of men such as Nicholas of Cusa and Marcellus Palingenius. Nicholas of Cusa (1401–1464), probably the most versatile and original mind of his day, was deeply aware of the importance of the study of nature and in this respect he followed the example of Roger Bacon, Albert the Great, Robert Grosseteste, John Buridan, and Nicholas of Oresme. There is no doubt that he held the traditional picture of the universe, and there is nothing to justify the conclusion that he disputed the correctness of the geocentric view of the world or the existence of the heavenly spheres. It is, therefore, out of the question to consider him as an actual precursor of Copernicus. There is, nevertheless, clear evidence of a desire on his part to break through the narrow cosmos of the Middle Ages,[4] even though his thoughts on this matter tend to be more philosophical than scientific. Despite the fact that there is no trace in his writings of an astronomical foundation of a new world picture, he undoubtedly helped to create a climate of thought in which a new investigation into the structure of the universe was made possible. Even more so than Copernicus, he was aware of the serious consequences of such a new enquiry. One wonders in vain whether Copernicus realized the revolutionary character of his theory. Nicholas of Cusa, however, clearly stated that there is an indissoluble bond between our view of the world and our conceptions of God and man, and consequently, that a change in world picture must lead to a new self-understanding of man. In all this he was much more modest than his predecessors. In contrast to the self-confidence with which the scholastics posited their definitive theses, he postulated the notion of learned ignorance; against the scholastic claim that truth consisted in the agreement between reason and reality, he argued that such an agreement was unattainable and that we had to be content with conjecture; in these and in many other matters he was a champion of common sense. This critical attitude towards scholasticism undoubtedly helped to bring about a favorable climate for renewed investigation.

In his readiness to explore new territories of the mind, he gave consideration to the following questions: If our cosmos is surrounded by the heavenly spheres, what lies beyond these spheres? Is there nothing to be found there or can we assume there is an infinite number of worlds about which we have absolutely no idea? And then, concerning the bond between theology, anthropology, and cosmology on which the whole medieval world of thought is founded, are we entitled to unite all three so closely? Can the cosmos serve as a starting point to understand man and God? Is it the task of the world to prove God's existence and is it not beyond its powers to do so? Is it not a mistake to have the structure and properties of the cosmos function as premises of our knowledge of God? Although Nicholas of Cusa maintained the bond between God, man, and world, he nevertheless conceived of this connection as less rigid and opened the way for a more autonomous investigation into the nature of man and God as well as of the world.

As to the nature of the world, he seemed to have been well aware that we cannot form an objective and uniform picture of the universe.

Though he never offered any actual scientific critique of the prevailing world picture, he plainly could not tolerate the picture of a limited, closed world. According to him the world is "interminate," which does not mean that it is infinite, because the latter is an attribute of God alone. It is precisely on account of its "interminate" character that we can only have a partial knowledge of the world, and even this is mere conjecture inasmuch as all concepts employed by the prevailing cosmology are inadequate and open to criticism. These seemingly contradictory concepts such as motion and rest, center and circumference, ultimately coincide, so that every fixed picture of the universe will finally be shown to be meaningless. In this view the whole world appears as a sphere whose center is everywhere and whose circumference is nowhere.[5]

Nicholas of Cusa was, moreover, severely critical of the hierarchical structure of medieval cosmology. By what right, he asked, is the earth assigned an inferior position in the universe while the heavenly bodies are exalted? His criticism of this hierarchical structure was, however, founded exclusively on philosophical considerations and in no way modified the prevailing astronomical conceptions. He merely ascribed as much dignity to the earth as to the heavenly bodies. But insofar as he disputed almost all the concepts of medieval cosmology, he can be said to have prepared the way for a more critical approach to the world picture.

Marcellus Stellatus Palingenius (1500–1543) was the author of a singularly didactic poem, *Zodiacus vitae,* which became very popular soon after its publication in Venice in 1534, and was translated into English and French. It has been said that he enunciated the theory that the universe is infinite, but this is evidently a mistake, because as far as we know this view was first proclaimed by Giordano Bruno. On this matter Palingenius betrays considerable ambiguity: on the one hand glorifying God's infinite creative power, maintaining what Lovejoy has called the principle of plenitude whereby everything in the cosmos is filled by the abundance of creation, and on the other hand, retaining the Platonic concept of a limited and closed world. He was a great admirer of Plato, whose influence on him is very clear, though his work also contains elements of Christian origin, mixed with all sorts of astronomical and mythological reminiscences. Moreover, he greatly emphasized the idea of a cosmic hierarchical order, considering the Creator as the divinity of order and all earthly things as a faint shadow of the world of ideas. Palingenius also held the opinion that life is possible on other heavenly bodies and that there are probably other beings to be found beyond the vault of heaven. After his death he was accused of heresy and in 1558 his book was put on the Index. Under Paul II his bones were disinterred and cremated.[6]

In the period preceding Copernicus there were doubtless many attempts to make improvements in the Ptolemaic conception of the universe. We mention here the names of Nicholas of Oresme,[7] Celio Calgagnini (1470–1541), and Girolamo Fracastoro (1483–1553). But all these attempts were only designed to improve certain details of the old world picture, not to make any basic changes or to reject it completely. Even Copernicus only set out to improve the old view and not to destroy it, but the corrections he proposed were so fundamental that they prepared the way for an entirely new view on the structure of the universe at the same time bringing to an end a world picture that had governed Western thought for nearly two thousand years.

At first sight the old picture of the universe, with the earth in the center and the heavenly bodies revolving around it, reflected our desire for perfect order and harmony. The most noble and worthy was at the top, with a gradual descent to the least worthy at the very bottom. In this way the earth was in a somewhat paradoxical situation, being at the same time, in the words of Pascal, the glory and the refuse of the universe. Glory because it was the place where man lived and where Christ had fulfilled his work of Redemption; and refuse because it consisted of the most imperfect matter.

The old picture contained another ambiguity that was much more difficult to resolve. The earth was at the bottom of the hierarchical world order and at the same time it was seen to be the center of the universe. But can the center of a circle be considered the least worthy position? Is it not, in fact, just the reverse? Is the center not the most important position in a circle, no matter what Aristotle had to say about this? For all radii meet in the center, and the circumference only exists by virtue of its relation to the center. How, then, could one explain this contradiction? Why was the least worthy to be found in the place of honor? The difficulty was actually even greater than it seemed at first, when it was pointed out that hell was in the center of the earth and in the center of hell was the throne of Lucifer! This certainly seemed to be blasphemous: the world had become, as Lovejoy explains, diabolocentric.[8] It was not God but the devil who occupied the place of honor in the universe.

Traces of this contradiction in the medieval world picture are to be found in Dante's *Divina Commedia*. When the poet has descended into the depths of hell, Virgil, his guide, inspires him with courage:

> Lo Dis, and lo the place
> where thou must arm thyself with fortitude . . .

Nevertheless, the sight of the three-headed monster strikes terror in the poet:

> How frozen I grew, how weak, through fearfulness,
> ask me not, Reader: wherefore should I strive
> to write what words are powerless to express?

Virgil then offers further explanation for what the poet sees and calls the devil:

> the evil worm which through the earth doth bore[9]

This unbearable contradiction was immediately brought to an end by the heliocentric picture of the universe, for the sun was the most obvious symbol of God, so that it was no longer the devil but God or the symbol of God that occupied the place of honor in the cosmos. But Dante was wholly captive to the old world picture and had not dared think of such a solution. The only way he saw of getting around this problem was to conceive the Heavenly Rose in his Paradise as the counterpart of the circles of hell: God was to be found in the center of heaven around which the petaled rings of the angels revolved. In this way the picture of the cosmos was practically turned inside out.

With the help of traditional mathematics and supported by the observations of his predecessors, Copernicus (1473–1543) applied himself to the task of demonstrating that the heliocentric picture of the universe was completely defensible.[10] His chief merit lies not so much in the field of astronomical observations—where he made little contribution—as in the field of cosmological theory. Since the system he devised was predominantly based on earlier observations, especially those of Ptolemy, we can say that he was mainly concerned with giving a new interpretation to what was already known, an interpretation that he believed corresponded better to the phenomena than those of his predecessors. It is difficult to know when he first acquired the heliocentric world picture. As his biography, written by his disciple Georg Joachim Rheticus, has been lost, we have extremely little information on his life and intellectual development, but it is supposed that he formed his opinion on this matter when studying in Italy. Though his principal work, *De revolutionibus orbium caelestium*, only appeared in 1543, it was in all probability already written in the years 1530–31. In the letter to Paul III which precedes this work, he stated that he had long held the ideas developed in his book. Moreover, many years before he wrote *De revolutionibus*, he had defended similar views in a smaller work, *Commentariolus*, various copies of which were distributed among friends.[11] The idea that the sun and not the earth was the center of the universe was not entirely new,[12] and Copernicus explicitly mentions his predecessors in the school of Pythagoras. Credit is due to Copernicus, however, for being the first to develop the heliocentric picture of the universe into a workable theory just as useful as the theories of Aristotle and Ptolemy had been, so that the position of the planets could still be calculated in advance on the basis of the heliocentric view.

In the center of everything there was the sun, around which the six planets were ranged: Mercury, Venus, Earth with its satellite, Mars, Jupiter, and Saturn, each moving in an orbit according to its own laws. Around this, but much higher than was previously thought, we find the motionless sphere of the fixed stars, by which the universe was enclosed. There is no doubt, then, that Copernicus retained the existence of the celestial spheres. Except for placing the sun in the center of the universe, he remained fundamentally loyal to the Ptolemaic system. But it was precisely this exception that signified a veritable revolution, ordering the destruction of the old system.

It has often been suggested that, for fear of the Aristotelians and the theologians, Copernicus presented his theory as a mere hypothesis, whereby he simply defended the feasibility of the heliocentric view as one of several possibilities without wishing to affirm anything about reality. On the contrary, he was thoroughly convinced that his theory was correct and firmly desired that it be presented as such, even though he was aware of the opposition it would meet and of the annoyance and even indignation it would provoke in certain circles. He therefore observed a certain caution but never gave the slightest impression of any ambiguity in his attitude or hesitation as to the correctness of his views. The responsibility for any possible misunderstanding on this matter rests entirely with Andreas Osiander, who wrote an introduction to *De revolutionibus orbium caelestium* without Copernicus's knowledge and even against his express desire. Osiander, himself a Protestant, realizing that this book, which he greatly admired, would cause a sensation and meet with opposition in all circles, suggested that Copernicus write an introduction to invalidate all criticism in advance with the aid of a subtle distinction between appearance and reality. In Osiander's view science only described things as they outwardly appear and was set up, as Plato had said, to save external appearances. Scripture and theology, on the other hand, were concerned with the hidden reality that is made accessible by Revelation. A scientific theory, therefore, did not have to agree with the views of Scripture because the scientist operated on the level of appearance and the theologian on the level of reality. From this viewpoint it was even possible to place various "scientific" theories next to each other, each being considered of value as long as it was able to offer a coherent explanation of the external appearance of things.

Although we do not have Copernicus's reply, we know from Kepler, who had read it, that Osiander's proposal was firmly rejected. Far from acknowledging such an ambiguity, which was contrary to his deepest convictions, Copernicus wrote to Paul III, arguing that science had the right and obligation to describe things as they are in reality, even though this gave rise to an apparent contradiction with certain statements in Scripture. But then the Bible did not intend to teach natural science and merely employed ordinary language.

Owing to various circumstances Copernicus and Rheticus were unable to see personally to the publication of *De revolutionibus,* so that unknown to them Osiander nevertheless added an introduction, expounding his own ideas and thus creating the impression that Copernicus shared his viewpoint. It must have been a bitter disappointment for Copernicus to receive the first copies of his work on his deathbed and to discover that his meaning had been entirely misrepresented in this manner.[13] What made things worse was that Osiander had not put his signature to the introduction, thereby creating the impression that Copernicus himself had written it.[14]

Through his heliocentric picture of the universe Copernicus caused the complete disruption of the splendid hierarchy of the medieval worldview. In his system the world actually had two poles: the sun in the center and the sphere of fixed stars on the outer edge, with the planets and the earth moving between both poles. But nowhere in the Copernican system do we find the perfect hierarchical world order that had counted as a sacred and unassailable principle for the scholastic theologians. One can readily understand that the theologians did not easily abandon their old position and did all they could to resist for as long as possible a theory that they felt to be a threat to their theological system. Opposition to this new world picture came not only from the theologians but also from the astronomers who, with a few exceptions, for a long time continued to maintain the Ptolemaic system. Even a scholar such as Tycho Brahe (1546–1601), who was responsible for numerous important discoveries and who can perhaps be considered the builder of the first modern observatory (Uranienburg, Hveen), was reconciled to the views of Copernicus only with much difficulty. What he did was to devise an ingenious system intended to harmonize the new view with the old by placing the earth in the center of the universe around which the sun moved. The planets, however, were said to revolve in a wide orbit around both the earth and the sun. Initially this amphibious theory, whereby the earth and the sun were situated together in the center of the world, met with considerable success because it appeared to many to satisfy advocates of both the heliocentric and geocentric views.[15]

The attitude of Johann Kepler (1571–1630) was entirely different. In his first work, *Mysterium cosmographicum* (1595), he already showed himself to be an enthusiastic advocate of the Copernican system.[16] In the preface to this work he declared he had seen that the old view was untenable from the time he had been a student of Michael Maestlin in Tübingen. The task he assigned himself was to prove that the Copernican theory was superior to the Ptolemaic, by appealing to arguments partly derived from his predecessors and partly devised by himself. In his opinion the Copernican doctrine was not only completely correct but was also necessary: "I do not hesitate to affirm that everything Copernicus has proved a posteriori, both on the basis of observations and with the help of geometry, can also be proved a priori, without appealing to subtleties." Kepler was thoroughly convinced that had the Copernican doctrine been available to Aristotle, he would have fully subscribed to it. The universe had thus to be conceived as completely spherical with the sun in the center. Two sorts of lines were to be distinguished in a circle or sphere: the curve on the surface and the straight line from the center to the outer edge. "Why," Kepler asked, "has God chosen the distinction between curved and straight lines, and the nobility of the former, as fundamental to the creation of the world? For what other reason than that it was absolutely necessary for the most perfect Creator to produce the most perfect creation. It is not fitting (as Cicero, in imitation of Plato's *Timaeus*, had said in *De Universitate*) and never has been for the best to bring forth something that is not the most beautiful of all".[17] In this view one had to see a symbol of the Blessed Trinity in the structure of the universe: the center representing the Father, the circumference, the Son, and the radius, the Holy Spirit.

About ten years after the publication of *Mysterium cosmographicum* Kepler published a second work, *De astronomia nova*,[18] that contained perhaps even more new and revolutionary elements that led to the further destruction of the old world picture. Of old it had counted as an indisputable axiom that a circle possessed an absolute superiority over all other lines or motions. As one had to ascribe the highest possible perfection to the world, and the circle or sphere was the most perfect form, it followed that one had to conceive the world as spherical and attribute a circular orbit to the planets. Kepler delivered a mortal blow to this view. By coincidence or, as he believed, by divine Providence, he came into contact with Tycho Brahe, at whose request he embarked on a complete study of the planet Mars and its motions. The fact that he concentrated his attention on this planet was indeed of outstanding importance. For it soon became evident that the earlier view that had attributed a circular orbit to Mars and all the other planets was completely untenable. The orbit of Mars was now clearly seen to form not a circle but an ellipse. Kepler hesitated for a long time before yielding this point, because it appeared to him a reckless and sacrilegious venture to doubt or contradict the teaching of the ancients on this matter. But the observations of his teacher Tycho Brahe and his own calculations took precedence over the authority of earlier writers. Immediately an entirely new view on the structure of the universe was born: the planets moved in an elliptical orbit round the sun. This new picture was not of course immediately accepted by all, and for many it was simply impossible to abandon the earlier view of circles and epicycles. A Dutch amateur astronomer wrote to Kepler:

> With your ellipse you abolish the circularity and uniformity of the motions, which strikes me as more preposterous the more I think of it'. . . . If you could only preserve the completely circular orbit and justify your elliptical orbit by another small epicycle, it would be much better.[19]

Kepler, however, did not consider returning to the earlier view: his studies had revealed that the "dignity of the circle" was a fanciful idea for which there was no foundation in reality. In this way he also demolished the view that had governed Western thought from the time of Aristotle.[20]

The planets were thus seen to move in an elliptical orbit around the sun. But by what force were they moved? Where was the cause of this motion to be sought? To answer these questions Aristotle had appealed to the celestial spheres that were set in motion by "separate intelligences." This explanation was quite unacceptable to Kepler who did not consider celestial spheres or separate intelligences as sufficient to account for planetary motions. It seemed to him that the solution to the problem should rather be sought in the sun itself:

> As to motion, the sun is the first cause of the planetary motions and the first motor of the universe, and this by virtue of its material nature. In the intervening space we find the movable bodies, that is, the spherical planets; the realm of fixed stars grants the planets their position and a foundation upon which they can rest as it were, naturally a motionless foundation, in comparison with which motion can be observed.[21]

It was especially in his later work, *Epitome astronomiae copernicanae* (1617–1621), considered by many as his most mature and systematic work, that he formulated the three laws that were to account for planetary motion and which Newton later defined more exactly; the first two laws also appeared in his previous work:

1. The planets follow an elliptical orbit, the sun being in one focus of the ellipse.

2. The line connecting a planet with the sun will sweep out equal areas in equal times.

3. The cube of a planet's mean distance from the sun is in constant ratio to the square of the time required for all planets to complete such an orbit.

With this Kepler came very close to the discovery of the universal attraction of bodies. Strictly speaking, however, he never took this decisive step. Arthur Koestler gives the following explanation for this:

> The whole notion of a "force" which acts instantly at a distance without an intermediary agent, which traverses the vastest distances in zero seconds, and pulls at immense stellar objects with ubiquitous ghost-fingers—the whole idea is so mystical and "unscientific," that modern minds like Kepler, Galileo and Descartes, who were fighting to break loose from Aristotelian animism, would instinctively tend to reject it as a relapse into the past. In their eyes, the idea of "universal gravity" would amount to much the same kind of thing as the anima mundi of the ancients. What made Newton's postulate nevertheless a modern Law of Nature, was his mathematical formulation of the mysterious entity to which it referred. And that formulation, Newton deduced from the discoveries of Kepler—who had intuitively glimpsed gravity, and shied away from it. In such crooked ways does the tree of science grow.[22]

In Kepler's opinion the study of the heavenly bodies was preeminently a religious concern. The true purpose of astronomy was, he believed, to discover what thoughts had been on the Creator's mind in drawing up the plan of the world, how he had arranged planetary motion, and which mathematical laws and physical forces were involved in this. Since God had created the world in supreme wisdom, the study of creation could not help but reveal the wisdom of the Creator.

Following the direction indicated by Copernicus and Tycho Brahe, Kepler achieved important results on many points. The planets moved around the sun in an elliptical orbit; the velocity of this motion was proportionate to their distance from the sun—the closer they were, the greater their velocity. But what was the sense of all this? Why had God placed the planets at various distances from each other and from the sun? Why did their velocity increase as they came closer to the sun and decrease as they moved farther away? At the end of many years of study Kepler finally came to the conclusion that God had created the world not only as a divine geometrician and architect but also as a divine musician. It seemed to him that each planet produced a particular note, varying acccording to the position of the planet. Between the various planets there were equal distances just as between the tones of a stringed instrument. Now if the planets were to move in a circular orbit they would always produce the same tone, which would certainly make a perfect chord, but the same chord, however perfect, eventually becomes monotonous. By prescribing an elliptical orbit for the planets, it was possible to have various tones and thus variation in the sound they produced. The universe became a continuous concert to the praise of God and the delight of the angels and the blessed. The planets were thus seen to form a gigantic orchestra, in which the earth produced *mi* and *fa*—and rightly so, remarked Kepler, when one considers that this is the place where *mi*sery and *fa*mine belong! Convinced that he had finally discovered the harmony of the spheres, of which Pythagoras had dreamed, Kepler was deeply moved and thanked the Creator in the conclusion to *Harmonices mundi libri V*[23] for having assigned him, an earthworm, the task of announcing to men the secret of the world:

> Now it only remains for me to put aside the planetary tables and direct my attention to the Father of all light, praying: God, who through the light of nature kindles in us the desire for grace, that we might thus be raised to the light of glory—I thank you, Lord

and Creator, for having delighted me by the sight of your creation and having filled me with jubilation whenever I beheld the work of your hand. In this way I have fulfilled the task assigned to me by virtue of my profession, using all the mental powers you have granted me. To those who read these pages, I have revealed the glory of your work, at least insofar as my limited understanding has been able to grasp something of the infinity of your work. My soul has zealously applied itself to the task of reasoning as correctly as possible. But if I, an earthworm, born and raised in the mire of sinfulness, should have said something unworthy of the decrees which you wished to reveal to man, enlighten my mind that I might correct my work. If I, carried along by the wonderful beauty of your work, have hurried on recklessly, or if let myself by tempted to strive after my own fame in a work destined for your glory, forgive me with leniency and compassion. Finally, grant that these argumentations may be conducive to your glory and to the salvation of souls, never bringing harm on them in any way.[24]

This is clearly indicative of the spirit of the man, disclosing at the same time just how closely connected, in his opinion, science and religion were. In the same strain as the writings of the medieval theologians, Kepler's inquiry was concerned with guessing the thoughts of the Creator which were concealed behind observable phenomena. What is more, he considered it man's task as a creature to contemplate the work of God and through this contemplation to reach his destiny.

In the revolution that started with Copernicus and culminated in the work of Isaac Newton, an outstanding role was played by Galileo Galilei, not in the first place on account of his conflict with the Inquisition, but more so on account of his invaluable contribution in the purely scientific field. Though his influence extended over many areas, we shall confine ourselves to his work in astronomy and cosmology.[25]

Writing to Kepler, Galileo refers to those people who "think that philosophy is a sort of book like the *Aeneid* or the *Odyssey*, and that truth is to be sought not in the universe, not in nature, but by comparing texts!"[26] From this we can readily see his primary concern that natural science be founded not on the authority of earlier writers but solely on observation and experiment. Besides being his principal concern, it was also his greatest merit to establish the correct scientific method.

In a manner quite unlike anyone of his day he challenged those who continued to appeal to the authority of Aristotle or Ptolemy by defending the view that in the field of natural science only facts are conclusive and these are only established by observation and experiment. His main opponents were the Aristotelians and the theologians[27] whose arguments were based on authority and thus ignored the evidence provided by observation. Galileo's particular contribution was not only to establish proper scientific method but to employ instruments whereby the phenomena of nature could be observed more accurately. Though he did not invent the telescope, he was the first to use it for astronomical observations, thereby opening up an approach that proved to be of utmost importance for the further development of natural sciences.[28]

The results he achieved filled him with pride and enthusiasm, as we can see from *Sidereus nuntius* (The Message of the Stars) where he made public his first discoveries:

> The message of the stars—a grand and stupendous spectacle . . .
> observed by Galileo Galilei, a citizen of Florence . . ., by means of
> a "perspicillum" he recently made . . ., things which no one has
> known until now and were now observed for the first time by the
> author.

The book, which appeared in 1610, naturally caused much commotion. What were the things Galileo had seen? First, that there were many more stars—ten times more, he wrote—than had hitherto been thought. Second, that the moon's surface was not smooth but rough and mountainous. And finally, strangest of all, the four moons of Jupiter. There was no record of these things in Aristotle or the earlier astronomers. Had they remained entirely ignorant of these phenomena? What confidence, then, could one still have in their science? And if their science was unreliable, how had one to judge a philosophy founded on this science? It is clear that the discoveries of Galileo could not fail to cause a crisis without precedent in the history of Western thought. Leaving aside the philosophical and theological questions that were raised, the conflict in the scientific field centered on two questions: first, whether the phenomena had been correctly observed. Had Galileo not made a mistake? What confidence could one have in that odd instrument, the perspicillum? Second, if the facts were correct, how had they to be interpreted? Could they be accounted for in the prevailing world picture or had the old geocentric picture to be abandoned for the heliocentric picture of Copernicus? Since Galileo had only the telescope at his disposal, one simply had to look to see whether he was speaking the truth or not. This was precisely the problem, however, because there was question over the value of this instrument. All sorts of tricks were played by quacks and conjurers who swamped the fairground. It was important, therefore, not to be too readily convinced. Many Aristotelians even refused to look into the telescope, whose reliability was certainly not equal, in their opinion, to the tried authority of Aristotle. When one considers that the first telescopes were distributed in the marketplace and were extremely primitive, one can understand why many people were skeptical of such a novelty. According to Magini, an authoritative astronomer at the university of Bologna, the whole thing was no more than an optical illusion. But others, like Kepler, immediately saw the value in this new method of observation, which was tested by the laws of optics.[29]

There was, however, considerably more disputation on the question of what significance ought to be attributed to the observed facts. Galileo excluded all possible doubt: his discovery of the moons of Jupiter and his later discovery of the phases of Venus were for him convincing arguments that the earth was also a planet and consequently that only the Copernican system was correct. In March 1611 he went to Rome, where he was received with honor, and for a year he delivered lectures and participated in discussions. The general of the Jesuits issued an order stating that the Aristotelian doctrine had to be maintained and defended as long as possible. Galileo's arguments were really not conclusive: strictly speaking, neither the rough surface of the moon nor the moons of Jupiter nor the phases of Venus provided convincing proof of the earth's motion.

Shortly after *Sidereus nuntius* Galileo published two smaller works, one on floating bodies and one on sunspots, which were discovered at about the same time by Father Christopher Scheiner and himself. But after the success of *Sidereus* he diverted his attention from the study of nature to entirely devote himself to the dissemination of his ideas. According to Geymonat, his intention was to bring about a general awareness of the revolution started by the new discoveries in our way of thinking about the world and which opened up such grandiose perspectives for the future. He was not a philosopher and always distinguished himself from Giordano Bruno, who was more concerned with the metaphysical implications of the Copernican system. Galileo thought only of the significance of the new science and its unlimited possibilities. Since he wished to impart to others his faith in science, he attempted to gain the support of the civil and ecclesiastical authorities. He received help and protection from the powerful Medicis and initially obtained promises of support from numerous ecclesiastical authorities. He remained relentless in his effort to propagate his faith in science until 1633, when he was condemned by the Inquisition. It was only after this that he confined himself to strictly scientific research. He was, moreover, completely won over by the ideas of Copernicus, the confirmation of which he found in his own discoveries. But even though his most brilliant opponents, like the Jesuit Clavius, acknowledged that his observations were correct, they nevertheless would not concede that these contained a confirmation of the Copernican system. They were simply not prepared to forsake Aristotle, whose philosophy was so closely related to the theology of the time, and they did their utmost to defend him. Just how zealous they were in this endeavor can be seen from the following example. Whereas Aristotle had taught that the moon's surface was perfectly smooth, it was evident from Galileo's observations that it was rough and mountainous. A bewildering explanation was offered by Clavius: the moon's crust was mountainous, but its valleys were filled with a subtle matter invisible to the human eye! Galileo remarked dryly that there was indeed no theory to resist such an argument.

Before long, however, the attacks of his opponents became more vehement. The history of these attacks is too complex to be related here. In 1616 the Holy Office made a decision whereby two theses were considered to be contrary to the teaching of sacred Scriptures: 1) that the sun is the center of the universe, and consequently does not change place; 2) that the earth is not the center of the universe and is not motionless, but is in motion as a whole and in its daily rotation. This decision of the Holy Office was made over to the congregation of the Index who decided on March 3: (1) that the books of Copernicus and Diego de Zuniga were banned until they had been corrected; (2) a book of Father Foscarini was completely banned and condemned; (3) all books proclaiming a similar doctrine had to be banned.

Immediately striking is the fact that there is no explicit mention of Galileo. Only several sentences were deleted from the work of Copernicus, namely, a passage from his dedication to Paul V where it is stated that his doctrine was not at variance with sacred Scriptures. The two others who were explicitly named had attempted to show that the heliocentric world picture was in no way contrary to Christian doctrine. Though nothing was said about the writings of Galileo, it is clear that the whole affair was indirectly aimed at him. The eminent scholar was evidently to be respected. He had an interview with Cardinal Bellarmine who informed him of the decision of the Holy Office, and he was later given a papal audience. From Cardinal Bellarmine he received the following certificate:

> We, Roberto Cardinal Ballarmine, having heard that it is calum-
> niously reported that Signor Galileo Galilei has in our hand abjured
> and has also been punished with salutary penance, and being re-
> quested to state the truth as to this, declare that the said Galileo
> has not abjured, either in our hand, or in the hand of any other
> person here in Rome, or anywhere else, so far as we know, any
> opinion or doctrine held by him; neither has any salutary penance
> been imposed on him; but that the only declaration made by the
> Holy Father and published by the Sacred Congregation of the Index
> has been notified to him, wherein it is set forth that the doctrine
> attributed to Copernicus, that the Earth moves around the Sun,
> and that the Sun is stationary in the center of the world and does
> not move from east to west, is contrary to the Holy Scriptures and
> therefore cannot be defended or held. In witness whereof we have
> written and subscribed these presents with our hand this twenty-
> sixth day of May, 1616.[30]

After the first trial Galileo clearly did not renounce any of his doctrine,
but stood firm, hoping that the great significance of the Copernican
discovery would be recognized sooner or later. However, he does
seem to have bound himself not to defend his doctrine in public.[31] He
was in any case more cautious.

An important event in 1623 raised Galileo's expectations: Cardinal
Maffeo Barberini was elected pope and chose the name Urban VIII.
Barberini was a cultured man with a lively interest in science and the
work of Galileo in particular. Would the new pope be willing to revoke
the condemnation of the heliocentric world picture and at the same
time grant the new science its rightful position? Impelled by the desire
to look after the needs of the Church as well as of science, Galileo
wanted to risk another attempt. It would not have been difficult for
him to go abroad, beyond the reach of the Roman authorities, and
quietly carry on his work. But as a sincere believer he was also concerned wih the future of the Church. What was clear to him was that
the ecclesiastical authorities had made a grave error in condemning
the heliocentric world picture and that sooner or later this would turn
against the Church. There could no longer be any doubt that the
Copernican doctrine was correct. If need be, science could manage
without the Church, but the Church could not cope without science.
Urged on by his old dream of reconciling faith and science, Galileo
ventured another attempt at persuading the ecclesiastical authorities
to review the whole matter. For this purpose he wrote his major work,
Dialogue on the Great World Systems, which appeared with an impri-
matur in 1632 and in which he compared the Ptolemaic and Coper-

nican systems, clearly giving preference to the latter. The book was written in Italian and not in Latin in order to invite discussion from a wide public. Its publication led to the notorious trial at which Galileo was compelled by the Holy Office, against his deepest conviction, to retract his doctrine and to accept the punishment imposed on him on account of his disobedience. The short-sightedness of his judges could not, however, prevent his works from being distributed in all parts of Europe and being quickly translated into various languages. During his house arrest at his country seat in Arcetri, near Florence, he concentrated his attention on the purely scientific field, especially mathematics and mechanics. This he did until his death in 1642.

Discussion of the Copernican doctrine was nevertheless continued on a purely scientific level. A great number of writings appeared in this period, both for and against the Copernican system, without, however, introducing any essentially new elements as far as the general world picture was concerned. Throughout the seventeenth century the phenomena of nature were studied with an increasing intensity, culminating in the work of Isaac Newton (1642–1727), who can be considered as having concluded the Copernican revolution.

To explain planetary motion, Plato had appealed to a world-soul, Aristotle to separate intelligences, the medieval theologian to angels, and Descartes to the notorious vortices or ethereal whirlpools carrying the stars and planets along in their revolving motion. All these conceptions were finally obliterated by the work of Newton.[32]

As legend has it, it was an apple falling from a tree that drew Newton's attention to the strange phenomenon of gravity. Many scholars like Copernicus, Kepler, Christian Huygens, Galileo, and Descartes had already studied this phenomenon. It was a common experience that bodies tended to the center of the earth, but the question was how far this force extended. As far as the moon? Could the attraction of the earth offer a possible explanation for the fact that the moon continued to circle the earth and was not hurled away by centrifugal force? Could it be this mysterious attraction that held the moon in its fixed orbit around the earth and the planets in their path around the sun? Following his account of the general laws of motion in the first and second part of his principal work, *Philosophiae naturalis principia mathematica* (1687), Newton proceeded in the third part of the book to show how gravity offered a balanced explanation for the elliptical orbit that was described by the planets and by which the attraction of the various heavenly bodies affected each other. The name of Newton is thus closely associated with the well-known law that bodies attract each other in direct proportion to their mass and in inverse proportion to the square of their distance apart. Owing to its simplicity and general validity it still remains an unequalled model of what we understand by a law of nature. Although other scholars, like Kepler, Huygens, Wendelinus, and Robert Hook had come close to this formula, it was the work of Newton that gave it its present form and made possible a new conception of the universe. We shall later have occasion to investigate the repercussions of this discovery on philosophical and theological thought.

It would, however, be an error to think that Newton's theory gained the immediate approval of the scientific world of his time. For many years it was vehemently contested, especially by the Cartesians who asserted that it contained no explanation for the fact that the planets were in motion. Even if it influenced the orbit of the planets, the attraction of gravity in no way accounted for the fact itself of planetary motion.

Moreover, what was this mysterious force which Newton rated so highly? Was it not a regression to a medieval manner of explanation whereby an appeal was made to all sorts of mysterious and unverifiable forces (occult qualities)? Newton's theory also met with fierce opposition from Leibniz and many others who refused "to kneel before the idol of attraction."[33] Alexander Pope wrote the famous verse:

> Nature and Nature's law lay hid in the night,
> God said: let Newton be! and all was light.

The study of the universe was now established for good. As telescopes were improved, new worlds were disclosed. Even the vault of heaven (the firmament) which the ancients believed enclosed the cosmos was proved to have been a fanciful idea, and with this the crystalline heaven and the empyrean immediately disappeared into nothingness.

In this way the old world picture was gradually effaced. The central position of the earth, the perfect circular orbit of the heavenly bodies, the higher dignity of the heavenly, the intervention of heavenly spirits, and the firmament marking out the world—the entire world picture of antiquity and of the Middle Ages, that had formed the basis of philosophy and was so closely bound to the whole culture, and had moreover served as background to fifteen centuries of Christian thought—this world picture now turned out to have been a complete mistake. What happened in the period between Copernicus and Newton is rightly considered to be one of the greatest revolutions in the history of humankind. It was inevitable that such a revolution in the world picture soon influenced all areas of human thought and evoked all sorts of reactions, not the least in religious circles. Its impact was felt not only in the purely scientific field but also in philosophy, morality, political theory, theology, and man's whole self-understanding. The beautiful and harmonious synthesis between cosmology, anthropology, and theology, which had been so well established in the Middle Ages, was henceforth doomed to destruction. It was, therefore, unavoidable that the collapse of the old world picture also caused a crisis without precedent in human religious feelings, at the same time posing a threat to all religious certainties. Through the work of Newton the way was open for further investigation of the universe. By a more precise statement of these laws and calculations, Laplace succeeded in making important improvements in the Newtonian system. Newton had not been able to offer a perfectly satisfactory explanation for planetary motions. In his opinion certain irregularities had occurred almost of necessity, which, in the course of time, could only be put right by God's intervention. Just as a clock can run perfectly well for a long time but sooner or later must be checked and, if need be, wound up, so, according to Newton, the motion of the planets had to be rectified from time to time by God's intervention so that they would continue to move in the right orbit. But Pierre-Simon Laplace (1749–1827) showed by his calculations that such interventions were completely superfluous and that all planetary motions could be fully explained by the law of universal attraction.[34] This explains why, in answer to Napoleon's question as to the place of God in his system, Laplace is reported to have said that he had no need of such a hypothesis, by which he meant that his system operated perfectly well without special intervention of God to rectify any eventual irregularities.[35]

Although there were many other prominent figures in the history of astronomy who contributed to the gradual widening of our knowledge of the universe, we shall now have to turn our attention to another science which greatly influenced our contemporary view of the world with results that were no less revolutionary than those of astronomy. While astronomy renewed our outlook on the spatial order of the universe, biology prepared the way for a new conception of time. With the fusion of both these views, an entirely new concept of cosmic reality was made possible, but not without demolishing another aspect of the medieval world picture.

Enthusiastic disciples of Charles Darwin (1809–1882) have often considered his principal work, *On the Origin of Species* (1859), to be the cause of a veritable revolution in the field of biology, comparable to that of Copernicus in astronomy. Like Copernicus, however, Darwin had many precursors, perhaps in a more real sense than in the case of Copernicus. The notion of evolution was not discovered by Darwin but has a long history, the first traces being found in Greek antiquity.[36] In the eighteenth century there was evidence of the idea of development in the various forms of life as a possible hypothesis in the work of scholars like Buffon (1707–1788) and Erasmus Darwin (1731–1802). Even Linnaeus (1707–1778), who initially seemed to belong to the "fixed-type" school, supposed that new species had come into being in the course of time. One of the first significant attempts to give a scientific basis to the evolution of the forms of life and to offer a possible explanation for this phenomenon is to be found in the *Philosophie zoologique* (1809) of Jean-Baptiste Lamarck (1744–1829). At the end of the eighteenth century the idea of the gradual development of nature received much attention from the philosophers of the Enlightenment, notably Herder in his *Ideen zur Philosophie der Geschichte der Menschheit* (1784). In his review of this book, Immanuel Kant wrote that there was undoubtedly a relationship between all beings, but the view that one species came from another or all species originated from one single species, was completely opposed to reason.[37]

Kant thus clearly realized that such a view had far-reaching consequences, even though he was not then able to discuss the matter. Hegel explicity rejected any doctrine of biological evolution,[38] while Goethe, who was deeply concerned with natural science, showed considerable interest in the theory of evolution and continued to follow the progress of Lamarck's work. With his doctrine of metamorphosis Goethe came very close to the problem for which evolutionism attempted to provide a solution.[39]

It is evident, then, that the pioneering work of Darwin has to be seen against this background. Darwin himself, like most of his contemporaries, initially held the view that species were immutable and in the course of time had always preserved the very same properties and characteristics. However, careful study of vast amounts of material, mostly collected during his voyage in *The Beagle*, led him to other insights, as he gradually came to the conviction, based on extremely accurate observations, that the theory of the immutability of species was untenable and that in the course of time mutations had taken place in the morphology of plants and animals. In *The Origin of Species* he not only provided an abundance of scientific observations that clearly pointed in the direction of an evolution, but at the same time developed a theory to explain this phenomenon. It seemed to him that new species came into being as a result of a natural selection, a consequence of the constant struggle for life and the survival of the fittest (an expression Darwin borrowed from the philosopher Herbert Spencer). The explanation of the mechanism of evolution undoubtedly signified an advance over previously devised theories and met with great success. Unlike Lamarck, who had appealed to the principle of adaptation to environment, Darwin taught that the simple principle of natural selection contained a universal explanation for the fact of evolution. The "law" of natural selection has often been compared to Newton's law of universal attraction,[40] because in both cases a rather simple concept has made it possible to provide a generally valid explanation for a series of phenomena that were previously held to be inexplicable. Only later was it acknowledged that Darwin's system could not boast a similar completeness and accountability. Credit is neverthelesss due to Darwin for having definitively introduced the idea of evolution into biology.

In *The Origin of Species* Darwin restricted his treatment of evolution to animals and plants. The problem of the origin of man was only touched upon in one brief sentence where it was affirmed that the theory of evolution could readily be applied to the origin and history of man. It was just this statement, however, which caused a stir and was vehemently contested, though it also had its advocate in the person of Thomas Huxley, who in his book *Man's Place in Nature* (1863), immediately extended Darwin's theory to man. In 1871 Darwin himself published his *Descent of Man and Selection in Relation to Sex*, attributing the origin of man to the same principles which had led to the origin of new species in the plant and animal kingdom.

If the work of Copernicus and Newton mainly endangered cosmology, the work of Darwin caused serious and irreparable damage to traditional biology and anthropology. Those who belonged to the "fixed-type" school, which held that species are immutable and were thus created as they are now, were gradually compelled to abandon their position. The principle of evolution is nowadays regarded as the only workable hypothesis in biology. Although there are still many questions to be solved concerning the history and mechanism of evolution, there is no longer any doubt as to the historical fact of an evolution in the forms of life. What is more, all recent discoveries in the field of animal and human palaeontology evidently confirm the evolutionary hypothesis, while discoveries in comparative anatomy, embryology, genetics, etc. point in the same direction.

Two of the most significant achievements of the nineteenth century were the hitherto unknown progress in the natural sciences and the development of the historical method. Though initially there seemed to be no connection between these two worlds, by the end of the century the theory of evolution had succeeded in bridging the gap by introducing historical awareness into our view of nature. More and more nature acquired the appearance of a gigantic historical process in which all things were interconnected. This signified the destruction of the last remnant of the old world picture—the existence of a static, immutable world order—and opened the way for an entirely new view of reality. Belief in a perfect, immutable, hierarchical, and anthropocentric world order was now finally abolished.

Chapter Five

CRISIS IN RELIGIOUS THOUGHT

For many centuries, indeed from its origin, theological reflection on faith attempted to interpret the Christian salvation mystery as perfectly as possible within the framework of the generally accepted geocentric world picture and the resulting image of man. The culmination of this endeavor is to be found in the thirteenth century when Christian doctrine and the prevailing world picture were seen to be in complete harmony. In this way an entire doctrinal system was established in which faith and science made a balanced contribution to the construction of an all-embracing Christian view of the world that remained valid in the centuries that followed.

With the Copernican revolution, however, the very foundations of the Christian world picture were shown to be unsound. From the new insights concerning the structure of the universe it was evident that the earlier picture was quite worthless and had to be abandoned. When one considers that this entailed the total dissolution of the admirable synthesis which had only been achieved by the work of many eminent scholars throughout the ages, one can readily understand the determination on the part of many Christians to defend the old world picture at all costs.

It is plain that this was not merely a theological concern, but essentially involved the entire culture, man's complete self-understanding and whole thinking, especially in religious matters. Aquinas once made the pithy remark that any error about creation also leads to an error about God.[1] Once it was evident that the old world picture was fundamentally wrong, did this not imply that the traditional notion of God had to be reconsidered? Since there is clearly an inevitable correlation between a philosopher's conception of God and his picture of the universe, there had to be a new concept of God to correspond to a new world picture. For this reason the traditional idea of God was subjected to severe criticism in the course of the seventeenth and eighteenth centuries, giving rise to new conceptions such as pantheism, deism, and atheism, whereby the whole of Christianity came under attack. Was not the God of Christianity the God of the old world picture, the God of the Bible, identical to the God of Greek philosophy? Did not the alliance between Christian theology and the old world picture also necessitate the downfall of this theology and evoke a deep distrust in everything that appealed to its authority? It was inevitable, then, that such a situation should provoke an unprecedented crisis in religion.

But the consequences of the Copernican revolution were also felt in the moral sphere. For centuries morality had been closely allied to a concept of order largely subject to the prevailing cosmology. Thus in his conduct man had to respect the same perfect, hierarchical order that the Creator had established in the world. However, it was just this perfect and hierarchical order that had now become problematic. Was the old idea of order still an acceptable criterion to distinguish good and evil? And if not, on what basis was morality to be founded? This concern for a new morality naturally gave rise to all sorts of views.

Finally, there was the threat posed to the very structure of society. It had previously been thought that society had to observe the same hierarchical order exemplified in the cosmos. This demand seemed to have been met by the medieval feudal system and later by the power, authority, and divine right of kings. What happens to such a polity, however, when it turns out that this hierarchical order in no way appears to be postulated by the natural world order? On what grounds can subjects be obliged to submit to such an authority? Although those in power undoubtedly attempted to maintain their position as long as possible, defending themselves precisely by appealing to the order that God had willed, new ideas nevertheless came to light, giving rise to an entirely new conception of society whereby the source of all rights was found to be the people and not the monarch.

A revolution in astronomy thus resulted in a revolution throughout the entire culture. Perhaps there was some truth in the claim that man's destiny was written in the stars, but then in an entirely different sense than the ancients had supposed. It took a considerable length of time of course, even more than the century and a half between Copernicus's *De revolutionibus orbium caelestium* and Newton's *Philosophiae naturalis principia mathematica*, before the consequences of the collapse of the old world picture were fully realized. Like science, philosophy made only slow progress, and it required no less effort to discover the consequences of the new cosmology than it had initially done to secure victory for the new insights concerning the structure of the universe. Once these consequences started to become clear, one had the impression of awakening for the first time to a true conception of reality, experiencing this insight as an enlightenment. The break with the medieval tradition was now complete. There were, of course, other factors such as the Renaissance and the Reformation which contributed to this intellectual revolution by creating a new cultural climate. Yet it cannot be denied that the disintegration of the old world picture played an extremely important role here, and for this reason many historians rightly consider this event as the beginning of modern thought,[2] without however underestimating the importance of the Renaissance, humanism, and the Reformation.

Initially the cultural climate continued to be governed by the old world picture, even though certain isolated thinkers soon began to explore the far-reaching implications of the new picture. It is a well-known sociological phenomenon that new ideas permeate a society only slowly, gradually disclosing all the consequences that are involved. Throughout the sixteenth century the old world picture was still maintained as an intellectual framework, in spite of the fact that scholasticism had fallen into decay and had become an object of ridicule. In Erasmus's (1649–1553) *In Praise of Folly* the scholastics are accused of captious hairsplitting. Luther (1483–1546) denounced them in the name of the pure Gospel, while Rabelais (1490–1553) regarded them as a laughingstock, bluntly casting them aside,[3] and Montaigne (1533–1592) withdrew into a skeptical consideration of the nature of man.[4] All these protests, however different, reveal a certain nostalgia for the old order, which was seen to be betrayed and severely crippled.[5] With Shakespeare (1564–1616) we also find clear indication that the old world picture continued to exercise considerable influence. It is only against the background of the prevalent desire for order and balance, that we can appreciate his portrayal of the chaotic world of the passions, of moral and social degeneracy. The often cited passage from *Troilus and Cressida* (I,3) which describes the hierarchical structure of the world order is but one example of the many allusions to the world picture of the age:

> The heavens themselves, the planets, and this center
> Observe degree, priority, and place,
> Insisture, course, proportion, season, form,

Office, and custom, in all line of order;
And therefore is the glorious planet Sol
In noble eminence enthron'd and spher'd
Amidst the other; whose medi'cinable eye
corrects the ill aspects of planets evil
And posts, like the commandment of a king,
Sans check, to good and bad. But when the planets
In evil mixture to disorder wander,
What plagues and what portents, what mutiny.
What raging of the sea, shaking of earth,
Commotion in the winds, frights changes horrors,
Divert and crack, rend and deracinate
The unity and married calm of states
Quite from their fixure. Oh when degree is shak'd
Which is the ladder to all high designs,
The enterprise is sick. How could communities,
Degree in schools and brotherhoods in cities,
Peaceful commerce from dividable shores,
The primogenitive and due of birth,
Prerogative of age, crowns, sceptres, laurels,
But by degree stand in authentic place?
Take but degree away, untune that string,
And hark, what discord follows. Each thing meets
In mere oppugnancy. The bound waters
Should lift their bosoms higher than the shores
And make a sop of all this solid globe:
Strength should be lord to imbecility,
And the rude son should strike his father dead . . .
This chaos, when degree is suffocate,
Follows the choking.

According to Shakespeare, then, all disorder in society is to be attributed to man's failure to appreciate the hierarchical order or "degree" that is exemplified in the cosmos. In the *Duchess of Malfi* (written about 1614) John Webster, like many others before him, ascribed man's infatuation to the influence of the planets:

> We are merely the stars' tennis balls
> struck and bandied
> Which way please them.[6]

In sharp contrast to this fatalistic view, is Shakespeare's defense of man's freedom and responsibility in *Julius Caesar*:

The fault, dear Brutus, lies not in our stars
But in ourselves, that we are underlings

And this, of course, is completely in line with the view of the medieval theologians who repeatedly argued that human freedom was not controlled by the planets.

In his brief but illuminating study, *The Elizabethan World Picture,* [7] Tillyard has shown how the basic medieval idea of order continued to govern the Elizabethan age. He argues that the greatness of the age was that it maintained the old idea of order in spite of the fact that the educated Elizabethan was well informed about the new cosmological conceptions originating from the work of Copernicus.[8] As no one was inclined to reject an idea that was so fundamental to the whole culture, the old order remained very much alive, retaining its validity in the work of Vondel (1587–1679) and Milton (1608–1674), for example, and was adhered to as long as possible throughout the seventeenth century.[9] Yet a feeling of uncertainty started to take possession of man, gradually replacing the quiet certainty that had once characterized his existence with a feeling of distrust in the wisdom of previous ages. As we read in Hamlet, "there are more things in heaven and earth, than are dreamt of in your philosophy."

Although this was not yet a rejection of the old world picture, it did signify the beginning of doubt and dissatisfaction. It is true that the old philosophy that had developed from the Greek worldview was still taught at schools and universities, but there was a general feeling of discontent with an education that failed to take into account the new view of the world. Evidence of this is to be found in the writings of Gilbert, Galileo, Bacon, Descartes, Webster, Hall, Hobbes, Glanville, Boyle, Locke, and Newton, all of whom expressed dissatisfaction with the education they had received.[10]

At the beginning of the seventeenth century there was already considerable commotion resulting from the collapse of the old world picture. From a purely scientific point of view, the matter was far from being resolved, but to many people the old picture of the universe no longer seemed so reliable as had previously been thought. A clear example of this growing skepticism is found in John Donne's *Anatomy of the World:*

New Philosophy calls all in doubt,
The element of fire is quite put out;
The Sun is lost and th' earth; and no man's wil
Can well direct him where to looke for it.

And freely men confesse that this world is spent,
When in the planets, and the Firmament
They seeke so many new; then see that this
Is crumbled out again in his Atomies.
'Tis all in pieces, all coherence gone;
All just supply and all Relation. [11]

For most people the new discoveries were a source of concern and even horror—the old world picture appeared to be disintegrating, and with that all coherence was gone. How was the cosmos to be pictured? What was the place of man in this mysterious universe? How had one to understand the traditional dogmas of Christianity which had been formulated in terms derived from the Greek world picture? Since Christian doctrine was so closely interwoven with the old world picture, it was inevitable that a revolution in cosmology should be the cause of such confusion.

Just how confounded Christians were can be seen from the writings of Pascal (1623–1662), whose intellectual and religious work is inconceivable without the cosmological background. Unlike Descartes, who looked forward to the future with confidence, and for whom the new science did not pose a threat to faith, Pascal was deeply aware of the problems that the new discoveries raised for the religious man. In contrast to the quiet, secure existence of the medieval theologian, Pascal was torn between the new science and traditional belief, wishing to hold onto both but unable to reconcile them. As to his views on the new cosmological conceptions, we find the following surprising statement in his *Pensées:*

I think that is is a good thing not to probe the opinion of Copernicus: . . . It is important for one's whole life to know whether or not the soul is immortal. [12]

What is immediately apparent in reading the text is that Pascal diverts his attention from cosmological problems and becomes absorbed in the problem of man, considering it much more important for man to know whether his soul is immortal than to know whether or not the sun revolves round the earth. Though he says that one should not go too deeply into Copernicus's opinion, it is not quite clear how he viewed the heliocentric picture of the universe. In a fragment entitled *Sur l'infini* he speaks about the planets revolving round the earth. Perhaps he preferred the doctrine of Tycho Brahe, which was accepted by many people after the condemnation of Copernicus and Galileo, and according to which the planets revolve around the sun as well as the earth. Most remarkable of all, however, is the fact that Pascal seems moved by an instinctive anxiety not to occupy himself with this subject. In the words of Alexander Pope (1688–1744): "Proper study of mankind is man."[13]

But this is just the question—Can man know himself without including the planets in his considerations? Pascal was also unable to avoid this question: "The parts of the world are so interrelated and their connection with one another such that I believe that it is impossible to know one without the other and without the whole."[14] If all things are interconnected and one thing cannot be known without the other, how can we understand ourselves without also knowing the world in which we exist ? What is the place of man in this infinite universe? "What is man in nature?"[15] Pascal was the first to give such a moving description of the wretchedness of man, lost as it were in the infinite, impenetrable universe:

> When we behold the blindness and wretchedness of man, when we look on the whole dumb universe, on man without light, abandoned to his own devices and appearing as though lost in some corner of the universe, without knowing who has placed him there, what he is supposed to be doing, what will become of him when he dies, incapable of all knowledge, I am overcome by fear like a man who has been carried off during sleep and deposited on some terrifying desert island who wakes up without knowing where he is and without any means of escape. And I am amazed that people do not fall into despair over such a wretched state.[16]

According to Pascal, only faith can free man from this miserable and desperate situation. The question remains, however, how we are able to situate ourselves in this mysterious universe. The only thing that can be said is that we stand between the abyss of the infinitely great and the abyss of the infinitely small. Man's dignity does not depend on whether he is to be found in the center of the universe, but on his rational nature:

> It is not from space that I must seek my dignity. By means of space the universe contains me and swallows me up like a speck; by means of thought I comprehend the universe.[17]

Man is but a thinking reed. But the fact that he can think is the basis of his superiority over the vast universe.

Medieval man felt secure in the center of creation, surrounded by the safety of the heavenly spheres and the object of God's concern; everything was made for man and all beings revealed God's wisdom, power, and goodness, so that everything was seen to have a deeper meaning. Pascal had a completely different view of the cosmos. Instead of speculating on the perfection of the world and the hierarchical order in the cosmos, he saw the world as an unintelligible and somber mystery, which we should think of as little as possible, because we cannot ever understand it. Neither do we have any idea as to our place in the universe. We can only attempt to understand ourselves: paradoxical beings who find ourselves in a tragic situation. Pascal describes this fear and anguish of our experience in the world: "The eternal silence of these infinite spaces terrifies me."[18]—an entirely different attitude from that of medieval man who heard the voice of God in all things. It is of little consequence whether Pascal is here describing the feelings of the unbeliever or expressing his personal experience. But if faith should succeed in overcoming this fear and horror, then it will in any case be a form of faith that is no longer related to any cosmology, a faith in God who does not reveal himself in the cosmos but in history.[19]

Pascal did not approve of Descartes and the new science. According to the testimony of his sister he seldom discussed the natural sciences, but when the occasion arose he did not conceal his opinion. He agreed with Descartes that animals are machines or automata, but this was about the only thing that met his approval. For the rest he repeatedly affirmed that he could not forgive Descartes for wanting to do without God in his philosophy: he believed that apart from having set the world in motion by a mere flick, God was of no further interest to Descartes.[20] This is clearly an unfair judgment, for the place Descartes attributes to God in his philosophy is certainly much greater than Pascal implied.

From a religious point of view, Pascal regarded the new science as a source of confusion and annoyance. He exemplified the tragedy of the age and was deeply moved by problems which continued to govern the seventeenth and eighteenth centuries and gave rise to the most divergent views. This signified the final breakdown of Christian unity and the beginning of the great debate on God, Providence, and the foundations of morality and society.

As to the concept of God, there were three schools of thought: the pantheism of philosophers like Giordano Bruno and Spinoza; deism, which in the wake of Newton was defended by many philosophers and was made known on the continent through the writings of Voltaire in particular; and atheism, which emerged in the eighteenth century with authors like Diderot, d'Holbach, and others. Many people undoubtedly retained and defended the traditional Christian idea of God against dissident views, either by adopting new approaches, like Descartes and Leibniz, or in a more traditional manner such as by continuing to hold to scholastic doctrine. But for a great many thinkers in this period Christianity seemed to be so closely allied to the old world picture that once the latter was brought into discredit Christianity also lost all credibility. They therefore began to look out for a natural religion or rejected every religion. One can always raise the question as to what might have happened had the Church immediately accepted the Copernican system, but to this there is no answer. What cannot be denied, however, is that the Church's rejection of the new world picture did promote an anti-Christian tendency.

With the downfall of the old world picture, the theory of the "two books" was also brought into disrepute. As has already been pointed out, this theory, which we first find in Augustine and in the Alexandrian School,[21] was particularly liked by the medieval theologian who regarded the Book of Nature and the Book of Sacred Scriptures as the integral Revelation of God. But what happened when the picture of God that was to be found in the new cosmology seemed to contradict the picture presented by the Bible? In such a situation the obvious choice for many people was to rely on nature and science to resolve the problem of God.

Pantheism

But what picture of God emerged from the Copernican cosmology? This question was raised at the end of the sixteenth century by Giordano Bruno (1548–1600), a fascinating figure who had entered the Dominican order at an early age and received a traditional scholastic education with which he was most dissatisfied, even though he retained much appreciation for Aristotle and Thomas. An entirely new view of the world was revealed to him upon reading Copernicus's *De Revolutionibus Orbium Caelestium,* in spite of the fact that he had no real background in mathematics. From then on his fate was decided: he left the monastery in Naples and wandered through Italy, France, England, and Germany, and finally, arrived in Venice where he fell into the hands of the Inquisition. Sentenced to death on account of heresy, he died at the stake on 17 February, 1600, on the Square of Flowers in Rome, where a statue was erected for him after the unification of Italy in 1870.

The case of Giordano Bruno is of particular importance in that it clearly shows how much the Copernican revolution led to a revolution in philosophy and, especially, the picture of God. Scholars are agreed that Bruno's philosophy is inconceivable without the Copernican cosmology, from which it derived its original significance and true unity.[22]

For Copernicus the universe was still a closed and limited one since he also considered the solar system to be surrounded by the starry heavens enclosing the entire cosmos. It is not altogether clear who first advanced the idea of an infinite universe. According to some, the notion is derived from Thomas Digges, at least in the sense that he conceived the universe as an open universe.[23] However, Bruno must be considered the first to defend the idea of a completely decentralized, infinite, and infinitely inhabited world. In his view our universe is but one of countless similar solar systems making up the universe. This thesis was not found in the Copernican cosmology nor could it be deduced from astronomical observations, an area that Bruno never studied in any case. The fullness of the universe is beyond all imagination. The universe, argues Bruno, must be infinite because it was created by an infinite God. An infinite God can only create an infinite world, and only an infinite world is in accordance with the dignity of an infinite God. The starting point for such reasoning must rather be sought in the neo-Platonic school of thought, bearing in mind that Bruno regarded Plotinus as "the prince of philosophers." Bruno's world picture can thus be described as an odd mixture of Copernican and neo-Platonic elements.

Conceiving the world as infinite also implies a new formulation of the relationship between God and the world. For centuries infinity had been considered a divine attribute. But if the universe is infinite, should it not then be considered divine and identified with God? Bruno undoubtedly draws a distinction here: the infinity of the world is extensive and pluralistic. Compared to God, the universe is but one point and no more. From this one could therefore conclude that Bruno maintains God's transcendence and rejects pantheism. On the other hand, he also raises the question whether infinities can exist alongside each other. "It is," he replies, "neither appropriate nor possible to posit two distinct infinities because one could never imagine where the one begins and the other ends. Moreover, it would be difficult to think of two beings which would be on the one hand limited and on the other hand unlimited."[24] It is understandable, therefore, that Bruno has sometimes been interpreted as a monist and at other times as a theist. Copleston is perhaps right when he says that Bruno's thought tended in the direction of monism, but that he de facto continued to believe in a transcendent God. His considerations on the cosmos led him to strongly emphasize divine immanence, but that is not to say that he therefore only paid lip service to divine transcendence. It would be better to regard his philosophy as a stage on the way leading from Nicholas of Cusa to Spinoza.[25]

There seems to be no doubt that Bruno exercised some influence on Baruch or Benedict (de) Spinoza (1632–1677). Though none of Bruno's writings appear in the catalogue of works in Spinoza's library, it is quite evident from certain pages of the *Tractatus brevis de deo et homine eiusque felicitate* (the *Short Treatise*) that he was long acquainted with Bruno's thought. Another indication of this influence is to be found in the use of the distinction between *natura naturans* and *natura naturata* which was common to both philosophers.

In addition Spinoza also assigned a central position to the problem of the relation between an infinite world and an infinite God. Whereas Bruno was still somewhat vague and hesitant on this point, Spinoza gave a clear and unambiguous answer. God and the world are not two infinities, for there is but one infinite and all-embracing substance: God or Nature. This divine substance exists in itself and is explained through itself, that is, without reference to anything else. All beings that we can perceive are only modes, that is, passing states, of this infinite substance with its essential and infinite attributes. If God and the world were distinct, argues Spinoza, then there would be two substances, neither of which would be infinite, because the one would be limited by the other. "Whatever is, is in God, and nothing can exist or be conceived without God."[26] All finite beings must be conceived as modifications of the one infinite substance. God possesses an infinity of attributes, two of which are known to us, namely, thought and extension. Man's intellect and the extension of matter are only modifications of these two divine attributes. "Particular things are nothing else than modifications of the attributes of God, or modes by which attributes of God are expressed in a certain and determined manner."[27] All these things follow of necessity from the divine nature.

But is there any connection between Spinoza's conception of God and the cosmological revolution which was then in progress? Spinoza was ten years old when Galileo died and his own death occurred before the publication of Newton's *Philosophiae Naturalis Principia Mathematica*. It is well known that he had a lively interest in the natural sciences and through his reading of Descartes in particular he came into contact with the new scientific views. Yet at first sight there appears to be little influence of the new world picture on his philosophy.

The starting point of his philosophical method is certainly not to be found in concrete facts or observations, but rather in general definitions and axioms, as in geometry. Propositions are then formulated and proven on the basis of the given definitions, and the argumentation is concluded by a formula of exposition as in geometry's Q.E.D., which is mostly accompanied by several corollaries. The whole thing seems to be the most perfect deductive method one could imagine. Furthermore, he completely rejected the inductive method of his opponents, reproaching them for taking their starting point in creatures and not in God. He believed that they failed to observe the proper order of philosophical argument: "For the divine nature, which they ought to have considered before all things, because it is prior to knowledge and nature, they have thought to be the last in the order of knowledge and nature, and things which are called the objects of the senses they have believed to be prior to all things."[28] Upon being asked by his friend Henry Oldenburg what he considered to be the main defects of philosophers like Descartes and Bacon, he replied that they had "strayed so far from the knowledge of the first cause and origin of all things."[29]

Spinoza's method would thus seem to imply a refusal on his part to relate the results of the natural sciences to his philosophy. Dismissing the cosmological proofs for God's existence, he invoked what can be regarded as a variant of Anselm's ontological proof. And when he did advance an a posteriori argument, for God's existence, he immediately asserted that this was only to clarify his first argument, which was based on the absolute perfection of the divine nature.[30] One therefore has the impression that Spinoza consciously endeavored to separate the proofs of God's existence from any cosmological consideration, a procedure that only acquires its full significance when it is situated in the cultural climate of the age. Arguments from motion and from the hierarchical order in the universe were thus clearly pushed aside and any teleological consideration was explicitly rejected. According to Spinoza, it is a mistake to look for meaning and purpose in nature, for the order of nature follows necessarily from the nature of God. Such an error is readily accounted for by the fact that human beings tend to act with an end in view and are therefore inclined to interpret God or Nature in the light of their own experience. Owing to mathematics, however, "which does not deal with final causes but with the essence and properties of things" we have had to learn to observe another standard of truth. Just as it makes no sense to ask about the purpose of a triangle when the only thing we can do is to study its properties, so we have to content ourselves with studying the properties of things without asking why things are as they are or for what purpose they have been brought about, because there is no such purpose in nature.[31] This was plainly a rejection of medieval cosmology and comes very close to current views in natural science.

In eliminating final causality Spinoza developed a world picture in which there was no place for uncertainty, purpose, spontaneity, or freedom: everything in nature was seen to follow from an eternal necessity and to have been produced by the supreme perfection of God.[32] And it is in contemplation of this infinite immutable substance that man was said to find true happiness and peace of mind.

According to Hegel, Spinoza's doctrine ought to be considered not so much as a form of atheism as a form of "acosmism," since the cosmos is completely absorbed, as it were, in God. Schleiermacher, on the other hand, believed that the universe was Spinoza's "one and only love." Perhaps it would be more true to say that for Spinoza love of God and love of the universe were fused into one love. In this way the seventeenth century—a period governed by astronomy and cosmology—saw the emergence of a philosophy in which the cosmos was raised to the sphere of the divine and God was revealed in the form of the universe.

Except for a few small circles, especially in north Holland, Spinoza's doctrine initially received little attention. It was only at the end of the eighteenth century that he was rediscovered by authors such as Jacob, Herder, Novalis, Heine, Goethe, and by German romanticism in general. In the wake of Newton's discoveries in particular, Western thought was for more than a century governed by another view of the relation between God and the world that formed the basis of a "natural religion"—in the opinion of many philosophers, a form of religion more in keeping with the new discoveries.

Deism

It has rightly been said that deism was more a general attitude of mind than a clearly defined system and it is therefore difficult to know just when it started.[33] As a whole it can be considered an attempt to bring religion into line with the new scientific views. While it rejected every form of revealed religion—and Christianity in particular—as incompatible with science, it also endeavored to construct a natural religion containing a doctrine on God as well as an ethical system. But the God of deism was no longer the God of Christianity who is concerned with the events of every day. Instead, God was only seen as the architect of the universe, leaving the course of events to the laws which he had imposed on nature and which science gradually helps us to discover. For the true deist one had to worship God not by outward ceremonies that have no meaning whatsoever, but only by an eminently moral life lived according to principles that are found in nature itself.

In its rejection of revealed religion and in its proposal of a natural religion, deism was closely connected with the new view of the cosmos based on the work of Galileo, Descartes, and Newton. What is remarkable is that these scholars remained loyal Christians, while their work provided a most powerful weapon for those who vehemently opposed Christianity.[34] At least one conclusion could clearly be deduced from their work, namely, that the medieval world picture had been a mistake and that Aristotelian science was no longer reliable. What, then, was one to think of the Church, which stubbornly clung to the medieval picture of the universe, using every means available to oppose the new insights? How could one continue to accept a religious doctrine so closely allied to a discarded world picture—and in the eyes of Church leaders, inseparably connected with it. There are undoubtedly several reasons to account for the Church's loss of influence and credibility during this period, but it must be acknowledged that a significant role was played by this emergence of a new cosmology and by the determination on the part of official ecclesiastical authorities to hold onto a world picture that had become obsolete. Besides Church authority the Bible also came under attack, for its geocentric picture of the universe had been proven false by science. And if the Bible had been mistaken on one point, who could give any assurance that it did not contain mistakes on other matters? It thus became common to look for errors in the Bible, which suddenly appeared to the deists to be bristling with contradictions. This thoroughly undermined the authority of Scripture in the eyes of intellectuals so that Catholic exegetes and apologists were hard pressed to deal with the questions that arose.

Over against the Church, which continued to cling to an antiquated world picture, and the Bible, which seemed to warrant such an error, the deists put forward a "natural religion." It was, they claimed, not the Bible but nature that had to be consulted to know how to think about God. Not wishing to yield to Christians in respect for the Supreme Being, they boasted of possessing a much purer conception of God, insisting, moreover, that it was precisely out of love for God that they rejected the false images of Christianity and other "revealed religions."[35] As many people were not only averse to the endless disputes and theological discussions between Catholics and Protestants, and disappointed in a Church that continued to adhere to medieval ideas, but were moreover confused by the discovery of the higher religions of India and China, there was a growing desire for a kind of natural religion that would be beyond all human disputes and directed to all people without distinction. It was, then, with much zeal that a wide variety of people set out to establish such a religion.[36] This had a decisive influence on philosophy of religion and even on Catholic and Protestant theologians from the second half of the seventeenth century until the end of the eighteenth century. For many, Christianity was seen as the continuation and culmination of the "natural religion" that had been drawn up by reason and they therefore interpreted the Christian conception of God in terms of deism.[37]

An important role was played here by Newton's doctrine, albeit against his will.[38] Newton always regarded himself as a Christian, belonging, as he saw it, to the Socinians or antitrinitarians. As is apparent from the number of writings he devoted to theology, he was as much fascinated by theological problems as by those of natural science.[39] When, after the publication of *Philosophiae Naturalis Principia Mathematica*, he was suspected in some circles of being an atheist, he reacted by stating quite explicitly in the second edition of his work that his world picture implied the existence of God: "You ascribe to me a rational soul because you perceive order in my words and actions; acknowledge then the existence of a supreme intelligent Being whenever you behold the order of the universe."[40] The order in the universe, so splendidly demonstrated in the law of universal attraction, was for Newton a clear indication of the existence of a Supreme Wisdom which had granted the cosmos its fixed laws. Neither the existence of the world nor the regular motion of the planets was conceivable without the intervention of the Creator.

Newton was regarded as the idol of deism. Having established a perfect unity of science and religion he was an excellent example for all. For the name of God was never to be mentioned without deep respect.[41] The nucleus of what the deists considered to be an irrefutable argument for the existence of God[42] is to be found in Newton's doctrine concerning the order that is so clearly present in the universe.[43] Belief in the existence of God is consequently much to be preferred to atheism, which must be dismissed as simply absurd.[44]

But who is the God worshiped by the deists? According to Samuel Clarke, we can distinguish four kinds of deists. First, those who professed to believe in an eternal, infinite, independent, and intelligent Being, but denied Providence. Then we find others who believed in an infinite and perfect Being and accepted Providence but refused to accept that God concerned himself with man's moral conduct. Next there were those who, though they believed in God, in Providence, and in the obligatory character of morality, denied the immortality of the soul. Finally, there were those who held a pure conception of God (and were thus actually quite close to Christianity), even though they rejected the whole idea of Revelation.[45] Such a conception of God can at one time be reduced to a vague belief in a Supreme Being, and at another time, to a consciously professed belief in a God to whom one can pray and whom one can, like Voltaire's Vicaire savoyard, appreciate in the beauty of nature.

The question arose, however, whether this God—the ingenious architect or able clockmaker who had framed the universe—still cared about his creation. Newton had irrefutably shown how the cosmos was governed by laws to which all things in heaven and on earth were subject. Was it meaningful under such circumstances to make mention of a Providence arranging everything for man's benefit, as Christians were apt to say? The theme of Providence naturally became one of the main discussion points in an age when man first began to see the world in the light of immutable laws.[46] According to Leibniz, God could have conceived and realized an infinite number of worlds. If God has chosen this world with the order we find in it, then we must conclude that this is the best of all possible worlds. On account of his goodness and wisdom, argued Leibniz, God was, as it were, obliged to make such a choice.[47]

Further evidence of such optimism[48] is to be found in Pope's *Essay on Man* (1733):

> Cease then, nor ORDER imperfection name:
> Our proper bliss depends on what we blame.
> Know thy own point: this kind, this due degree
> Of blindness, weakness, Heaven bestows on thee,
> Submit—In this, or any other sphere,
> Secure to be as blest as thou canst bear:
> Safe in the hand of one disposing Power,
> Or in the natal, or the mortal hour.
> All Nature is but Art, unknown to thee;
> All chance, direction, which thou canst not see;
> All discord, harmony not understood;
> All partial evil, universal Good:
> And, spite of pride, in erring reason's spite,
> One truth is clear: Whatever is, is RIGHT

Any impression we might have of disorder in the world is thus a mistake which is to be attributed to a lack of understanding on our part. For the deist such a view was simply insupportable. Who could believe that an infinitely wise and almighty God could devise nothing better than this world where we find so much disorder and suffering? Does it not seem as if man is completely subject to blind forces of nature that are by no means attuned to his happiness? Following an earthquake in Lisbon in 1755 that caused widespread destruction, countless writings[49] appeared dealing with this very question. Voltaire's *Poème sur le désastre de Lisbonne* met with such a wide response that it was reprinted twenty times in one year.[50] Was this then the best of all possible worlds? Was Lisbon a worse town than London or Paris and was the world any better as the result of its destruction? It was certainly to be hoped that all would one day be well, but to claim that this was already so was no more than an illusion.[51] With the publication in 1759 of Voltaire's *Candide*, a parody of the optimism of Leibniz and Pope, we can, writes Paul Hazard, consider the case to have been tried—and lost.[52]

The God of deism was thus seen as a God who had created the world and imposed fixed laws on nature, but for the rest let things take their course, leaving man to his own devices. Man is therefore to take his destiny into his own hands.

Atheism

Pantheism and deism were not the only reactions to the emergence of the new cosmological conceptions. At the end of the seventeenth century and during the eighteenth there was an increasing number of people, mostly small groups of intellectuals, who adhered to atheism, even though they were a small minority compared to the deists who governed the entire eighteenth century. Atheism has a much longer history of course and atheists were to be found in Greek and Roman antiquity as well as in the Italian Renaissance. But it was not until the eighteenth century that atheism came into prominence,[53] when the intellectual climate, created by Copernicus and Newton, seemed favorable for another radical denial of the existence of God. From the new cosmology the deists had undoubtedly derived a new picture of God, which they held onto with much conviction. It has been said, however, that a deist was really an atheist who did not have the courage to take the final step. Although this was certainly not true of men like Bolingbroke, Pope, and Voltaire, who consciously rejected atheism, it is a fact nevertheless that for many people deism paved the way for a radical atheism. Common to both atheism and deism was the rejection of any form of revealed religion. Atheists, especially in France, were moreover just as relentless as the deists in opposing

Christianity in a most hostile manner. What is more, both shared an unrestricted cult of the new science that was chiefly represented in the work of Newton. But why still hold onto a vague conception of God that no longer had any practical value for man? To explain the origin of the world? Was it at all meaningful to ask questions about the beginning and end of the cosmos? What could human reason say about this? Could one not just as well put forward the hypothesis that the universe had neither a beginning nor an end, and thus a Creator was superfluous? Or was the deistic conception of God necessary to account for the order in the cosmos? There was undoubtedly a certain order to be perceived in the cosmos, but did not a careful consideration of the world reveal as much disorder? Both these views could be accounted for by the atomism of Epicurus and Lucretius. For from the properties of matter, to which a vague intelligence could perhaps be ascribed—as Locke and Maupertuis had done—one could derive both an incidental order and an equally incidental disorder.

Belief in God thus appeared to be quite superfluous and even harmful to man. Religions were seen to create divisions among people, having given rise in the past to disputes, persecution, oppression, and war. They were also the cause of much hypocrisy, fanaticism, and stupidity. What seemed to be clear in any case was that religion alienated man from his most urgent and exalted task: to contribute to the progress of humankind. In contrast to Dostoevsky, who a century later declared that nothing astonished him more than the fact that an insignificant creature like man proved to be capable of conceiving such a sublime idea as the notion of an infinitely perfect God, the atheist of the eighteenth century proclaimed this to be the most nefarious idea man had ever invented.

Among the many people who openly or secretly adhered to atheism during this period Diderot, d'Holbach, Helvetius, and d'Alemberg can be considered the main representatives, as they were responsible for making a major contribution to the dissemination of materialistic atheism (under the cover of science) by their principal work, *L'encyclopédie*. It was undoubtedly their deepest aspiration to construct an all-embracing world picture, presenting on the basis of a radical materialism a view of man and the world in which religion would no longer have any part.[54]

Moral and Political Theory

The collapse of the old cosmology and the emergence of a new science involving the principles of Bacon and Galileo gave rise to the great debate on the problem of God that governed both the seventeenth and eighteenth centuries. Besides pantheists, deists, and atheists there were still many more people who retained the Christian idea of God, which—perhaps to its disadvantage—also enjoyed official support in most European countries. Traditional theism was upheld both by those who, in the wake of Descartes, advocated a new philosophy and by those who continued to adhere to scholasticism. An extensive apologetical literature thus came to be written.[55] How Catholic theology responded to the challenge of the new trends of thought will be considered in the next chapter.

In addition to the idea of God, the new world picture had serious implications for the problem of human nature and its place in the totality of things, especially as it related to the standards that had to be applied to human actions. Could man still be understood in terms of the Greek and medieval conception of matter and spirit or was he not rather to be considered a machine, just as La Mettrie (1709–1751) claimed in *L'homme—machine*? Was matter not the only reality, so that man's psychic life could, according to Hartley (1705–1757) and Priestley (1733–1804), be conceived as a kind of physics of the nervous system? What was one to think of the value of human thought after all the mistakes that had been made in the past? Were all men equal, as Helvetius and Rousseau claimed, or was there a fundamental inequality, as Diderot and d'Holbach believed. All these questions were discussed in this period with renewed interest and in a totally new climate of thought.

Attention was naturally drawn to the problem of morality. What was the basis of the moral obligation? What criteria did one possess to distinguish good and evil? Until the Copernican revolution morality had been so closely connected with the medieval world picture that it was seen as the transposition into human conduct of the perfect order God had imposed on his creation. Morality was plainly a question of order. Man was virtuous whenever he respected the order God had established and sinful whenever he was at variance with it. The basis of morality, therefore, was the belief in a perfect, immutable, and hierarchical order. Since this order was conceived as the expression of God's will, man had to respect it in all things. The task of the moralist thus consisted in tracing this order and discovering its implications for human conduct.

But with the changes the new science introduced into our view of the world, this concept of order now appeared problematic. For even though Newtonian science taught us to distinguish fixed laws in physical phenomena, this had little to do with the perfect, hierarchical order of the earlier world picture. Many people thus felt an urgent need for a new foundation to morality, all the more because the new view of the world seemed to many to be a pretext for libertinism.[56] The problem of morality was the subject matter of endless discussions in the seventeenth and eighteenth centuries, especially among the deists and atheists. As far as the disciples of Spinoza were concerned the matter had already been settled in the *Ethics,* where it was argued that man's actions had to be attuned to true bliss, which consisted of the placid and beatific contemplation of the eternal and immutable substance that granted man his greatest freedom by freeing him from the clutches of earthly and transitory things and uniting him with the supreme good. Besides laying the theoretical foundation of this mystical conception of morality, Spinoza also gave it a concrete dimension by his example of detachment.

With the deists and atheists, however, things were entirely different. It was clear to them that morality raised particular difficulties that could readily be brought forward against their system. For how could one still maintain the binding character of moral law if one denied the existence of God and the immortality of the soul or conceived of God in such a way that he no longer had anything to do with man and the world? And if every binding moral law were rejected, would this not lead to utter chaos in society and to the degradation of man just when it had been intended to raise him to a higher perfection?

It was not long before certain authors appeared who were not disturbed by these consequences and did not hesitate to demand total freedom in the moral sphere, claiming that man himself was the only law in the fields of thought and action. So not only Christian doctrine but also Christian ethics had to be completely eradicated. At first timidly defended by only a few isolated thinkers, this view soon became widespread, especially during the eighteenth century, and created a climate of profligacy that could only be compared to the decadent period of the Roman Empire. Thus Libertinism in thought was consequently allied with libertinism in behavior, as can be seen from people like La Mettrie and Sade.

But the vast majority of deists and atheists had no desire to be thought of as amoral. When Leibniz expressed the opinion that the increasing immorality in England was the result of the doctrine of Newton and Locke, many people were offended and could not help responding to such an accusation. It was left to Samuel Clarke, a friend of Newton, to refute this charge by in turn accusing Leibniz of being irreligious.[57] Both in England and in France the question was raised whether there were eternal and absolute laws that man had to observe and how these could be known by us. Since human reason had succeeded in discovering the laws that govern the physical world and to which all motion of material things is subject, could it not also discover if there are any universal laws intended to regulate man's conduct? Atheists like Diderot and Holbach considered La Mettrie and his kind as an abomination because by their immorality they compromised the cause of atheism in the eyes of the public. As to the deists, they were as relentless in their search for a natural morality as they had been in their attempt to draw up a natural religion. What happened, however, was that instead of a natural morality, a number of ethical systems came into being that contradicted each other.[58] For medieval man it had been a simple matter to deduce the order God willed from nature, but then this was done in the light of Revelation. Now, without the help of Revelation, it was suddenly evident that nature was open to many interpretations and that the order which had been presupposed was extremely difficult for people to discern, even though they did not despair that this order would sooner or later be discovered.

In the opening words of *L'esprit des lois* (1748) Montesquieu solemnly declared that, "In the widest meaning of the term, laws are necessary relations derived from the nature of things. And in this sense all beings have their laws: Divinity has its laws; the material world has its laws; intelligences superior to man have their laws; animals have their laws; man has his laws." Concerning the laws governing nature science could provide us with a decisive answer, whereas there could be endless discussion concerning the laws man had to observe. Ought man to be guided by self-interest, something that he well understood? By pleasure? By the general welfare? Could nature serve as a line of action for man, teaching him to distinguish good and evil, or was man completely free to do whatever he pleased? But, what was the actual meaning of the word "nature"?[59] Each author had his own explanation for this term so that it could signify nearly anything and had only to exclude Christian ethics, but for the rest it scarcely had a positive content anymore. It was in fact so vague that it was possible for almost everyone to offer his ethical theory in the name of being true to nature, whether it be the utilitarianism of Thomas Hobbes (1588–1679) or the renewed epicureanism of Saint-Evremond (1616–1703) or Jonathan Bentham (1748–1832). In *Système de la nature, ou des lois du monde physique et du monde moral*, one of the most widely known works of the eighteenth century, Holbach maintained that "virtue is everything that is truly and continually useful to human beings living in a society; vice is everything that is harmful to them."[60] Like many of his contemporaries, Holbach preached a moral theory but denied freedom, so that morality was often reduced to a description of the mechanism regulating our actions: "the actions of senseless people are just as necessary as those of the most prudent."[61] But if man is not free, what is the sense of proclaiming a theory that is prescribed as a standard for human conduct? Why does a virtuous action deserve more esteem than an evil one?

While it was unanimously agreed that the earlier conceptions of freedom and morality were to be rejected, there was much diversity of opinion among the deists and atheists once they attempted to provide a positive solution to these problems. With the dissolution of the old world picture, man's place and function in the cosmos had been upset, giving rise to a great many difficulties that could not readily be resolved.

Besides challenging our view of man the new cosmology also had serious implications for our view of society. Since the order in medieval society had been based on the analogy of the hierarchical order in the cosmos, it was evident that the repudiation of the latter by the Copernican world system would have grave consequences for the structure of society. For by what right could monarchs and nobility continue to appeal "to the order God had willed"? Should not all citizens have a say in matters of common interest? In this way the disintegration of the old world picture seems to have been a necessary condition for the emergence of a new conception of the state.

Initially there was no desire to abolish the monarchy as such, since the deep-rooted respect for royal authority could not be eradicated all at once. The most urgent need was for a new foundation for organizing the state. Since authority could no longer be based on a supposed hierarchical order in the cosmos, it seemed to many that authority was derived from the people, who instructed a ruling body to govern society in the interest of common good.

The theory of social contract seemed to offer a good solution here and met with the most success. In his natural state man was free and independent. But by virture of a sort of tacit agreement he joined other individuals to form a society which required a minimum of authority and organization to be able to function properly. Political authority was delegated by the people who could as well appoint another executive if they so wished. The main representative of the doctrine of social contract was undoubtedly Rousseau (1712–1778), even though the same idea was maintained by others and was in keeping with the general pattern of the political theory of the Enlightenment. There was a tendency to restrict authority as far as possible, for experience had shown that the accumulation of authority in the hands of one individual was extremely dangerous and led to an abuse of power. Man was seen to be corrupted by the feeling of power, and the greater his power, the more he was exposed to corruption and degeneracy. For this reason, as Montesquieu (1689–1755) argued, it was preferable to share power as much as possible and to invest no one with the fullness of authority.

From this revolution in political theory practical conclusions were drawn leading to political developments which went further than most theorists had dreamed. In North America there was the War of Independence (1775–1783), while in Europe the French Revolution of 1789 dealt a fatal blow to the old conception of the state. The slogan Liberté, Egalité, Fraternité implicitly contained the radical rejection of the earlier principle of hierarchy from which the Ancient Régime had derived its strength and inspiration. This paved the way for a new structure of society that only laboriously found its definite form but was in any case as radically different to the previous structure as the Newtonian world picture was to that of the Middle Ages.

For medieval man the created world bore clear and unambiguous testimony to the existence of God. From the order and beauty of nature the mind could read the true nature of God by means of what Bonaventure called "contuition." What is more, from a common world picture medieval theologians also derived the same picture of God, helped naturally by the Revelation found in sacred Scriptures. Now, however, more and more people abandoned this view, adopting instead a pantheistic, deistic, or atheistic explanation of the world. The earlier unanimity concerning the idea of God thus made way for confusion and dissension.

An attempt had already been made by Descartes to separate natural theology from cosmology, with which it had long been connected, when he considered the idea of God to be an innate idea in the mind. In Descartes' view religion was thus finally rescued from the clutches of an ever-changing natural science. A similar attempt was made by Kant (1724–1804) at the end of the eighteenth century. As far as he was concerned, there were two objects of wonder and admiration: "the starry heavens above and the moral law within." But like Descartes, Kant regarded cosmology as unsuitable to bring us to God. It was also clear that the laws imposed on human action were no less wonderful than those governing the motion of the heavenly bodies. Moreover, the existence of a moral obligation could not be sufficiently

accounted for without postulating the existence of a supreme authority. It was, therefore, practical reason that led to the recognition of
God's existence.

Kant's endeavor to separate the problem of God from cosmology,
connecting it instead with the moral order, met with a wide response.
Even greater, perhaps, was Hegel's attempt to approach the problem
of God from a new standpoint. It is remarkable how little consideration Hegel gives in his writings to cosmological questions, even
though he was much concerned with the problem of God.[62]

Hegelian philosophy can perhaps best be characterized as an impressive attempt to integrate man into the whole of reality. It thus
corresponds to one of the deepest aspirations of the human spirit,
which likewise finds expression in most religions and is a permanent
theme of Western philosophy. Over against the mysterious and hostile world around him, man feels he is a stranger, inwardly divided
and alienated from himself. The whole aim of Hegel's philosophy is
to overcome this tragic opposition, reconciling man and the world by
situating the human spirit in the deepest reality of the cosmos.

It appeared to Hegel that the natural sciences could be of little service here, for, he remarked, the stars in the sky deserve no more
attention than the freckles on a man's face.[63] The human spirit can
only feel at home in a reality of a spiritual nature which is not yet to
be perceived in the material world. We must therefore look elsewhere
if we are to find a way to integrate ourselves into the world as a whole.

The area where the deepest reality of the world is revealed to us is
the history of humankind. It is only in history that mind comes to
consciousness of itself, that the deepest spiritual reality can be discovered. We can distinguish three levels in the history of humankind.
The first level, the most superficial, is formed by the events and in-
cidents of everyday life. This is reflected in diaries, novels, chronicles,
and newspapers. A second, already deeper level comprises the great
changes that have taken place in the life of states and cultures. This
is the domain of the historian whose attention naturally only turns to
the more important events of the past. Finally there is in the historical
process a still deeper level—the gradual awakening of the Idea in the
depth of humanity as a whole. It is to this, the deepest level of history,
that the philosopher must direct his attention. The study of the other
levels is of interest to him only insofar as it helps him to understand
the deepest level. Only here do we find God, the absolute Idea.[64]
Hegel thus conceived the *logos* of history as analogous to the *logos* of
the cosmos, which governed Greek thought and which had, he believed, become completely unthinkable after the emergence of the

new cosmology and historical consciousness. Hegel's *logos* of history displays the same properties as the *logos* which the Greeks perceived in the cosmos: everything that happens in history is rational and meaningful.[65]

Hegel was always an avowed opponent of the theory of evolution, which in his time had not yet acquired a really scientific basis: "Mind which perceives and thinks must free itself from such nebulous ideas that are actually only rooted in feeling, as for instance, the theory that plants, animals, and the higher organisms develop from lower organisms."[66] Evidently this idea did not fit into his system, where nature had such an inferior role. For it is not in the material world, but in spiritual reality—which constitutes the deepest reality—that human consciousness has to be integrated. Only here can the thinking subject feel at home. Consequently we must look for God not in nature but in history where mind comes to itself and realizes itself.

The philosophical significance of evolutionism, which was soon to have a great impact through the work of Darwin and his followers, can perhaps be seen in the fact that it once again overcame the opposition between nature and history. Through the theory of evolution, history was once more brought into nature, while the latter was seen more and more in a historical perspective. This, moreover, created a new possibility of situating man in the whole of reality, without detracting from his spiritual aspect.

The attempt to separate the problem of God from cosmology assumed many other forms that cannot be considered here. From what we have seen, however, it is quite evident how much the revolution in the world picture, started by Copernicus, Kepler, Galileo, and Newton, also caused a serious crisis in the doctrine of God and had a profound influence on the religious thought of Western man. Henceforward pantheism, deism, and atheism, besides a purified form of theism, laid claim to the approval of the new cosmology. But we shall now have to trace the reaction of Catholic theologians to this revolution in the world picture.

Chapter Six

THE NEW WORLD PICTURE AND THEOLOGY

As we have seen, medieval theology employed the thought-categories derived from the world picture of the time to formulate Christine doctrine in a systematic manner. An important role was played here by the concept of order which is found everywhere: in the doctrine on God, Providence, creation, man, original sin, the Incarnation, Redemption, grace, and the four last things. Christianity was thus seen to be in harmony with a perfect, immutable, hierarchical and anthropocentric world order. With Copernicus, however, this world picture came under fierce attack. We shall now consider how theologians reacted to this situation which threatened not only the background to but also the thought-patterns of medieval theology.

In the seventeenth and eighteenth centuries theology was largely dominated by controversy and polemic, involving much lively discussion with Protestants, Anglicans, Jansenists, Quietists, Gallicanists, Diests, etc. Traditional Catholic theology appeared to be threatened on all sides and in this way a theology developed that was more concerned with invalidating the arguments of its opponents than with deepening its own doctrine. What concerns us here, however, is not how Catholic faith was defended but what was actually defended. In other words, how did Catholic theologians formulate Christian doctrine after the disintegration of the medieval world picture? What concepts did they employ? And in what cosmological framework did they situate Christian doctrine? The impact of the Copernican system was felt not only in the natural sciences but in philosophy and in the entire cultural life of the period. Could we speak of a revolution in theology comparable to that of the thirteenth century when Aristotelian science was introduced into theology? What was the reaction of leading theologians in the Catholic Church to the new science and to the new world picture in particular?

Theology on the Eve of Galileo's Condemnation

The theologians of the sixteenth century and especially the main commentators on the *Summa* of Aquinas had no objection whatsoever to the old world picture. Fundamentally their picture of the universe and interpretation of Christianity were the same as that of the Middle Ages. The concept of order acted as a guarantee of the unity in interpretation of doctrine. Initially there was no sign of a direct influence of Copernicus on theology. An important figure in the controversies of the age, particularly in the De Auxiliis question, was Leonardus Lessius, author of *De perfectionibus moribusque divinis libri XIV* (1620).[1]

As in the Middle Ages, cosmology is discussed in the treatise on Providence (bk. II). Chapter seven is entirely devoted to the question of how God guides the motion of the heavenly spheres. It is by this motion, writes Lessius, that God mainly governs the material world. There are four things to be considered in this motion: velocity, diversity, uniformity, and efficacy. The sun, for example, is said to move at a speed of 1.1 million miles per hour, while a star from the eighth sphere has a velocity of 42 million miles per hour. With such astounding velocities, asks Lessius, we may wonder what velocity is to be found in the highest moving sphere. But the diversity of the motions is no less stupendous, with each sphere of planets having a different motion. There are also all sorts of strange epicycles which are difficult to investigate. We must also admire the uniformity of these motions. Any irregularity we may observe in the motion of the planets is due to epicycles or the elevation (greater or smaller) above the earth, and is therefore not a real disparity but only in relation to the center of the earth. For in relation to their own center epicycles always observe the same velocity.

At this point Lessius raises the question whether the motion of the celestial spheres is caused by angels. In his opinion this is not the case, even though many eminent scholars hold the opposite view. According to Lessius, the motion of the heavenly spheres is directed directly and continuously by God himself, since it is not fitting that such an important and universal task be consigned to inferior beings like the angels, who are in any case unable to move the gigantic heavenly bodies. Moreover, if angels were to be responsible for this motion they would be so engrossed in their work that they would have no opportunity to go now and then to the empyrean or to visit people on earth. And this appears to be irreconcilable with the beatific freedom that has to be attributed to the angels. What is more, as free beings it would be possible for them to stop the motion of the heavenly spheres, and what chaos would this not cause in the cosmos? As this is a matter of supreme importance, on which the welfare of the lower beings depends, it cannot be entrusted to created beings, even if they are angels. It is therefore more reasonable to suppose that the admirable motion of the heavens with its far-reaching consequences is directly guided by God's mighty hand.[2] On this question Lessius clearly deviates from the view of most medieval theologians.

Finally, with regard to the efficacy of the motions of the heavenly spheres, Lessius accepts the position that all material changes that take place on earth must be ascribed to the heavenly bodies. An exception must be made for the motions of the free will and possibly also for some things that are attributed to the imagination of animate beings, even though the heavenly bodies can play a role here also, not so much by coercion, as by evoking a particular inclination in the organism.[3]

Except for the intervention of the angels, the cosmology presented here by Lessius is identical to that of Aquinas and most scholastics. And yet one can raise the question whether Lessius did not purposely adhere to the traditional view in this book on account of the condemnation not long before, in 1616, of the Copernican system. In an earlier work, *De providentia numinis et animi immortalitate libri duo adversus atheos et politicos*, written in 1612, he shows considerable interest in the new discoveries. Though he does not mention the book, there is no doubt that he had read Galileo's *Sidereus nuntius* and that this had made a profound impression on him.

De providentia numinis is aimed at atheists and those who supported Machiavelli. Part one contains a series of arguments—many of which are derived from the cosmology of the time—for the existence of God and his guidance of the world. The second argument is based on the motion of the heavenly spheres.[4] Here Lessius tells of the recent invention in Holland of a peculiar instrument, fistula dioptrica, with which astounding things can be observed in the sky: the moon is seen to have a spongy appearance; the planet Venus, like the moon, has different phases; Jupiter is surrounded by four smaller stars, at one time preceding, at another time following the planet, from which it can be concluded that they move in small orbits around the planet; there are many spots to be observed in the sun, continually changing place and at one time appearing to be less numerous than at another time. From this it is evident that they are not really part of the sun but are rather small stars between us and the sun, round which they move in small orbits. "With the aid of this instrument," writes Lessius, "I myself have been able to observe all these things."[5] It is clearly a question here of the same phenomena as are described in *Sidereus nuntius*. On one occasion it seems as if Lessius declares himself in favor of the heliocentric world system, when having mentioned the phases of Venus he concludes: "from this it appears to be quite evident that the planet Venus moves in a great epicycle *round the sun*."[6] Galileo had also regarded this phenomenon as a proof of the heliocentric world system. But one can of course interpret Lessius's text within the framework of Tycho Brahe's view.

In any case the text as a whole clearly displays much enthusiasm for the new discoveries, even though there is no evidence that Lessius was aware of the consequences of these views. In his later work, written after the condemnation of 1616, we find no more than a re-statement of traditional views. It is especially in the earlier work of 1612 that we learn about the astronomy of the time, for which Lessius had a particular liking, constantly alluding to the vast dimensions of the universe and the splendid order to be seen all around him:

> When we behold a magnificent palace, perfect in every detail and designed with utmost precision, exhibiting the most perfect proportions and symmetry so that it leaves nothing to be desired in the way of architecture, there is no one who doubts that it is the work of an extremely competent architect. Who, then, could doubt that the universe, each part of which is perfect and in harmony with the whole, which is moreover so richly adorned that it received the name "cosmos"—who could doubt that this world has a supreme Creator?[7] Is the creation of the world not also then the greatest of all miracles?[8]

A similar openness of mind is also to be found in Cardinal de Bérulle (1575–1629). In 1622 the founder of the Oratory in France published his most important work, *Discours de l'estat et des grandeurs de Jésus*, in which he also discloses his inclination towards the new cosmology:

> A brilliant mind of this century has attempted to maintain that the Sun and not the Earth is at the center of the World; that it is motionless and that the Earth, in keeping with its round shape, moves in relation to the Sun: by this contrary position satisfying all appearances which compel our senses to believe that the Sun is in

> constant motion around the Earth. This new opinion which is not popular in the science of stars is useful and should be popular in the science of salvation. For Jesus is the motionless Sun in its grandeur, moving everything . . .[9]

While obviously in favor of the heliocentric system, the author does not express his opinion on the value of the new conception but simply mentions that it has only a few followers in the scientific world of the time and that it will correspond to the truth. For the rest, he merely uses the heliocentric cosmology as a basis of comparison in proclaiming a theological doctrine. It was clearly not his task to pronounce judgment on a purely scientific question. Yet his choice of comparison bears testimony to an openness that betrays an unspoken sympathy and at the same time paves the way for the introduction of the new world picture into theology. With C. Ramnoux, one can rightly ask whether the Church might not have been spared a serious conflict of conscience had the theologians in Rome shown the same openness of mind.

It was clear to Cardinal de Bérulle that Aristotelian science and philosophy were now obsolete. He therefore advised his followers to look to Plato:

> The Platonists, who are the most educated of the pagans in the knowledge of things sublime, being truly divine among naturalists and theologians among philosophers, speak of nothing so divinely as unity; and in the elements and secrets of their doctrine they teach their disciples that the divine essence and fecundity are in unity.[10]

He silently hoped for a Christian thinker who would present the Church with a new philosophy to replace a discredited scholasticism. It is probable that he set his hopes on the young Descartes, whom he never failed to encourage.[11]

From the examples of Lessius and de Bérulle we can see that some prominent theologians were initially willing to include the new cosmological conceptions in their theology. It was undoubtedly a question here of very modest attempts by people who had been educated in and were still entirely captive to the old world picture, but who were nevertheless sufficiently open-minded to look upon each new discovery with interest. But with the Holy Office's condemnation of the heliocentric system, this situation was brought to an abrupt end.

The Theological Background
to the Condemnation of Galileo

We must now take a closer look at these condemnations, for what was involved had such a bearing on theology that it cannot be underestimated. Owing to this pronouncement by the highest ecclesiastical authority—both decrees were issued with papal approval—every new attempt to include the heliocentric theory in theological speculation was for a long time completely blocked, while the geocentric theory of the universe was granted a validity that appeared to many as binding.

The questions that can be raised in connection with this condemnation are numerous and often complex. In view of our present theme, we can restrict ourselves to those questions directly related to the theological aspect of the case, leaving aside the historical circumstances of the condemnations, which are dealt with in other works. At the time when the heliocentric theory emerged, no longer as the harmless speculation of an isolated scholar but as a forceful current, Christian faith was predominantly explained in a way that can be called the medieval paradigm. This involved a form of Christian self-understanding whereby Revelation was wholly interpreted within the framework of a very concrete world picture whose thought-categories served to formulate the truths of faith in a systematic and rational manner. The fundamental thought-category of this world picture was undoubtedly the concept of order: the universe formed a perfect, immutable, hierarchical, and anthropocentric order. It was precisely this idea of order, derived from a particular cosmology, that became the central concept of scholastic theology. As has already been pointed out, all the basic dogmas of Christianity were interpreted and formulated with the help of this concept. This manner of interpreting faith was still completely intact at the beginning of the seventeenth century, despite the Reformation and humanism, and must have appeared to many as the only possible interpretation of faith. At any rate such a conviction formed the background to the prevalent theology and all theologizing took place within this paradigm.

In such a situation one can readily understand that the heliocentric theory was thought to be revolutionary and extremely dangerous in many respects, posing a threat to the very foundations of the whole system. It was to be expected, then, that there would be fierce opposition, irrespective of the particular characters involved in the condemnation. Even without Bellarmine, Paul V, the Dominicans, and Jesuits, there would have been strong protest against the heliocentric theory, which was seen to undermine the spiritual foundations of the community. That one ought to have made a distinction between doctrine on the one hand and the interpretation of doctrine worked out by scholasticism on the other hand, had not yet been realized. Doctrine was thus identified completely with the interpretation of doctrine, a misunderstanding that was later repeatedly found.

Therefore much was at stake. Each community had the task of creating a particular order within which life could proceed harmoniously.[12] For many centuries Christianity had endeavored to construct such an order, using every effort to build a spiritual edifice that was perfect in all respects. And it was just this magnificent achievement that was now threatened with distintegration. So when it was objected that Copernicus had abased the sun and undeservedly glorified the earth by placing it among the imperishable heavenly bodies, this was not just a whim but the expression of a clear conviction that the heliocentric theory endangered the whole world order and thus undermined all existing certainties.

Apart from this general threat, there were other aspects of the worldview of the time that came under attack from the heliocentric theory. In the first place there was the authority of Scripture. As we have seen, the Bible had long been interpreted within the framework of the Greek world picture. In commentaries on the Book of Genesis and on the creation story in particular, the biblical world picture had been identified with that of Greek science. The latter seemed to confirm the biblical world picture, which in turn consolidated Greek science, conferring upon it an almost sacred character. But if Copernicus could show that Greek science had been mistaken on a fundamental issue, did this not also effect the credibility of the Bible? This obviously became a focal point of discussion, since the authority of Scripture was unanimously accepted both by those for and those against the heliocentric theory. How could a Christian accept the new world picture in such circumstances without thereby endangering the principle of biblical "inerrantia" and at the same time putting himself under suspicion of heresy?

Next there was the authority of Aristotle. It was true of course that a follower of Christ did not necessarily have to be a disciple of Aristotle. Still, since the time of Aquinas, the Stagarite had acquired an unsurpassed authority in ecclesiastical circles so that his scientific and philosophical views were firmly established in all universities and theological schools. "Theology," writes Descartes in a letter to Mersenne, "is so completely under the power of Aristotle that it is practically impossible to present another philosophy which does not create the impression of being contrary to faith."[13] One hundred years earlier Erasmus had accused some theologians of appearing to put Aristotle and Christ on the same level, making the truth of the Gospel, which in the words of St. Paul is folly in the eyes of the world, inferior to Greek philosophy.[14] For many centuries the integration of Greek thought and theology had led to a Christian self-understanding that gave many people perfect intellectual satisfaction. As one might suspect, it was the doctrine and authority of Aristotle, even more so than that of Scripture, that constituted the greatest obstacle to the acceptance of the heliocentric theory.[15] When the general of the Jesuits issued directives in 1612, laying down that his order ought to defend Aristotelian doctrine at all costs, this was undoubtedly because he was convinced that there was an extremely close connection between Christianity and Aristotelian doctrine and that by defending the latter one rendered the Church a service. Even later, in the years 1650–1660, we find James Dupont advising his students at Cambridge that whenever they appeal to the authority of Aristotle in any of their discussions to see to it that they quote him in his own words and in his own language. It was argued that the authority of Aristotle will not be lightly repudiated as long as his own words justify a favorable and sure interpretation.[16] Throughout the seventeenth century there was persistent conflict concerning the authority of Aristotle, which gave rise to numerous polemical writings,[17] the theologians mostly opting for the Greek philosopher by virtue of their attachment to scholasticism. Instinctively it was felt that undermining the Aristotelian world picture would pose a grave threat to the entire theological system.

In addition to the credibility of Scripture and the authority of Aristotle, the generally accepted order of sciences also came under attack from the introduction of the heliocentric theory of the universe. Instead of the sharp distinction between natural science, philosophy, and theology that we know today, natural science was at that time mostly conceived as part of philosophy and the terms philosopher and scientist were not always clearly distinguished.[18] Philosophy, in turn, was subservient to theology and had at all times to be subject to faith. In the theoretical field Aquinas had undoubtedly drawn clear dividing lines but, as he also believed, this did not exclude the fact that all areas of knowledge exhibited a hierarchical order. It did not occur to anyone to cast doubt on "the reduction of the arts to theology," so beautifully described by Bonaventure. All sciences were subject to the supreme authority of theology since the latter occupied the highest place in the order of sciences. The Christian view of man and of the world still formed a harmonious whole, displaying the same hierarchical structure as was found in the entire cosmos. And just as in a hierarchically structured universe all direction originates with the highest celestial spheres, so in the classification of sciences there ought to be a supreme authority somewhere, a function for which only theology is eligible since it alone is founded in God's word.

It was precisely this hierarchical structure of sciences that was threatened by the Copernican system. For the appeal to observation and experiment as the supreme authority in the natural sciences challenged the position of theology. One can readily accept that this emancipation of cosmology from theology was felt in ecclesiastical circles as a dangerous precedent, since in the medieval way of thinking the idea of an autonomous science was completely objectionable.

From all this it is evident that the question of whether the sun revolves around the earth or the earth around the sun was by no means a secondary matter but rather an essential concern affecting the foundations of traditional theology. With the acceptance or otherwise of the new world picture an entire theological system was decided. The choice confronting the ecclesiastical authorities and the theologians could not help but have far-reaching consequences: either hold onto an age-old but now unstable synthesis or open the way for a totally new interpretation of Christianity within the framework of the new world picture.

At this decisive moment in history the Church preferred to defend the traditional theological system at all costs. The authority and the efforts of a man like Galileo, who was thoroughly aware of the danger to the Church, were inadequate to break through the conservatism and incomprehension of his judges. It was the tragedy of his life that he was not permitted to succeed in protecting the Church he loved from its own mistakes and in preserving it from approaching calamity.

But is one justified in explaining this error of the Roman judges only in terms of conservatism and short-sightedness? Were there no other motives which deserve more appreciation? Leaving aside the fact that these judges were also products of the age—an age still completely governed by medieval ideas—we can have regard for the concern they showed to uphold the authority of Scripture and Church tradition. Perhaps their decisions were to a certain extent also motivated by pastoral concern. The new discoveries had naturally been the cause of much doubt and unrest. Moreover, after the commotion and tension of the Reformation, the ecclesiastical authorities were anxious to restore order and tranquillity to those who had remained loyal to Rome. Cardinal Bellarmine, for example, devoted all his energy to achieving this end. But just when his work started to bear fruit there was a new threat of confusion and unrest—the Copernican system. The Church authorities plainly felt they had to adopt a clear standpoint in the conflict concerning the heliocentric theory of the universe. We shall now have to examine the grounds on which they based their intervention.[19] Only one of the motives we have mentioned is clearly expressed in the decree of 1616: the heliocentric theory contradicts the teaching of Scripture. It is to be noted that those authors named in the text of the decree were condemned not so much because they defended the heliocentric theory but because they claimed that this theory was consonant with the teaching of Scripture. In this way only those sentences were deleted from the works of Copernicus and Diego de Zuniga, in which it was stated that the new cosmology was not incompatible with the teaching of Scripture. The heliocentric theory was thus repudiated, not on the basis of scientific arguments but on the basis of what was thought to be an indisputable interpretation of Scripture. By shifting the whole case to the field of biblical interpretation, it was immediately affirmed that the scientist had to submit himself to the Church, the genuine authority in matters of biblical interpretation. This document has plainly to be seen against the background of the medieval world of thought. It was a question of defending this world thought in its entirety—the Bible and Greek philosophy were so clearly connected here that for many people the one was not conceivable without the other.

Galileo and his friends pointed out in vain that the Bible did not pretend to teach science. Neither did it use scientific language. It simply employed ordinary language and this included expressions which were not scientifically justified, but at which no one took offence. It was of no avail. In the eyes of the theologians an expression such as "Sun, stand thou still" (Joshua 10:12) had to be understood literally as affirming that the sun, and not the earth, was in motion, as earlier expositions had held. What is more, it was believed that this amounted to an irrefutable argument.

The second trial of 1633 is of less importance from a theological standpoint. With a skill that is peculiar to many ecclesiastical authorities, the whole affair was this time transferred to the province of obedience. Galileo was accused of disobedience to the ecclesiastical authorities and of failing to keep previous promises not to speak any more about the heliocentric theory. To what extent he was obliged to keep silent is, from an historical standpoint, not altogether clear, but this question is beyond the scope of the present work.[20]

In this way the ecclesiastical authorities totally rejected the Copernican system for a second time. Whether there was a third condemnation, perhaps relating to Tycho Brahe's system, is difficult to ascertain.[21] The decisions that were taken were in any case strictly enforced. To ensure that they were precisely executed, directives were sent to the inquisitors and nuncios, while the Catholic universities bound themselves never to allow the "foolish and perilous" heliocentric theory to be taught within their walls.[22] All possible means were employed to protect the old world picture and to safeguard the foundations of the traditional view of life.

The Copernican theory undoubtedly contained a challenge for Catholic theology. But instead of acccepting the challenge and reflecting on faith in a new perspective, the Church opted for an easy conservatism, keeping the enemy at bay by means of its anathemas. This failure to accept the challenge of a new world picture was a great loss to the Church and to Christianity.[23]

The Scholastic Tradition
after the Condemnation of Galileo

There is a tendency among some historians to minimize the consequences of Galileo's condemnation as if it were simply a question of an accidental error which, though naturally regrettable, was for the rest of no fundamental importance.[24] It would seem, however, that the consequences of Galileo's condemnation were, on the contrary, quite disastrous and can still be felt today. Although the condemnation was not able to save the old world picture or arrest the further progress of science, it did have an adverse effect on the Church's prestige and on the development of theology. Not only did it give rise to the view of the Church as the enemy of science but it also consolidated a theology that excluded all dialogue with the growing natural sciences, and thus became more and more estranged from the world.[25]

It has been said that the condemnation of Galileo, together with the Eastern and Western schisms, must be counted as the three greatest disasters that have ever befallen the Church.[26] As a result of this condemnation, the world of science turned away from the Church and went its own way without any regard for religious problems. Much has still to be done to bridge this gulf between the Church and modern culture.

What possibilities were open to the Church in such a confused situation where Aristotelian science and philosophy had been completely discredited? Even prior to the emergence of Copernican astronomy Aristotelianism had lost much of its earlier influence and prestige. In the sixteenth century some humanists like Pomponazzi and the school of Padua, on a closer examination of the authentic text of Aristotle, had pointed out that the Greek philosopher did not actually hold that God created the world or that the soul is immortal. Moreover, by proposing a radical division between faith and reason, they were able, on the one hand, to keep up an appearance of orthodoxy in matters of faith and, on the other hand, to go their own way as philosophers. Many people then turned against Aristotle, especially in the area of philosophy, and their critique had considerable influence and met with wide approval outside of Italy as well .[27] But the final blow to the already waning authority of Aristotelianism came when it became evident from the work of Copernicus and Galileo that Aristotle had been fundamentally mistaken in the field of cosmology.

As far as theology was concerned, there now seemed to be three possibilities open. The first consisted in abandoning Aristotle in order to turn once again towards Plato. There was at this time considerable interest in Platonism, which escaped the criticism leveled at Aristotelianism. As we have seen, this attitude was recommended by Cardinal de Bérulle. Then again, one could also forsake the whole of antiquity to look for new ways, just as Descartes did, and attempt to construct a new theology on the basis of his doctrine. Finally, one could also row against the stream, clinging obstinately to Aristotelianism and scholasticism. Of the three, only the third possibility received the support of the ecclesiastical authorities. With regard to the other alternatives, Platonism, which was closely associated with Augustinianism, was adhered to for a long time, especially by the Oratorians, but was very much compromised by the Jansenists, while Cartesianism was vehemenently opposed by Bossuet. Scholasticism, on the other hand, was strongly encouraged by the authorities and found many adherents among the Jesuits, Dominicans, and Franciscans. The condemnation of Galileo obviously played a significant role in this. Initially the scholastic tradition (both Thomism and Scotism) was integrally maintained, inclusive of medieval cosmology. But as the latter was shown to be more and more impossible, an effort was made to separate Aristotle's philosophy from his views on natural science, which then gradually disappeared from theological treatises. For the rest, however, the spirit of medieval scholasticism was maintained as faithfully as possible.

If we attempt to define the general character of Catholic theology in the seventeenth and eighteenth centuries, we can say that, though initially shocked by the Copernican revolution, theologians were soon reassured by the condemnations of 1616 and 1633, enabling them to continue their work within the framework of the Thomistic or Scotist tradition. What they produced generally displayed little originality and was mostly intended as a commentary or summary of earlier writings, so that apart from vehement discussions on the problem of grace, we basically find a restatement of what the theologians of the thirteenth century had done with such skill. There was still no mention of rethinking Christian doctrine within the framework of the new world picture. Neither was there any change brought about in this respect with the emergence of positive theology, since those engaged in this field were of the opinion that the study of the Church Fathers and Christian writers had chiefly to serve as a support and confirmation of the scholastic tradition, they also held this view with regard to the old world picture.

At the same time, however, the ideas of Galileo and Newton gradually gained ground, as it became clear that Aristotle and his cosmology had to make way for a totally new view of the world. And yet we seldom find an explicit repudiation of the medieval world picture—but then no one openly admits defeat. A respectful silence was observed on cosmological problems, while the scholastic interpretation of Christianity was passed on just as before. What is clear is that opposition to the Copernican system was only reluctantly abandoned and consequently there was no real attempt to integrate the new cosmological conceptions. Adopting the view that there was no essential connection between Aristotle's metaphysics and his views on natural science, theologians felt they could now discard the latter but still hold onto the former, which allowed them to continue their work unperturbed by the findings of science. Anything that could be ascribed to the natural sciences had, therefore, to be deleted from medieval theology, while the remainder could continue to hold good as the "perennial theology." Medieval theology had been constructed on the basis of data derived from Revelation, metaphysics, and the natural sciences. Now that the latter was no longer discussed, theology was conceived of as an interpretation of doctrine with the help of a modified Aristotelian metaphysics.

One can readily imagine the result of such a method. The theological writings of this period presented Christianity as a fossilized and abstract system that had lost all contact with life. Not surprisingly, therefore, this period in the history of theology is known as "the decline of scholasticism."[28] One of the causes of this decline was undoubtedly the refusal on the part of theology to take into account the new insights in the natural sciences and the new philosophical problems which these raised. A typical example of this attitude is to be found in the notorious *Mémoires de Trévoux*, a periodical published by the Jesuits in France (1701–1762) and intended as a counterpart of the then celebrated *Journal des Savants,* in which the scientific life of the period was followed with considerable interest. The periodical mainly contained extensive reviews of the most important scientific publications of the period. As to the theological ideas expressed in these reviews, Alfred R. Desautels considers that the contributors to the periodical were "open to the ideas of the age and were influenced by them but nevertheless maintained a narrow, fossilized, and traditional orthodoxy, which purposely excluded every consideration that might compel them to question their own views. There was no need to go beyond the Church Fathers and Aristotle. . . . To the Christian who was alarmed and confused by the new theological problems, they gave the chilling reply: when one believes, one does not try to understand."[29] This, moreover, was the predominant attitude in theological circles at that time.

We shall now briefly consider three principle commentators on Aquinas: Joannes a Sancto Thoma, Gonet, and Billuart. Earlier theologians such as Bañez (d. 1604) and Suarez (d. 1617) cannot be said to have participated in the cosmological debate or to have deviated from the medieval view on this matter. Joannes a Sancto Thoma (d. 1644) had little to say on the cosmological issue, despite the fact that he was a contemporary of Galileo. In his principal work, *Cursus philosophicus thomisticus,* and in his treatise *De meteoris,* he simply reproduces all aspects of the cosmology of the thirteenth century without the slightest hesitation. As to the new cosmological conceptions he briefly remarks: "I also add that just as a certain opinion of Copernicus and others concerning the natural motion of the earth in an orbit was condemned by a decree of the Holy Office, issued by Pope Paul V, so also, as I learned from a reliable source, the opinion that the earth undergoes certain oscillations was condemned by Gregory XV, as contrary to sacred Scriptures which teach that the earth remains forever (Ec. 1: 4) and that God has set the earth on its foundations so that it should never be shaken (Ps. 104: 5)." He evidently considered this to be the end of the matter and could therefore repeat what his predecessors had said. The "world machine" was also described by him in the most traditional manner.[30]

A similar attitude is to be found in the celebrated theologian J.B. Gonet (d. 1681) whose *Clypeus theologiae thomisticae* makes no reference whatsoever to the cosmological conceptions of Copernicus and Galileo. Since it never occurred to him to doubt that the world picture of the Middle Ages—and of Aquinas in particular—was unassailable, he continued to hold this view, considering the universe as a perfect hierarchical order and employing the terms microcosm and macrocosm in a thoroughly medieval fashion.[31] The angels were seen as constituting an integral part of the universe[32] and as instruments of God in directing the world,[33] while the heavenly bodies played the same role as in the medieval view of the world.[34] Here too the influence of the condemnations of 1616 and 1633 was clearly felt: the theologian must not concern himself with the new cosmological conceptions which were condemned by the Church, but can safely proceed as if nothing had happened.

In C. R. Billuart's detailed commentary on the *Summa* of Aquinas, *Summa sancti thomae hodiernis academiarum moribus accomodata sive cursus theologiae* (1746–51) we find a slight change in attitude. There is far less mention of the celestial spheres and heavenly bodies and, though Billuart still holds Aquinas's doctrine, he does not give explicit consideration to his world picture. The universe is represented as a splendidly ordered whole[35] and the angels have the same role as in medieval cosmology.[36] But there is no mention of Copernicus, Galileo, or Newton.

In the same strain, Billuart also wrote a summary of his major work, *Summa summae S.Thomae sive compendium theologiae,* which was used as textbook in many seminaries until the beginning of the twentieth century. From these three outstanding representatives of the Thomistic school, we can conclude that the old world picture was explicitly maintained by the vast majority of theologians in the seventeenth century, gradually receiving less consideration until it almost disappeared in the course of the eighteenth century. And yet there was no allusion to the new world picture.[37]

What has been said of the representatives of Thomism also applies to the Scotists. As a counterpart to Gonet's work, Bartholomy Durand (d. 1720) wrote *Clypeus Scotisticae Theologiae,* while Jerome de Montefiore (d. 1728) produced a Scotist *Summa Theologiae* that can be considered as a counterpart to Billuart's work. There was in fact a stream of Scotist textbooks in this period. Common to all these Scotist and Thomistic writings was the fact that the Christian salvation mystery was treated against the background of the medieval world picture, whether the latter was explicitly mentioned or tacitly assumed. Since most of these writings were actually textbooks, they obviously had a decisive influence on the theological formation of the clergy. Such conservatism was clearly contrary to the spirit of the thirteenth century. One can only assume that this fossilization of theological thought was closely connected with the condemnation of the heliocentric world system which obliged theologians to hold onto the old world picture. The condemnation of Copernicus remained valid until 1757, while the work of Galileo was not removed from the Index until 1822.

We shall now consider a few theological writings of the period. Dionysius Petavius (1585–1652) was renowned in his time and is considered one of the founders of positive theology. It is hardly conceivable that he was completely unaware of Copernicus and Galileo. He evidently avoided all discussion of the new world system. In his treatise on Providence[38] he holds that the world consists of two parts: heaven, with its eternal spheres, and the sublunary world, which is composed of the four elements. Both were created in supreme wisdom and are miraculously directed by God's Providence.[39] After this general affirmation Petavius attempts to support his thesis, first with regard to the universe. This he does by means of a long quotation from Cicero (*De natura deorum, II*). The celestial spheres were created, as this was necessary for the life of plants and animals.[40] God's wisdom, concern, and ingenuity are especially evident from the great diversity of the motions of the heavenly bodies. To substantiate this claim he appeals to Lactantius (*Divinae institutiones* 11, 1. 11, c. 5), Theodoretus (*De providentia, 1*) Socrates (*Xenophon, IV, Apomemnon*) and the peripatetic Alexander (*De providentia*). God's Providence can be seen not only from the motion of the heavenly bodies but also from earthly things. Petavius then quotes Gregory Nazianzen, Paulinus Nolanus, Nemesius, Ambrose, and Julius Firmicus. God's Providence is also apparent from the fact that all people have a different face: just imagine if this had not been the case, then a man would not even recognize his own wife and criminals would always be at large! Furthermore, animals are able by the sense of smell to distinguish a poisonous plant from the rest. There then follows a long discussion on the question of whether God is also present in the imaginary space beyond the heavenly spheres.[41]

Petavius emphatically rejects the thesis that God's Providence is only concerned with the heavenly spheres and does not extend to the sublunary world.[42] God also shows his direct concern for the smallest matters on earth. But the influence of the heavenly bodies does not extend to man's free will.[43] The whole cosmos was created for man and God can constantly alter the course of events, otherwise prayers of petition would be meaningless.[44]

Petavius retained the validity of the medieval world picture. Further evidence of this is to be found in his work on the creation story, *De sex primorum mundi*,[45] where we can clearly see how he derives his cosmology from biblical texts and supports it with numerous quotations from the ancients. His positive method is aimed at finding support for scholastic theology in the Fathers of the Church, thereby granting the traditional world picture a new credibility.

Throughout the seventeenth century, theology—whether Thomistic or Scotist—remained tied to the medieval picture of the universe, so that Christianity was still interpreted within the framework of a perfect, immutable, hierarchical, and anthropocentric world order. It would appear that the condemnation of the Copernican world system had such a binding force on the leading theologians of the period that they found it superfluous to pay any attention to the new cosmological theories.

This was clearly the case with Bossuet (d. 1704), a major figure in ecclesiastical life in France for a great part of the seventeenth century. Though he was well grounded in theology, based on a wide knowledge of Scripture, Patristics (especially Augustine), and the main representatives of scholasticism, he was extraordinarily reserved on matters relating to cosmology, and this at a time when such issues were being hotly debated and philosophers were raising questions as to the consequences of the new world picture for the concept of God. Did he feel he was incompetent to form an opinion on these matters or did he believe them to be totally insignificant? It has been said of Bossuet that he, in contrast to Fénélon, looked more to the past than to the future.[46] Perhaps this accounts for the fact that he remained reticent on questions of cosmology, preferring to read the writings of the ancients where he found a world picture that he consciously or unconsciously made his own. If truth has been given to man once and for all, why go in search of novelties? The Christian, he believed, has nothing to look for. What Bossuet entirely failed to notice was that Christian doctrine in spite of its immutability was capable of growth and development.[47] Holding the view that immutability was the chief characteristic of truth, Bossuet argued that Protestant doctrine was false since it had repeatedly undergone changes of one kind or another[48]—to which Protestants could reply that change was a sign of vitality and love of truth. His writings show that he was acquainted with classical antiquity, history, literature, philosophy, mysticism, politics, and ethics and that he dealt with all matters in any way related to the Church at that time. And yet he made no mention whatsoever of people like Copernicus and Galileo. In Descartes he saw a pernicious threat to Christianity.[49] Bossuet's view of creation was that of the thirteenth century and he particularly defended the idea of a perfect hierarchical world order in which everything had its proper place and all things displayed a perfect harmony. Evidence of supreme wisdom is everywhere to be found, even in the smallest details.[50] All disorder that is thought to be discovered is only an appearance, for in reality the Creator has arranged everything in the most perfect manner. It is man's duty to respect his order.

The same concept of order also permeates Bossuet's political theory. Convinced that a completely hierarchical order must prevail in the state just as it was seen to do in the cosmos, Bossuet did not hesitate to defend the absolute authority of the monarch. All authority comes from God. Therefore no human intervention may in any way restrict the power of the king, which can only be tempered by goodness and wisdom. It must not be impeded in its exercise by any earthly authority.[51] With regard to the Church, he also maintained the concept of hierarchical order, even though he did not believe in papal infallibility and felt compelled as a Frenchman to make several concessions, however, moderate, to Gallicanism. Bossuet thus embodied a system which was based entirely on the traditional world picture and which interpreted Christian doctrine in this context. For this reason he can rightly be considered a classic representative of seventeenth-century theology and its refusal to have anything to do with the new world picture.

Except for the many controversies of this period—Protestantism, Jansenism, Quietism, Gallicanism, etc.—the theology of the seventeenth century contained little original thinking and was mostly a matter of commentaries or textbooks. (We shall later discuss Cartesianism and its influence on theology.) The new ideas in cosmology clearly did not give rise to a renewed reflection on Christian doctrine nor was there any interest in Copernicus and Galileo at the Catholic universities, chiefly on account of the condemnation of the heliocentric theory. In the faculty of arts preference was mostly given to Tycho Brahe's system, which was believed to be consonant with the letter of Scripture. At the university of Louvain we find a typical example of what then took place at Catholic universities. In 1616 Libert Froidmont, a professor at Louvain, published a work entitled *Saturnalitiae coenae*,[52] in which he at least reacted very favorably towards the doctrine of Copernicus and Galileo. At the time he wrote this work he was apparently unaware of the condemnation issued by the Holy Office in the same year. We find an entirely different attitude in his later works, *Metereologica* (1626) and *Anti-Aristarchus* (1631), where he even felt compelled to defend himself against the accusation that he had ever adhered to a condemned doctrine.[53] He therefore declared himself to be a follower of Tycho Brahe, whose doctrine he made his own. One can hardly avoid the impression that this reversal must to a great extent be attributed to the condemnation by Rome. Till the end of the seventeenth century the university of Louvain felt obliged to oppose the doctrine of Copernicus and Galileo. It was only then that Copernicus and Descartes were introduced into the curriculum, as a result of the efforts of Martin Van Velden, but not without considerable opposition and all sorts of difficulties. Ultimately, however, there was a greater openness in this matter.[54]

Apart from the many controversies, the theology of the seventeenth century was largely a poor rendering of that presented by the scholastics of the thirteenth century. There is little evidence of any real dialogue with the new science after 1616, while those who were interested gradually discarded theology to concentrate on science.[55]

Cartesianism and Theology

It is a common sociological phenomenon that ideas which run counter to the generally accepted social pattern or scientific paradigm are initially repelled with considerable force. But if after a lapse of time it becomes utterly impossible to deny or to suppress any longer the newly discovered facts, then the community will eagerly concentrate on fitting the new data into the existing paradigm, making them harmonize as far as possible with the old schema. If this also proves ultimately to be impossible, then the only solution is that of total revolution whereby the old paradigm is replaced by the new. Such a phenomenon is then described as a cultural or scientific revolution.[56]

Progress in science is not achieved by adding new facts or insights to what is already known but by showing the previously accepted paradigm to be worthless and by replacing it with a new paradigm. This progress is the result of revolution rather than evolution. Once the new paradigm has been clearly defined, scholars will continue working for some time within this framework, making small additions and improvements, until another genius appears and the revolutionary process can be repeated.

An interesting example of this is provided by the subject concerning us here. As soon as the new world picture of Copernicus and Galileo was felt as a threat to the existing patterns, it met with fierce opposition and almost widespread rejection. Both the ecclesiastical authorities and the scientific world labeled the new world picture as foolish and pernicious. But when it became clear that the new cosmological theory had a sound basis, attempts were made to fit the new data as best they might into the old framework. At the end of the seventeenth, and for a great part of the eighteenth century, theologians of the scholastic tradition did try to save the old paradigm by removing everything clearly reminiscent of the earlier world picture, without endangering the old schema. It was not long, however, before thinkers appeared who plainly realized that it was quite impossible to consider the new facts as merely adventitious and therefore introduced a total revolution in human thought, a revolution which ultimately had to extend to the field of theology.

This was the attitude adopted by Descartes (1596–1650), the father of modern philosophy. While he expressed his gratitude for the education he received from the Jesuits at La Flèche, he was nevertheless most dissatisfied with what he felt to be a complete divorce of the natural sciences and philosophy. Since Aristotelian science had been shown to be totally unreliable, how could one still have confidence in a philosophy so closely connected with this scientific view? Though he never managed to free himself completely from its influence,[57] there could, in his opinion, be no doubt that scholasticism had to be discarded to make way for a totally new interpretation of reality. Henceforth he was to be guided by a twofold ideal. First, he devoted all his energy to the experimental and mathematical sciences, making a significant contribution in these fields, especially with regard to analytical geometry. Then he attempted to build up a new philosophy that would correspond as closely as possible to the newly acquired insights in the scientific field and fulfill the same role vis-à-vis modern science as Aristotelian metaphysics had done vis-à-vis Aristotelian science. In this endeavor he also seems to have been inspired by a religious concern.[58] It appeared to him that the Church had an urgent need of a new philosophy as substructure for its theology and, encouraged by a dream, he felt he was called to present the Church with such a philosophy. The words of Cardinal de Bérulle had also strengthened him in this conviction. He was, then, impelled by the desire to be a new Aristotle.

In the realization of this ideal, Galileo's doctrine concerning both scientific method and the structure of the universe constituted a significant starting point. Descartes intended to treat the whole of physics in one of his first books, entitled *Traité du monde et de la lumière*, which he worked on with much enthusiasm:

> For two or three months I have been very deeply involved in the firmament; and after satisfying myself with regard to its nature and that of the stars we see there, and several other things which I had not dared hope for several years ago I have become so bold that I now dare look for the cause of the position of each fixed star. For

> even though they appear to be scattered very irregularly here and
> there in the heavens, I nevertheless have no doubt whatsoever that
> there is a natural order among them, which is regular and deter-
> mined; and the knowledge of this order is the key to and foundation
> of the highest and most perfect science that man could have . . .[59]

Descartes was aware that this task was really beyond man's power.
As he looked for works dealing with astronomy, he learned that Galileo had published his *Dialogue on the Great World Systems*, but that this
had been condemned by Rome. He immediately wrote to his friend
Mersenne for further information. Was this book condemned because
Galileo defended the heliocentric theory or for some other reason? In
the former case Descartes felt this also affected him, for the helocentric
theory formed the basis of his doctrine concerning the universe: "I
confess that if it is false, all the foundations of my philosophy are too,
for it evidently may be taken to pieces by them. And it is so closely
connected with all parts of my treatise that I would not be able to
separate it from them, without rendering the rest entirely defective.
But for nothing in the world would I wish to be responsible for a
discourse containing the slightest word that was disapproved of by
the Church, and so I prefer to suppress it than to make it appear
lame."[60] When Descartes learned that Galileo had in fact been condemned on account of his heliocentric theory, he did not hesitate to
give up his work: "I wished to suppress my treatise completely and
lose nearly four years' work, as an act of total obedience to the Church
. . ."[61] Still he continued to cherish the hope that this condemantion
would not be endorsed by the pope or a council and it would not
therefore be a question of faith. It was his hope, then, that the Church
would one day see things differently.[62] Had not the existence of an-
tipodes formerly been condemned? This theme was resumed in a later
work, *Principia philosophiae* (1644), where he gave a detailed account
of his view of the material world.[63] As to his views on this there can
be no doubt. Cartesianism was in the first place an expression of
jubilation at the wonders the new science had revealed to man and at
the power he thus acquired as "maître et possesseur de la nature."

Descartes clearly realized that this was the advent of a new era for
humankind, an era in which the natural sciences would play a fundamental role. And the natural sciences in turn would, as far as physical reality was concerned, be dominated by mathematics; by means
of mathematics the whole of physical reality would be open to man.
For only that aspect of physical reality which can be expressed in
mathematical terms merited Descartes's attention, complying with his

desire for clear and distinct ideas.[64] Where Bonaventure pleaded for a "reduction of the arts to theology" Descartes advocated a "reduction of science to mathematics."

Experience, argued Descartes, has taught us to distrust two things: the doctrine of the scholastics and the testimony of our senses. Both held that the earth was stationary and that the sun revolved around the earth. Both were mistaken. Since these sources are suspect, we cannot but doubt anything that comes from them. If we are to reach the truth we must first and foremost erase all this from our mind and then start once again from the beginning. Descartes was no skeptic, however, for he employed methodic doubt not as an end but as a condition of attaining a more reliable knowledge of reality. What he strove after was a radical break with the past, with Aristotle, Aquinas, and their disciples. The new science clearly demanded a new philosophy.

It is precisely this initial attitude of Descartres that is significant as far as our present subject is concerned. While most theologians, supported as they were by the ecclesiastical authorities, consciously aimed at continuity with the past and with scholasticism in particular, Descartes aspired after a revolution. In the course of time those who carried on the scholastic tradition were certainly prepared to make a few minor corrections in their system and, if need be, to drop all allusions to the world picture; but the system as such had to be left intact. Descartes, on the other hand, wished first and foremost to reject the system as such and, if need be, was prepared to include some elements of the earlier doctrine in his new system. These two attitudes were clearly irreconcilable and naturally clashed with each other. Despite the opposition he met, Descartes retained the hope that the Church would one day realize the need to replace scholasticism with his philosophy.

It was this threat to scholasticism that made the Dominicans and the Jesuits hostile towards his doctrine. For even though many Jesuits were friends and admirers of Descartes, how else were they to react after such a recent condemnation of the heliocentric theory and after being told to defend Aristotelian doctrine as long as possible? In 1663, thirteen years after his death, the writings of Descartes were put on the *Index*, while a royal decree forbade the teaching of his doctrine at the University of Paris. Still this did not prevent his work from becoming well known and having a profound effect. In theological circles his ideas increasingly found support, albeit with reservations. Only at the end of the seventeenth century was Cartesian doctrine introduced into Catholic universities.

In contrast to the earlier manner of thinking, whereby cosmology and natural theology were closely related—God's existence being deduced from certain properties of the cosmos such as motion, order, perfection, etc.—Descartes opted for a complete separation of cosmology and natural theology.[65] According to Descartes the idea of God is innate to the mind of man and is by no means deduced from the contemplation of the world. This immediately implies that religion has nothing to do with science and thus makes every conflict a priori impossible. It seemed, then, that without the interference of theology the natural sciences would develop freely without impeding the renewal of theology.

Once this initial standpoint had been adopted, there were two ways to proceed. One could either emphasize the natural sciences and eventually come to the position of positivism and materialism, or one could as well develop the view that the idea of God is innate, as Malebranche would do. But the drawback to this whole undertaking was that the relation between God and the world would meet with difficulties just as the relation between body and soul had become an unsolvable problem in the doctrine on man.

Descartes himself did not explicitly deal with strictly theological problems, preferring to devote himself entirely to philosophy and the natural sciences, even though he was aware that this necessarily had certain implications for theology. It seems he consciously refrained from an actual rethinking of Christianity. The same must be said of Malebranche (1638–1715), whose work belongs more to the field of philosophy than theology, despite the fact that his philosophical writings often included theological problems which were dealt with in such a way that they were organically connected with his whole work.[66] In the area of philosophy he undoubtedly established a very personal and impressive metaphysical system, characterized by the affirmation of a predominating divine causality, exclusive of any secondary causality (the *causae secundae* of the scholastics). In the strictly theological field, however, his view of Christianity was that of scholasticism, even though he combined the latter with a different metaphysical system. He was preoccupied with the medieval idea of order and this was the basis of his interpretation of Christian doctrine: God created the world in perfect order and it was, Malebranche believed, quite unthinkable that the body was not completely subject to the soul in the original creation. But sin had upset the original order.[67] It is this order which Redemption and grace aim to restore. Malebranche thus acknowledged a perfect harmony and symmetry between the natural and supernatural order, so that morality consists in respect for the order God has willed. This order is grounded in God himself and is therefore eternal and immutable.[68] To reject this idea of order is to reject the whole of Christianity, for the one is inconceivable without the other. However original Malebranche may have been in establishing a new metaphysical system, his theological conceptions were strictly medieval. There was clearly no question of a rethinking of Christianity.

A great many theologians of the seventeenth and eighteenth centuries underwent the influence of Descartes and Malebranche. In some cases, such as Thomassin or André Martin, this influence was clearly perceptible, while in other cases it was more unconscious. But it was restricted to the philosophical arsenal that was employed to support or clarify the traditional conception of Christianity. The medieval interpretation of Christianity thus continued to live on under the veneer of a new metaphysics.

Natural Religion and Theology

As we have seen, deism can be considered an attempt to devise a "natural religion," a "natural morality," and a "natural conception of God" as opposed to the religion, morality, and conception of God which appeal to Revelation. With the support of the new sciences, represented by Newton in particular, it enjoyed considerable success in the eighteenth century.[69]

What concerns us now is not so much the grounds on which Catholic theologians opposed this tendency as the extent to which deism influenced the self-understanding of the Christian in this period. Did it have the effect of urging the theologian to review his traditional system or, on the contrary, did it merely result in an even greater determination on his part to cling to the traditional interpretation of Christianity? It appears that the latter was the case and that the theologian became more convinced he was right in holding onto the medieval conception of Christianity.

It is true that the eighteenth-century theologian was thoroughly aware of the fact that the deistic conception of God only partly agreed with the picture of God which the Christian had formed on the basis of Scripture. And though he also clearly realized the dangers involved, it seemed to him that deism, in contrast to pantheism and atheism, included certain elements that were acceptable to a Christian. First there was the possibility of conceiving this natural religion and natural conception of God as an introduction to Christianity. A number of theological textbooks and treatises were written in this strain.[70] More and more people became convinced that Christianity had to be conceived as the continuation and completion of "natural" religion, whereby the difference between both was minimized and Christianity was often given a deistic turn.[71]

The particular appeal of deism in the eyes of Catholic theologians was its emphasis on the order in nature. This was familiar ground, even if the deistic concept of nature concerned the laws of the phenomena of nature and not the medieval idea of the hierarchical structure of the cosmos. At any rate the deists rejected the notion that the present situation in the world can be explained by chance and acknowledged the existence of a transcendent intelligence that had granted creation a fixed and unshakable order.[72] Far from losing significance it seemed that the concept of order actually acquired a new luster. It is understandable that Catholic theologians, who for centuries had systematized Christian doctrine around the concept of order, felt impelled in such circumstances to persevere in the same direction, particularly when the new insights appeared to confirm rather than dispute the cosmological foundation of the medieval idea of order. On the side of theology it did not occur to anyone to challenge the central position of the concept of order in the systematization of Christian doctrine. A recurrent theme in apologetical and devotional literature was that of the admirable order in nature, in which context reference was not infrequently made to the new discoveries in the field of natural science. The emergence of romanticism also favored this trend.

In this way deism helped to promote the tendency of interpreting Christianity in the traditional manner with the aid of the concept of order. But there is another reason why deism contributed to the fossilization of theology. In addition to its positive side—the attempt to draw up a natural religion—there was a negative side to deism in which it concurred with atheism and pantheism, namely, the total rejection of every form of Revelation. From the time of the Renaissance there was evidence of an anti-Christian tendency that seemed to reach its climax in the eighteenth century, when each page from the Bible, every point of doctrine, every moral precept and institution of Christian origin was subject to inexorable criticism. The attack came from all sides so that theologians were hard pressed to answer the accusations of their assailants and consequently devoted their energy to polemic rather than to a rethinking of Christian doctrine. Most theologians felt it was better to maintain and to secure the traditional interpretation of Christianity, an attitude that was coupled with a growing antiintellectualism, which was already manifest in the middle of the seventeenth century, notably in Pascal, and which intensified in the course of time, finally resulting in fideism and traditionalism at the beginning of the nineteenth century.

Just how pronounced this fideistic tendency was can be seen from Desautels's study of *Les Mémoires de Trévoux*,[73] where he shows that the contributors to this periodical clearly betrayed a deep distrust of human reason, especially in matters relating to God and religion. It was argued that God has spoken to man through Revelation precisely because human reason is unable to attain the truth in such matters. Man must therefore submit himself unconditionally to Revelation and not attempt to understand what is beyond his powers of comprehension.

Whether in a moderate or a more extreme form, the theme of the limitedness of human reason and of the sole saving power of faith is repeatedly found in this period. An example of moderate antiintellectualism is Bossuet's posthumously published work, *La Connaissance de Dieu et de soi-meme* (1722), while we find its most extreme form in Pierre-Daniel Huet's *Faiblesse de l'esprit humain* (1723). In his youth a fervent follower of Descartes, Huet was alarmed at the growth of rationalism, and gradually became a most radical opponent by developing into a systematic doctrine the theme of the powerlessness of human reason and thus the necessity for a total and blind faith. His views did not win widespread approval at the time and were mostly rejected as shortsighted and exaggerated. For many people fideism was more a general attitude of mind: one should not reflect too much on religious matters but rather content oneself with faith and submission to the Church's doctrine. It was only in the nineteenth century that it received a more theoretical formulation in the fideism and traditionalism of men like L. E. M. Bautain, A. Bonnetty, A. De Bonald and F. De Lamennais, whose views were condemned during the First Vatican Council.[74]

The intellectual climate of the eighteenth century clearly did not provide a favorable atmosphere for a renewed interpretation of Christian doctrine. Certain obstacles proved to be insuperable. Contrary to the teaching and example of the scholastics of the thirteenth century, theologians rejected any attempt at a rational reflection on faith. And this, coupled with the fact that they held on to the concept of order, did not allow for the possibility of reviewing their interpretation of Christianity.

Evolutionary Theory and Theology

The idea of the immutability of the world order and of all created beings must undoubtedly be counted among those elements from the old world picture which held out the longest. But with the emergence of evolutionary theory this final pillar of the medieval worldview was demolished, so that the cosmos was no longer seen to display a fixed and unchangeable order to which man had unconditionally to submit himself.

Theologians were initially hostile towards Darwin's theory. It is true that during the second half of the nineteenth century and the first decades of the twentieth century there was no lack of intellectuals who endeavored to convince their fellow believers that evolutionary theory was indeed correct and that there was no need to fear it. One of the first to declare that he consciously ranged himself on the side of Darwin and could see no reason at all why his theory should be thought contrary to Christian dogma was J.H. Newman.[75] In spite of such efforts, and those of others like M. D. Leroy,[76] P. Zahm,[77] H. De Dorlodot,[78] and Jean D'Estienne[79] to allay the fears of Christians, the ecclesiastical authorities as well as the vast majority of theologians had a deep distrust of evolutionism. During a provincial council held in Cologne in 1860 the German bishops declared that the theory which explained the origination of the human body by evolution from the higher species of animals was contrary to Scripture and had to be rejected as irreconcilable with Christian doctrine.[80] The First Vatican Council (1870) confined itself to the rather banal principle that there could be no essential contradiction between faith and science, while the most authoritative theologians of the day, G. Perrone, C. Mazella, B. Jungmann, J. Katschaler, M. Scheeben, H. Huster, and others, totally rejected the idea that the human body originated by evolution and considered this theory heretical. Even until the 1930s there were theologians who defended the thesis that the human body was directly created by God.[81] Though evolutionism was never explicitly condemned, an atmosphere was nevertheless created in Catholic circles that was hostile towards the theory of evolution, particularly with regard to the origin of man. An attempt was made by Monseigneur Benigni to have evolutionism officially condemned but was prevented by the timely intervention of Cardinals Ehrle, Mercier, Bourne, and Maffi.[82] The doctrine of *humani generis* (1950) can be summarized as follows: the problem of the origin of the human body may, with the necessary caution, be further investigated; man's soul is directly created by God; so provisionally at least, monogeny ought to be maintained. A pamphlet written by C. Muller as an attempt to give a wider interpretation to the views expressed in this encyclical was put on the Index.[83]

This conflict was for a long time the cause of much turbulence. Science, philosophy, and theology were combined in the most unfortunate manner whereby both the scientist and the theologian often went beyond their own competency. As far as the theologians were concerned, evolutionism was often seen as a theory devised to undermine religion and Christianity. Ernst Haeckel (1834–1919) declared that the theory of evolution would signify a deathblow to Christianity. For some time, then, the whole problem was approached almost exclusively from an apologetical standpoint, so that instead of stimulating new reflection of Christian doctrine it actually favored a fossilization of the old positions.

The intellectual climate of the Catholic universities and seminaries during the last decades of the nineteenth century is clearly exemplified by the views of an authoritative theologian at the Gregorian University. In the preface to his *De Deo creante praelectiones scholastico dogmaticae*,[84] C. Mazella (d. 1900) declares that he has consulted not only the Fathers of the Church and earlier theologians but also the scientists of his day, not so much out of interest for science as to combat with appropriate means the abuse that had been made of the natural science.[85] Owing to his scholastic prejudices his attitude remains avowedly hostile. The same arguments are repeatedly advanced: it is only a question of unproved hypotheses, authors contradicting each other, and so forth, while scholasticism is presented as the only reliable doctrine. As to the creation of the world, Mazella holds that the "six days" of the Mosaic creation story can perhaps be conceived as "six periods" (Concordism), but his preference is for the former view.[86] Evolutionism finds no favor in his eyes and he accepts the archaic view that humankind has existed between five and seven thousand years.[87] What he regards as most certainly true, however, is that man—both body and soul—is directly created by God.[88] And to prove the old thesis that the entire cosmos has been created for man, he quotes a text of Aquinas in which the motion of the heavenly bodies is said to be aimed at the coming-to-be of plants and animals: and these are created for man. Man is thus the goal of the motion of the heavenly bodies.[89] Mazella finally refers to the pronouncement of Pius IX that it is an error to claim that the method and principles of scholasticism are not adapted to the demands of modern science.[90]

The theological textbooks of the period were plainly prejudiced against the theory of evolution, which was considered as a threat to faith and thus had to be vehemently opposed. Periodicals and popular writings also waged war against the new views.[91] With the revival of scholasticism there appeared to be an unconscious desire to maintain the spirit of the old world picture in theology, so that anyone who advocated the theory of evolution was immediately suspect and often prevented from teaching theology. It was not until the middle of the twentieth century that there was visible sign of change, despite the fact that Cardinal Ruffini published a book as late as 1948 opposing evolutionism, especially with regard to the human body.[92] Several years earlier, in 1941, Pius XII had claimed there was still no proof that the human body had originated from animal ancestors, and that only further investigations could throw light on this matter.[93] Any theologian favoring evolutionism at that time had therefore to take many precautions to avoid difficulties with the ecclesiastical authorities. There was nevertheless clear evidence of change. It was gradually acknowledged that there were no theological objections to the theory of evolution.[94] But as there was still no real attempt to rethink Christian doctrine in the light of these newly acquired insights, the scholastic interpretation of faith prevailed.

Summary

We have seen how medieval theology interpreted Christian doctrine within the framework of the world picture of the time and how a central role was played here by the concept of hierarchical order. God had created all things in perfect order: this order had been disrupted by sin but was restored by Christ's redemptive work. All this was fully intelligible so long as the same world picture served as a background to theology and the culture as a whole.

What is surprising, however, is that Catholic theologians continued to defend the medieval interpretation of Christian doctrine long after the world picture from which it derived its credibility had been discarded by the discoveries of the natural sciences. Apart from a natural conservatism characteristic of many ecclesiastical authorities and monastic communities, there was a quite understandable concern to preserve the traditional interpretation of Christianity, which appeared to many to belong to the very content of faith—or at any rate, to be so closely related to it that a separation would inevitably lead to faith itself being undermined. Moreover, now that Christianity seemed to be threatened on all sides, there appeared to be more urgent matters to attend to than a quiet reflection on Christian doctrine. Finally, it cannot be denied that the condemnation of the heliocentric world system by the highest authorities in the Church greatly impeded theologians, especially during the seventeenth century, and made them even more convinced that it was better in such circumstances to hold onto earlier positions.

However one might wish to account for the attitude of Catholic theologians, the fact remains that, apart from allusions to the world picture, the interpretation that theologians of the eighteenth and nineteenth centuries gave to Christianity was practically identical to that of the thirteenth century. The principle of order, derived from belief in a perfectly ordered world—an expression of God's supreme will—continued to dominate this interpretation of faith, even when development in the natural sciences had shown such a principle to be completely meaningless. Pius XII's last Christmas message (1957) is a case in point.[95] Detailed consideration is given to "the universal world order": God is said to have created the world in a state of perfect order and harmony so that a supreme and eternal law is to be found in all things.[96] Though the sin of Adam has upset this order and harmony, a return to the original state is possible and necessary.[97] The end of the world is moreover referred to as the day of the universal return to the original state.[98]

What, then, is the task of the Christian in such a world? In the first place, says Pius XII, the Christian has to love and admire this world order and proclaim it everywhere.[99] The divine world order must then be defended and it is the right and obligation of all Christians to see that it remains intact. For it is not sufficient for them to delight in the contemplation of the beauty of the world. They are called to continuous action in all areas of life and it is therefore their indefensible right to intervene in worldly affairs when it is a question of defending the divine world order.[100] The order and harmony in the world must be treated with absolute respect[101] and should form the starting point of all human activity and the framework within which it takes place.[102]

What is remarkable is that there is no mention here as to what constitutes this important order. It is also striking that Pius XII describes his picture of the world as "the *Christian* concept of the cosmos,"[103] without making clear the grounds on which this assertion is based. The question can rightly be raised whether such a world picture is not more appropriate to Plato than to the Bible, for the existence of a "perfect" world order is hardly mentioned in Scripture. Such a view at any rate belongs to the Middle Ages and not to the world in which we now live.[104]

Our survey of the period from the first half of the seventeenth century until the middle of the twentieth century reveals that the interpretation of Christian doctrine, both from the most authoritative theologians and in theological instruction in general, remained fundamentally the same as that of the thirteenth century. The only difference is that the world picture that was central to the medieval world of thought gradually disappeared. For the rest there were few changes. The result was, of course, an antiquated theology that became more and more estranged from the world.

It is precisely in the concept of hierarchical order that this fossilization process can clearly be seen. What was once an imaginative concept that stimulated man's intellectual, moral, and political activity, was on account of the new view of the cosmos gradually deprived of its intrinsic value, and it finally became a meaningless notion incapable of evoking a response in modern man.

Part Three

THE CONTEMPORARY WORLD PICTURE AND THEOLOGY

The theme of Cosmology, which is the basis of
all religions, is the story of the dynamic effort
of the World passing into everlasting unity, and
of the static majesty of God's vision, accomplishing
its purpose of completion by absorption of the
World's multiplicity of effort.

Alfred North Whitehead

A new day seems to be dawning in religious thought,
which for several centuries has been struggling to
free itself from the intellectual chains in which
Aristotelian and so-called Platonic or neo-Platonic
influences have long held it confined.

Charles Hartshorne

The outstanding achievement of medieval theology was its remarkable synthesis of Christianity and the then generally accepted world picture, whereby cosmology and Christian doctrine were seen to form a perfectly balanced whole that was thoroughly credible in the eyes of intellectuals as well as the ordinary faithful. With the downfall of the medieval world picture, however, this favorable situation, as far as Christianity was concerned, was brought to an end. But even though the rejection of the old picture of the universe paved the way for a totally new interpretation of reality, theologians were, as we have seen, most reluctant to accept the challenge that was now presented to them. After a futile attempt to preserve the medieval world picture, they devoted their energy to rescuing as much of the old picture as could be saved. The medieval theological system was therefore retained but without the cosmological background from which it had previously derived a great deal of its vitality, so that theology gradually became estranged from the world, as the gulf between faith and modern culture became increasingly wider.

The philosophers of the Enlightenment are said to have had the feeling that their age was totally different from anything that had previously been known.[1] Might the same not be said of our age—and with even greater justification? For as a result of the achievements in the natural and the human sciences we see ourselves and our place in the world in an entirely different perspective than that of any previous age.

Theological thought clearly cannot fail to be influenced by this cultural climate. What is urgently required is a renewed reflection on

Christian doctrine, the more so because of the lack of normal development in the theology of the preceding centuries. A living theology, as has repeatedly been said, constantly moves between two poles: the lasting data of faith on the one hand and the changing cultural situation on the other.[2] Theology can thus be described as a dialogue in the consciousness of the believer between his religious aspirations and his experience of reality. At the present time speculative theology is thoroughly aware of this situation. Its major concern is to give careful consideration to contemporary images of man and of the world in interpreting Christian doctrine, and in this sense it is a continuation of what was striven after by the theologians of the thirteenth century.

This immediately gives rise to the question of precisely what we understand by the contemporary world picture. To answer this question we must carefully consider what philosophy and the natural sciences have to say on this matter. Leaving aside the question of whether the term "world picture" still has a concrete content, we shall in any case have to make a clear distinction between the significance attached to the term "world" in the natural sciences and in existential phenomenology. This will be dealt with in chapter seven.

Of the many attempts in recent times to construct a more coherent view of man and of the world, the contribution of Teilhard de Chardin merits particular attention, not only because his views met with a wide response but also because he was explicitly concerned with the problem of the relation between our world picture and theology. Chapter eight will therefore be devoted to a more detailed consideration of his ideas on this matter.

In the final chapter of this book we shall examine from a more general standpoint the problems which the contemporary view of man and of the world raises for theology. The medieval interpretation of faith, so closely related to the then generally accepted world picture, is clearly no longer acceptable to the contemporary Christian. It would seem that a period in Christian history, which has to a great extent been dominated by Greek thought, has now been brought to an end and any attempt to maintain this situation is bound to fail. There is, moreover, no sense in bemoaning what has been lost.[3] Only renewed reflection on the enduring value of the Gospel message can give new support to the believer and at the same time open the way to the future for Christianity.

Chapter Seven

THE 'WORLD' IN PHILOSOPHY AND IN THE NATURAL SCIENCES

The terms "world" and "world picture" are used frequently today. Besides the many introductions to "the world picture of the natural sciences," we find philosophers arguing that we are essentially involved in the world and that the present age is "the age of the world picture."[1] During the second half of the twentieth century, the way we think about the world has undergone a profound change, as significant, if not more so, as that which took place in the days of Galileo and Newton. With the progress of the natural sciences, many new facts have come to light concerning the properties and structure of matter and the origin and development of life, as well as the dimensions and structure of the universe, in comparison with which all previous views appear to be fanciful ideas. From all these new discoveries a totally new view of matter, life, and man have gradually developed which could conveniently be called the world picture of the natural sciences. But the results that were thus achieved also raised a number of questions. For in spite of all our efforts not only is our knowledge of the world still extremely limited, disclosing a great many gaps and uncertainties, but, moreover, the question has increasingly been raised in scientific circles as to the actual value of the scientific approach to reality. Critical reflection on the method and results of the natural sciences has thus compelled us to define more closely the limits of scientific knowledge and to be aware of its relativity.

In the philosophical literature of our age the term "world" has acquired a meaning that differs profoundly from its usual meaning in the natural sciences. Since the time of Edmund Husserl (1859–1938) philosophy has become increasingly interested in the study of the prescientific "life-world" (Lebenswelt) in which man lives as a conscious being and with which he is inseparably connected.[2] The life-world is said to be prescientific not only because it precedes the scientific investigation of nature but also because the latter is only possible on the basis of our ordinary experience of the world. The relation between the "subjective" world in which we live as conscious beings and the "objective" world, which the natural sciences strive after, forms one of the most important problems of contemporary philosophy.[3] The world of everyday experience displays different structures, properties, and dimensions in space and time than those with which the natural sciences are concerned. It is, therefore, of utmost importance that both these concepts be clearly distinguished. We shall now briefly consider each of these in turn, without losing sight of the connection between them.

The World Picture of the Natural Sciences

In the course of the past centuries scholars have brought to light a great number of phenomena, devising many theories to explain these phenomena and to show how they are interrelated. The question immediately arises as to what extent all this can be united to form a coherent whole, in such a manner that we can speak of a scientific world picture. Is there such a thing as a scientific world picture? In his discussions with Rudolph Bultmann, Karl Jaspers dismissed the possibility on principle.[4] What concerns us here is not whether the discussion is due to a misunderstanding of Bultmann's meaning but whether the expression "scientific world picture" can be used meaningfully and what content can be given to this concept.

Let us first see what the expression "scientific world picture" does not mean. It clearly cannot mean that the natural sciences are capable of giving us a complete picture of reality. What we possess is limited information concerning a limited number of aspects of reality. Concerning reality as a whole, however, we are almost completely ignorant. For this reason we are sometimes inclined to say that the concept "the world in its totality" belongs more to the sphere of mysticism than to that of the natural sciences.

Yet we are not dealing here with a purely factual impossibility but rather with what is in principle impossible, originating from the very nature of the scientific method. It is true that from time immemorial man has endeavored to see the world as an ordered whole in which everything had its proper place. With the emergence of science this dream was by no means destroyed. On the contrary, the hope was cherished that ultimately the whole of reality, in every detail, would be made visible for our comprehension. The Greek philosophers had formulated this hope and expectation in a striking manner when they proposed the ideal that our mind should reflect the total world order. And according to the French positivist Berthelot, there were no longer any mysteries but only problems that would eventually be solved, so that we would in the course of time be able to explain the world and human existence in a satisfactory manner. Today, however, scientists wonder whether such an expectation does not belong to the realm of illusion. For experience shows that each new discovery gives rise to further problems that are increasingly more difficult to solve. Moreover, in science everything is open to revision. What was once held to be certain can be cancelled by new discoveries. The history of science reveals a constant iconoclasm, a continually returning revolution, relating not only to restricted parts but to whole areas of science.[5] It is precisely in this permanent self-criticism, the constant questioning of results that have been achieved, that we find the strength and the principle itself of the scientific method. No result can be regarded as final. For this reason it would be an illusion to think that the natural sciences can ever give a definitive picture of reality as a whole.

Furthermore, the expression "scientific world picture" cannot mean that science can achieve a completely objective picture of reality. Again this is not just a matter of circumstances or the inadequacy of scientific instruments, but concerns the very nature of scientific procedure. However one looks at the matter, science is always the work of people and this implies that the subjective element cannot be eliminated. The reality which science lets us see is reality as seen through the eyes of man. With the help of scientific method we question nature and if we are persistent we receive an answer. But we never fully succeed in removing the subjective element, for it is ultimately man who always raises the questions and there is nothing or no one to guarantee that the questions are right. Scholars such as Werner Heisenberg and C. P. von Weizsäcker have rightly argued that what we see in the constructs of science is more a reflection of the human mind than of nature.

The fact that science involves the cooperation of man and nature has led some theoreticians to accentuate man's role to such an extent that it completely outweighs nature's part, which is reduced to a minimum. This view is held, for example, by advocates of instrumentalism like S. Toulmin, F. P. Ramsey, and G. Ryle. Generally influenced by analytic philosophy, they regard scientific theories, laws, and concepts as mere instruments or useful fictions, which enable the scientist to find his way in the chaos of phenomena and to predict some future phenomena, so that he acquires a certain power over them. Man's part receives even greater emphasis from advocates of idealism (Eddington, Jeans, Milne, and the Neo-Kantians Cassirer and Margenau) for whom science is only a construct of the mind which we spread over reality like a web. According to Eddington, science follows footprints in the sand of phenomena and comes to the discovery that these are our own footprints. "The mind may be regarded as regaining from nature that which the mind has put into nature." Over against this radical emphasis on the subjective element in science we find "realists" like Planck, Einstein, Campbell, Whitehead, the Neo-Thomists, and Nagel and Smart, defending the priority of the objective element. Though the description of reality offered by science is partly a creation of man, it is equally true that the world as such does not lend itself to every arbitrary description. There is a reality which precedes human perception. The convergent character of scientific theories can only be accounted for if we acknowledge the influence of objective reality on our thought and perception. It appears reasonable, therefore, to say that a real encounter takes place in science between man and nature, in which both play a positive role and make an essential contribution, however one might assess their mutual share.[6]

From what we have seen it is evident that the possibility of a scientific world picture is closely related to the question of what value is attributed to the findings of science from an epistemological point of view. In any case it is clear that a naive realism must make room for critical reflection on the degree of objectivity that can be ascribed to scientific insights.

Thus by "scientific world picture" we do not mean that present-day science makes it possible for us to grasp and to form a clear picture of the whole of reality; neither do we mean that every subjective element can be eliminated from our picture of the universe. Finally, this expression does not mean that we ascribe an absolute and definitive value to the results of the natural sciences. For it is the nature of science to look out for new possibilities and in this way it shares in the historicity of human existence. It is not inconceivable that contemporary science will in ages to come be looked down upon just as we look down upon the science of the Greeks or of the Middle Ages. When, therefore, we speak today about the world picture of the natural sciences, it is with the necessary modesty and the awareness of the limitations and relativity of our knowledge, however much we may rejoice about the progress that has been made in all fields by the efforts of scientists in the course of the last centuries. But this confronts us with another question. Is it conceivable that the science of the future will reject our vision of the universe as radically as we reject the medieval world picture? We can readily accept that our worldview be supplemented or corrected in certain parts. We witness new discoveries every day. These, however, are an extension of what is already known, signifying a supplement or correction and by no means a destruction of the fundamental principles on which science is based. Is it conceivable that these basic principles and the most fundamental insights of our physics, chemistry, astronomy, biology, etc. will one day also be found to be wrong? We are of course inclined to think that such a thing is utterly impossible, for the simple reason that these insights are rooted in experience and are repeatedly confirmed by countless observations. It seems totally unthinkable that we would be mistaken. But the question remains whether man will not one day view things in a different perspective and reach a different view of reality than that with which we are familiar. We attempt to understand the world and to explain phenomena. What does it mean to understand something, to explain something? Opinions on this matter have changed radically in the course of history. In Greek antiquity and in the Middle Ages it was thought that one had explained something when its essence or nature had been clearly formulated so that the thing or being in question could be situated in the general world order. With Galileo and Descartes another view emerged: to explain something meant to measure, weigh, and compare. The whole of reality was immediately described with mathematical formulae. One was thought to have explained something when one was able to define its properties in an exact manner.

In course of time to explain something came to mean: to analyze in detail, to trace its last components. Yet another meaning was acquired when the historical dimension of nature came more into the foreground: to explain meant to bring to light the origin and history of a particular phenomenon. It was thought, for example, that man had been explained when one had described his origin and evolution. In the light of these changes who is to say that a different attitude of mind cannot tomorrow lead to an entirely new conception of "understanding" and "explanation"?

We have so far attempted to indicate the limits within which the use of the expression "scientific world picture" or "world picture of the natural sciences" ought to be situated. It cannot mean that we possess an all-embracing picture of reality; nor that our picture has any claim to absolute objectivity or an unassailable and definitive validity. But within these limits there is still an entire area that is open for our observation. However limited our possibilities, we cannot help thinking about the universe and reflecting on our place in the world around us. For our existence as conscious beings is simply inconceivable, detached from the world to which we are intrinsically related. The natural sciences, which are but a particular manifestation of our essential involvement in the world, have revealed important aspects of reality of which we were previously unaware and which have considerably influenced not only our actions but also our self-understanding. Bearing in mind the limitations we mentioned above, we can say that the term "scientific world picture" denotes the totality of these aspects which the natural sciences have disclosed to us.[7]

There is a tendency among many authors to focus almost entirely on theoretical physics in attempting to define the concept of world picture, since this is where the experimental mathematical ideal of the natural sciences was most recently extended.[8] This view is defensible but can lead to a certain one-sidedness, because the contribution of the biological sciences to the formation of our world picture can thus easily be overlooked—a contribution that is by no means inconsiderable and reveals essential aspects of reality not accessible to theoretical physics. Julian Huxley is surely right, then, when he wonders whethers we should not rather assign a central position to the study of evolution.[9]

But what of the contemporary view of the world? What positive content can be given to this concept? It would of course be meaningless to attempt to enumerate the conclusions and results to which the study of nature has led us in the last couple of centuries. We shall therefore try to synthesize the central ideas which we can reasonably expect to be confirmed in the further development of the natural sciences. Science is not a static phenomenon, but a dynamic one. More important than the results achieved at a particular moment, is the direction in which scientific investigation evolves and the trend which thus becomes visible. The medieval world picture was characterized by the idea of a perfect, immutable, and hierarchical world order. So what basic ideas, we might ask, are suggested by the insights we have now acquired concerning the nature and development of the reality surrounding us? From the scientific activity of the last couple of centuries there seem to be three fundamental characteristics of our experience of the world. Reality appears to be boundless, dynamic and organic, and the further science advances, the more visible the boundless, dynamic, and organic character of the cosmos seems to be. Let us now consider the precise meaning of these concepts.

The Boundless Universe

The natural sciences have undoubtedly widened our view in all directions—space and time, the infinitely great and infinitely small, the past and the future—to such an extent that we no longer hope to reach a limit in any direction. The ancients and medieval man believed the cosmos to form a closed space, surrounded by the sphere of fixed stars. Only at the end of the sixteenth century was this mistake realized and since then the spheres gradually disappeared from the human conception of the universe. In the eighteenth and nineteenth centuries we were proud of having investigated the solar system and having started the study of the galactic system. Not until the twentieth century did we discover extra galactic spiral nebulae, whose existence had already been supposed by Herschel in the eighteenth century. As our observations progress, we are more inclined to suspect that we live in a boundless universe. With the aid of enormous telescopes a space of two billion light years is covered, while with the aid of radio-telescopes, waves have been received whose source is as much as eight billion light years away. But who can say that we have reached the ends of the universe? Is it at all meaningful to speak in this way, unless in the sense intended by what Einstein called the cosmos?

The inability to reach the ends of the universe implies that we are incapable of determining our place in the universe and of answering the question whether we are near the center or the edge of the cosmos. In contrast to previous ages when there was a general feeling of security in a well-ordered world, man now feels completely lost in a boundless universe in which he does not seem to belong and which offers no support on which to base his existence.

It is likewise impossible for man to situate himself in time. We stand between the past and the future, but how far do the past and the future extend? The world was once thought to have been created about the year 4004 B.C. Now we wonder whether we can rightly speak of a beginning. The earth is about 4.5 billion years old, but the cosmos as a whole is much older. On the basis of our relative knowledge of the past, we can also hazard a guess about the future. This, however, does not lead us very far, so that we once again have to acknowledge our ignorance.

Our first impression on becoming fully conscious of the dimensions of the cosmos is that of being lost in the infinity of space and time. Confronted with the new world picture we immediately raise the question whether we are the only inhabitants of this mysterious universe. Is there no life, no human being to be found on other planets, with whom we could sooner or later enter into conversation and in this way feel less abandoned in the deadly loneliness surrounding us?

On this matter we have no more than vague suppositions. In our solar system no proof has so far been found for the existence of life on planets other than earth. But certain indications have recently been found that chemical processes have taken place elsewhere bearing a similarity to those which most probably led to the emergence of life on earth. In the Murray Meteorite (Kentucky, 1950) and the Murchison Meteorite (Australia, 1969) eighteen amino acids were found, which according to the theory of A. I. Oparin and J. B. S. Haldane played a role in the chemical processes that led to the origin of life on earth. And in the Orgueil Meteorite (France, 1864), which was only recently analyzed by a NASA team, six amino acids were found, relating to forms of life.[10] These meteorites are supposed to be 4.5 billion years old and to have come from the zone of Asteroids (between Mars and Jupiter). According to Oparin and Haldane, lightning or sunlight in an atmosphere of methane, ammonia, hydrogen, and other gases produced amino acids, which in turn led to the origin of life.

But traces of life are also sought outside our solar system. Plans are now being made to use radio-telescopes to pick up any possible signals from space that could come from intelligent beings. Half of the five hundred stars nearest to us appear to have planets and it is as good as certain that in each of these solar systems there is at least one planet in the zone where life similar to ours could be found. It is also of interest to note that Leonid N. Wellachew, of the Meudon observatory and the California Institute of Technology, has recently shown the presence of a hydroxyl group (OH) in extragalactic space. Very complex chemical processes, such as those that contributed to the origin of life on earth, have repeatedly been found to be present in our galaxy.

The question as to the existence of life on other planets is closely connected with the way one explains the origin of life on earth. There are two conflicting views on this matter. Some claim that it is mainly to be attributed to chance. It was, they argue, only by a most rare coincidence that the relevant chemical processes were brought about. Moreover, in the further development of life, which is chiefly governed by an inevitable regularity, there were several purely accidental changes. Man is the result of the interplay of chance and necessity, and should therefore be considered a rare exception, as an anomaly in the universe. Such a view can hardly include belief in the existence of life on other planets, because it is most improbable that there would be a repetition of what happened on earth.

Others, on the contrary, see life as an almost natural development of forces contained in matter. By virtue of its inner dynamic matter seems to be aimed at the formation of complex chemical processes which, when circumstances are favorable, have led in turn to the emergence of life. That is not to say, however, that accidental circumstances had no part in bringing about these complex processes and in the further development of higher forms of life through the mechanism of mutations and natural selection. It is a question of a more precise definition of the concept "chance." Chance ought then to be considered not so much as the negation of causality but as a more complex form of causality, which can be further analyzed with the help of statistics. On the other hand, one should bear in mind that the concepts "chance" and "finality" are not necessarily contradictory: something can be discovered or realized by chance despite the fact that it was consciously striven after. Sufficient examples of this are to be found in the history of the natural sciences, which can serve as an analogy here. It would seem that nature was driven to develop continually new forms of life, but that the emergence of these new forms was partly determined by fortuitous circumstances. If one regards life on earth as a "normal" consequence of forces in nature, one will readily accept the probability of life on all planets where the requisite chemical and climatological conditions are to be found. But that is not to say that primitive forms of life, had they already appeared elsewhere, must necessarily have led to the origin of humanoids. Distinguished scholars such as G. G. Simpson and T. Dobzhansky have rightly rejected such a view as unscientific, while J. C. Eccles considers the existence of humanoids on other planets as practically impossible.[11] There is, as Schroedinger remarked, no audience to attend the human drama. Reconnaissance flights outside our solar system seem to be completely out of the question and as to the picking up of signals, there has so far been no result.

As science now stands we are assigned to hypotheses, each of which has its adherents. In the meantime we are condemned to "cosmic solitude" and with Eddington we can ask whether nature, which allows millions of acorns to come into being to make one oak, might not also have called to existence countless spiral nebulae to let one planet in each fully develop . . .[12]

The Dynamic Universe

Contemporary cosmography points to a world in which man feels completely alone in an infinity of space and time. Further analysis reveals that this world is subject to motion and change. Whereas previous ages believed in a static, immutable world order in which everything had its fixed place from the beginning, man has now been astonished by the discovery that the entire cosmos is involved in a gigantic historical process.

Our view of the cosmos has been revolutionized by the discovery of time as a constitutive element of reality, possibly even more so than by the discovery of the dimension of space. The universe now appears as a four-dimensional continuum. Each phenomenon in the universe, each aspect of reality, has a history and cannot be understood without taking into account its historical origin and development. The atoms, stars and planets, life, plants, animals, and men—all have their history. All that we perceive today is the (provisional) result of a complex historical evolution, so that the universe now appears to consist of events rather than things or beings.

The word "history" is used here in a wide sense. Under the influence of Hegel, there are those who prefer to ascribe history only to man, since he alone consciously experiences and makes history. In a wider sense, however, history is present wherever something "happens," so that we can rightly speak of the history of nature.[13] Criticizing Hegel, Marx claimed that the history of man must be considered part of the history of nature.[14] That does not mean that there is no difference between the history of man and, for example, that of atoms or plants. History displays different properties in each sphere of reality and consequently there are important differences to be found in the concept of history. Nevertheless, there is a common content in that the term "history" points to the dimension of time that is present in all beings and phenomena without exception.

What we have said about history equally applies to the term "evolution," which is often used to denote the historical process in which all things are involved. Strictly speaking, this term belongs to biology, where it designates the mutations that have in the course of time taken place in the morphology of living beings. In a wider sense the word evolution is often used to describe certain changes that occur in the material world or in the world of mind. One can thus speak of the evolution of a spiral nebula or the evolution of an idea.[15] The evolution of life can therefore be seen as part of a wider evolution comprising the whole of reality.

The natural sciences have, as we said, made us particularly sensitive to the historical or evolutive aspect of reality. That does not imply that we are familiar with all aspects of the development of the cosmos, of life, and of man. But although many problems have yet to be resolved, the evidence we possess is such that no one would think of defending the earlier view concerning the immutability of things.

Cosmogony is a relatively new science and has only recently come to reflect on its basic principles and method.[16] We still do not have a generally accepted and completely satisfactory theory of the origin of the universe, even though one has to admit that such a theory does seem to be more and more within our reach and that there is a growing unanimity among scholars. Shortly before his death Einstein declared that everyone has his own cosmology and who can say that his is the correct one.[17]

Einstein himself was critical of all theories that were proposed, both the earlier theories of Weyl and Eddington and the hypothesis of the expanding universe of Friedmann, Lemaitre, and the later Eddington. He also rejected Milne's kinetic relativity as well as the more recent theories of Jordan, Bondi, and Fred Hoyle, which appealed to a static model where there was continuous creation of new matter.[18] In recent years the theories of Milne and Bondi-Hoyle have been increasingly abandoned in favor of the "big bang" theory, which most scholars at present prefer to any other cosmogonic model. Each science is of course open to revision if new facts are discovered. The latest findings seem, however, to point in the direction of the "big bang" theory.[19]

Besides giving us a plausible explanation for well-known phenomena of nature such as the origin of cosmic rays, the formation of atoms, the motion of spiral nebulae, etc., this theory also opens up tremendous perspectives for our understanding of the universe, because it implies the possibility of an alternately expanding and contracting universe, with the result that our present cosmos must be regarded as a phase in a process in which the explosion and reconstruction of the primeval atom can be repeated an infinite number of times. This is doubtless only a speculative hypothesis that can neither be proved nor refuted, but it ought nevertheless to be taken into consideration.[20]

We have thus come to see the cosmos as a gigantic historical process. But this process involves other phenomena which we are accustomed to classifying under physics, chemistry, or astronomy. Life originated on earth and has manifested itself in countless forms. This origin and development of the phenomena of life ought also to be considered part of cosmic evolution, which thus received a new dimension, as it were, gradually leading to the most astounding phenomenon in the cosmos: the awakening of consciousness and of freedom. With the origin of the phenomena of life, a series of processes started whose properties, however much they were also rooted in matter, differed profoundly from all that had hitherto appeared. We do not, it is true, have a completely satisfactory explanation for the way in which the first phenomena of life arose from "lifeless" matter. But there is no longer any real doubt that the necessary conditions for the origin of life were gradually realized in the material world by a number of physicochemical processes, so that the boundaries between the living and the lifeless became increasingly indistinct.[21]

Concerning the development of life on earth there are three fundamental questions that can be raised. The first is whether the forms of life have originated by "evolution," that is, whether species are immutable or have altered in the course of time. If the latter is the case, the question arises as to how this process actually evolved, in other words, whether we can describe the history of life on earth. Finally, there remains the difficult question concerning the mechanism of evolution: to which factors can the origin of new species be ascribed?

As to the first question, science answers in the affirmative. It is difficult to think of a biologist still doubting the historical fact of evolution. Evolution cannot, it is true, be called a scientific fact in the strict sense of the word, because it is not capable of being repeated and cannot be directly observed. But since the data of paleontology, biological geography, genetics, embryology, and other sciences point in this direction, it has become really impossible to doubt the historical fact of evolution. As far as the actual course of evolution is concerned, scholars are agreed on the main features of the process. There are undoubtedly many gaps in our knowledge of this area, but new discoveries continue to fill these gaps, basically confirming again and again what we already know.[22]

With regard to the mechanism of evolution there is general agreement that evolution is an extremely complex process that cannot be explained by any one factor but is rather the result of a number of interrelated factors such as mutation, selection, genetic and geographical isolation, etc. The "synthetic theory" is by far the most popular among biologists. For several years, however, doubt has arisen concerning the thesis that "accidental mutations plus natural selection" offer a complete explanation for the phenomenon of evolution, and distinguished scholars such as Bertalanffy, Waddington, and Whyte have raised the question whether there are no other, more fundamental factors involved. There is in any case no completely satisfactory explanation for the way in which the forms of life have originated.

This is particularly valid as far as man is concerned. For he is by no means an immutable being that was at a given moment introduced from without but is rather the product of the evolutionary process, and is closely connected with the material and living world which preceded him. Such then is the manner in which he was prepared for the power that was revealed in him, a power we could not previously detect and which in the course of time changed the face of our earth. In whatever direction we look we observe motion, change, development, and the emergence of new phenomena and new beings. All aspects or our world picture have clearly acquired a dynamic character.

The Organic Universe

The third distinctive property of the contemporary world picture is its organic character. This term can perhaps lead to some misunderstanding as a consequence of the fact that the development in cosmology has been described as "a mechanization of the world picture." Reference has already been made to the work of Dijksterhuis, which bears this title and is undoubtedly intended to emphasize that, since Newton, our picture of the universe has been characterized by regularity.[23] To this it can be objected that medieval writers often compared the universe to a gigantic machine, describing it as the "world machine," while contemporary science, on the contrary, seems to emphasize the organic coherence of all phenomena of nature. In both cases it is, of course, a question of analogy. Does the unity of the cosmos bear more resemblance to the unity we find in a machine or to that of an organism? A machine is artificially assembled after all its parts have been individually prepared, whereas an organism develops from within, gradually producing its various parts from the initial germ. The idea of evolution makes us see the world as involved in a gigantic process in which new phenomena are continually brought into existence and can be explained by previous conditions. In this sense we can rightly describe our world picture as organic.

The physical world already appears as a coherent whole and not at all as a loose collection of autonomous entities. All things are seen to be interconnected and governed by the same principle of order that manifests itself in an infinite variety of ways. It is only within the totality of the system and in total dependence on it that the various individual physical entities are brought about.[24] This impression of organic coherence becomes even more vivid when we look at living things. Here also we see clearly how the whole develops from its parts, which are in turn totally dependent on the whole, whether it be on the level of the individual and of the species or of the world in its totality. Even more than in the material world, we observe a perfect example of dynamic coherence, a continuous process of development and breakdown, decay and renewal, stability and change. What we find, then, is essentially an area of dynamic unity in which nothing is static, uniform, and undifferentiated, but in which all motion and change is aimed at order and coherence.[25]

The cosmos thus appears to be a coherent whole in which all things are interconnected and nothing can be considered a detached and autonomous being—a coherent whole which, by virtue of its inner coherence, suggests a still deeper and more mysterious order.[26] That is not to say that this organic unity is everywhere transparent and unproblematic. In the present state of the natural sciences it is more a question of a postulate than a clearly demonstrable fact—but, however, a postulate whose fruitfulness is confirmed each day by new discoveries and without which our science would be inconceivable.

There are two areas in particular in which this postulated unity of our world picture still poses a problem for contemporary science. The first concerns the connection between matter and life, and the second, the relation between matter and mind. We have already touched on the connection between matter and life when we established that though the problem of the origin of life had not been completely resolved, we nevertheless had the impression of being very near to a solution, so that we could, without fear of being mistaken, already speak of an actual transition from "lifeless" matter to the primary forms of life. As to the further development of life, such progress has been made in recent times, particularly in the field of molecular biology, that the connection between matter and life has become more evident than was hitherto known.[27] We may rightly raise the question of to what extent we are still justified in making a radical distinction between lifeless and living matter. In ordinary language we undoubtedly distinguish clearly between "dead" matter and material things on the one hand, and living beings, plants, animals, and man on the other hand. But is there a clearly demonstrable boundary between them? Does there not seem to be a gradual transition from the one to the other, so that we must think more in terms of continuity rather than of a distinction?

The relation between matter and mind is a somewhat different question. Where one previously spoke of a radical distinction, we are now more inclined to think that they are closely related. But how are we to conceive of this relation? This problem has always given rise to the most divergent views and is still far from being resolved. Since the advent of evolutionism the traditional problem of the relation between matter and mind has been coupled with another problem, namely, that concerning the origin and development of consciousness in living beings and of self-consciousness in man. Though both problems are no doubt related, they are different and consequently can be treated separately. The answer to the one will necessarily have repercussions on the way we attempt to resolve the other.

Contemporary philosophy has abolished Cartesian dualism and tends instead towards a matter-mind monism, whereby the mental and physical are seen as two aspects of one and the same reality. But what does this actually mean? It has rightly been pointed out by G. N. A. Vesey that the introduction of this metaphor has only changed our manner of speaking without resolving the problem itself: "What empirical difference is there between there being one process with two sides, mental and physical, and there being two kinds of events inexplicably associated with one another?"[28]

Neither has complete agreement been reached in the scientific field. Experiments have shown that our consciousness and the working of the brain are interdependent. But can we conclude from this that self-consciousness can be fully explained by physicochemical causes? There are those who hold this at least as an hypothesis. It is argued that if we could make a computer with the same degree of complexity as in man, the computer would also possess the same awareness and freedom as is to be found in man. Such a view is defended by Norbert Weiner and Karl Steinbuch, while it is vehemently opposed by other experts, such as the brain specialist John Carew Eccles and the biologists Waddington and Haldane.[29]

The problem thus remains unresolved. This, however, does not detract from our fundamental view that the universe ought to be considered an organic unity. For whatever theory one accepts, there is no doubt that self-awareness and freedom must have a place in the structure of reality and, since they are closely connected with physicochemical processes, they may not be conceived as heterogenous elements. But the study of these phenomena has scarcely begun.[30]

If the cosmos has indeed to be conceived as an organic unity, the question arises as to how far we can describe this unity as an ordered connection. What concept of order do we find in our present view of reality? What is clear is that the hypothesis of a universal world order underlies the scientific investigation of nature. Not only would natural science be impossible, but the very idea would not have come into our mind if our experience had not first suggested the existence of regularity and continuity, coherence and stability. By studying individual beings and phenomena we moreover discover a certain structure, from which they derive their existence and individual character. But none of these structures is totally isolated. They are always dependent on particular circumstances, influences, and causes, which are external to the individual structures and without which the structures would not exist. No particular structure is self-explanatory, but rather, always points to other more universal structures. It can be said, then, that the existence of particular structures implies the existence of a universal structure, which then suggests that there is a basic plan underlying the whole of reality.[31] The wonder we feel when we observe the reality surrounding us has its origin in the inevitable supposition that there is a deeper rationality, a coherent project at the basis of everything. The whole of science has developed from this sense of wonder.

Further study of reality reveals that this concept of order is by no means abolished by the existence of discontinuity, indeterminateness, or chance, but that these properties are, on the contrary, implicitly contained in and only made possible by this concept. According to classical physics, all physical phenomena are determined by fixed laws. The same principle was vigorously maintained by Einstein.[32] Just as the quantum theory of Max Planck introduced a certain discontinuity into physical reality, so Heisenberg's uncertainty principle was to a certain extent detrimental to the universality of deterministic laws. On the other hand, the concept of chance can be said to play a significant role in biology, because the mutations underlying the whole evolutionary process appear to occur completely arbitrarily and cannot therefore be foreseen.

The concepts of discontinuity, indeterminateness, and chance ought no doubt to be defined more accurately. But they cannot in any way detract from the fundamental unity and coherence of nature. Especially as far as the concept of chance is concerned, one has to bear in mind, as was said above, that this means not so much the absence of causality, but rather, a particular kind of causality that can be more closely defined with the help of statistics.[33]

The Concept of "World" in Existential Phenomenology

In the preceding pages we attempted to give a survey of the principle elements that determine our contemporary view of the world in order to outline the world picture found in the natural sciences. The cosmos now appears as a dynamic and organically structured whole whose space-time dimensions escape us entirely. This is the cosmos in which man lives. By his body man is quite insignificant, but by his consciousness he is open and amendable to the whole of reality.

But what is the concept of "world" in existential philosophy and how does it differ from that of the natural sciences? Unlike the natural sciences, existential philosophy is concerned with man as man. That is to say, it attempts to analyze what it means to exist as a human being, including what is unique about human existence.

On the basis of our self-experience we can say that four concepts are necessary to define the specifically human mode of being: self-consciousness, bodiliness, world, and intersubjectivity. None of the four can be omitted or reduced to one of the others. Our most fundamental characteristic is that of being consciously present to things: we experience ourselves as open to the whole of reality and our consciousness extends over all that exists. At the same time, however, we feel capable of making this very experience the object of our reflection. Our being is a being that is conscious of its own existence. But this self-consciousness is an embodied consciousness: existence is essentially being related to the world—a relatedness that is characterized by bodiliness and without this bodiliness is not conceivable.

It is not sufficient, however, to simply describe man as an embodied consciousness. For man does not exist in a kind of vacuum, but is inextricably connected with his particular world, with a milieu that is his very own. Each of us builds up his particular world from the experiences he has undergone. We each have a different world because each of us has a different past, different activities, and different experiences. Taken together, all these elements form a specific, coherent, and unique whole, constituting the world in which we belong and with which we are familiar—the "world" we can call our own, or, as Aldous Huxley describes it, "the home-made cosmos of intelligible symbols." Without this world we would no longer be what we are. It belongs to our very being and cannot be separated from it. In the words of Heidegger, to be man, is to be-in-the-world. To exist, therefore, is to be a conscious-being-in-the-world that is, moreover, a being-at-home-in-the-world.

But in the private world that is our own and (following Husserl) can be called the "primordial sphere," we cannot eliminate our relation to other people. Besides the fact that others often have the same or at least similar experiences, and as a consequence of which our private worlds have much in common, it is also true that the "other" belongs to my world not only as a bodily presence, as a "thing" alongside other things, but also as a conscious person with whom I can come into contact, enter into conversation, or share an activity. Its personal character notwithstanding, my world displays from the beginning a social dimension.

It is obvious that some people, by virtue of common experience, friends, or interests, feel mutually related in a special way, with the result that their worlds begin to show a number of common features. In this way we can speak of the world of the businessman, the world of the solicitor, the world of the art lover, etc. In his *Principles of Psychology*, William James refers to these worlds as "sub-universes" or "sub-worlds."[34] These are the contexts within which we experience what we call "reality"—"the multiple realities"—even though this includes imaginary things like myths, prejudices, dreams, and the most foolish inventions.

This subjective but real world, whether we consider it on the level of the strictly individual world or on a wider plane which includes intersubjective reality, is never simply given. It is chiefly a question here of the cultural or "artificial" world. In contrast to the animal whose world is given to it at birth, man has to devise and continually develop his own world which is never altogether complete. Man is never content with the world he has created. Owing to the inexhaustible creativity that is revealed in human beings, the world of each generation differs from that of previous generations. The natural sciences obviously play a significant role in these changes and will presently be discussed in more detail.

We thus live as conscious beings in a world constituted by cultural activity, and with which we are inseparably connected. This world cannot be eliminated from our existence. It forms for us the preeminent reality, demanding our attention, stimulating our interest, and involving the whole of our emotional and active life. It is real so long as it has our attention; without this it sinks into nothingness.[35] The fact that we live in different worlds greatly impedes mutual understanding. For real dialogue is only possible on the basis of what our separate worlds have in common. If we wish to have a conversation with a person we have met for the first time, we immediately look for common ground. From this we can conclude that, insofar as it is a question of our "subjective" world, we cannot really speak of a true world picture. Even with the supposition that we are able to express our world-experience in an ordered and coherent picture, there could at most be mention of "world pictures" but never of a single world picture.

However fundamental the role of our personal experience, the development of our world is by no means a purely individual concern. It has, on the contrary, a preeminently social character. Just as the development of the scientific world picture is not the work of one scholar but has grown out of the cooperation between a great number of scholars, so our world is the result of the intersubjective relations in which we are involved throughout our life. Looked at objectively, the society to which we naturally belong is a continuous dialectical process in which one can distinguish three moments that appear simultaneously: externalization, objectification, and interiorization. It is characteristic of man to express his thoughts, impressions, and feelings, etc. in all sorts of creations such as a particular social order, rules of conduct, and every kind of technical and artistic creation. Crucial to this whole process of externalization is the part played by language as a means of social intercourse.[36] These creations, which are born from the impulse to externalization, gradually acquire an objective existence of their own, quite independent of the person responsible for them in the first place. It is, moreover, possible for them to be taken up once again into the conscious life of others, being thoroughly integrated into their existence, so that they come to constitute a part of the world that these persons now experience as reality.

The process of interiorization begins with the individual. For the world the individual enters has already been organized and interpreted. It is a world that is already full of meaning. For this reason the individual's world is never purely personal but always a socially constructed world, irrespective of the order and meaning that the individual may later create.[37]

The Relation between the Life-world and the World of the Natural Sciences.

We cannot conclude this chapter without considering the relation between the life-world and the world picture of the natural sciences. Does our subjective world have any significance for our scientific interpretation of reality? And what is the impact of the scientific world picture on our everyday world? It is in any case clear that scientific investigation has its origin in our everyday experience of the world. As was mentioned at the beginning of this chapter, Husserl rightly described the life-world (Lebenswelt) as prescientific, not only because it is prior to the scientific study of the reality surrounding us, but especially because the everyday world gave rise to the development of the natural sciences. From his everyday experiences man came to devote himself consciously to a more exact study of certain phenomena with which he was confronted. The questions we now raise in the natural sciences ultimately have their origin in the fact that certain experiences or phenomena particularly fascinated us or were drawn to our attention for one or another practical reason. The objective world of the natural sciences thus has its origin in the subjective world of our everyday experience.[38] A number of questions arise, however, when it comes to defining the degree of objectivity that has to be ascribed to the results of the natural sciences. Husserl, for example, made an extensive study of these questions.

What is more important for our topic, however, is the question concerning the influence of the scientific world picture on our subjective world. The rise of the natural sciences, it need hardly be argued, had a profound effect on Western man, thoroughly changing his way of life and manner of thinking in many respects and now extending its influence to all people without distinction. By this we mean not only that the rise of the natural sciences and their application in all sorts of technical creations have altered the material conditions in which we live, but rather that certain insights derived from the natural sciences have become a constituent part of our subjective world and have transformed our attitude of mind.

One of the first changes to appear in our subjective experience of the world concerns the way in which we interpret the world around us. The belief in mysterious forces and occult sciences which dominated the world of primitive man has now been abolished to make way for the conviction that there is, in principle, a rational explanation for every phenomenon. This alone has changed the outlook of our everyday world. People have generally come to regard the world as an ordered and coherent whole, capable of rational explanation, whose underlying principles can be traced by the natural sciences. In this way the world of our everyday experience is no longer subject to fears of imaginary threats and to many forms of superstition. We now have explanations for phenomena which previously seemed to be inexplicable, and through the astounding creations of technology we have become utterly convinced that nature is subject to man's will and can be made intelligible. For the most part, then, nature has lost its magical character.

This naturalistic attitude has become a specific feature of our contemporary life-world. Closely related to this is the critical attitude that is taken for granted in our daily life as well as in scientific and philosophical method. Instinctively we turn against any form of credulity. Each statement is critically examined, each proposal carefully considered, and each theory closely analyzed and its credibility tested, with the result that there is deep suspicion and reserve whenever certain matters have not yet been sufficiently examined and found to be correct. This frequently results in a deep-rooted skepticism, as, for example, in neopositivism, which makes us reject everything that is not experimentally verifiable.

A third characteristic of our life-world is the development of historical consciousness, which also found a powerful ally in the natural sciences. The contemporary world is no longer a static world where everything has its fixed place and an undisputed order prevails. History, prehistory, cosmology, and the theory of evolution have taught us that change is the law of existence and that we merely represent a particular moment in a process whose beginning and end eludes us entirely. This point is well illustrated by Minkowski's suggestion that the frequently used definition of human existence as "being-in-the-world" be replaced by "becoming-in-the-world" or better still by "becoming-with-the-world."[39] The theory of evolution in particular has furthered the development of this historical awareness whereby we experience our existence as part of a universal process, and conversely, the experience of our historicity has done much to promote the credibility of the theory of evolution, so that it now belongs to the life-world of Western man.[40]

What is more, the growth of the natural sciences, and particularly the technical creations with which we come into daily contact, have given us a new feeling of power and self-confidence. What are the limits to what we can achieve? One thing seems certain to us: we have by no means reached the limits of our possibilities. For we realize that what was impossible yesterday can be reality tomorrow. The main thing is that we continue along the same road, taking our destiny into our own hands.

But where does this road lead us? Does it not perhaps ultimately lead to our downfall? This is the problem we have to contend with today and it raises the question whether it is at all meaningful for us to employ so much effort to end in self-destruction. For this reason our life-world is at once subject to optimism and pessimism, great expectations and deep disappointment, hope and despair. With the demystification of the cosmos and critical reflection on our own experience our power over nature has increased, while earlier religious views have gradually lost credibility and influence. We are thus left in a spiritual vacuum. Being completely abandoned to absurdity, we recall the words of Hamlet:

> Life's but a walking shadow, a poor player
> that struts and frets his hour upon the stage
> and then is heard no more: it is a tale
> told by an idiot, full of sound and fury
> signifying nothing.

The cultural creations with which we surround ourselves are, as André Malraux has said, no more than a "liturgy of nililism." It would be a mistake, then, to claim that man has lost all sense of mystery. For just as in the days of Plato and Aristotle, and as in Kant's celebrated statement, man now stands in silent wonder before the mystery of the cosmos and of his own soul. Modern science has not resulted in the destruction of our sense of mystery in all that surrounds us, but, on the contrary, in a deepending of it. It is unlikely that the scientist of today would endorse Berthelot's statement that there are no longer any mysteries but only problems. However much science has managed to explain, there is infinitely more that has yet to be fathomed. The contribution of science consists in exposing false mysteries and thereby creating the space for philosophy and religion to situate mystery in its rightful place. Of the many distinguished scholars of the age whom we could quote, we confine ourselves to two, the one a devoted student of cosmic reality, the other an authority on the study of the brain and of human consciousness. "The most beautiful thing we can experience," Einstein declared, "is the mysterious. It is the source of all true art and science. He to whom this emotion is a stranger, who can no longer pause to wonder and stand rapt in awe, is as good as dead: his eyes are closed. This insight into the mystery of life, coupled though it be with fear, has also given rise to religion. To know that what is impenetrable to us really exists, manifesting itself as the highest wisdom and the most radiant beauty which our dull faculties can comprehend only in their most primitive forms—this knowlege, this feeling, is at the center of true religiousness."[41] Einstein himself never ceased to be amazed at the superior rationality of nature and always held that "the cosmic religious feeling is the strongest and noblest incitement to scientific research . . ."[42]

And while Einstein expressed his amazement at the mystery of the cosmos, Eccles expressed the hope that he might "restore to his fellow-men a sense of the wonder and mystery of their own personal existence on this beautiful planet that is ours. . . ." "I believe," he wrote, "that we have to recognize that there are great unknowns in the attempts that have so far been made to understand the nature of man. And the further we progress in research, the more each of us will realize the tremendous mystery of our personal existence as a consciously experiencing being. . . . For me there is a profound mystery in existence. . . . Such fundamental problems as the mind-brain liaison in perception and free-will will be beyond any conceivable investigation."[43]

If the nature of man is defined in terms of his everyday experience of the world and if that experience has undergone a fundamental change under the influence of the natural sciences, it follows that we are in a sense essentially different than men of previous ages. Science and technology have thus produced a new type of human being. But he, like his predecessor, continues to ask what purpose he serves in the world in which he belongs and yet retains the feeling that he is a stranger.

Chapter Eight

WORLD PICTURE AND THEOLOGY IN THE WORK OF TEILHARD DE CHARDIN

W e have already indicated why it seemed desirable to devote a
chapter of the present work to the views of Teilhard de Chardin. Apart from the tremendous impact that his writings have had in
the most diverse circles, Teilhard is particularly relevant to us in view
of the fact that the problem of the relation between world picture and
theology has a central place in his work.

There is already an extensive literature on Teilhard, especially on
his theological views.[1] We must naturally confine ourselves to a brief
summary of his ideas on the contemporary world picture and his
interpretation of Christianity. It was his firm conviction that Christianity was increasingly losing influence and credibility in today's world
because its theological expression appeared to be linked to an outmoded and, to contemporary man, completely unacceptable picture
of the universe. When a religion clashes with our experience of reality,
it is inevitable that reality will get the upper hand. It is, then, of utmost
importance for the theologian to ascertain what world picture consciously or unconsciously forms the background to his theological
statements and what views concerning man and the world are presupposed in his interpretation of Christian doctrine. Only by a critical
investigation of the anthropological and cosmological elements contained in the traditional theological system can we expose the real
cause of the present crisis. We cannot, therefore, hope to build a living

theology without first making a thorough examination of the true structure of our experience of reality.

But, according to Teilhard, that is just what is lacking in traditional Catholic theology. For the message of Christ has been formulated in a manner that is still tributary to the medieval world picture and has not sufficiently taken into account our contemporary experience of reality. As a result of exaggerated conservatism on the part of theologians, the Church has become even further estranged from modern culture. Even the most sincere Christian, for whom contemporary culture constitutes a living reality, feels somewhat uneasy in a Church that continues to appeal to the thought-categories of a previous age. For many the only solution was to separate faith and science and in this way to avoid all conflict, an attitude that could ultimately be described as a kind of schizophrenia. In the past, apologists and theologians have concentrated on showing that there was no contradiction between faith and science. Teilhard considered such an endeavor, however praiseworthy, as totally inadequate. What he aimed to do was not so much to obviate all conflict as to build a new synthesis on the model that St. Thomas Aquinas had striven after in the cultural situation of the thirteenth century. For this purpose, argued Teilhard, it is by no means sufficient to make a few small corrections in our traditional textbooks. What is required is nothing less than a radical rethinking of Christianity within the framework of our contemporary experience of the world. That is to say, we have to return to the deepest roots of theological thought: the message of Christ as understood by the primitive Church and Christians in later centuries on the one hand, and the present experience of reality on the other. This of course is no mean task. But we should not be daunted by the difficulties involved in such a venture. Teilhard has tried first and foremost to make us aware that striving for such a renewal in theology is essential to the future survival of Christianity. His theological project was thus supported by pastoral concern.

The whole project was characterized by three fundamental principles that can be said to be traditional in Catholic theology. In the field of espistemology Teilhard believed in critical realism, even though he did not work this out systematically. The relation between faith and reason was seen by him as one of harmony in the sense that, far from there being any contradiction, they actually supplement and perfect each other. Finally, science and Revelation were said to point in the same direction, a convergence that paved the way for an eventual synthesis.[2]

It is not our intention to discuss the whole of Teilhard's thought. As we shall see, his work focuses on two themes which particularly demand our attention: man and his place in the whole of nature, and Christ and his significance for man and the world. Both themes have been widely misunderstood. We must therefore attempt to understand the basic categories of his thought as accurately as possible.

Man's Place in the World

Central to Teilhard's thought is his analysis of the phenomenon of man, to which he devoted a series of studies.[3] A first requirement for a proper understanding of his ideas is (as is generally the case when dealing with a scientific theory) that we consider the problem the author is addressing, the starting point for his investigations. For Teilhard, man is a problem because he is, on the one hand, at home in the world and yet he seems, on the other hand, somehow not to belong to this world. How are we to reconcile man and the world? Man is a being characterized by freedom and self-consciousness, neither of which are found in the material world. Owing to the theory of evolution we are clearly aware that man has not been introduced into the world from without but, that he has, on the contrary, gradually appeared, as it were, from within. But how could a world in which there is no self-consciousness produce a being characterized by self-consciousness? How could matter, which knows no freedom, call into existence a being that delights in its freedom and creativity?

In the vast expanse of the universe man occupies an extremely small place: a bit of mold on the skin of a planet revolving round a mediocre star, which is only one of the billions of stars in the galaxy and this in turn is but one of the billions of spiral nebulae that seem to make up the universe . . . But there is a paradox here. For how was such an insignificant being capable of exploring this immense universe?

The thing that distinguishes man from all else is his self-awareness. The whole world enters his consciousness, for consciousness, in principle, is coextensive with the universe. Past experience has taught us that the limits of our spatial and historical awareness constantly move and that our knowledge of the universe continues to increase. And just as our cognition is in principle unlimited, so also are our freedom and creativity. History once again reveals the spectacle of a being continually extending his power, making nature increasingly subject to his will. Man's consciousness thus displays an almost unlimited character in spite of the extremely limited body with which it is connected. We are confronted, then, with the most remarkable phenomenon in the universe: a being that has changed the face of the earth and who measures itself against the whole cosmos.[4]

The question of man's place in the universe is of course as old as mankind itself. Compelled by necessity, man attempts to situate himself among the phenomena surrounding him. This was precisely the aim of the ancient myths. As soon as more rational thought gets the upper hand, philosophical systems are devised, sometimes emphasizing the harmony between man and the world, and sometimes, the opposition between them. At one time man experiences his union with the cosmos, at another time he has the feeling of being a stranger, lost in the infinity of space and time, in search of a spiritual home. But there are many sides to the problem. It can be approached from the standpoint of philosophy and theology, but also from that of the natural sciences. Teilhard was particularly concerned with the latter, seeking to devise a scientific theory capable of explaining man's place in the universe. Since it appeared to him that the natural sciences had neglected this question by failing to give consideration to man's spiritual aspect, he decided to concentrate on the natural sciences, rather than philosophy and theology. What he wanted to achieve was a unified science that would include man and the world and provide an explanation for the existence of both. In this he came very close to the opinion of Aristotle, who declared that the study of the soul belonged to the field of the natural sciences. In Teilhard's view, even the theory of evolution has not gone far enough. For though it has shown how man is biologically connected with the animal kingdom, it has not given sufficient consideration to what is specifically human, namely, the emergence of self-consciousness.

It was clearly Teilhard's intention to extend the theory of evolution to man, considered not only in his biological but just as much in his spiritual aspect. Man as a whole belongs to the field of observable phenomena and must be included within the framework of our explanation of reality. The problem of man's place in the cosmos thus belongs to the field of the natural sciences, and must be approached with the help of the scientific method.

There is no disputing this fact. However, Teilhard's method has received considerable criticism, so that it is not superfluous to comment on this question. Generally speaking, a scientific problem is solved in the following manner: one first looks for a hypothesis from which the problem can be approached; with the help of observation and experiment this hypothesis is then tested by the facts; if the initial hypothesis is confirmed by observation and experiment, one can speak of a scientific theory. But a working hypothesis is not verified in the same way in all sciences. The natural sciences can be said to fall into two groups. On the one hand, there are the "historical" sciences, also called the palaeotiological sciences (Whewell), such as geology, paleontology, and the sciences concerned with the origin of the cosmos and of living beings, and on the other hand, the sciences which chiefly appeal to observation (geography, crystallography, etc.) and experiment (physics, chemistry, etc.). Observation and experiment do not play the same role in the first group as in the second, because phenomena of the distant past are not open to observation and experiment. The palaeotiological sciences attempt to reconstruct events of the past, and as these are not within our reach, one has to appeal to the principle of uniformity.[5] These sciences are thus situated between the "pure" sciences (based on observation and experiment) and historiography. The latter can appeal to human testimony, while the former can always refer to repeatable experiments. This, however, does not alter the fact that the palaeotiological sciences also merit our confidence and that, despite their difficult position, they succeed in giving a well-founded explanation for the present situation of the cosmos and of the phenomena found in it. For this purpose they naturally developed a method in which "analogical reasoning" has a significant role.[6]

The problem that Teilhard sought to solve must evidently be included in the sphere of the palaeotiological sciences. It is hardly surprising, then, that the evidence he presented was not that which is normally advanced in physics or chemistry and that he appealed not only to "scientific facts" but sometimes also to arguments from analogy. It would seem that such a method is, in principle at least, fully justified. The fact that some people have nonetheless reproached Teilhard for having used this procedure can only be explained by a lack of familiarity with the customary method of the palaeotiological sciences.

An important question that we must now consider concerns the working hypothesis adopted by Teilhard as a starting point for his research. In the Preface to *The Phenomenon of Man* he states that he had started from a twofold hypothesis: the primacy of psychism and of thought in the stuff of the universe, and the biological significance of the community. These two hypotheses must constantly be kept in view. If we cannot accept them, it would be better not to read the book.[7] For it is precisely in the choice of these working hypotheses that we find the originality of the work. There were also other occasions when Teilhard showed the importance of these hypotheses for reaching a good understanding of his thought. As has already been said, the problem that he sought to solve concerns man's place in the universe. To answer this question in a scientific way we have two possible approaches: we can either take matter as our starting point and attempt to ascend to man, or, we can take man as our starting point and descend to the level of matter. In other words, we can either accept the primacy of matter or the primacy of mind. Viewed a priori both hypotheses are equal: in each case it is a question of phenomena that belong to the sphere of existence; what we see are two ends of a series which can consequently be studied in both directions. Only the results will determine which method deserves preference.

The usual approach in scientific circles is to start with matter and then proceed to explain the origin of life and of man. But Teilhard judged the results of this method unsatisfactory. Apart from the obscurities surrounding the concept "matter," this approach has not succeeded in providing an adequate explanation for the origin of self-consciousness and freedom. Attempts to explain man from matter have only resulted in the reduction of man to an anomaly or a mere accident. In this way the most central phenomenon in the whole evolutionary process is regarded as an epiphenomenon, having nothing to say about the true nature of matter and of the world, and even as an unnatural product of the cosmos. As Teilhard recalled, however, it is not uncommon in the history of science for something which was initially regarded as an exception to turn out, on closer examination, to be absolutely essential and to pave the way for a totally new concept of reality.[8] A clear illustration of this is Kepler's discovery of the elliptical orbit of Mars. What was at first thought to be an exception opened the way for an entirely new outlook on the planetary system, teaching us to see the elliptical orbit as a characteristic of all planets without distinction. Similar events surrounded Henri Becquerel's discovery of radioactivity. Initially considered to be a special property of radium, it soon became evident that this was by no means an exception but rather a general property of matter, a discovery that made possible a completely new view of the nature of matter.[9] These comparisons help us to understand Teilhard's precise intention. This might be formulated as follows: could not the phenomenon of self-consciousness and freedom, hitherto regarded by most scholars as an epiphenomenon and an exception, perhaps constitute a central datum whereby our concept of the world and of matter could be thoroughly changed? *The Phenomenon of Man* is nothing other than an attempt to make this hypothesis plausible.[10] Starting from the hypothesis that life and self-awareness constitute a central phenomenon in the whole of the cosmos, Teilhard attempted to construct a scientific theory capable of reconciling man and the world and explaining the unity that exists between them. We must now take a closer look at this theory.

The natural sciences have taught us to view the world as an evolutive event, an historical process in which new phenomena continually appear. The question can be raised whether this evolution complies with certain laws or, in other words, whether we can distinguish a definite orientation in this process. It is characteristic of the natural sciences to look for regularity in the phenomena we observe. Careful consideration of the process of evolution that has occurred on earth reveals that evolution has always taken a particular direction, namely, that of increasing complexity and increasing consciousness. From the elementary particles and the primeval atom to the human brain we observe the origin of increasingly more complex structures, which, from the origin of the first forms of life, were coupled with an ever-growing psychism to achieve self-awareness and creative freedom in man. We could say, therefore, that the world appears to us as a succession of events in which we distinguish a double aspect: a growth of increasingly more complex structures (the exterior) and an increase of psychism (the interior) or a two-sided dynamic reality. However we view the matter, we cannot escape the impression that, despite all hesitations and fortuitous circumstances, evolution has de facto been moving in the direction of man, in whom we find the highest degree of complexity (the brain and the nervous system) and the highest degree of psychism (self-consciousness). Taken as a whole, the process of evolution thus displays a definite orientation. That is not to say that evolution follows a linear process. On the contrary, the history of life on earth shows moments of stagnation and regression; the forms of life, moreover, have evolved in the most capricious ways, with fortuitous circumstances not infrequently playing a significant role.[11] Life has sought its way most tentatively, trying every means and scanning all possibilities until self-consciousness finally emerged in man. Viewing evolution as a whole and considering the way it actually developed, it can be described as governed by the law of increasing complexity and increasing consciousness.

So far almost everyone can agree with this interpretation of the evolutionary process. Difficulties arise, however, over further interpretation of the process. Once again we face a dilemma: either we start with matter, thereby reducing man to an epiphenomenon, an anomaly in the whole of cosmic reality, or we start with self-consciousness as a central and fundamental datum. The option that is made here is decisive for the way in which one ultimately interprets the process of evolution. Teilhard's originality consists in the fact that he, contrary to the approach which is mostly taken in the natural sciences, chose the second hypothesis. He consciously made this choice not because he believed that evolution was directly aimed at man—which is certainly not the case—but because it seemed to him that it has its justification in the intrinsic value of self-consciousness as a phenomenon excelling all others. With the primacy of consciousness the course of the evolutionary process is not changed but acquires an entirely different outlook: what was seen in the first hypothesis as a fundamental reality now becomes a provisional and preparatory state; what was regarded as an exception or a by-product of evolution now becomes the central concern of the whole process.[12] It is a change of perspective, not a distortion of the facts. What Teilhard demanded was that we look at already known facts from a new standpoint, since he was convinced that this would lead to a better and more coherent view of reality. This proposal is of course objectionable to those who adhere to a preconceived materialist orthodoxy. The question must be raised, however, whether the time has not come to break through this dogmatism in the scientific field, even though it defends itself with a self-righteousness that is reminiscent of the Inquisition.[13]

Teilhard's theory has its strongest base in biological evolution, which, as far as the higher forms of life are concerned, shows a steady growth in complexity of structures and wealth of psychism. But on two points he felt obliged to extrapolate. First, the two-sided reality he had established in living beings was extrapolated in the direction of the past, namely, in the direction of matter, which was likewise attributed with a form of interiority. Of course, this thesis cannot be proven. It is merely a working hypothesis, which is of value only to the extent that it contributes to the solution of the problem and paves the way for a coherent explanation of the world, including man. The origin of consciousness remains a mystery for science. We have, therefore, no other possibility but to appeal to a hypothesis, as is customary in such cases when solving scientific problems. With the help of the hypothesis that psychism is already present in matter in one way or another; it is indeed possible to envisage the whole evolutionary process as a succession of events containing a double aspect: an exterior (a growing complexity) and an interior (a growth of psychism), both of which culminate in man.

The second extrapolation concerns the future. If the law of increasing complexity and increasing consciousness may be considered to be an accurate rendering of what has taken place in the history of our world, then it would appear to be acceptable to project this law into the future. For all science is based on the postulate of stability in the laws of nature, a postulate that is confirmed by our everyday experience of life. There is not a single reason for us to suppose that evolution is complete and that from now on everything will remain the same. Everything that happens today is only a moment in an evolutionary process which extends to the future. If the above mentioned law is correct, then one may reasonably expect that the future will be a continuation of the past, or in other words, that it will proceed in the direction of increasing complexity and increasing consciousness.

Such an increase of complexity and of consciousness is theoretically conceivable on two different levels: either within the present human species or outside it. The latter can be conceived in two ways: either from another branch of human beings or an extension of man that radically transcends him—the superman. On the basis of available data Teilhard felt justified in concluding that we must situate the future of evolution within the context of the present human species. Not only does the animal kingdom largely seem to be stagnating and at times even threatened with extinction, but the position of man is now so firmly established and he commands such a dominant power that it is most improbable that he would willingly allow himself to be expelled—in the supposition of course that he himself does not commit collective suicide. As to the possibility of a new species, the superman, we can say that while this idea did have some adherents in the nineteenth century, it now appears for the most part to have been abandoned. The human brain has reached such a high degree of complexity and displays such vulnerability that any modification would have disastrous consequences for the entire organism. Moreover, this has become completely superfluous now that man already has at his disposal all the conditions for widening the scope of his life in all directions with the aid of an increasingly more complex and more varied technology. Teilhard thus prefers the thesis that the future course of evolution is contained in the present human species. Only there do we find the profound changes that can be interpreted as a new stage in the growth of greater complexity and consciousness.

Let us carefully consider these changes. From a biological point of view the unity of humankind was never so sure as it is now and its vital power is far from being exhausted. Instead of branching off into various groups, as was the case in the plant and animal kingdom, the various human groups seem to grow towards each other, becoming attuned to each other's way of life. Despite all the difficulties and opposition, there is in humankind a profound feeling of human solidarity and mutual dependence, which accounts for the fact that we look for supranational institutions to enable us to live together in peace and in a spirit of cooperation. This urge for organic unity is accompanied by an unprecedented increase in intellectual activity. What is now being carried out in the fields of the natural sciences, technology, art, the social sciences, philosophy, and religion surpasses any achievements of the past. These and many other symptoms seem to indicate that evolution in the human species has become convergent rather than divergent, aimed at a central point which Teilhard called the Omega point and which denotes the moment in history when, in continuation with what is currently in progress, the highest possible degree of unification and consciousness will be attained. It is obvious that the value of this prospect is purely statistical. For Teilhard's ideas on the future are derived not so much from a theoretical view of the evolutionary process as from an analysis of what is presently going on in our world. Indeed, everything seems to indicate that man has entered a new phase in his history and that we are on the threshold of what could be called the socialization of humankind. To do justice to Teilhard one has clearly to take into account the fact that his image of the future is not based on purely speculative grounds but on a very concrete analysis of the vast changes now taking place, whose future course and ultimate result can be measured statistically.

Teilhard's whole project can be reduced to one question: Is man central to or merely a secondary phenomenon in the cosmos? Is self-consciousness no more than an epiphenomenon of matter or is it, on the contrary, the phenomenon par excellence, the central datum in the deeper structure of the world? This immediately presents us with the most fundamental issue in present-day science, the unsolved problem of the relation between man and the world, or the question of the significance of self-consciousness and creativity in a world that does not appear to have a creative consciousness at its disposal. It would seem that Teilhard's principal merit has been to highlight this problem in a stimulating manner, making us particularly conscious, moreover, of its far-reaching implications not only for our individual self-understanding but also for the future of humankind.

Having acknowledged this merit, one has to question the extent to which Teilhard's theory can be considered satisfactory. From a scientific point of view, a theory must satisfy two conditions: it has to offer a real explanation for the phenomenon in question, and it may not contradict any clearly recognizable fact. Does Teilhard's theory fulfill these two conditions? Our first impression is that the world picture outlined here is characterized by inner unity, so that the world which previously appeared to be incoherent and absurd is now seen to be coherent and meaningful. Underlying modern science is the postulate of cosmic unity, which is everywhere rigorously maintained. Matter, living beings, and man constitute a constant succession of events, mutually related and yet essentially different. In this picture of the world man does not appear as an inexplicable marginal phenomenon but as a central datum in which the most profound mystery of the cosmos is expressed—man is nothing less than the key to understanding the universe.

That is not to say, however, that all matters are satisfactorily explained by Teilhard's theory. The origin of self-consciousness still remains a difficult issue. To explain this Teilhard appealed to an unprovable hypothesis, namely, the existence of a psychical element in matter which continually expands as more complex structures are built up. But he was not the only one to do so. Eminent scholars such as C. S. Sherrington and J. Huxley have also appealed to this hypothesis, regarding it as indispensable to a coherent explanation of man. It perhaps deserves consideration as a working hypothesis, but this does not exclude the possibility that it can ultimately be replaced by a better hypothesis, even though we have at present no idea of what this might be. We can therefore only accept it with reservations. It seems that psychism has developed from matter by way of the plant and animal kingdom to human consciousness. But how are we to conceive of this transition from animal to human consciousness? There is, as Teilhard also explicitly stated, a fundamental difference between them, so that he spoke of a discontinuity in the continuity. We remain, then, very poorly informed about animal psychism.[14]

It would appear that there are considerable advantages to Teilhard's theory and that it is, as science now stands, perhaps the only workable theory. But that does not alter the fact that it has its weak points which demand further analysis. In this context we recall the statement of John Eccles that:

> No scientific hypothesis or theory today can be claimed to be completely true in itself. We must say it is the best we can do.[15]

The second condition each scientific theory must satisfy is that it may not contradict any clearly observed fact. This raises the question whether the theory presented by Teilhard is not perhaps in any way contrary to what are clearly recognized facts. Critical questions have been raised by G. G. Simpson and others and these must receive some consideration. Teilhard's theory presupposes, it is said, that biological evolution shows a definite orientation and was, as it were, directed at man from the beginning. However, careful study of the evolutionary process as we now know it points in a different direction. Evolution does not appear to have any definite orientation. Life has, on the contrary, developed in all directions. Wherever "biological space" was available appropriate forms of life developed to fill these places. There is, therefore, no trace whatsoever of a clear orientation towards man. Fortuitous circumstances have, moreover, often played a significant role, so that there is no sense in speaking of man as if he were the goal of evolution.

But what value can be ascribed to this criticism? It would appear that it stems from a misrepresentation of Teilhard's intention. For he has by no means denied that life has been "groping" its way, nor did he fail to acknowledge the significance of chance. Both these notions were explicitly included in his description of evolution and were in no way underestimated.[16] In studying the primary forms of life no one could predict the direction in which life would develop and what the final outcome would be. The only thing that one can readily ascertain is the fact that nature has the capacity to produce increasingly higher, more complex, and better structured organisms—a process that could be designated as "orthogenesis."[17] The evolution of life was a tentative search in all directions where biological space was available, and there is no sign of it being directly aimed at man. It was precisely from this tentative procedure that man emerged.[18] Only now can one raise the question as to the actual significance of the phenomenon of man in the whole of the evolutionary process. This process clearly acquires a different outlook depending on whether it is viewed from its starting point or its final result. When we look at it from its starting point we see only a chaotic diversity in life forms developing in all directions. Looked at from its final result the process gains a different meaning and perspective: that which preceded man now appears as a preamble to the emergence of self-consciousness. What Teilhard proposed, then, was a change in perspective and by no means a misrepresentation of scientifically established facts. All in all, his theory can be seen as a working hypothesis that undoubtedly has its weak points but is extremely useful, as science now stands, for further study of the problem. For instead of ultimately reducing man to a mere anomaly or marginal phenomenon as the materialist theory does, Teilhard's theory shows the unique value and central significance of consciousness to its full advantage.

The Significance of Christ

In our brief account of Teilhard's view of the problem of man's place in the universe we have seen how Teilhard was fundamentally impelled by the idea of fully integrating man into the very structure of the world. By taking man as the starting point for his inquiry and establishing self-consciousness as the most central phenomenon, the cosmos acquired an entirely different perspective than before. It is, argued Teilhard, precisely in man that the true nature and profound energy of matter finds expression, that the true face of the cosmos is shown to us.

As we pointed out, this is primarily a scientific theory. One can readily see, however, that such a theory is also of particular importance to theology. In the first place, it touches upon one of the most fundamental presuppositions of Christianity, namely, the dignity of man. Secondly, it contains elements that seem as if they might be useful for constructing a new interpretation of Christianity.

It is then, precisely as a scientific theory that Teilhard's theory is concerned with man. The cultural developments of the last centuries have repeatedly reduced man's significance. With Copernicus man lost his central position in the cosmos. With Darwin it became clear that man is not independent of his natural environment. And from the discoveries of Freud we have come to realize how much man is governed by the dark forces of the unconscious. In this way the image of man that we find in classical antiquity, in the Middle Ages, and in humanism has been continually exposed to all sorts of dismantlement. Moreover, there is the treatment to which man has been subject as a result of industrial and political revolutions, whereby he has been made into an extension of a machine or into a blind and powerless instrument of political and economic forces. For many this is a cause for concern. In the scientific as well as in the philosophical and political fields there has been a call to restore respect in the human person without thereby detracting from the splendid insights we have gained from the natural sciences. Man's dignity and significance has become our common concern.

The theologian is by no means indifferent to which image of man emerges from the natural sciences. Clearly not every view of the cosmos and of man is consonant with the fundamental principles of Christianity. While Christians firmly believe in the meaningfulness of creation and in the dignity of man, it is precisely these issues which are at stake in contemporary culture. Teilhard's work is concerned with such problems. To many people it has extended the hope that renewed insight into human dignity is ultimately attainable from a scientific point of view.

There is, however, another reason why Teilhard's work is particularly relevant to the theologian. From our study of medieval theology and its further development after the Copernican revolution it has become evident how significant a role the generally accepted world picture has in the interpretation and systematization of Christian doctrine. As we have seen, all points of faith were formulated within the framework of the concept of hierarchical order. This idea of order had a profound influence, not only on the Christian conception of God, creation, and Redemption, but equally so on the Christian understanding of morality, grace, and the sacraments. Initially there was an explicit appeal to the prevalent cosmology. Even after the Copernican revolution, and as a direct result of the condemnation of Galileo, there was little or no change in this situation, on the understanding that all reference to the old world picture was avoided, but the spirit of the old world picture and the conclusions that had been drawn from it were left intact. Teilhard opposed this state of affairs. He criticized the prevalent theology of his day for proclaiming the God of the medieval world picture. To Teilhard it was clear that the Christ of a small and closed world was totally inadequate to meet the religious needs and expectations of our age, with its entirely new view of the world and of man. What is more, these mysterious links with an antiquated world picture only widened the gap between the Christian view of the world and modern culture: the religious sense of modern man, having grown out of his cosmic experience, could not, it seemed to Teilhard, be reconciled to a Church that continued to cling to medieval theology. For this reason many of our contemporaries have turned away from Christianity and many others have come to feel uneasy about the Church in spite of their reverence and respect for the Gospel message.

Clearly, then, there is no more urgent task for theology than to free Christianity from the grip of the past. What is required is a new interpretation of Christian doctrine within the context of our contemporary experience of the world. And today, just as in the Middle Ages, cosmology must provide the key concept for this reconstruction of Christianity. We have seen how Christianity became the religion of order. In keeping with the medieval world picture, scholasticism made the idea of hierarchical order absolutely central to its interpretation of Christian doctrine, which thus became credible in the eyes of all. This explains the success of scholasticism. But the key concept which has arisen from the contemporary picture of the universe is that of evolution, of progress and development in every field. For contemporary man Christianity is only conceivable as the religion of evolution, as a doctrine and attitude towards life that derives its meaning and orientation from history.

Teilhard thus endeavored to show that Christianity is the religion of evolution. The God he sought is no longer the God of a static world order but the God of a world in the process of becoming, and the Christ he desired to follow is only the Christ who can lead the world to its final completion. Yet Teilhard's writings, however eloquent, can hardly be considered strictly theological. For many theologians they even constitute a stumbling block. They are, nevertheless, particularly relevant to theology. In the first place they bear testimony to what is going on in the deeper layers of Christianity. Teilhard himself considered it his task to make generally known the aspirations and expectations of many people both within and outside the Church.[19] It is understandable, therefore, why so many people could identify themselves with him, why his writings met with such a wide response, and why the same writings were vehemently opposed by others. Teilhard's true significance is only disclosed when we see him as testifying to what is actually taking place in the womb of Christianity. A period in the history of Christianity is, as he saw it, now definitively closed. A new period is beginning that is thoroughly different from the preceding period, so much so that we can speak of a "neo-Christianity."[20] His writings on these issues have to be seen as the first laborious attempts to give shape to the dream of a renewed Christianity as the religion of humankind on the way to its final completion. Until now Christianity has been the religion of order, the doctrine of a return to an original world order. Henceforth it would become the religion of progress, of humankind feeling its way towards the future. One could hardly imagine a more radical change.

This obviously implies a fundamental revision of theology. What Teilhard primarily strove for was not so much a new theological synthesis, but rather a modification of the question preceding every theological synthesis. St. Thomas Aquinas raised the basic question: What does Christ mean to a world which had been created in perfect order and disrupted by original sin? The entire *Summa* attempts to give an answer to the question, an answer that was for centuries considered to be satisfactory: Christ has restored the original world order. Teilhard did not reject the validity of this answer. It was, however, totally irrelevant to him, because he regarded the question itself as meaningless. The question we raise today is no longer that of Aquinas. Christians are now concerned to know: What does Christ mean to a world in evolution, a world like the one that emerges from the work of Darwin, Marx, and Einstein? This is the only relevant question. Teilhard is of vital importance to contemporary theology precisely because he gave a new and clear formulation to the fundamental question of all speculative theology and made us aware of this necessary reformulation. For a new question must necessarily produce a new answer. A theory is always determined by the question it is designed to answer and this holds good for the natural sciences as well as theology. Traditional theology started from a question that had become meaningless to us. A theory or system is not necessarily affected because another theory or system is placed alongside it. At most this leads to a conflict which gives rise to long discussions. A theory or system is only dealt a mortal blow whenever one alters the question from which it has arisen and derived its validity. This immediately clears the way for a new stage in the evolution of thought.

A few remarks are in order here. In the first place it is to be noted that Teilhard's question has its starting point in faith and not in the natural sciences. It was certainly not his aim to ground a theological theory in the natural sciences. The question he raised is not primarily whether the pronouncements of Christianity are acceptable and can be justified by present-day science, but rather concerns the Christian's self-understanding.

Teilhard's inquiry is preceded by faith in the divine Revelation of Christ. His scientific views certainly play a role in his solution to the problem, but the issue would never have been raised had faith not already been present on other grounds. It would seem, then, to be a mistake to claim, as some have done,[21] that Teilhard grounded his theological views in the natural sciences.

A second remark concerns the place given to the cosmic element in his inquiry. Generally speaking, there is little room for cosmological considerations in the philosophical and theological thought of our time, not least because the development of the natural sciences have made it increasingly more difficult to situate man in cosmic reality as a whole. Having lost our central position in the cosmos, we tried at least to find a hold in history. It soon became evident, however, that this attempt was also doomed to failure. This resulted in a radical decosmization. Man was thus thrown back upon his own resources. In this way existentialism came into being which, whether in its atheistic or Christian form, having given up all hope of a meaningful integration in a natural or historical order, left man to his own devices—a situation that was moreover explained as a fundamental characteristic of human existence.[22]

An entirely different viewpoint was adopted by Teilhard. In his opinion contemporary science opens the way for a new integration of man into the cosmos and into history, thanks to the idea of evolution, which includes both the cosmos and history. Existentialists regard this as old-fashioned. Just as Newton was accused of reverting to the medieval theory of occult qualities, so Teilhard was suspected of resorting to an eighteenth-century philosophy of nature. Teilhard's theological thought is doubtless aimed at reintegrating cosmology into theology, measuring the significance of Christ within the context of a concrete view of reality such as that now made accessible by the natural sciences. A theology which merely sees Christianity as a "clarification of existence" in the existentialist sense simply did not appeal to Teilhard. He was not concerned with how Christ has helped clarify human existence, but rather with the place of the historical Christ in the structure of the total reality that has become visible to us. It is against this background that his interpretation of Christianity must be seen. Only then is objective criticism of his theology possible.

Teilhard and Aquinas thus shared the same conviction with regard to the relationship between theology and the world picture. Both were entirely convinced that a true theology always implies or, rather, presupposes an outlook on the cosmic reality, not in the sense that it produces a religious doctrine (cosmic religiosity) but in the sense that each doctrine, irrespective of its origin, only becomes relevant and efficient when it can function in harmony with the totality of our world experience. Where this does not occur there is always the danger that religious doctrine either languishes completely or is reduced to a marginal phenomenon that can still be upheld sociologically and psychologically for some time, but increasingly loses all hold on the individual and the community.

There were two main difficulties facing Teilhard. There was the fact that from its first systematic formulation Christian doctrine was very closely connected with a cosmology which is no longer generally accepted. Unlike Aquinas, Teilhard could not build on an already established tradition. He had in fact to dissociate himself from this tradition, considering it his primary task to separate the original core of the Gospel message from an age-old theological tradition without thereby abandoning any of its essential content. In the opinion of some people like Urs von Balthasar, Teilhard has gone too far in this respect, and has accordingly lost certain fundamental elements in his synthesis, while others who adhere to an existential theology criticize him for not going far enough, arguing that his interpretation of Christianity still retains too many mythical elements.

The second difficulty concerns what one is apt to call the contemporary "world picture." We have already indicated the numerous questions this concept raises. If we are dissatisfied with a purely existential interpretation there are two options open to us: we can either restrict ourselves to the general characteristics, which are clearly held by the natural sciences to be indisputable, and endeavor to reformulate Christian doctrine within this context, or we can, on the basis of a very concrete and specific interpretation of the world, aim at a new integration of Christian doctrine and a particular world picture. The second option clearly involves certain risks, because the final result is totally dependent on the value attributed to the particular world picture.

Teilhard consciously took the second option. Convinced that his theory, at least as far as its main features were concerned, was able to resist all criticism, he purposely focused his attention on the question of the significance one had to attach to Christ within the context of a concrete view on the structure of the cosmos. On the basis of certain premises, he achieved a Christological interpretation of the world that is characterized by considerable inner coherence and, irrespective of all possible criticism, represents a unique achievement in contemporary theology. This Teilhardian Christology has given rise to a number of studies.[23] It will be sufficient for us, however, to consider its main features in order to shed some light on its chief implications.

Dominating Teilhard's theology is, as has already been said, the question of the relation between Christ and the world. Both terms are clearly defined. Christ is the Christ of tradition: the historical Jesus who preached the Kingdom of God, was crucified, and rose from the dead, and who is expected to come again at the end of time. The concept of world is also clearly defined: it is a world-in-evolution with man as its dynamic center, a world that Teilhard believed had become visible in the light of contemporary science. In his view, the relation between Christ and the world could not be purely accidental, for this could hardly account for such a wonderful event as the Incarnation. There simply had to be an intrinsic connection between them: Christ had to belong in one way or another to the very structure of the cosmos. Creation and the Incarnation could not be thought of independently of each other. They had to be so closely related that the Incarnation could be seen as the continuation and culminating point of creation. This was by no means a novel idea in theology. It was already defended by Duns Scotus in the thirteenth century and is repeatedly found in later theologians who considered that the reason for the Incarnation was not only the restoration of the world order which had been disrupted by the sin of Adam, as Aquinas had held, but that it would also have taken place independently of the Fall, because Christ was the goal of creation and in him creation had to find its completion. To support such a view reference was made to certain statements of St. Paul which clearly point in this direction (Col. 1:15–20; Eph. 1:9–10).

Teilhard's originality does not consist in the fact that he reintroduced this doctrine, but that he related it to his view of an evolving world. One can rightly say that he fully incorporated this doctrine of Christ's primacy into the framework of his view on the deeper structure of the cosmos. It seemed to him that it was precisely this deeper structure of the cosmos that demanded a personal center without which evolution could not function until the end. The cosmos is evolving and in its human phase evolution displays a convergent character, pointing in the direction of what one could call an Omega point, the final phase of the whole process. The main characteristic of the human phase of evolution is freedom. How, in spite of all difficulties, sacrifices, and misfortunes, would man find courage to persevere until the end in pursuit of unification and spiritualization, had there not been a guarantee somewhere that this goal could be achieved, that it was already present in principle? By virtue of the dynamic structure of the world one could already suppose that there had to be such a source of energy, or magnetic pole. Christianity holds that this source of energy is to be found in the person of Christ, whom Christians expect will return at the end of time. In this perspective, then, the Parousia and the Omega point must ultimately coincide.

It is, moreover, the identification of the Omega point with the Parousia that forms the keystone of Teilhard's theological system. This reveals the close connection that exists between Christ and the world. As would be expected of the Omega point, Christ was in the first place the unifying principle in the cosmos, since in him everything ultimately held together; then, secondly, the energizing principle, since all motion originates from the final object; and, finally, the principle of completion, since everything finds its ultimate perfection in him. Christ and the cosmos are essentially and organically attuned to each other. In God's plan they constitute a whole: the Christified world, a world built on the Christic principle.[24]

This has significant consequences for the construction of a new theology. First, that the main emphasis in Christian theology should be on the future, not on the past. In this way one can immediately distinguish between a theology in the framework of a dynamic world picture and a theology in the framework of a static world picture.[25] For traditional theology all important moments appeared to be in the past: Creation, the Fall, the Incarnation, and the Redemption. Eschatology, on the other hand, generally received little attention. The fact that Aquinas was not able to complete his *Summa* only partly explains why his followers and commentators did not have much interest in the theme of eschatology. It would seem that the orientation to the past was the weak point in the scholastic synthesis.

By contrast, Teilhard's view is directed towards the future, while the past is only of importance insofar as it teaches us to understand the future. Of the three questions which Kant considered ought to govern all human reflection—What can I know? What must I do? What may I hope for?[26]—it is the third that is the most important, according to Teilhard, since it gives direction to our actions and can inspire action. Humanly speaking, we have, it is true, no certainty whatsoever of ever reaching such a goal. We can only hope. As man is free, it is within his power to let the whole thing fail: the completion of the world in Christ is not imposed on us as a necessity but is offered to us as a possibility that will not be realized without our cooperation. The further evolution of humankind ought to be our main concern. But this future expectation must not be understood solely in terms of an ideal state on earth nor simply in terms of the desire for the hereafter. The way we have to follow is that of earthly progress in the direction of spiritual unification in order to reach our final destiny, which undoubtedly lies on another plane, but is not therefore detached from the world. According to Teilhard, the Parousia is only meaningful when it is linked to a humanity that is prepared for this transformative event by its inner unity and spiritualization:

> When all things are subjected to him, then the Son himself will be subjected to him who put all things under him, that God may be everything to every one (1 Cor. 15:28).

Besides its emphasis on the future and on the eschatological character of Christianity, Teilhard's theology is also concerned with giving a new religious significance to human activity, with creating an entirely new type of Christian who would find in his relationship with Christ a deep source of inspiration for all his activity in the world. If the cosmos is an evolving cosmos and if man has a creative role in this evolution, this creative activity has to acquire a totally different meaning now that Christ is the center and final purpose of the cosmos. To work for the improvement of the world is to contribute to the completion of the world in Christ. All human activity can thus be said to be intrinsically religious. This idea was further developed in *Le Milieu Divin* where Teilhard made it a guiding principle for Christian spirituality. But it was repeatedly discussed in many other writings. Teilhard glorified human toil, granting man's creative power a cosmic dimension whereby it was seen to belong to the very structure of the world. For the world is an evolving world in which man has an essential contribution to make. A significant role has been played by the achievements not only of science and technology but also of social and political thought. All these forms of human activity had ultimately the same aim in view: the unification of humankind, the growth of commmunal consciousness, the completion of the evolutionary process in the Omega point. The success of cosmic evolution was plainly dependent on human cooperation. Without this contribution everything was doomed to failure. The ultimate significance of human toil was thus to be found in its cosmic dimension—a cosmic dimension to which a profoundly religious meaning was ascribed by the Christological perspective.

Such a philosophy and theology of labor immediately pointed to a new morality and a new humanism. From Greek antiquity until long after the Middle Ages morality had been founded on the concept of order: in all things there was a fundamental and immutable order that was derived from the wisdom and will of the Creator. It was man's duty to respect this order. For this purpose he had in the first place to trace the order willed by God in all things and then to observe this order in his actions. Reference has already been made to Augustine's definition of eternal law as "the divine reason or will commanding that God's natural order be preserved and in no way disturbed."[27] This was generally considered to be the fundamental principle of all morality. Morality was thus a question of order. Humanism was also conceived along these lines, a humanism of equilibrium where the ideal was to achieve a well-balanced and harmonious development of all one's faculties. This held good not only for the intellect and will but especially for literary and artistic taste. It seemed to Teilhard, however, that both these views were now obsolete and had to be replaced by a new morality and a new humanism: a morality and humanism of progress, human toil, and creative activity. A truly moral and humanistic attitude thus implied constant concern for the progress of humankind and the development of the world, so that the value of a particular action was not determined by the extent to which it agreed with or failed to agree with a preconceived concept of order, but rather by the extent to which it contributed to this progress. Our greatest admiration is for those who have contributed to the spiritual growth of humankind. There is no preestablished order to which we are subject, for man has been created as a free being and must therefore build up his world in freedom, devising for himself the order that is required for his development. The course of history is not predetermined. Even the Omega point is only a possibility, not a certainty, in that all prospects concerning the future course of history merely have a statistical value, interpreting the deepest longings of mankind. But the realization of those longings depends entirely on whatever we decide in the awareness of our freedom and responsibility. In this way a morality of order and a humanism of equilibrium must make way for a morality of progress and a humanism of creative activity, both of which acquire religious significance for the Christian, in that they are intrinsically concerned with building up Christ's world.

The two characteristics of Teilhard's theology which we have so far discussed—its orientation towards the future, with particular emphasis on eschatology, and its concern with human activity—can only be fully understood when they are linked to the third characteristic, namely, a thoroughgoing personalism.[28] Teilhard believed that the person was at the center of cosmic evolution, and this for various reasons. First, because the whole evolutionary process was, as we know from the study of the past, in reality attuned to the human person, characterized by self-consciousness and freedom. For it is in the human person that cosmic evolution reveals its greatest energy and most profound significance. The personalistic character of this view also comes to light in the fact that a person, namely the person of Christ, constitutes its driving force and culminating point. In Teilhard's conception the person of Christ dominates the whole cosmic event, forming the central point to which everything is ultimately attuned. It is in Christ that all things achieve their ultimate unity and completion. What is more, it is in him that the cosmos acquires a personal dimension, becoming as it were a living person, and as such it can be the object of our supreme love. Just as our whole body shares in the person that is peculiar to each of us, so the whole cosmos shares in the person of him who is its center and crowning point. The world is a Christified world, a whole that has itself become a person.[29] The cosmos is his "pleroma," his fullness and his glory. Without Christ the world is not complete, but neither is Christ complete without the cosmos. Both are completely attuned to each other, constituting a whole such as that formed by the head and members. This was powerfully formulated by Augustine as "the whole Christ, both head and members," even though it was at that time restricted to those who are united with Christ in the Mystical Body. With Teilhard, however, this unity is extended to the whole cosmos. Christ is in the fullest sense of the word the "cosmic" Christ, in whom the cosmos acquires an all-surpassing personal character.[30]

Here we touch upon what one could call the mystical element in Teilhard's theology. In Christian mysticism such as is found in the works of Eckhart, Tauler, Ruusbroec, and St. John of the Cross, the union of man with God is described as a turning away from the visible world to come close to God by means of contemplation. The first condition for union with God was that of a radical renunciation of the world. Only then was it possible for the soul to experience God's presence and to see all things transformed by him. Teilhard's view is quite different. Instead of considering the world an obstacle to union with God, he regarded it as the proper way to attain the goal of mystical union. What is required, in his view, is insight into the world and not renunciation of the whole visible world. By consciously uniting ourselves with the world, we unite ourselves with God, because Christ, who is the way to all union with God, is present in this world.[31] To embrace the world is to embrace Christ, for it is one with him. By devoting ourselves entirely to the world through our work and study, through our social and political action and all our human activity, we unite ourselves with Christ. Love of the world and love of God are thereby fused into one love. Teilhard's mysticism can rightly be called a mysticism of the earth and of action, which does not exclude the fact that he also retained the full significance of prayer and self-denial.

From this perspective the experience of Christianity acquired a totally different outlook. A new type of Christian emerged—one whom Teilhard envisaged as devoted to building up the world as an expression of his love of Christ and of God. Such a Christian does not turn away from the world and consider all cultural activity as worthless from the viewpoint of eternity; neither does he disapprove of all innovation, trusting only in what stems from the past. On the contrary, he is thoroughly concerned with his freely chosen task in the world and is completely open to every new idea, irrespective of where it comes from. He is, moreover, fully involved in developments in science and technology, paying particular attention to social justice and the spiritual growth of mankind. Such a Christian clearly does not regard the cosmos as meaningless and absurd, but firmly believes in its deeper significance and ultimate destiny. By virtue of his Christian faith he believes in the rationality of the world.

In addition to his description of the new Christian, Teilhard was deeply concerned with sketching an outline of a new concept of God. The present age has often been characterized as atheistic. It would, argued Teilhard, be more true to say that we have not yet found an appropriate concept of God: we suffer from an "unsatisfied theism," from a concept of God that bears too many traces of an antiquated vision of the universe and is, as it were, imposed on us from without, having no connection with our deepest expression of reality. We have yet to find a name for the mysterious presence that we suspect among the phenomena of our evolving world. Teilhard's whole life was directed towards discovering the concealed Presence, the "diaphany of the divine in the world." It seemed to him that previous conceptions were unsatisfactory as the world from which they had originated no longer cohered with our experience of reality. He sometimes referred to his concept of God as a "Christian pantheism," not because he underestimated the transcendence of the divine, but because he wished to emphasize the presence of God in all things, particularly in the evolutionary process that took place in the world. His God was a God who had become immersed in his creation, struggling together with his creation for its completion; a God who had become incarnate in his creation so that the Incarnation became coextensive with the duration of the world.[32] Contemporary man can only kneel before a God in whom he has recognized the organic center of his evolution. The whole aim of humankind today is to discover such a God.

Teilhard's work undoubtedly represents a remarkable attempt to free Christian doctrine from the grip of an outmoded theology which has lost all credibility because its cosmological premises had turned out to be completely worthless, with the result that it had in fact become an acosmic theology. What is new in his theological project is the reintroduction of the cosmological element into theological reflection, where it had virtually played no part since the end of the Middle Ages. The depth and intensity of Teilhard's renewed Christian cosmic sensibility is comparable only to that which is found in some of the Greek Fathers such as Gregory of Nyssa or Maximus the Confessor.

Today, however, we are somewhat apprehensive of this cosmic element. Except for the work of several major poets, it has largely disappeared from modern thought. Science has become conscious of its limitations and doubts whether it will ever be possible to grasp the universe in its totality, while philosophers, recalling how much they were disillusioned with previous attempts to encompass the world and history in brilliantly devised systems, prefer to concentrate on the mental and social aspects of human existence. Are we able to overcome this fear and hesitation , and, now that we have entered the age of space travel, do we dare raise the question once again as to our place in the whole of the cosmic order? Though there are a few indications that this will indeed be possible, it will be some time before theology succeeds in constructing a Christian view of the cosmos in any way comparable to that of the Middle Ages.

Turning our attention to the world picture devised by Teilhard, we must also ask whether such a picture of the universe has sufficient scientific basis to serve as the foundation of a speculative theology. As far as the past is concerned, Teilhard's theory would appear to be scientifically defensible, but there is some hesitation when it comes to the future. Does evolution really have a convergent character? There are no doubt many symptoms pointing in this direction. Yet no one will dare claim that these indications are sufficient to remove all doubt on this issue. It is, however, precisely the vision of the future that is essential to the whole system. Scientifically speaking, the matter is by no means resolved. While it is possible that Teilhard will be proven right on this point also, it is understandable that some theologians are for the time being reluctant to adopt a definite position. But that does not alter the fact that many other aspects of Teilhard's work have an impact on present-day theology.

Finally, there is the question of Teilhard's identification of the Omega point with the Christ of the Parousia. Such an identification is only meaningful of course in the supposition that Teilhard's view of evolution is found to be correct. There is, moreover, the question as to whether we are to conceive the biblical notion of eschatology in a realistic or in a more existential sense. This question has given rise to a variety of opinions, even though it would appear that, in spite of all demythologizing, the realistic interpretation is more in line with Christian tradition. These and many other questions demand further investigation. It is clear, however, that having met with such a wide response, Teilhard's ideas are bound to stimulate continued discussion of these fundamental issues.

Chapter Nine

THE NEW CONFRONTATION BETWEEN WORLD PICTURE AND THEOLOGY

Theology, it has often been said, is never a definitive statement of religious doctrine but only a temporary expression of the manner in which this doctrine has been defined by a particular community at a particular moment in its history. Bearing this in mind, we have looked at earlier theological conceptions in an attempt to trace the influence of the prevailing world picture. Starting with St. Thomas Aquinas and his belief in a static and perfect world order we have finally reached Teilhard de Chardin and his view of convergent evolution. In the preceding chapters we have seen how a total revolution took place in the picture of the world around us, so that nothing remains of the medieval view concerning the structure of the cosmos. The world that has emerged is entirely new and unexpected and the cultural climate we live in differs profoundly from that of antiquity or the Middle Ages. But how has theology fared in all this? Has it been able to cope with these changes? Have we succeeded in breaking away from the medieval interpretation of faith and in speaking a language that can be understood by contemporary man? Do we already possess an interpretation of Christianity that is in harmony with the cultural situation in which we now find ourselves? This question is by no means easy to answer, but it should in any case arouse the interest of the theologian and of anyone concerned with religion.

Before we deal directly with this then, it would be useful to look back over the way we have come in order to clarify our present situation. As we have seen, the medieval theologian concentrated on integrating Christian doctrine as perfectly as possible into his total view of cosmic reality. It did not occur to anyone to doubt the validity of this explanation of the world, since it appeared to be warranted not only by Greek and Arabian science but equally so by biblical and patristic tradition. In this way an interpretation of Christian doctrine developed that was fully adapted to the prevailing world picture, from which it derived considerable credibility. But it was precisely this cosmology that soon turned out to be based on an illusion. With the emergence of a totally new view of reality in the seventeenth century the fate was sealed for a world picture which had dominated Western thought for almost two thousand years and which had never failed to influence the interpretation of Christian faith. But the condemnation of Galileo and the attitude of the ecclesiastical authorities towards the heliocentric system created the impression that the old world picture was inseparable from Christianity and that the resulting interpretation of faith was the only correct one. Thus profound changes took place in all spheres of culture—except theology. Generally speaking, theologians simply retained the conceptions of medieval theology. For although the old cosmology disappeared silently from theological handbooks, the spirit of the traditional world picture was left intact. Theologians were, on the whole, given little freedom: the doctrinaire attitude of the Roman authorities clearly did not allow them sufficient scope for a thorough rethinking of Christianity. It seemed as if the old picture of the universe continued to exercise its influence as a kind of archetype in the subconscious of the Church. What had originally held good as an expression of a true religious experience was thus unconsciously converted into a codified and dogmatic theory, a rigid and complicated system, that was henceforth considered the only possible expression of Christian faith, with the result that change and development were only thought to be possible if they occurred within the framework of this system.[1]

There was certainly no lack of isolated thinkers—one need only think of Newman or Guardini—who repeatedly demanded more openness towards modern thought, but, on the whole, the situation we have described seemed to characterize Catholic theology as late as the eve of the Second Vatical Council. Time will tell whether Vatican II signifies a real turning point. When we look closely at certain documents such as the *Dogmatic Constitution on the Church* and the *Pastoral Constitution on the Church in the Modern World,* we can, it is true, find several allusions and formulations that point to a change in the traditional world picture. To conclude from this, however, that the new world picture has been consistently accepted would be a gross exaggeration.

The Protestant theologian George A. Lindbeck, an observer at the Second Vatican Council, has explicitly raised the question of which world picture governed the Council.[2] It seemed to him that Vatican II has to be seen as a transitional council in which the old and the new come together. Though the documents themselves are often ambiguous, forming a hodgepodge of old and new ideas, with only sporadic references to present-day science and modern biblical exegesis, it would appear that the views of the Council Fathers increasingly evolved in this direction. Evidence of this is to be found not only in the documents but in the private discussions which took place and in which the name of Teilhard de Chardin was heard more often than that of any other modern thinker. All in all, however, any mention of an avowedly new outlook seems to be immediately replaced by archaic ideas. This is the case, for example, in the *Dogmatic Constitution on the Church* where we find a beautiful description of the eschatological nature of the Church (Art. 48), but are then thrown back upon traditional thought-categories (Art. 49–51). The realistic eschatological view of the Council is most clearly evident in the *Pastoral Constitution on the Church in the Modern World* (Art. 43). But we cannot speak of there being a consistent rethinking of Christianity within the framework of the modern world picture.

From all of this we can see that Catholic theology is in a critical period of transition. The medieval interpretation of Christianity has become obsolete, while the new interpretation has yet to find a definite form, with the result that there is much confusion and uncertainty. W. H. van de Pol has rightly characterized our age as "the end of conventional Christianity." There will, of course, be those who close their eyes to the changes that have taken place in our understanding of man and the world and cling to earlier conceptions. But such an attitude is no longer viable. An increasing number of Christians, seeing that earlier formulations of faith have become entirely unsatisfactory, clearly realize that the question of the meaning of Christianity must be raised in a totally new way. What is currently going on in the Christian world is not simply the emergence of a new trend in theology or a new school of thought in the closed little world of academics, but rather an essential change in the deeper layers of Christian consciousness itself, a search for a new concept of Christ and of his significance for the life of humankind, a desire for a new concept of God that is consonant with our contemporary experience of reality. This process has only started and, like every process, it is not immediately discernible, but is for that reason no less real. What strikes us at the moment is, of course, the collapse of traditional theology and the institutions and practices which invoked its authority.

The sooner we rid ourselves of these antiquated conceptions, the sooner there will be a fresh opportunity for Christianity. The primary task of present-day theology is, therefore, to free Christ and his work from the grip of an obsolete theology in order to demonstrate from a new foundation his true and lasting significance for the moral and religious life of humankind. Far from detracting from Christian tradition, this actually deepens and refines the traditional insight into faith.

This work is now in full progress in theological circles of all denominations. With a devotion equal to that of previous ages, and with all the resources of the natural and human sciences, an effort is currently being made to build a new theological synthesis, which even though it is not yet complete has already recorded significant results. Inevitably, there have also been some mistakes, but this is the price of progress in any field.

It is certainly not our intention to review the many attempts of recent years to rethink Christianity in the context of our contemporary experience of the world. Reliable information concerning present-day theological currents can readily be found in the works of H. Zahrnt,[3] John Macquarrie,[4] J. Sperna Weiland,[5] or T. M. Schoof.[6] Neither do we intend to treat all the questions that arise in such an undertaking, but shall have to restrict ourselves to asking how much our present view of the world has a role to play in our search for a new concept of what Christianity has to say about Christ and God. In answering this question we must also confine ourselves to a few provisional suggestions.

From our earlier considerations it should be evident that a study of the relationship between man's changing world picture and theology is particularly helpful in gaining a better insight into the history of theology. The same has to be said of the present situation in theology. For it is precisely the changes in our world picture which compel us to review previous positions in an attempt to find a new formulation for the content of faith.

In the introductory chapter to the *Pastoral Constitution on the Church in the Modern World* there is explicit mention of the fact that contemporary man has undergone a radical change, with a further allusion to the changes that have taken place in our view of the world. Contemporary man has, it is said, increasingly abandoned the "static" conception of the order of things, turning instead to a "dynamic" and "evolutive" view of things. And this, of course, has given rise to many new problems.[7] One of these would appear to be the central problem of a contemporary formulation of Christianity, even though the Second Vatican Council did not actually go into this vital matter.

We have already recalled the golden rule of A. C. Crombie with regard to the manner in which a scientific theory has to be studied: before judging a scientific system of thought, it is important to trace the question it was meant to answer, for only when we have properly understood the problem can we judge the answer. What holds good for the study of a scientific theory equally applies to the study of theology. A precise formulation of the question a theory is designed to answer is, then, of utmost importance, the more so because the question is seldom made fully explicit. Bearing this in mind, we must ask what it was that led theologians of previous ages to systematize Christian doctrine in the way they did. What was the precise question they started from when they constructed their theology?

Crucial to their inquiry was, of course, the question of the teaching and the person of Christ, whose appearance on earth had left such a lasting impression. It is to be noted, however, that the question as to the significance of Christ was raised by people in very concrete historical and cultural circumstances—the well-defined situation of one who knows he lives in a world which had originally been created in perfect order and beauty but which had in some mysterious way been abandoned to chaos through the guilt of the first man. The fundamental question of classical Christology can therefore be formulated as follows: what significance must we ascribe to Christ in a world created in perfect order but then disrupted by original sin? What did Christ have to offer such a world? The theological answer to this question is well known: Christ came into the world to restore order, to return man and the world to original justice and perfection.

It is important to take a closer look at this question and answer, for they constitute the basic framework within which all theological interpretation of Christian doctrine was carried out for many centuries. The question presupposes two things: that the world had been created in perfect and immutable order and that this order had been disrupted by the Fall. Christ's life and death were thus seen against the background of a world picture whose main features were vividly present in the medieval mind. Theological treatises gave a most detailed analysis of the inner order and perfect harmony of the first man, culminating in a system of natural, preternatural, and supernatural gifts which made him into a kind of "superman," favored with impassibility and immortality, free of all inordinate desire and sanctified by divine grace. It was precisely because this point was felt to be so important that it received such extensive treatment in earlier theological writings. While there were subtle controversies on matters of lesser importance, such as the theoretical possibility of a man with a pure nature,[8] the general picture had to be left intact. What was beyond all doubt was that man and the world had been created in the highest conceivable perfection and that this perfection was destined to last throughout the ages.

But the second element in the question was no less significant and likewise gave rise to detailed consideration, and elaborate speculation. From the time of St. Augustine in particular, attention was increasingly paid to the Fall and its consequences for humankind, in spite of the fact that very little had been said of this in Scripture and in the earliest Christian writings. The theme of the Fall thus developed into a matter of outstanding importance to theology. Though there were differences of opinion concerning matters of minor importance, one did not tolerate any doubt with regard to the issue itself: that on account of the Fall the original order had been disrupted and humankind had lost all preternatural and supernatural gifts. There was at the same time much discussion as to what extent original sin also affected man's natural qualities—a theme which became popular especially during the Reformation and for a long time afterwards.

Only in the supposition of a perfect order disrupted by original sin, it was argued, could one truly understand the deeper significance of Christ's appearance on earth. St. Thomas Aquinas also held, at first somewhat hesitantly, but later quite resolutely, that the Incarnation would not have taken place had there been no original sin. While Duns Scotus did not share this view, he still remained faithful to the traditional schema: that Christ's appearance as the suffering and humiliated Messiah could be accounted for by original sin which required atonement. The greatest care was taken in formulating and defending these two presuppositions—the basis of the whole theological system.

What we have so far described could be labeled in Kuhn's terminology as the paradigm of traditional Christology. For despite all theological disputes of the past and despite all changes in the generally accepted world picture, the paradigm was left intact, with all theological controversy both in the Catholic Church and between the Protestant Churches remaining within this framework. But it is precisely this situation which now seems to be coming to an end. The present debate concerns the paradigm itself that is no longer considered to be tenable. The more we are influenced by the modern world picture, the more the traditional paradigm loses all credibility. How can we still believe in the existence of a perfect world order at the beginning of time, when all that modern science has to tell us about the past of man and the world points in a different direction? All attempts to preserve the traditional view of the state of paradise have failed,[9] because it is clear that there never has been a perfect, hierarchical, and immutable world order. Thus our modern world picture, however incomplete, compels us to reject the traditional question as simply irrelevant.

Having compelled us to abandon the traditional paradigm, the new picture of the universe also provides us with the means of reformulating the fundamental question of theology. It is, moreover, our right and obligation to raise the question of Christ's significance from the situation in which we now find ourselves. The basic question for present-day theology can thus be formulated as follows: what significance does Christ have for a world that is characterized by evolution? Such a change in the basic question must necessarily produce a new interpretation of Christian doctrine. But only a radical reflection can restore credibility in Christianity.

The focal point of our contemporary world picture is undoubtedly the idea of evolution. As a result, today's Christian lives in an entirely different world, a totally new intellectual climate in which the earlier question and answer no longer have any meaning. For this reason the question of Christ's significance can only be raised within the context of the world as we now know it—thanks to the work of Darwin and Mendel, Marx and Freud, Einstein and Heisenberg, Nietzsche and Wittgenstein.

This change in the fundamental question raised by theology also explains why there is now so little interest in the theological disputations which formerly held the attention of the various Christian Churches. For whether we are Catholic or Protestant, Anglican or Orthodox, the same question confronts us all, obliging us to come together to reflect on the most fundamental issue for present-day theology: the meaning of Christ in today's world. This question is, moreover, relevant to the humanist and the Marxist as well, in that the figure of Jesus Christ indisputably belongs to the tradition of Western culture: his teaching is connected with the ideals which have remained with us throughout the ages, such as the sense of truth and humanity and the desire for justice, peace, and intellectual freedom. For all of us, then, the question is significant.

The Polish Marxist philospher Leszek Kolakowski has drawn attention to the unique position of Christ in Western cultural tradition, pointing out how a number of fundamental values which constitute the wealth of this tradition are inseparably connected with the name of Jesus Christ. To separate these values from Christ, even outside a Christian context, is a kind of cultural deprivation, For this reason, argues Kolakowski, criticism of Christianity must not go so far as to fail to appreciate these values and the fact that they have their origin in Christ. To claim that the same values can also be found elsewhere is not to the point, for in Western culture they are in fact associated with the name of Jesus Christ. Any attempt, therefore, to abolish Christ from our culture on the pretext that we no longer believe in the God in whom he believed is quite ridiculous. It is nothing but the work of unenlightened minds, convinced that a vulgar atheism not only suffices as a view of the world, but also gives them the right, by virtue of their doctrinaire program, to mutilate any given cultural tradition by depriving it of its source of life.[10] It cannot be denied that Jesus of Nazareth has played a significant role in the spiritual evolution of mankind. Besides the millions of people who have recognized in him the true teacher of the authentic life, there are millions of others who have unconsciously profited by his influence, perhaps much more than they themselves suppose or are willing to admit. Christ has in fact given history a new orientation, equivalent to a revolution infinitely more profound than anything ever achieved by political or social reformers, because his teaching was not in the first place aimed at change in outward living conditions but at the inner liberation of man, paving the way towards a richer human existence.

Many writers, from Renan to Bloch, have recognized the revolutionary character of Christ's life, even though it has not always been properly understood. The fact that his teaching contained criticism of the society of his day is clear from the earliest writings about him. But to claim that he primarily strove for political revolution, as Bloch believes, is at least a one-sided view. Christ's concern was with a new way of life, a reversal in the established scale of values, a radical conversion whereby human existence acquired a richer quality and wider dimension. His followers have rightly felt his teaching as a "liberation" or "redemption": redemption and liberation from the prevalent views of their surroundings, from the narrow-mindedness of the Scribes and Pharisees, from oppressive social conventions and hollow traditions, from all mysterious powers which violate man's conscience; redemption and liberation from the illusions to which we are exposed, such as the illusion of power, money, and wealth and from all forms of self-delusion, conceit, and self-righteousness.

It was Christ's desire that his followers should become truly free. This was clearly seen by Paul: "For freedom Christ has set us free"

(Gal. 5:1) and thus we are to rise above our surroundings and our-selves.[11] While some people rejected Christ for this reason, condemn-ing him as a dangerous rebel who undermined the foundations of the established order and had therefore to be made away with, others decided to accept the Gospel and to recognize the superiority of Christ's teaching above all that had previously been held to be true, even if it came from Abraham, Moses, or the prophets. The followers of Christ would triumph over all persecution, and even death, for in him a new form of "life" had emerged, which henceforth presented humankind with its definitive dream, its highest aspiration, showing the way towards its further completion.

This evangelical concept of freedom was greatly impaired, however, by the medieval conception of the world, which submitted both the individual and society to a fixed order willed by God. From this view a whole set of directions, laws, and institutions was distilled and im-posed in the name of God, restraining human freedom on all sides. Even when the modern concept of freedom was discovered and man was no longer seen to be dependent on a predominating world order, but had, in the words of Kant, the feeling of coming of age for the first time, theology refused to accept the challenge of the Enlighten-ment and continued to maintain the old paradigm in disguised form as the criterion for all human activity and the framework for inter-preting Christian doctrine. In this way religion become divorced from culture—a situation that has continued to this day.[12]

The idea that man had to submit himself unconditionally to an im-mutable cosmic order has, as such, nothing to do with Christianity. Christ never once appealed to such a scheme to support his teaching. If Christianity became involved in the cosmization process at an early stage, this was the influence of the Hellenistic culture with which it came into contact and which had considerable impact on its further development. Moreover, the Hellenization process was so gradual that many were perhaps not even aware of it and came to hold its final result in scholasticism as an authentic interpretation of the Gos-pel. But the Gospel is not concerned with situating man in a fixed cosmic order: man is always seen as an autonomous being that has to determine his attitude towards God and his fellow man in complete freedom, letting himself be guided only by love and respect. In the Gospel man is not confronted with the cosmos but with himself, with his conscience, with his desire for truth, justice, and authenticity. To make this freedom possible, God had to conceal himself, becoming a "hidden God," in this way allowing room for an autonomous human existence. That is not to say that man's desire to situate himself in the world as a whole has to be rejected as simply irrelevant. Yet it has nothing to do with Christianity as such. Christianity soon managed to disentangle itself from Jewish law and traditions; it must equally free itself from the influence of the Greek concept of cosmos and its resulting casuistry. This is an important aspect of its redemptive and liberating power.[13]

Twice in its history the Jewish people avoided the temptation of being absorbed into an alien culture: the exodus from Egypt and the return from Babylon. On each occasion it was a question of a highly developed culture characterized by a cosmic religiosity wishing to subject man to a general cosmic order, but Israel continually refused to subscribe to such a view, preferring to wander about in the desert than to renounce its spiritual freedom and autonomy. Yet it was precisely in the teaching of Jesus that this striving after spiritual freedom found its highest expression. If Christianity in its later development still accepted a concept of cosmic order, it was not by virtue of its inner logos, but as a result of the logos that was already found in Greek thought and increasingly dominated the Christian concept. A new exodus is taking place in Christianity today, which once again must free itself from a concept of cosmic order in which it is incarcerated.

A concrete manifestation of this is found in what we are now apt to describe as a secularization process. When nowadays a number of aspects of human existence lose their religious aureole or are withdrawn from the Church's influence, this can be seen as one aspect of a dealienation process in the sense given to this term by Peter Berger. Today we witness the end of what has clearly been a cosmization process in Western cultural tradition. For man is again becoming conscious of the need to take his destiny into his own hands, instead of being guided by an imaginary concept of cosmic order that can prescribe any line of conduct whatsoever. This immediately provides Christianity with a fresh opportunity to find its true form again and rid itself of any foreign elements which have been added. The present crisis in the Church can thus rightly be considered a purification process.

The meaning of the statement "the truth shall make you free" is not only that truth finds its completion in freedom, but that freedom is actually the touchstone of truth. Anything that does not lead to true freedom must be rejected as untrue. For this reason the Gospel is a constant call to freedom, an invitation to shape our own lives rather than allow ourselves to be influenced by an imaginary world order or to have any code simply thrust upon us.

It will not be easy to free Christianity from the Greek paradigm with which it has long been so closely connected and with which it is still unconsciously identified by many people. Indeed it will take some time before we are actually able to rid ourselves of all the consequences of this dangerous and undesirable alliance. A radical change is now taking place in this respect. The rediscovery of the evangelical concept of freedom is the main concern of the present theological debate, the outcome of which will most certainly be decisive for the future of Christianity.

But there are many aspects to this rediscovery of Christian freedom. If the Gospel message implies the "liberation" of man from the domination of an imaginary world order, confronting him once again with his own conscience and responsibility, the question immediately arises as to the meaning of this freedom: freedom for what? (Camus). "Freedom of" clearly has meaning only when it leads to "freedom for." What purpose does freedom serve? Is it only a "useless passion," as Sartre believes, or does it have a deeper meaning?

Since man emerged in the cosmic evolution as a new being, entirely different from everything that preceded him, this cosmic background is not able to prescribe a fixed line of conduct or provide any definite idea as to how he should shape his life. Man must therefore proceed tentatively to an unknown future, entirely free to determine his own path of life as the "first free man of nature" (Herder). In this situation the Christian again asks himself how he shall use the freedom he has acquired and what inspiration the Gospel can give to his creative power. What does it mean to be a "free" man in the world and to live this freedom in a Christian sense?

This question is a fundamental concern of contemporary theology, in particular the "theology of hope" or "eschatological theology" and "political theology" or the "theology of revolution," which are not so much two different trends as part of the same trend. Indeed it is striking how the innovators of the theology of hope gradually evolved in the direction of political theology.

The theology of hope has its starting point in the conviction that Christianity is entirely directed towards the future and has something essential to tell us concerning man's destiny. It is the vision of the future and not of the past that characterizes the Christian attitude to life, according to Jürgen Moltmann whose book *Theology of Hope* (1964) provides the first systematic presentation of this school of thought. Doubtless inspired by *The Principle of Hope* (1959), the pioneering work of Ernst Bloch, who approached the theme of hope from a Marxist viewpoint, Moltmann's work met with immediate success in both Catholic and Protestant circles, giving rise to an extensive literature on the subject.[14] For many this rediscovery of eschatology as a theological category of the first order constitutes one of the most significant events in the theology of our time, an event which gives a totally new orientation to Christian self-understanding.[15]

One can readily subscribe to the statement that hope for the future plays an important role in the life of each individual and of each culture. Though it is often said that we make the future, there is as much right to claim, as does Professor Polak,[16] that it is the future which makes us. For the future is not something that appears unexpectedly; in a certain respect the future is already present, "an anticipation we have previously conceived in outline, which acts as a magnet drawing the present towards itself, and which, insofar as we, realizing our responsibility, do not yet choose differently, already contains the germ of future history in conformity with its own previous shadow . . . It is not simply a question of the past determining the future, for it is equally true that the future determines the present."[17]

The conception of the future as a determining factor of the present is very much alive in present-day theology. In the traditional handbooks of dogmatic theology, by contrast, the doctrine of the four last things comes at the very end and is dealt with as if it were a matter of secondary importance. Contemporary theology has reversed this position, in the belief that the apocalyptic idea was, as Ernst Käsemann so rightly pointed out, "the mother of all Christian theology."[18] Christianity has clearly arisen out of hope, out of expectation, out of trust in the future, out of the conviction that human existence does not result in nothingness, but in the Revelation of a divine Presence. It is essentially antinihilistic. What we learn from Christ is that we must never give up our faith in the future, but always maintain confidence, amidst all disappointment and misfortune, in the ultimate realization of a completed world in the Kingdom of God.

This immediately places the believer in a very peculiar situation. It is no longer possible for him to be content with the past, or with existing situations. Faith in the promised Kingdom puts an element of unrest in the heart of our existence, a feeling of discontent with the present that makes us look forward eagerly to what is to come, to the distant horizon of our existence. For this reason a Christianity which only swears by "respected traditions," which only believes in the established order (mostly an established disorder) is no more than a parody of the Christianity we find in the Gospel. For it is precisely in the Gospel that the opposition between old and new assumes particular significance. The division of Scripture into the Old and the New

Testaments already points in this direction. The Gospel tells us that we must look forward to "a new creation," a "new heaven and a new earth," for "The Lord says: behold, I make all things new." Looking forward to things that are to come, to radical renewal, plainly constitutes an essential characteristic of Christian existence. The Christian attitude to life consequently rejects any form of pessimism, firmly convinced that human endeavor will not come to nothing.

The coming of the Kingdom of God was undoubtedly the principal theme of Christ's preaching. Today, however, this expression does not appear to have any concrete content, so that our notion of ultimate reality remains totally vague and indefinite. It is simply said that it concerns a situation, already present as a possibility, which will only be realized in an undefined future. But should we not see in this extremely vague description an expression of respect for the freedom of man? For a concrete description would imply a restriction of our freedom and would immediately throw us back into a situation where we would merely have to carry out a predetermined plan for the future. As it is, however, it is left to us to use our own initiative to give concrete shape to our vision of the future. "Providence," wrote Cardinal de Bérulle, "has placed man in the hands of man." This applies to the future as well as the present. Hope immediately refers us to our own creative ability, to our own efforts, so that there is no question of us having to wait passively. A theology of hope had, therefore, necessarily to result in what is now called "political theology."[19]

This expression has given rise to much misunderstanding.[20] It reminds some people of a kind of "political Catholicism" of former years (Charles Maurras) or the "political theology" of Carl Schmitt, while others recall the lack of political courage among some Church leaders during and after the Second World War, a strong indictment of whom is to be found, for example, in Hochhuth's *The Representative*. But all this has little or nothing to do with the "political theology" which found an avowed champion in J. Metz.[21]

Political theology as is envisaged here has its starting point in the conviction that Christianity must prove itself not only in the distant future or in the hereafter but here and now, in this world. It has nothing to do with politics based on Scripture (in the strain of Bossuet), but wishes to take into account the fact that political reality constitutes the comprehensive and crucial field in which Christian truth has to be actualized.[22] To put an end to the view that religion is a purely private matter, political theology accentuates the social, political, and cultural dimension of faith, seeking to clarify the Church's responsibility in shaping society.

The reality within which we live is primarily a social reality. For it is not the stars and planets but the social and political structures of the society in which we were born that determine our possibilities in life by forming the framework within which we can develop our activity. But these political and economic structures which we have inherited form previous generations were devised under different circumstances from ours and are based on values and views we no longer share. Generally they were the work of a small minority and were explicitly or covertly intended to safeguard the position and privileges of this minority and to serve its interests—which explains why they show such grave deficiencies and gave rise to much injustice. A perfectly just society will perhaps always remain a utopia, but nevertheless a utopia which we must constantly bear in mind, the more so, the further we are from it.

Just as in recent times we have become increasingly conscious of the abuses and injustices that exist in the world and are maintained by existing structures and institutions, so within the Church we have, especially since the Second Vatical Council, become more aware of the responsibility we share in this situation. Are we as a Church community not accessory to the continuation of injustice and oppression? It was long held as a sound axiom that the Church had to observe absolute neutrality in political matters and this was rightly considered to be an improvement over previous ages when the Church was all too often involved in struggle for power. But is neutrality really possible and is it always justified?

The churches are, whether they like it or not, an important factor in the social order. For neutrality is mostly no more than an appearance. In reality it signifies direct or in any case indirect support for the status quo; it can easily be interpreted as tacit approval, thus helping to maintain the existing situation. But do we as Christians have the right to remain neutral in the midst of injustice, when the poor are oppressed and the weak are exploited? It is the precise intention of those who, out of evangelical concern, advocate a "political theology" to unmask the ambiguity of this so-called neutrality and to emphasize the obligation we have to take sides in major issues when human dignity and the general public well-being is at stake—an obligation that is not fulfilled by vague and noncommittal statements that allow everyone to conclude whatever he pleases. What is more, advocates of political theology desire all churches to adhere to the great spiritual aspirations of humankind, particularly those derived from the Enlightenment: the dream of a society founded on true freedom, equality, and fraternity, the dream of the truly free man. Do these ideals not actually contain some truly Chrisitian elements? Yet the churches have always been most hesitant to take part in this endeavor, preferring to lend their support to established positions and remnants of the old order and thus creating the impression that they were ultimately unmoved by the ideal of the liberation of man. Political theology can therefore be said to constitute a critique of the Church in the name of the Gospel, but, however, a critique from within that is not inspired by animosity but by a real concern to see the Church remain faithful to her true vocation.

It will be immediately clear that this is not a purely speculative or theoretical matter. The real intention behind political theology is to strive for practical action and to take a definite position in major issues and in this way to induce church authorities (and their members) to adopt a different attitude towards the great social problems of our time. Instead of being a pillar of counterrevolution as often appears to be the case, the churches, it is argued, ought to be a driving force of the social and spiritual revolution that is now in progress. Largely under the influence of conditions in Latin America, political theology evolved more and more in the direction of a theology of revolution and of liberation.[23]

The word revolution has also given rise to much misunderstanding. For many people it calls to mind the horrid events associated with the French Revolution or the Russian October Revolution. But liberation theology does not advocate a repetition of such atrocities. The term revolution here signifies those moments in history when profound changes have taken place in the social and cultural situation—any outbreak of violence and public rage being considered as secondary to these changes. In the world in which we now live there are many indications of vast changes in social organization. In the Third World, and in Latin America in particular, opposition is growing between the rich minority solely intent on maintaining the status quo and the vast majority who are exploited by this minority and desperately look forward to a change in the present situation. Many experts believe tension between both groups is continually mounting so that one can speak of an increasing polarization with the result that both sides will adopt more rigid attitudes.

More and more Christians are coming to realize that they cannot remain indifferent to such a conflict and that they ought resolutely to take sides, espcially now when the possibility exists of creating decent living conditions for all and when the present inequality in the distribution of goods is by no means inevitable. Is it not our duty in such circumstances to bring about a radical change, working together with all who strive for renewal and the desired revolutionary change? In previous ages the churches were mostly on the side of the ruling powers, and this not only because of the intergration of Church and state since Constantine, but also because of the conviction that there was a fixed world order that had not to be tampered with. But now that this belief in an unassailable world order has come to an end and churches are no longer tied to political instututions, Christianity is once again free to develop into a revolutionary force in the world as it originally was.

Theology of revolution assigns itself the task of reviving and illuminating these revolutionary elements that are to be found in Christianity. Does Scripture not constantly take the side of the poor and oppressed? Do the Beatitudes not favor those who are persecuted? Does the Magnificat not tell us how God casts the mighty from their throne and raises the poor and lowly, how he fills the starving with good things and sends the rich away empty-handed? Christ did not come as rich and powerful but as poor and outcast, thereby establishing a new scale of values. As Ernst Bloch so rightly claimed in *Im Christentum steckt die Revolte*.[24] What a caricature of Christianity it would be if the churches were to become the reservoir of all those who are apprehensive of change (Richard Shaull)!

Theology of hope, political theology, theology of revolution . . . The disintegration of the old world picture with its belief in an immutable world order has clearly paved the way for a new Christian self-understanding.

But the influence of the modern world picture on contemporary theological thought naturally extends much further. Such a radical change in our world picture as that which has taken place in recent years can only result in an equally radical change in theology. The problem of God remains the most vital issue here. But does the change in our view of cosmic reality not also make possible a new approach to this problem? As we have seen, the world picture of a particular period is always closely related to its idea of God. Has the present age with its new view of reality already been able to formulate its concept of God with sufficient clarity? To answer this question would demand a long investigation. What seems clear, however, is that seldom in the history of philosophy has the problem of God aroused so much interest as it does today, not least among those who call themselves atheists. Even under the surface of a naive materialism one can often discern an unmistakable search for a deeper explanation of ultimate reality. All this would seem to confirm Newman's prediction that just as the problem of Christ occupied a central place in the nineteenth century, so the problem of God would become a focal point of twentieth-century thought.

Of the many philosophical currents that have come to light in our time attempting to give a coherent interpretation of our experience of reality, there is none perhaps so worthy of attention as that which has its origin in the work of the distinguished mathematician and metaphysician Alfred North Whitehead. As with many of those who preceded him—one need only think of philosophers like Henri Bergson, Samuel Alexander, Charles S. Pierce, and William James—the idea of evolution occupied a central place in Whitehead's thought. It seems to us, however, that he developed this idea with greater exactitude and more attention to its fullest implications than any of the others. What is clear in any case is that his work belongs to the most outstanding achievements of our time in the field of metaphysics. Moreover, his views have had such a profound effect on theological thought that one can rightly speak of an actual school of thought known as process philosophy and chiefly represented by writers such as Charles Hartshorne, Schubert Ogden, and John B. Cobb, Jr.[25]

While fully aware of Hume and Kant's criticism of the traditional proofs for God's existence, Whitehead and his followers nevertheless believe that a concrete analysis of cosmic reality leads to the recognition of a divine activity in the world from which all phenomena derive coherence and direction. Starting from a philosophical cosmology that is intricately connected with the data of the natural sciences they have opened up entirely new perspectives for philosophical thought and introduced ideas which differ on significant points from those hitherto held good in traditional Western philosophy.

All knowledge has its origin in experience; all concepts have an experimental basis. Yet experiences and experimental observation is preceded by the perception and experience of our own existence as percipient subject.[26] This fact, which Whitehead calls "the reformed subjectivist principle," is fundamental for a proper understanding of the theory presented here. But it is just this elementary fact which, according to Heidegger and Whitehead, has been largely overlooked in traditional metaphysics. Once the starting point of metaphysics was held to be the perception of the world around us and not the experience of self-consciousness, it was evident that the model used to describe reality should be derived from the perceived "objects." Thus we find a predominance of concepts like "being" and "substance" conceived as self-contained with no internal relation to anything whatsoever. Most of the same categories were employed to describe the self, which was consequently understood to be a special kind of substance, a being or thing. On closer analysis, however, we see that the self cannot be described with the help of such concepts, for my *self* is not a thing, a completely self-contained being, but is intrinsically related to other aspects of reality. The self is essentially relational or social. It is, moreover, a constant movement embracing past, present, and future. To exist as a self means always to be related to something else, first and foremost one's own body and then the world perceived by the senses. Moreover, it means a continual process of growth in which successive impressions, experiences, and decisions have an active role and without which the self is not conceivable. Thus the reality which comes to light in the experience of my own self must be described as a dynamic process of growth, intricately connected with the world around me, a process of growth characterized by creativity and mutual relations. The experience of self-consciousness thus provides a different model than that employed in traditional metaphysics. As Ogden rightly remarks, the change from a thing-model to a self-model must signify a veritable revolution in the field of metaphysics, where the main category is no longer the concept of being or substance but that of a dynamic and relational process.

But can reality as a whole be described with the help of this new model? It would seem that this is not only possible but that such a method is actually more in keeping with the view of reality that we have gained from the natural sciences than the earlier method based on a thing-model. Two discoveries in particular have determined our contemporary view of reality: Darwin's evolutionary theory and Einstein's theory of relativity. Evolutionary theory has taught us to see life not as a system of immutable and mutually independent species but as a stream of events in which new forms which are genetically related to each other continually appear. Owing to the theory of relativity and further development in quantum theory and the field theory, we have come to understand subatomic reality as a flow of energy and a network of mutual relations. In this way creativity and relativity determine our view of reality. The world as we see it today does not consist of things placed next to each other, of totally independent objects, but rather of mutually dependent events. It is, then, in this creative process that Whitehead sees the most precise expression of reality; this becomes for him the most universal category, "the Category of the Ultimate," the "universal of universals." We see the world as a system of mutually related events, not of things placed alongside each other. The latter are only moments in the universal process of becoming—"actual entities" or "actual occasions"—that is, they are characterized by creative synthesis. That is not to say that the philosophy of becoming rejects the concept of being; it merely emphasizes the fact that in our world all being is a being-in-becoming and thus implies constant renewal.

The world is clearly a process of becoming and this process is reality itself. To describe this reality we should, as we have said, preferably employ the self-model that is more appropriate to the results of contemporary science. But what does this model teach us about the deeper nature of the process of becoming going on in and around us? Analysis of human existence reveals, first and foremost, that man creates himself by the many decisions, big and small, that make him what he is. Each moment implies a choice and the succession of decisions making up our lives constitutes our spiritual stature. Man is thus "a self-creative creature," "a creative becoming," the experience of which process we are apt to describe with the term "freedom." Man is consequently a creature that creates himself in freedom. Yet this self-creative activity which we see in man is by no means an exception. Indeed, it is everywhere to be found in the world around us. The evolution of material and biological phenomena continually involves "decisions" whereby one of the many possibilities present in nature is realized and the others rejected—take for instance the uncertainty principle in physics or "arbitrary" mutations in biology. The world is also a series of decisions and in this sense we could say that freedom forms a dimension of the universe. Freedom must be seen as the essence of reality and not merely as a particular case. To exist, therefore, means to create oneself and thereby also bring about the self-creation of those by whom we are known.[27] So not only man but the whole world is a self-creative reality. Similarly, all events that take place in this process of self-creation are mutually related and cannot be separated from this network of relations. Creativity and relativity are thus the fundamental properties of reality.

This also holds good with regard to the ground of reality we call God—who must therefore be seen as eminently self-creative and universally related. In Aristotelian metaphysics, which described reality with the help of an object-model, God was considered a being, albeit as the Supreme Being. But God is not a being alongside other beings, however dependent on him the latter are thought to be. The world does not consist of beings but of events. In a metaphysics which describes reality in terms of a self-model or in terms of our most direct experience of reality, God can only be thought of as the supreme Creativity and universal Relation.[28] The question arises, however, whether further analysis of reality actually leads us to the recognition of such a divine reality and whether or not this has to be conceived as a "person."

Reality is, as we have said, a continuous process of self-creation in which new events constantly appear on all levels. But all these events exhibit an undeniable unity and cohesion. What keeps the many "decisions" underlying the universal process of becoming from resulting in total chaos or radical conflict? The world is certainly not a perfect order but even less is it a total chaos inasmuch as most events can be reasonably foreseen forming an infinite variety and yet coherent whole that fills us with awe. How are we to account for this aspect of reality? Is it entirely a matter of chance or does it happen spontaneously or through an innate goodness or wisdom? Or, rather, is the cohesion and fundamental orientation found in the world not attributable to the presence of a universal power of attraction, to the influence of a supreme creativity on all phenomena? Yet this influence and power of attraction must not be thought of as cancelling the freedom and power of decision in all phenomena, for it is conceived by Whitehead as an invitation, as an enticing voice that gives the world a definite orientation. Thus the whole world is seen as an interplay of the individual forms of self-creativity and the eminent form of divine self-creation which is related to all phenomena by virtue of its universal power of attraction. As each person forms a center of relations and is constituted by these relations, it is reasonable to call this supreme self-creativity a "person" in the most eminent sense of the word on account of its universal relation to all phenomena. Taking a closer look at this new concept of God that we find in the contemporary view of reality we can see that traditional atheism and traditional theism are what Harthshorne describes as two sides of the same error, which is, moreover, one of the most characteristic errors of human thought.[29] Over against atheism and theism process philosophers propose a concept of God often denoted by the term panentheism—to be distinguished from both pantheism and theism. While they recognize an essential distinction between God and the world they consider them as so closely connected that our mind cannot conceive the one without the other. Returning to reality as it reveals itself to us we everywhere perceive events which form a harmonious and therefore aesthetic whole and, though there are clearly degrees of harmony, nowhere do we find complete chaos or radical contradiction. Yet pure creativity and pure potentiality are of themselves insufficient to produce unity, cohesion, and harmony, so that a third factor is required to give phenomena their inner cohesion and order. An analytical description of reality thus forces us to recognize that an order-creating principle is constantly at work. God is that ordering element whereby creativity assumes specific characters, and without which no actual occasions of experience are possible. God, in this function, is the infallibly-present ground of experience.[30]

In his primordial nature God is infinite and the eternal ordering-principle of all possibilities; but in his consequent nature, that is to say, in his relation to the concrete world, we must recognize contingency and change, because the evolutive world affects God just as what is known affects the knowing subject. The distinction between God's primordial and consequent nature is rather subtle and demands considerable elucidation.[31] The main difficulty is the concept of "perfection" which appears to be inseparable from the concept of God. How is change reconcilable with absolute perfection? Greek philosophy, which saw in being the principal element of reality, considered change as a sign of imperfection and consequently irreconcilable with the concept of God. It was argued that anyone who loses a perfection (act) is no longer perfect, while anyone who gains a perfection was previously imperfect: God had therefore to be conceived as pure act. But this only applies to a metaphysics in which being is the predominant concept. In a metaphysics of becoming, however, it is not being but becoming that is absolute perfection and this implies growth, change, movement. Moreover, God is, in the words of Scripture, a living God, and life without change can no longer be called life. A metaphysics of being clearly results in contradiction when it comes to explaining God's knowledge of free actions in the future. On the one hand, it is obliged to exclude from God any new acquisition of knowledge, as this would entail a change in God; on the other hand, it cannot be said that free actions in the future are already decided, for how then can they still be called free actions? All sorts of solutions were proposed. Aristotle held that God did not know novel decisions that take place in the world and was thus consistent with his concept of perfection, while Spinoza adopted the opposite viewpoint, claiming that there was essentially nothing new in the world. Mainly for theological reasons, scholasticism attempted to find a mean that would respect man's freedom as well as the imperishableness of God's knowledge, but never reached unanimity on this point—one need only recall the conflict between Banez and Molina—declaring that it was ultimately a mystery and not a matter of contradiction . . . A metaphysics of becoming makes a radical choice of a new concept of perfection, seeing in God eminent self-creativity and the infinite ordering-principle of all possibilities. Insofar as he is related to the concrete world (his consequent nature) one has to recognize limitedness and change in God because these are implied in concrete phenomena. What only exists as a possibility can only be known as a possibility.

But as soon as a possibility becomes reality something essentially new is born and thus makes new knowledge possible. Owing to the fact that he is related to the world we must recognize in God new knowledge, new relations, and even a certain dependence—not that dependence and perfection exclude each other, for does the doctrine of the Trinity not hold that the Son is dependent on the Father and yet no less perfect than the Father? In this respect we can rightly say that God and the world "live very closely together" and can readily confirm Whitehead's statement that God is "the great companion—the fellow sufferer who understands."[32]

Conclusion

In the preceding pages an attempt was made to trace the influence of man's evolving world picture on the current interpretation of Christianity. While this study could doubtless have been extended to include other areas such as the changing images of man, socioeconomic relations, or the theology of other Christian churches, it seemed imperative, precisely because of the extensiveness of the subject matter, to impose certain restrictions. Some important conclusions have nevertheless come to light and the most relevant of these may be mentioned in brief.

First, we have clearly shown that Christianity was very soon influenced by the dominant world picture of the Hellenistic period. This was the geocentric picture of the universe which had been devised by early Greek thinkers and was later to find its classic representation in the work of Ptolemy. The medieval world picture can then rightly be described as an odd combination of Graeco-Roman elements and biblical data.

Moreover, the same world picture impressed its own type on an interpretation of Christianity which remained valid until the seventeenth century and was for a long time afterwords to a great extent able to hold its own, having considerable impact on theological thought as well as ecclesiastical institutions. It need hardly be repeated that the fundamental thought-categories of this interpretation were based on a cosmology which proved to be a mistake.

From chapter three it became evident just how much the then generally accepted world picture affected the interpretation of Christianity: from a religion in which love was held to be the supreme value, Christianity became a religion in which order was placed above all else—an order modeled on that believed to be present in the cosmos.

A second obvious conclusion concerns the gulf that has arisen since the seventeenth century between Christianity on the one hand and modern culture dominated by the natural sciences on the other. Clinging to an outmoded world picture (or at least to the spirit thereof) has proven to be extremely harmful and has promoted a growing alienation. Though other factors certainly played a significant role in creating this gulf, there is no disputing the fact that the condemnation of Galileo and the mentality it expressed, whether or not other elements were involved, greatly impaired the normal development of Christianity.

For Plato and many philosophers after him, the relation between contemplation of the starry heavens and religious experience is most subtle and delicate. It is, then, at our peril that we neglect the invisible bond between cosmology and theology.

Finally, it should be clear from our survey that considerable efforts are currently being made to rethink Christianity within the framework of our present experience of reality. But this task is still far from complete and is, moreover, much more significant than many suppose.

Present-day theology can be said to be confronted with three important authorities: the natural sciences, the human sciences and social theory, not to mention history and the hermeneutics of biblical texts and documents of the past. None of these can be neglected. Yet we are simply scratching the surface, for what is actually involved is no less than a new discovery of the Christian tradition of faith, or rather, a new interpretation of the Gospel message within the framework of our contemporary experience of reality which differs profoundly from that of previous ages.

NOTES

Introduction

1. See Karl Löwith, *Gott, Mensch und Welt in der Metaphysik von Descartes bis zu Nietzsche* (Göttingen, 1967), p. 9.

"Die Titel Kosmologie, Psychologie und Theologie—oder die Dreiheit Natur, Mensch, Gott—umschreiben den Bereich, darin alles abendlandische Vorstellen sich bewegt, wenn es das Seiende im Ganzen nach der Weise der Metaphysik denkt." Martin Heidegger, *Nietzsche* (Pfüllingen, 1961), p. 59.

2. "The whole of modern philosophy springs from the concept of self-consciousness." K. Rosenkranz, *Hegels Leben* (1844), p. 202; cited by Löwith, op. cit., p. 27.

3. Löwith, op. cit., pp. 9–29. This thesis is also to be found in other works of the same author. See *Gesammelte Abhandlungen zur Kritik der geschichtlichen Existenz* (Stuttgart, 1960).

4. Guido Maertens, *Augustinus over de mens: een visie op de menselijke innerlijkheid tussen Hellenisme en Christendom*, Verhandelingen van de Koninklijke Vlaamse Academie voor Wetenschappen, Letteren en Schone Kunsten van Belgie, Klasse der Letteren, XXVII, 54 (Brussels, 1965).

5. Ibid., p. 2.

6. See in this connection A. P. Orban, *Les Dénominations du monde chez les premiers auteurs chrétiens* (Nijmegen, 1970).

7. Albert Schweitzer, *Christianity and the Religions of the World*, trans. Joanna Powers (London: Allen and Unwin, 1939).

8. Karl Barth, *Kirchliche Dogmatik*, Vol. 3, *Die Lehre von der Schöpfung*, Part 2, (Zurich, 1948), pp. 2–6.

9. Peter Berger, *The Sacred Canopy* (New York, 1967) p. 121.

10. As, for example, Christopher Dawson, *The Historic Reality of Christian Culture* (New York, 1960), p. 60: "As I have shown in *Religion and Culture* and elsewhere, all the great civilizations of the ancient world believed in a transcendent divine order which manifested itself alike in the cosmic order—the law of heaven; in the moral order—the law of justice; and in religious ritual; and it was only insofar as society was coordinated with the divine order by the sacred religious order of ritual and sacrifice that it had the

right to exist and to be considered a civilized way of life. But today this ancient wisdom is forgotten. . . ."

The idea of order forms the basis of Theodor Haecker's anthropology: one need only recall the oft-repeated cry "We are hierarchists." *Was ist der Mensch?* (Berlin, 1959), p. 124.

11. On the basis of these considerations Berger comes to the following empirical definition of religion, which is clearly dependent on the work of Rudolf Otto and Mircea Eliade: "Religion is the human enterprise by which a sacred cosmos is established. Put differently, religion is cosmization in a sacred mode." (*The Sacred Canopy*, p. 25). Or again: religion is "the establishment, through human activity, of an all-embracing sacred order, that is, of a sacred cosmos that will be capable of maintaining itself in the ever-present face of chaos." Ibid., p. 51.

12. See Clifford Geertz, "Religion as a Cultural System," in *The Religious Situation*, ed. Donald R. Cutler (Boston, 1968), p. 669: "This symbolic fusion of ethos and world view is involved in any religious ritual, no matter how apparently automatic or conventional." See also by the same author, "Ethos, World View and the Analysis of Sacred Symbols," in *Antioch Review* (1957–1958), pp. 421–37.

13. Berger, op. cit., p. 27.

14. For a critical view of Berger's ideas, see Philip E. Hammond, "Peter Berger's Sociology of Religion: an Appraisal," in *Soundings* 52 (1969): 415–24; John Wilson, "The Dealienation of Peter Berger," in *Soundings* 52 (1969): 425–33.

15. *Gorgias*, 507e–508a, ed. E. R. Dodds. (Oxford: Clarendon Press, 1959).

16. *Memorialia*, I. 1. 11.

17. On this, see Orban, op. cit., pp. 1–7.

18. Ibid., p. 89.

19. A. J. Festugière, *La Révélation d'Hermès Trismégiste*, Vol. 2, *Le Dieu cosmique* (Paris, 1949).

20. *Naturalis historia*, II. 1: "mundus sacer est, aeternus, immensus; totum; infinitus et finito similis; omnium rerum certus et similis incerto; extra, intra, cuncta complexus in se; idemque rerum naturae opus et rerum ipsa natura." cf. Löwith, op. cit., p. 14.

21. *Almagest*, I. 7. 17–24.

22. Berger, op. cit., p. 156.

Part One Introduction

1. "Alii cursus et positiones siderum, et caeli conversionem quibusdam instrumentis manifeste describunt." Hugh of St. Victor, *De vanitate mundi*, lib. I. PL 176, 709 (*Patrologia Latina*, ed. Migne; henceforth abbreviated as *PL*).

2. General literature: Pierre Duhem, *Le Système du monde: Histoire des doctrines cosmologiques de Platon à Copernic* (Paris, 1945–59); especially vol. 3. P. M. Schedler, *Die Philosophie der Macrobius und ihr Einfluss auf die Wissenschaft des christlichen Mittelalters*, vol. 13, No. 1 (Münster, 1916); H. Liebeschutz, "Kosmologische Motive in der Bildungswelt der Frühscholastik," in *Vort. Bibl. Warburg* 3 (1923–24) pp. 83–148; G. Paré, A. Brunet, P. Tremblay, *La Renaissance du XXe siècle: les écoles et l'enseignement* (Paris and Ottawa, 1933); "L'Homme et son destin d'après les penseurs du Moyen Age," Actes du premier congrès international de philosophie médiévale, 1958 (Louvain, 1960); "La Filosofia della natura nel medioevo" (Atti del terzo congresso internazionale di filosofia medioevale, 1964 (Milan, 1966); F. Van Steenberghen, *La Philosophie au treizième siècle* (Louvain, 1966); Hans Meyer, *Abendlandische Weltanschauung*, vol. 3, "Die Weltanschauung des Mittelalters" (Paderborn, 1952).

3. M. D. Chenu, *La Theologie au douzième siecle: Etudes de philosophie medievale* 45 (Paris, 1957): 19–51.

4. See J. M. Parent, *La Doctrine de la création dans l'école de Chartres* (Paris and Ottawa, 1938), p. 146.

5. Pierre Boyance, *Etudes sur le songe de Scipion* (Limoges, 1936); *Macrobius, Commentary on the "Dream of Scipio,"* translated with an introduction and notes by William Harris Stahl (New York, 1952); *Proclus, Commentaire sur le Timée*, traduction et notes par A. J. Festugière (Paris, 1966–67); *Chalcidii Timaeus ex Platonis dialogo translatus et in eumdem commentarius*, Fragmenta Philos. Graecorum II (Scriptorum Graecorum Bibliotheca LV) (Paris, 1881).

6. "The chief problems before the historian of science are, therefore: what questions about the natural world were men asking at any particular time? What answers were they able to give? And why did these answers cease to satisfy human curiosity? An obsolete system of scientific thought, which may appear very strange to us looking back from the 20th century, becomes intelligible when we understand the questions it was designed to answer." A. C. Crombie, *Augustine to Galileo: The History of Science A. D. 400–1650* (Cambridge, Mass., 1953), p. xiii.

7. André von Ivanka, *Plato Christianus* (Einsiedeln, 1964), pp. 189–222. See also W. Beierwaltes ed., *Platonismus in der Philosophie des Mittelalters* (Darmstadt, 1969).

8. In his *Geschichte der Katholischen Theologie seit dem Ausgang der Väterzeit* (Freiburg im Breisgan, 1933), pp. 53–56 Martin Grabmann reduces medieval theological literature to four groups: (1) commentaries on the Bible; (2) commentaries on Peter Lombard's *Sentences*; (3) quaestiones disputatae, or quodlibeta; (4) summae theologicae. The question could be raised whether the Hexaëmeron commentaries may not be considered as a separate group. Indeed, they can hardly be included in one of these four groups, and in any case they exceed the category of biblical commentary. One need only think, for example, of St. Bonaventure's *Collationes in Hexaëmeron*.

9. M. D. Chenu, "Nature ou Histoire? Une controverse exégétique sur la création au XIIe siècle," in *Archives d'histoire doctrinale et littéraire du Moyen Age* 20, (1953), p. 25. See also J. M. Parent, op, cit.; T. Gregory, *Anima mundi: la filosofia di Guglielmo di Conches e la scuola di Chartres* (Florence, 1955).

Chapter One

1. See Werner Jaeger, *Paideia: the Ideals of Greek Culture*, vol. 1, (New York, 1945), pp. 150–184. "The idea of the Universe plays such a central role in ancient thought that one could say it is characteristic, and that modern thought is distinguished from ancient thought precisely in the fact that the idea of the universe is out of use." From J. Moreau, *L'Idée d'univers dans la pensée antique* (Turin, 1953), p. 5. See also W. Kranz, "Kosmos," in *Archiv für Begriffsgeschicte*, II, 1 & 2 (1955, 1957).

2. H. Diels, *Fragmente der Vorsokratiker*, 12th ed. (Dublin and Zurich, 1966). At Diels's request the later editions of his work give more prominence to a number of texts devoted to the theme of cosmology, thereby showing even more clearly how Greek philosophy was from the very beginning closely connected with cosmology. See also the useful work of K. Freeman, *The Pre-Socratic Philosophers: A companion to Diels's "Fragmente der Vorsokratiker,"* 2nd ed. (Cambridge, Mass., 1966); and G. S. Kirk and J. E. Raven, *The Presocratic Philosophers* (Cambridge: At the University Press, 1963). Upon being asked about the purpose of his life, Anaxagoras is reported to have replied: "to behold the sun, the moon, and the vault of heaven." See Diels, op. cit., vol. 2 p. 5.

3. Of the many works dealing with the history of Greek cosmology the following are of particular interest: M. Sambursky, *The Physical World of the Greeks* (London and New York, 1956), *Physics of the Stoics* (London and New York, 1959), and *The Physical World of Late Antiquity* (London and New York, 1962); René Taton, *Histoire des sciences*, vol. 1 (Paris, 1957); Duhem, op. cit; J. L. E. Dreyer, *A History of Astronomy from Thales to Kepler*, rev. W. H. Stahl (New York, 1953); Charles H. Kahn, *Anaximander and the Origins of Greek Cosmology* (New York and London, 1964); W. Kranz, "Kosmos und Mensch in der Vorstellung des frühen Griechentums," in *Nachrichten der Gesellschaft der Wissenschaften zu Göttingen*, Philol.–hist. Klasse, Fachgr. 1, N. F. 2 (1936–38): 121–61, and "Kosmos als philosophischer Begriff frühgriechischer Zeit" in *Philologus* 93 (1938): 430–48.

4. On Arabian cosmology in the tenth and eleventh centuries, see Seyved Hossein Nasr, *An Introduction to Islamic Cosmological Doctrines* (Cambridge, Mass.: Harvard University Press, 1964).

5. See especially Erich Frank, *Plato und die sogenannten Pythagoreer* (Halle, 1923); A. W. E. Taylor, *Commentary on Plato's "Timaeus"* (Oxford 1928); A. Rivaud, "Le Système astronomique de Platon," in *Rev. d'hist, de la philos.*, 8 (1928); Francis Macdonald Cornford, *Plato's Cosmology: The "Timaeus" of Plato Translated with a Running Commentary* (London, 1937); A. Olerud, *L'idée de macrocosmos et de microcosmos dans le Timée de Platon* (diss., Uppsala, 1951); I. M. Crombie, *Examination of Plato's Doctrines*, 2 vols. (New York, 1962–63); H. Allers, "Microcosmos, from Anaximandros to Paracelsus," in *Traditio* 2 (1944): 319–407; G. Lanczkowski, "Makrokosmos und Microkosmos," in *Religion in Geschichte und Gegenwart*, 3d ed. (Tübingen, 1957); A. J. Festugière, *La Révélation d'Hermès Trismégiste*, vol. 3, *Le Dieu cosmique* (Paris, 1949), pp. 92–152; J. Moreau, *L'âme du monde de Platon aux stoiciens*, Coll. d'études anciennes (Paris, 1939); *Iamblichi Chalcidensis in Platonis Dialogos Commentariorum Fragmenta*, edited with translation and commentary (Leyden: Brill, 1973); C. Von Korvin-Kransinski, *Makrokosmos und Mikrokosmos in religionsgeschichtlicher Sicht* (Düsseldorf, 1960).

6. Plato, 30b/c, 30d, translated by B. Jowett, *The Dialogue of Plato* (Oxford University Press, 1931), p. 450.

7. *Timaeus* 90a

8. "Plato . . . the father of all Greek religious thought": A. J. Festugière, *La Révélation d'Hermès Trismégiste*, vol. 2 (Paris, 1949), p.xvii.

9. Plato, *Laws* in B. Jowett, trans., *The Dialogues of Plato* (Oxford: Clarendon Press, 1964), (3:) 181.

10. See Festugière, op. cit., and *Personal Religion among the Greeks* (Berkeley: Univ. of California Press, 1954), pp. 105–21.

11. This translation by Robert Bridges is to be found in *The Oxford Book of Greek Verse in Translation*, p. 621. See F. Boll, "Das Epigramm des Claudius Ptolomaeus," in *Sokrates* ix, 1921.

12. Francis Macdonald Cornford, *Plato's Cosmology* (London, 1957), p. 6.

13. See F. M. Cornford, *From Religion to Philosophy: A Study in the Origin of Western Speculation* (New York, 1957), p. 211.

14. *Almagest*, I 7, 17–24.

15. Seneca *Ep.* 59. 16.

16. D. J. Allan, *Aristoteles de Caelo* (Oxford, 1936); W. K. C. Guthrie, *Aristotle on the Heavens* (London, 1945); Friedrich Solmsen, *Aristotle's System of the Physical World: A comparison with his predecessors*, (New York: Cornell Univ. Press, 1960); J. De Tonquedec, *Questions de cosmologie et de physique chez saint Thomas d'Aquin* (Paris, 1950). Abraham Paulus Box, *Een onderzoek naar de cosmologie van Aristoteles in de eerste jaren van zijn wijsgerige activiteit* (proefschrift, Univ. Amsterdam, Filosofisch Instituut, Free University of Amsterdam, 1971).

17. A. Mansion, "La genèse de l'oeuvre d'Aristote d'après les travaux recents," in *Revue néoscolastique de philosophie* 29 (1927): 307–41, 423–66, "Aristotelesliteratuur," in *Tijdschrift voor Phil* 2 (1940): 403–26, and "Vooruitgang in de studie van Aristotles' wijsgerige ontwikkeling," in *Tijdschrift voor Phil* 7 (1945): 117–148. For a survey of more recent developments, see Jean Pépin, *Théologie cosmique et théologie chrétienne* (Paris, 1964), pp. 4–11, and, in more detail, Leo Elders, *Aristotle's Cosmology: A Commentary on "De Caelo"* (Assen, 1966).

18. A. Konrad, *Das Weltbild in der Bibel* (Graz, 1917); J. Simons, "De voorstelling van het heelal bij de Psalmist," in *Studiën* 116 (1932): 145–79; G. Schiaparelli, *L'Astronomia nell' A. T.* (Milan, 1903); E. W. Maunders, "The Astronomia Biblica," in *Rendiconti del Seminario matematico e fisico di Milano* 10 (1936): 143–82. See further under "Kosmos, Planet, Weltbild" in *Bibellexikon* (Einsiedeln: Benzinger, 1951); Evode Beaucamp, *The Bible and the Universe* (Westminster, Md, 1962). Concerning the biblical world picture, Thorleif Boman considers that "In short, what we call the cosmological ideas of the Bible are virtually the cosmological ideas of the Middle Ages; they are neither Hebrew nor Greek, but a naive mixture of both," *Hebrew Thought Compared with Greek* (Philadelphia; Westminster Press, 1960), p. 183. See also Michael Landmann, *Ursprungsbild and Schöpfertat: zum platonisch–biblischen Gesprach* (Munich, 1966), pp. 142–71. C. Houtman, *De hemel in het Oud Testament: een onderzoek naar de voorstellingen van het oude Israel omtrent de cosmos* (Francker; Wever, 1974).

19. See Hermann Sasse's account of the term *cosmos* in G. Kittel, ed., *Theological Dictionary of the New Testament* (Grand Rapids, Mich.: Eerdmans, 1965).

20. H. Junker, *"In principio creavit Deus caelum et terram:* eine Untersuchung zum Thema Mythos and Theologie," in *Biblica* 45 (1964): 477–90; H. Renkens, *Israel's visie op het verleden* (Tielt, 1958), p. 39, passim; and *De godsdienst van Israel* (Roermond and Maaseik, 1962), p.28.

21. L. Wächter, "Der Einfluss platonischen Denkens auf rabbinische Schöpfungsspekulationen," in *Zeitschrift für Religions– und Geistesgeschichte* 14 (1962): 36–56.

22. Hans-Friedrich Weiss, *Untersuchungen zur Kosmologie des hellenistischen and palästinischen Judentums* (Berlin, 1966), pp. 248–82; Ursula Früchtel, *Die kosmologischen Vorstellungen bei Philo von Alexandrien: ein Beitrag zur Geschichte der Genesisexegese,* Arbeiten zur Literatur und Geschichte des hellenistischen Judentums, vol. 2 (Leyden: Brill, 1968).

23. Werner Jaeger, *Early Christianity and Greek Paideia* (Cambridge, Mass.: Harvard Univ. Press, 1961), p. 54; Jean Daniélou, *Message évangélique et culture hellénistique* (Tournai, 1961). The transition from ancient paganism to Christianity has been tersely described by Georges Gusdorf: "Christianity substituted itself for Greek religion without breaking with the inspiration of astral piety." *Les Sciences humaines et la pensée occidentale,* vol. 3, *La Révolution Galiliéenne* (Paris: Payot, 1969), 1: 76. This appears to be a correct interpretation.

24. On the use of terms such as *cosmos, mundus, saeculum,* and their significance for early Christian writers, see Orban, op. cit.

25. Festugière op. cit., vol. 2, p. 258; P. Wilpert, "Die aristotelische Schrift: Über die Philosophie," in *Autour d'Aristote,* Recueil d'études offert à Mgr. A. Mansion (Louvain, 1955), pp. 99–116.

26. Festugière, op. cit., pp. x–xi.

27. Clement of Rome, I. Cor. 20, *The Epistles of St. Clement of Rome and St. Ignatius of Antioch,* translated and annotated by James A. Kleist, in *Ancient Christian Writers,* I.; W. C. Van Unnik, "Is I. Clem. 20 purely Stoic?" in *Vigiliae Christ.* (1950), p. 181 ff; Werner Jaeger, *Early Christianity and Greek Paideia,* p. 14: " ... we see Clement refer in that wonderful twentieth chapter of his letter to the cosmic order of all things as the

ultimate principle established by the will of God, the Creator, as a visible model for human life and peaceful cooperation." See also Karlmann Beyschlag, "Clemens Romanus und der Frühkatholizismus: Untersuchungen zu 1. Clemens 1-7.," *Beitrage zur historischen Theologie* 35 (Tübingen, 1966): 21 ff.

28. See E. Wilhelm Möller, *Geschichte der Kosmologie in der griechischen Kirche bis auf Origenes* (Halle, 1860; facsimile Frankfurt-Main, 1967); H. Bientenhard, *Die himmlische Welt in Urchristentum und Spätjudentum* (Tübingen, 1951).

29. J. M. Pfättisch, *Der Einfluss Platons auf die Theologie Justins des Martyrers*(Paderborn, 1910), esp. pp. 93–103; C. Andreisen, "Justin und der mittlere Platonismus," in *Zeitsch. f. neutestam. Wissenschaft* 44 (1952–53): 157–95; L. W. Barnard, *Justin Martyr: His life and Thought* (London, 1967).

30. "The characteristic thing about Origen was that he ... more than any other Christian thinker before St. Thomas, came to see the world as a single whole". J. Daniélou, *Origen*, trans. W. Mitchell (New York, 1955), p. x; see also H. Cornelis, *Les Fondements cosmologiques de l'eschatologie d'Origène* (Paris, 1959), and the works of Richard A. Norris and E. W. Möller already cited.

31. Emile Bréhier, *Histoire de la philosophie*, vol. 2, Part 1, *Plotin*, (Paris, 1926), pp. 452–453. See also Paul Henry's introduction to the English translation of *The Enneads*, 3d ed. trans. Stephen MacKenna, rev. B. S. Page (London, 1962), p. lxx; Paul Henry, *Plotin et l'Occident*, (Louvain, 1934); W. R. Inge, *The Philosophy of Plotinus*, 3d ed., 2 vols (London, 1929); A. H. Armstrong, *Architecture of the Intelligible Universe in the Philosophy of Plotinus* (Cambridge: At the University Press, 1940); E. Bréhier, *La Philosophie de Plotin*, 2d ed. (Paris, 1951).

32. *De div. nominibus*, c. 7, a. 3. *PL* 122, 1155; see also *De cael. hier*, c. 4. *PL* 122, 1047, and c. 5. *PL* 122, 1096.

33. On the cosmology of the Church Fathers, see P. Duhem, *Le Système du monde*, vol. 2, pp. 393–494, and vol. 3, pp. 3–37.

34. *De Consolatione Philosophiae*, Lib. I, 4a., ed. Ludovicus Nieler, Corpus Christianorum 94, (Turnhout, 1957): 7.

35. Ibid., Lib. IV, pp, 77–84.

36. *De civitate Dei*, X, 9. *PL* 41, 387.

37. See Jean Pépin, *Theologie cosmique et théologie chrétienne*: Ambroise L.I, 1–4 (Paris: P.U.F., 1964).

38. F. Cayré, "Les preuves courantes de l'existence de Dieu," in *Rev. Univ. Ottawa*, 21 (1951): 397–413.

39. *Enchiridion*, c. 9. *PL*, 40. 235.

"When then the question is raised, what is that content of belief which pertains to religion, there is no call to pry out the secrets of the natural universe as those do whom the Greeks call physicists, nor any need for a Christian to fear to be ignorant of something concerned with the function and number of the elements, the movement and order and phases of the heavenly bodies, the shape of the heavens, the species and natural attributes of animals, fruits, stones, fountains, rivers and mountains, the measurements of space and time, and the signs of imminent tempests, or of innumerable other facts concerned with those matters which such persons either have discovered or think they have discovered . . . ."(Chap. 9). *Saint Augustine's Enchiridion*, translated from the Benedictine Text with an introduction and notes by Ernest Evans (London: S.P.C.K., 1953).

40 *De actis cum Felice Man.*, 1, 10.

41. "Comm. in Gen. ad Litteram," IV, 3–7; See W. J. Roche, "Measure, Number and Weight in Saint Augustine," in *The New Scholasticism*, 15 (1941): 350–76; On Augustine's attitude toward the natural sciences, see H. I. Marrou, *Saint Augustine et la fin de la culture*

antique (Paris, 1938–39), pp. 148–58, 678. See note 137 in next chapter on work of H. Krings.

42. One of St. Augustine's early writings, written shortly after his conversion, deals with the order in the universe: *De ordine libri duo, P.L* 32, 977–1020; See also *De civitate Dei*, XIX, 11–13; J. Rief, *Der Ordobegriff des jungen Augustinus* (Paderborn, 1962).

holistic, symbolistic and psychological microcosmos." See R. Allers, "Microcosmos, from Anaximandros to Paracelsus," in *Traditio* 2 (1944): 319–407. On this theme, see G. Lanczkowski, "Makrokosmos und Mikrokosmos," in *Religion in Geschichte und Gegenwart* (Tübingen, 1957).

44. R. Leys, *L'Image de Dieu chez Saint Grégoire de Nysse* (Brussels and Paris, 1951); G. B. Ladner, "The philosophical Anthropology of Saint Gregory of Nyssa," in *Dumbarton Oaks Papers*, Vol. 12 (Cambridge, Mass, 1958), pp. 558–94; J. Gaith, *La conception de la liberté chez Grégoire de Nysse*, Etudes de philosophie Médiévale 43 (Paris, 1953); E. Mühlenberg, *Die Unendlichkeit Gottes bei Gregor von Nyssa: die christliche Kritik am Gottesbegriff der klassischen Metaphysik* (Göttingen, 1967).

45. See the excellent work of Lars Thunberg, *Microcosm and Mediator: The Theological Anthropology of Maximus the Confessor* (Lund, 1965); also, Urs von Balthasar, *Kosmische Liturgie. Maximus der Bekenner: Höhe und Krisis des griechischen Weltbildes* (Einsiedeln, 1961); W. Völker, *Maximus Confessor als Meister des geistlichen Lebens* (Wiesbaden, 1965).

46. André Benoit, *Saint Irénée. introduction à l'étude de sa théologie* (Paris, 1960); A. Houssiau, *La Christologie de Saint Irénée* (Louvain, 1955).

47. *PL* 90, 187–278.

48. Ibid., 91, 9–190.

Chapter Two

1. Alfred North Whitehead, *Adventures of Ideas* (Cambridge: At the University Press, 1961), p. 19.

2. In contrast to our culture, which is ultimately based on experience and observation, medieval culture was chiefly founded on the writings of the ancients. Thus C. S. Lewis rightly speaks of "the overwhelmingly bookish or clerkly character of medieval culture." *The Discarded Image: An Introduction to Medieval and Renaissance Literature* (Cambridge: At the University Press, 1967), p. 5.

3. Duhem, op. cit., vol. 3, pp. 20–23.

4. *PL* 122, 439–1022. On this see M. Cappuyns, *Jean Scot Erigène* (Louvain and Paris, 1933); H. Liebeschutz, "Kosmologische Motive in der Bildungswelt der Frühscholastik," in *Vorträge Bibl. Warburg*, esp. 3 (1923–24), pp. 85–110; Henry Bett, *Johannes Scotus Eriugena* (New York, 1964), pp. 48–50, 114–16; E. von Erhardt-Siebold and R. von Erhardt, *The Astronomy of Johannes Scotus Eriugena* (Baltimore: Johns Hopkins Univ. Press, 1940); Duhem, op. cit., vol. 3, pp. 44–62; J. O'Meara and Ludwig Bieler, eds., *The Mind of Eriugena*, papers of a colloquium, Dublin, 1970 (Dublin: Irish University Press, 1973).

5. R. L. Poole, "The masters of the schools at Paris and Chartres in John of Salisbury's Time," in *Engl. Hist. Rev. 35* (1920): 338–39; B. Haureau, *Notices et extraits de quelques manuscrits latins de la Bibliothèque Nationale* 1 (1890): 45–69; Liebeschutz, op. cit., pp. 111, 114; Eduard Jeanneau, *Lectio Philosophorum: recherches sur l'Ecole de Chartres* (Amsterdam, 1973).

6. In Migne *PL* we find one version of this work ascribed to Honorius of Autun (*PL* 172, 39–102) and another included in the works of Bede the Venerable (*PL* 90, 1127–1178). On William of Conches, see the works of J. M. Parent, T. Gregory, and M. D. Chenu already cited.

7. Edited by Parent, op. cit., pp. 142–77; see also K. Werner, "Die Kosmologie und Naturlehre des scholastischen M. A. mit spezieller Beziehung auf Wilhelm von Conches," *S. B. der Wiener Akademie* 75 (1973): 314 ff.

8. Parent, op. cit., pp. 16–17; E. Gilson, "La Cosmogonie de Bernardus Silvestris," in *Archives d'histoire doctrinale et littéraire du moyen âge* 3 (1928): 5–24. Brian Stock, *Myth and Science in the Twelfth Century: A study of Bernard Silvester* (Princeton, N. J.: Princeton University Press, 1972). Winthrop Wetherbee, *The Cosmographia of Bernardus Silvestris: A Translation with Introduction and Notes* (New York and London: Columbia Univ. Press, 1933).

9. Hugh of St. Victor, *PL* 175–77, "Because of these facts, astronomers have divided the world into two parts: into that, namely, which stretches above the sphere of the moon and that which lies below it. The superlunary world, because in it all things stand fixed by primordial law, they called "nature," while the sublunary world they called "the work of nature," that is, the work of the superior world, because the varieties of all animate beings which live below by the infusion of life-giving spirit take their infused nutriment through invisible emanations from above, not only that by being born they may grow but also that by being nourished they may continue in existence. Likewise they called that superior world 'time' because of the course and movement of the heavenly bodies in it and the inferior world they called 'temporal' because it is moved in accordance with the movements of the superior. Again the superlunary from the perpetual tranquillity of its light and stillness, they called *elysium*, while the sublunary, from the instability and confusion of things in flux, they called the underworld or *infernum*." *The Didascalicon of Hugh of St. Victor: A Medieval Guide to the Arts*, translated from the Latin with introduction and notes by Jerome Taylor (New York and London; Columbia Univ. Press, 1961), bk 1, chap. 7.

10. Godfrey of St. Victor; see P. Delhaye, "Godefroy de Saint-Victor," *Microcosmos I, Texte, II Etude théologique* (Lille, 1951).

11. Andrew of St. Victor; see B. Smalley, *The Study of the Bible in the Middle Ages* (Oxford, 1952), Chap. 4.

12. Honorius of Autun, *PL* 172. In his *De imagine mundi* he merely wishes to state what is recommended by tradition: "Hic nihil autem in eo pono nisi quod majorum commendat traditio." *PL* 172, 119. The world is first conceived in the mind of God: ". . . ante tempora saecularia immensitas mundi in mente divina concipitur, quae conceptio archetypus dicitur." *PL* 172, 121. This world is conceived as a piece of music: "Caelestis musica mensuratur, ad cujus exemplum nostra inventa affirmatur." *PL* 172, 140. "Minor mundus [= man] dicitur, dum sic consono numero caelesti musicae par cognoscitur." Ibid. The number seven also plays a significant role; among the many cases involving the number seven he also states that Adam and Eve stayed only seven hours in paradise. *PL* 172, 165.

13. Gerhoh of Reichersberg, *PL* 194.

14. Arnold of Bonneval, *PL* 189.

15. Alan of Lille, *PL* 210.

16. Adelard of Bath; see C. H. Haskins, *Studies in the History of Medieval Science* (Cambridge, Mass.: Harvard Univ. Press, 1927), pp. 20–42.

17. Peter Abelard, *PL* 178.

18. P. Glorieux, "Répertoire des maîtres en théologie de Paris au XIIIe siècle," in *Etudes de théologie médiévale au XIIIe siècle* vols. 17, 18 (Paris, 1933–35). Some examples of the latter: Bernard of Trillia, *Questiones in spheram Joannis de Sacro Bosco*, I, 155; Thierry of Freiburg, *De universitate entium; de animatione caeli; de elementis in quantum sunt partes mundi; de intelligentiis et motoribus caelorum*, I, 162–165; Henry of Ghent, *Opus sex dierum*, I, 388; Peter of Auvergne, *De caelo et mundo*, I, 413; Arnold of Villanova, *Compendium*

astrologiae de judiciis infirmitatum secundum motum planctarum; quaestio de possibilitate et veritate imaginum astronomicarum, I, 323–429; Philip of Thory, *Speculum astronomicum*, I, 292, (authorship uncertain); Henry Bate of Malines, *Magistralis compositio astrolabii; Aequatorum planetarum: Liber de mundo vel saeculo*, I, 409–11; Roger Bacon, *De Cometis; Tractatus de astrorum judiciis; Naturalis philosophia*, II, 60–69; Raymond Lull, *Liber de astronomia; Liber de natura*, II, 147–91; Petrus Auriolus, *Tractatus de principiis naturae*, II, 244; Aegidius of Rome, *De materia caeli contra Averroystas*, VII, 301; James of Viterbo, *Quaestio de animatione caelorum*, II, 310.

19. E. Heck, *Roger Bacon, Ein mittelalterlicher Versuch einer historischen und systematischen Religionswissenschaft*, Abhandlungen zur Philosophie, Psychologie und Pädagogik 13 (Bonn, 1957). See also D. E. Sharp, *Franciscan Philosophy in the Thirteenth Century* (Oxford and London, 1930).

20. A typical example is Michael Scot (d. 1236), the chief astronomer of Emperor Frederik II and much favored by Honorius III and Gregory IX. See Haskins, op. cit., pp. 272–98. On this whole period, see the works of G. Sarton and Lynn Thorndike.

21. M. Grabmann, "Der Einfluss Alberts der Grosse auf das mittelalterliche Geistesleben," in *Zeitschrift für Kath. Theologie* 25 (1928): 153–82; On his significance for the natural sciences, see G. Sarton, *An Introduction to the History of Science*, vol. 3, pp. 934–44, and Lynn Thorndike, *A history of Magic and Experimental Science*, vol. 2 (New York: Columbia University Press, 1923), pp. 517–92.

22. See, for example, the sermon of Alan of Lille in *Sermones octo*, PL 210, 214 (sermo VII), or that of William of Auvergne, Bishop of Paris (d. 1249), on the order in the cosmos that is given as an example for man to follow (M. M. Davy, "Les sermons universitaires parisiens de 1250–1251," *Etudes de philosophie médiévale* 15 (Paris, 1931): 149–53), or the sermon of magister Guiardus, in which monks are compared to the stars: "(Stella) non movetur moto proprio sed sequitur motum firmamenti, sic et veri claustrales non debent moveri propria voluntate sed motu firmamenti, scilicet Dei. Sed multi motu contrario moventur, sequentes proprias voluntates, et propter hoc dicit Daniel (8:10) 'Cornu arietis dejecit de stellis et conculcavit eos.' . . . Stella . . . in uno loco fixa est, sic religiosi et clerici fix debent esse ut loca sua non mutent. . . .Sed quidam sunt qui contrarium faciunt . . . ." Davy, op. cit., pp. 231–37. ("Just as a star does not move by its own motion but follows the motion of the firmament, so true monks ought not to move by their own will but by the motion of the firmament, namely of God . . . But many, following their own will, move by a contrary motion, and for this reason Daniel says, 'And some of the host of the stars it cast down to the ground, and trampled upon them.' (Dan. 8:10). . . And just as a star is fixed in one place, so too religious and clerics ought to be fixed in order that they do not change place. . . . Yet there are those who do the opposite . . . ."). In one of his sermons Bernard of Siena (d. 1444) gives a detailed account of the traditional cosmology, taking it as a starting point for his moralizing views: sermo VIII, sabbato post cinerem, *Opera omnia*, ed. Ad Aquas Claras Florentiae, vol. 3 (1956), p. 135 ff. On another occasion the theme of macrocosm solidus: macrocosm/microcosm is discussed, and this in connection with the text "Qui preest, in sollicitudine." (Rom. 12:8): *Tractatus de beatitudinibus evangelicis*, sermo v, art. 1, c. 3, *Opera omnia* 4:405. Further examples are to be found in A. M. Landgraf, *Dogmengeschichte der Frühscholastik*, II, *Die Lehre von Christus*, vol. 1 (Regensburg, 1953), p. 63.

23. General literature : J. C. Bougerol, *Introduction à l'étude de Saint Bonaventure* Bibliothèque de théologie, série I, Théologie dogmatique, vol. 2 (Paris and Bruges, 1961); Romano Guardini, *Systembildende Elemente in der Theologie Bonaventuras. Die Lehre von Lumen mentis, von der Gradatio entium und der Influentia sensus et motus*, Studia et Documenta Franciscana, III (Leyden: Brill, 1964); J. Ratzinger, *Der Geschichtstheologie des hl.*

Bonaventura (Munich 1959); A. Schaefer, "The position and Function of Man in the Created World according to Saint Bonaventure," in *Franciscan Studies* 20 (1960): 261–316, 21 (1961): 233–382; further bibliography will be found in F. Van Steenberghen, *La Philosophie au XIIIe siècle* (Louvain, 1966); J. A. Wayne Hellmann, *Ordo: Untersuchung eines Grundgedankens in der Theologie Bonaventuras* (Munich: Schöningh, 1974).

24. *Brevil.*, p. II, c. III, no. 1. See also II *Sent.*, d. 2, II, a. 1, q. 1; d. 14, p. I, q. 1 and p. II, a. 1, q. 3.

25. See II *Sent.*, d. 2, p. II, a. 1, q. 1.

26. This was the generally accepted theory since the twelfth century; see Thomas Litt, *Les Corps célestes dans l'Univers de Saint Thomas d'Aquin*, pp. 255–58. In St. Augustine's *De civitate Dei*, c. 9. *PL* 41, 287 we learn that the term *empyrean* (loca empyrea) was already used by Porphyry.

27. II *Sent.*, d. 24, p. I, a. 1, q. 1, conclusion.

28. Ibid., d. 14, p. I, a. 1, q. 1.

29. "I know a man in Christ who fourteen years ago was caught up to the third heaven . . . ." 2 Cor. 12:2.

30. "Caelum videtur habere figuram orbicularem," II *Sent*, d. 14, p. I, a. 1, q. 1, conclusion.

31. *Coll. in Hexaëm.*, visio III, coll. 4, nos. 10–11. There are also seven periods in the history of the world. *Brevil.*, Prologus, art. 3 and II, 2, no. 5. In his commentaries on the Dream of Scipio, Macrobius deals at length with the significance of the number seven (Chap. 6), which is called "the key to the universe" (no. 34).

32. "Utrum caelestium et terrestrium una sit materia quantum ad esse. Corporum caelestium et terrestrium una fuit materia, secundum esse incompletum, quod materia ante productionem habuit; sed post productionem et secundum esse completum different eorum materia . . . . Absque dubio differt materia caelestium et terrestrium quantum ad esse, tum quia sub una forma est corruptabilis, sub alia incorruptabilis, quia sub una forma est subjecta privationi, sub alia non." II *Sent.*, d. 12, a. II, q. 1.

33. Ibid., d. I, I, 12. Cf. Van Steenberghen, op. cit, pp. 224–26.

34. *Coll. in Hexaëm.*, visio IV, coll. 1, no. 1.

35. II *Sent.*, d. 17, a. 2, q. 1.

36. "Locum paradisi in alto situm, usque ad lunarem circularem pertingentem." Ibid.

37. Ibid., d. 17, a. 2. Dubia circa litteram magistri. Dubium IV.

38. For example, *Breviloquium*, Prologus, a. 3, no. 4: "For there is great beauty in the world machine"; see also p. II, c. III, 1. *Brevil.*, p. II, c. 2, p. II, c. 4, 5.

39. "Deus et motor caeli est immobilis," II *Sent.*, d. 2, p. II, a. 1, q. 1.

40. "Sicut influentia Dei movet firmamentum, sic quietat empyreum," Ibid.

41. "Deus movet primum mobile mediante alqua virtute creata, cui ipse immediate cooperatur," Ibid., d. 14, p. I, a. 3, q. 1.

42. "Caelum non est animatum, sed vel movetur a propria forma, Deo defectum virtutis supplente, vel a Deo mediante angelo," Ibid., q. 2.

43. "(Angeli) habent enim virtutes quibus regulant motus orbium," *Coll. in Hexaëm.*, visio I, coll. 2, no. 26.

44. See H. de Lubac, *Surnaturel: études historiques* (Paris, 1946), pp. 216–17.

45. "Nomine intelligentiae hic utimur pro nomine angeli," *Coll. in Hexaëm.*, visio I, coll. 2, no. 26; II *Sent.*, d. 14, p. I, a. 3, q. 2. "Angelos sive intelligentia," *Coll. in Hexaëm.*, visio I, coll. 2, no. 26.

46. "Conveniens tamen est quod intelligentur motus superiorum fieri administratione intelligentiarum. *Coll. in Hexaëm.*, visio I, coll. 3 o. 26. II *Sent.*, d. 14, p. I, a. 3, q. 2b.

47. II *Sent.*, d. 2, p. II, a. 1, 1. 1. *Brevil.*, p. VIII, c. 4, no. 2. *Brevil.* p., VII, c. 4, 7.

48. "Sicut congruum est, Angelos deputari ad ministerium hominum, sit etiam congruum est, deputari ad motum et regimen caelorum," II *Sent.*, d. 14, p. I, a. 3, q. 2.

49. *Brevil.*, p. II, c. 3, no. 5.

50. Ibid.

51. Ibid.

52. "Caelestia (corpora) influunt in terrestria et elementaria quantum ad distinctionem significationum temporum, scilicet dierum mensium et annorum", *Brevil.*, p. II, c. 4., no. 1.

53. Ibid. See also II *Sent.*, d. 2, p. II, a. 1, q. 2, and d. 14, p. II, a. 2, q. 2 ff.

54. "In istis enim proprietatibus (claritas, subtilitas, impassibilitas et agilitas) caelestibus corporibus assimilatur," *Brevil.*, p. VII, c. 7, no. 4.

55. Ibid., p. II, c. 4, no. 4.

56. Ibid., p. II, c. 4, no. 1.

57. *Coll. in Hexaëm.*, visio II, coll. 3, no. 3.

58. "Qui igitur tantis rerum creatarum splendoribus non illustratur aecus est; qui tantis clamoribus non evigilat surdus est; qui ex omnibus his effectibus Deum non laudat mutus est; qui ex tantis indiciis primum principium non advertit stultus est." *Itinerarium*, c. 1, no. 15.

59. *Coll. in Hexaëm.*, visio IV, coll. 1, no. 8.

60. *Brevil.*, p. VII, c. 4, no. 3.

61. ". . . oportet ut contemplativus fixus sit et manens . . . habens oculos. . . aquilinos, fixus in gradibus hierarchicis," *Coll. in Hexaëm.*, visio IV, coll. 1, no. 13.

62. Ibid., visio I, coll. 4, no. 14.

63. Ibid., coll. 3, nos. 14–19, 20–23.

64. "Illae quatuor virtutes conjunctae cum tribus cardinales cum theologicis gyrum faciunt imperturbabilem." *Coll. in Hexaëm.*, visio I, coll. 4, nos. 18–2, Cf. Gregory Magn., *Moral.*, XXIX, c. 31, nos. 68–72. *PL* 76, 515.

65. *Coll. in Hexaëm.*, visio IV, coll. 4, no. 24.

66. Ibid. coll. 1, no. 25.

67. "Omne quod non habet ordinem in universo, non est dicere quod est." *Quaestio de existentia angelorum.* See Ferdinand Delorme, *S. Bonaventurae Collationes in Hexaëmeron et bonaventuriana quaedam selecta,* Ad Claras Aquas Florentiae (Florence, 1934), p. xxii. The above quotation appears in the "Videtur quod non," no. 4, p. 296, but it is also included in the "Respondeo," p. 301.

68. *Coll. in Hexaëm.*, Principium, coll. 2, no. 27. Ibid., visio I, coll. 2, no. 25.

69. *Itinerarium mentis ad Deum*, I, no. 14.

70. Thomas Litt, *Les corps célestes dans l'Univers de Saint Thomas d'Aquin* (Louvain, 1963). Reviewed by John L. Russell, "St. Thomas and the Heavenly Bodies," in *The Heythrop Journal* 8 (1967): 27–39.

"The world system adopted by St. Thomas is entirely tributary to the pseudo-metaphysical hypotheses of Aristotle and the Peripatetic School: without the slightest criticism he fully accepts the theory of the four elements, the theory of the heavenly spheres and all their applications . . . ." F. Van Steenberghen, *La Philosophie au XIIIe siècle* (Louvain, 1966), p. 345.

71. *In octo libros physicorum expositio* (probably after 1268), *In libros de caelo et mundo e posito* (ca. 1272), *In libros de generatione et corruptione expositio* (1269–71).

72. For example, *De judiciis astrorum ad fratrem Reginaldum Socium suum carissimum; de mixtione elementorum ad magistrum Philippum; de occultis operibus naturae ad quemdam militem.*

73. "It is impossible to know a thing perfectly unless we know its operation: since

from the mode and species of its operation we gauge the measure and quality of its power, while the power of a thing shows forth its nature . . . ." *Summa contra gentiles,* II, 1, in *The "Summa contra Gentiles" of St. Thomas Aquinas,* literally translated by the English Dominican Fathers from the latest Leonine edition (London: Burns Oates & Washbourne, 1923).

74. "This meditation on the divine works is indeed necessary in order to build up man's faith in God." Ibid., II, 2.

75. ". . . through meditating on His works we are able somewhat to admire and consider the divine wisdom. For things made by art are indications of the art itself, since they are made in likeness to the art . . . . Hence we are able to gather the wisdom of God from the consideration of His works." Ibid.

76. ". . . this consideration leads us to admire the sublime power of God and consequently begets in men's hearts a reverence for God . . . and this admiration makes us fear and reverence God." Ibid.

77. ". . . this consideration inflames the souls of men to the love of the divine goodness. For whatever goodness and perfection is generally apportioned among various creatures, is all united in Him universally, as in the source of all goodness." Ibid.

78. " . . . this consideration bestows on man a certain likeness to the divine perfection . . . there results in man a certain likeness to the divine wisdom." Ibid.

79. "For errors about creatures sometimes lead one astray from the truth of faith, insofar as they disagree with true knowledge of God. This happens in several ways." Ibid., II, 3.

80. "This consideration of creatures is likewise necessary not only for the building up of faith, but also for the destruction of errors." Ibid.

81. "Man. . . through ignoring the nature of things, and consequently the order of his place in the universe, thinks himself to be beneath certain creatures above whom he is placed: as evidenced in those who subject man's will to the stars. . . ." Ibid.

82. Litt, op. cit., p. 7.

83. "Quod aliter considerat de creaturis philosophus, et aliter theologus." *S. c. g.,* II, 4.

84. "For philosophers consider such things as belong to them by their own nature: for instance that fire tends upwards. Whereas the believer considers about creatures only such things as belong to them in respect of their relation to God: for instance that they are created by God, are subject to God, and so forth." Ibid., II, 4.
"Any matters, however, that the philosopher and the believer in common consider about creatures, are delivered through different principles on the one hand and on the other."Ibid.

85. " . . . sometimes divine wisdom argues from the principles of human philosophy: since also among philosophers the First Philosophy makes use of the teachings of all sciences in order to establish its purpose." Ibid.

86. "Accordingly it is clear that the opinion is false of those who asserted that it mattered not to the truth of faith what opinions one holds about creatures, so long as one has a right opinion about God." Ibid., II,3.

87. See Litt, op. cit., pp. 268–80.

88. A good description of the Thomistic world picture is to be found in J. De Tonquedec, *Questions de cosmologie et de physique chez Aristote et chez St. Thomas d'Aquin* (Paris: Vrin, 1950); H. Braun, "Der hl. Thomas und der gestirnte Himmel oder die Stellung des hl. Thomas von Aquin zu den astrophysikalischen Doctrinen seiner Zeit," in *Angelicum* (1940), pp. 32–76. Cf. Litt, op. cit., pp. 16–17, 20–21.

89. Litt, op. cit., p. 362.

90. *De caelo*, I, 1. 4, no. 36.

91. "Wherefore of all figures the circles and of all movements the circular, are the most perfect, because in them a return is made to the beginning," *S.c.g.*, II, 46.

92. "The truth is that he shared with his contemporaries commonly accepted ideas on the structure of the universe, without discerning the phenomena actually observed and that rational interpretation of these phenomena was still hypothetical, fully dependent on the presuppositions of the time." Litt, op. cit., p. 366.

93. *Summa theol.* I, 66, 2. c. see Litt, op. cit., pp. 44–53.

94. This proposition is repeated thirty-seven times in the works of St. Thomas; see Litt, op. cit., pp. 59–79.

95. "In corporibus caelestibus . . . forma perficit totam potentiabilitatem materiae." *S. th.*, I, 9, 2, c. Further references are to be found in Litt, op. cit, pp. 74, 76, 78, 89. In this respect the form of heavenly bodies is more perfect than the human soul.

96. *S.c.g.*,II, 93, and numerous other places; see Litt, op. cit., pp. 91–98.

97. Aristotle considered the heavenly bodies as animate beings, whereas St. Augustine always remained in doubt about this matter. Aquinas followed the latter's example. Litt, op. cit., p. 108.

98. See Litt, op. cit., pp. 99–108 (*De causis*, lectio V).

99. II *Sent*, d. 14, I, 1, 3, 6.

100. E.g. *S.c.G.*, III, 23.

101. *Ad. Mag. Joh. de Vercellis*, q. 3.

102. *S.c.g.*, III, 22, 23. See Litt, op. cit., pp. 100–106.

103. ". . . besides the first movement, there are many such movements in the heaven, as is proved by the observations of astronomers. . . . Now the heavenly movements proceed from an intellect . . . . Therefore there are several intellectual substances that are not united to bodies." *S.c.g.*, II, 91.

104. "Seemingly the order of the universe requires that whatever is more noble among things should exceed in quantity or number the less noble: since the less noble would seem to be for the sake of the more noble. Hence the more noble things, as existing for their own sake, should be as numerous as possible. Hence we find that incorruptible, i.e. the heavenly, bodies so far surpass corruptible, i.e. the elemental, bodies, that the latter are inconsiderable in quantity as compared with the former . . . . Therefore separate intellectual substances surpass in number the whole multitude of material things." Ibid., II, 92.

105. Ibid.

106. On this see Litt, op. cit, pp. 110–241.

107. *De caelo*, II, 1, 4, no. 342.

108. *S.c.g.* II, 29.

109. "Caelum per motum suum causat generationem et corruptionem in istis inferioribus. . . . II *Sent.*, 2, 2, 3, c.

110. See Litt. op. cit., p. 198.

111. *S. th.*, I, 79, 4, c., and I, 118, 1 ad 3.

112. *In Matth.*, c. 2, no. 170.

113. *S.c.g.*, II, 87.

114. *Opusc. responsio ad Fr. Johannem Vercellensem, generalem ministrum ordinis de articulis*, XLII, art. VII. If man could move his body "without the motion of the heavenly bodies," this would point to an exceptional intervention of God. Litt, op. cit., pp. 213–14.

115. Litt, op. cit., pp. 214–19

116. See, for example *S. th.*, II, 95, 5.

H. Braun, "Der hl. Thomas von Aquin und der gestirnte Himmel oder die stellung des hl. Thomas von Aquin zu den astrophysikalische Doctrin en seiner Zeit," in *Angelicum* (1940), pp. 32–76; Ph. Schmidt, "Die Stellung des hl. Thomas zur Astrologie," in *Stimmen der Zeit* (1954–55), pp. 65–69; L. Thorndike, *A History of Magic and Experimental Science*, vol. 2, (New York, 1929), pp. 593–615.

117. II *Sent.*, 15, 12 ad 5.; *S. th.*, I, 70, 1 ad 2. Further references are to be found in Litt, op. cit., pp. 220–40.

118. II *Sent.*, 11, 2, 6, ad 3.

119. As, for example, in medieval paintings and miniatures, where heaven is represented as a spring landscape.

120. *Divina commedia*, trans. Geoffrey L. Bickersteith (Oxford: Basil Blackwell, 1955), final verse.

121. For example, P. Duhem, *Le Système du monde*, and the works of G. Sarton and Lynn Thorndike already cited.

122. This work is often ascribed to Albert the Great and can therefore be found in his *Opera omnia*, ed. Borgnet, vol. 34 (Paris, 1895), pp. 1–261.

123. See M. Grabmann, *Mittelalterliches Geistesleben* (Munich, 1926), pp. 147–221.

124. As, for example, J. Duns Scotus, Peter of Tarantasia (later Pope Innocent V), Richard of Middleton, Durandus of Santo-Porciano, Francis de Meyronnes, Nicholas Oresme, Denis the Carthusian, Siger of Brabant, Gabriel Biel, and, in general, all commentators on Peter Lombard's *Sentences*.
A typical example is to be found in the writings of Opicinus de Canistris. See R. Salomon, "Das Weltbild eines avignonesischen Klerikers," in *Vorträge der Bibl. Warburg, 1926–27* (Leipzig, 1930), pp. 145–89, and *Opicinus de Canistris: Weltbild und Bekenntnisse eines avignonesischen Klerikers des 14. Jahrhunderts*, Studies of the Warburg Institute, IA and IB (London, 1936).
See also Lewis, op. cit, pp. 92–121.

125. On this point both Aquinas and Bonaventure differ from St. Augustine. See J. Ratzinger, "Der Mensch und die Zeit nach Bonaventura," in *L'Homme et son destin d'après les penseurs du Moyen Age*, Actes du premier congrès international de philosophie médiévale (Louvain and Brussels, 1958; Louvain and Paris, 1960), pp. 481–82.

126. On the concept of microcosm in the Middle Ages, see P. Delhaye, *Le Microcosmos de Godefroy de Saint-Victor* (Lille, 1951); M. D. Chenu, *La Théologie au XIIe siècle* (Paris, 1957), pp. 38–43. Though the term *microcosm* was not employed by Peter Lombard in his *Sentences* (Liber Sententiarum), it still became generally known, especially after the emergence of Aristotle, in whose writings the term is to be found: *Phys.*, VIII, 2, 252, b. 26. See G. Lanczkowski, "Makrokosmos und Mikrokosmos," in *Religion in Geschichte und Gegenwart*, 3. ed. (Tubingen 1957). Robert Javelet, "Image de Dieu et nature au XIIe siècle," in *La Filosofia della natura nel medioevo* (Milan, 1966), pp. 291–92. See also Fritz Saxl, "Macrocosm and Microcosm in Medieval Pictures," in *Lectures* (London: Warburg Institute, 1957), vol. I, pp. 58–72; II, pp. 34–42, 166b, 169b.

127. This is a wrong translation, which we find in the Vulgate. The correct translation of the Greek text reads: "Let every person be subject to the governing authorities. For there is no authority except from God, and those that exist have been instituted by God." Rom. 13:1 (RSV).

128. William of Conches. See Parent, op. cit., p. 148.

129. St. Bonaventure, *Quaestio de existentia angelorum*, in Delorme, op. cit., p. 300.

130. Like Aristotle, Aquinas believed it was man's highest perfection to reflect the whole world order, and its final causes in his mind and spirit. "Haec est ultima perfectio ad quam anima potest pervenire, secundum philosophum, ut in ea describatur totus ordo universi, et causarum ejus. *De veritate*, II, 2.
See also *De malo.*, XVI, 9; *De spirit creat.*, 8, *S.c.g.*, III, 76.

Hans Meyer, *Thomas von Aquin* (Bonn, 1938), p. 583.

"Sine unitate ordinis, non est unitas universi.": J. Duns Scotus, *De primo princ.*, ed. M. Muller (Freiburg im Breisgan, 1941), p. 57.

131. *S. th.*, I, 44, 3, and I, 103, 3c.

132. St. Bonaventure, II *Sent.*, d. 2, p. II, a. 1, q. 2.

133. *De divinis nominibus*, c. 7, a. 3. *PL* 122, 1155. Cf. *De cael. Hier.*, c. 4 *PL* 122, 1047; c. 5 *PL* 122, 1016.

134. St. Bonaventure, *Brevil.*, Prologus, a. 3. 1.

135. Ibid., a. 3. 2.

136. The fact that Scotus sees Christ as the goal of creation does not detract from the anthropocentric character of his cosmology; for he also believes that the whole world is directed to man, and only through man is it directed to Christ.

137. On the medieval concept of order, see Hermann Krings, *Ordo philosophisch— historische Grundlegung einer abendlandischen Idee* (Halle, 1941). According to Krings, the medieval concept of order was especially influenced by Wisd. 11:21.

See *Deutsche Vierteljahrschrift für Literaturwissenschaft und Geistesgeschichte* 18 (1940): 238 ff.

E. R. Curtius, *Europäische Literatur und Lateinisches Mittelalter* (Bern, 1948), pp. 495–96.

138. St. Bonaventure, *Coll. in Hexaëm.*, Principium, coll. 3. nos. 10–12; *Brevil.*, II, 4, 5. St. Thomas Aquinas, *S.c.g.*, II, 22. "If, therefore, the movement of the heaven is directed to generation; and all generation is directed to man as the last end of this genus: it is evident that the end of the heavenly movement is directed to man as its last end in the genus of things subject to generation and movement. This is expressed (Dt. 4:19) where it is said that God made the heavenly bodies *"for the service of all nations."* The "Summa contra Gentiles" of Saint Thomas Aquinas,* the third book, part 1, chapter 22. Literally translated by the English Dominican Fathers from the latest Leonine edition (London: Burns Oates & Washbourne, 1928). Johannes Zahlten, *Creatio Mundi. Darstellungen der sechs Schöpfungstage und naturwissenschaftliches Weltbild im Mittelalter* (Stuttgart: Klett-Cotta Verlag 1979) 2 vol.

139. C. S. Lewis is surely right when he claims: "The human imagination had seldom had before it an object so sublimely ordered as the medieval cosmos." Op. cit., p. 121.

Chapter Three

1. Jacques Le Goff, *La Civilisation de l'occident médiéval*, Les Grands civilisations (Paris, 1965); see also the works of Hermann Krings and Hans Meyer already cited, and J. H. Wright, *The Order of the Universe in the Theology of St. Thomas Aquinas*, Analecta Gregoriana 89 (Rome, 1957). It is not easy to explain this urge for order and harmony so clearly present in the Middle Ages. Psychologists speak of two types of people: the classical and the romantic. while the former is more sensitive to order, equilibrium, rest, and harmony, the latter is more responsive to motion, conflict, adventure, and change. This distinction is already to be found in the opposition between Parmenides and Heraclitus. To each temperament there is a corresponding view of the cosmos.

See Hélène Tuzet, *Le Cosmos et l'imagination* (Paris, 1965), p. 10 ff.; A. Lovejoy, *The Great Chain of Being* (Harvard, 1936); M. H. Nicolson, *The Breaking of the Circle* (New York, 1949); Arthur Koestler, *The Sleepwalkers* (London, 1959).

2. For the early scholastic period, see Henri Cloes, "La Systématisation théologique pendant la première moitié du XIIe siècle," in *Eph. theol. lov.* 34 (1958): 277–329. This study is particularly concerned with the manner in which theological problems are arranged; the author distinguishes historico-biblical problems, logical problems, and a combination of both.

3. "The lack of eschatological sense . . . represents . . . the most decisive defect in the theology resulting from scholasticism." H. de Lubac, *Exégèse médiévale*, I–II (Paris, 1959), p. 642. See also F. G. Fessard, *De l'actualite historique* (Paris, 1959–60), where the same view is expressed.

4. St. Augustine, *Sermones*, 126, 6.

5. St. Augustine, *Didascal.*, 7, 3 *PL* 176, 814.

In explan. cael. hier. magni Dionysii, I. *PL* 175, 926. The allegorical interpretation of nature flourished in the Middle Ages, especially in the works of spiritual writers but equally so in painting and sculpture.

With St. Bonaventure the theory of two books acquires a slightly modified form: "Duplex est liber, unus scilicet scriptus *intus*, quae est aeterna Dei ars et sapientia; et alius scriptus foris, mundus scilicet sensibilis." *Brevil.*, II, 11, 2.

6. For example, Hugh of St. Victor, *Quaest. in epist. Pauli ad Rom* 34 (Pseudo-Hugh) *PL* 175, 440. St. Thomas Aquinas, *S.c.g.*, II, 2.

7. *The Divine Comedy; Paradise*, trans. Geoffrey L. Bickersteith (Oxford: Basil Blackwell, 1955), Canto 1, vv. 103–111. On Dante's picture of the universe, see Willy Krogmann, "Die Welt in Dante's 'Divina Commedia,' " in *La Filosofia della natura nel Medioevo*, (Milan: Vita e Pensiero, 1966), pp. 509–17.

8. See F. Cayré, "Les Preuves courantes de l'existence de Dieu," in *Rev. Univ. Ottawa* 21 (1951): 397–413.

9. A. R. Motte, "A propos des 'cinq voies,' " in *Rev. sc. phil. théol.* (1938), pp. 577–82; J. M. Dorta-Dugue, *En torno a la existencia de Dios: genesis y evolucion historica de los argumentos metafisicos de la existencia de Dios hasta Santo Tomas* (Santander, 1955);—F. Van Steenberghen, *Dieu caché* (Louvain and Paris, 1961), pp. 165–88. On the order and beauty in the world, see Alexander of Hales, *Summa theol.*, 1, 2, p. 1, inq. 1, tract. 2, q. 3.—1. 5; St. Albert the Great, *Summa theol.*, II, XI, 66.

10. Thomas Celano, of *Vita S. Francisci*, II, 29: "Who can describe the joy he experienced when he contemplated the wisdom, power and goodness of the creator in created things? For it was precisely this consideration which so often filled him with awe and ineffable joy, as he looked up to the sun, beheld the moon, or watched the firmament and the stars." See also St. Bonaventure, *Vita S. Francisci*, c. 5 and 8.

11. See A. Mens, *L'ombrie italienne et l'ombrie brabançonne*, Etudes Franciscaines 17 (1967, supplément): 57–60. The quotation from the "Life of Blessed Ida of Nivella" is to be found in C. Henriquez, *Quinque prudentes virgines* (Antwerp, 1630), p. 276.

12. See J. Huizinga, *Verzamelde Werken*, vol. 6 (Haarlem, 1950): 212–15.

13. For a fuller treatment, see A. Mens, *Oorsprong en betekenis van de Nederlandse Begijnen—en Begardenbeweging* (Antwerp, 1947), pp. 9, 104–10, 133–34, 147, 200. Also P. Pourat, *Spiritualité chrétienne*, vol. 2, *Le Moyen Age* (Paris, 1919–28). Chapter 4 is devoted to the school of St. Victor.

14. "Whether divine Providence arranges the inferior bodies by means of the heavenly bodies." *De veritate*, VI, 9;

"That the inferior bodies are ruled by God by means of the heavenly bodies." *S.c.g.*, III, 82.

15. St. Thomas Aquinas, in Litt, op. cit., esp. pp. 174–85. For Albert the Great, see *Summa theol.*, II, tr. XVII, q. 68 (Borgnet, 32, p. 695). For Bonaventure, see Guardini, op. cit., pp. 93–124. The idea that Providence especially

asserts itself in the motion of the heavenly spheres constitutes a significant part of the Aristotelian conception of the relation between God and man. The same idea is repeatedly to be found in his commentators. See Pierre Thillet, "Un Traité inconnu d'Alexandre d'Aphrodine sur la Providence dans une version arabe inédite," in *L'Homme et son destin d'après les penseurs du Moyen Age* (Louvain and Paris, 1969), pp. 313–24.

16. Albert the Great, *Summa theol.*, 22, tr. XI, q. 66 (Borgnet, 32, p. 623). St. Thomas Aquinas, *S.c.g.*, II, 45.

17. Albert the Great argues that God would not have allowed the Fall had he not immediately seen to a remedy to restore this order. *Summa theol.*, I, tr. XI, q. 63 (Borgnet, 32, p. 697) In the same passage (q. 63) he also argues that some forms of disorder can be used as a means to restore order.

18. Albert the Great, *Summa theol.*, II, tr. XI, q. 66. (Borgnet, 32, p. 622).

19. See, for example, St. Bonaventure, *Brevil.*, II, c. 6, no. 3. Cf. Guardini, op. cit., pp. 104–24, which also deals with the history of the concept "gradatio entium," or the hierarchical order of beings. St. Thomas Aquinas, *S.c.g.*, II, 96, and *Summa theol.*, I, 50, 1 in c.

20. F. M. Cornford, *Principium Sapientiae* (New York), p. 147, note 2.

21. T. Gregory, *Anima Mundi: la filosofia di Guglielmo di Conches e la scuola de Chartres* (Florence, 1955). William of Conches, Thierry of Chartres, Peter Abelard, and Arnold of Bonneval all identify Plato's World-Soul with the Holy Spirit without however falling into pantheism.

For St. Thomas Aquinas, see *Summa theol.*, I, 3, 8, c. Albert the Great, *Summa theol.*, II, XI, 66. (Borgnet, 32, p. 623). Augustine did not dare to take a stand on this issue. *De consensu evangelistarum*, I, 23, no. 35. *PL* 34, 1058. Conrad Bonifazi, *The Soul of the World: An Account of the Inwardness of Things* (Washington, D.C.: University Press of America, 1978).

22. "That God is not the form of a body." *S.c.g.*, I, 27.

23. *Quodlib.*, XI, 8.

24. See Litt, op. cit., pp. 108–9.

25. A. J. Festugière, *La révélation d'Hermès Trismégiste*, Vol. II, *Le Dieu cosmique* (Paris, 1949).

26. Aquinas devotes no less than five chapters (41–45) to this question. "If again we grant that the spheres of the separate substances are causes of movement, and that by their movement they cause the forms of sensible things, this mode of knowing separate substances through sensible things, does not suffice for knowing their quiddity. . . . The powers of separate substances surpass all the sensible effects that our intellect understands, even as a universal power surpasses a particular effect. It is therefore impossible through understanding sensible objects to arrive at understanding separate substances." S.c.G., III, 41, translated by the English Dominican Fathers (London: Burns Oates & Washbourne, 1928).

27. Albert the Great, II, *Sent.* 3, 3, and 3, 1.

28. See H. De Lubac, *Surnaturel: etudes historiques* (Paris, 1946), pp. 216–17. St. Bonaventure, I. *Sent.*, 7, 1, q. 2. in c. See Guardini, op. cit., p. 101.

29. *Quaestio de angelicis influentiis.* This text is to be found as an appendix to *S. Bonaventurae collationes in Hexaëmeron et Bonaventuriana quaedam selecta*, ed. F. Delorme, Ad Claras Aquas, (Florence 1934), pp. 363–417.

30. Albert the Great, *Summa theol.* I, XVIII, q. 75, solutio (Borgnet, 31, p. 785).

31. St. Bonaventure, *Coll. in Hexaëm.*, visio I, coll. 2, no. 27.

32. St. Bonaventure, *Brevil*, II, 4, no. 5; ibid., VII, 4, no. 3. Also *II Sent.*, 15, 2, 1. 1.

and 16, 1, 1. 1. in c.; *Coll. in Hexaëm.*, principium, 3, nos. 10–12. The same idea is also to be found in Hugh of St. Victor: "For if God has made all things on account of man, man is the cause of all things." *PL* 176, 205b.

33. St. Thomas Aquinas, *Summa theol.*, I, 96, 3 in c; II, IIae, 64, 1:III, 26, 7 ad I.

34. See St. Bonaventure, *Coll. in Hexaëm.*, principium, coll. 3, nos. 10–12; *Brevil.*, II, 4, 5. St. Thomas Aquinas, *S.c.g.*, III, 22.

35. Albert the Great, *Liber de natura et origine animae*, I, 1, *Opera omnia*, vol. 12, ed. B. Geyer (Aschendorff, 1955), p. 3.

36. M. D. Chenu, "Cur homo? Le sous-sol d'une controverse au XIIe siècle," in *Mélanges de sciences religieuses* 10 (1953): 195–204: "With Honorius of Autun man is seen to have his own value, integrating himself in the cosmos. This idea prevails in *Summa Sententiarum* and comes to fruition in St. Thomas Aquinas."—which does not alter the fact that Aquinas continues to hold that man has to take the place of the fallen angels.

37. Albert the Great, *Summa theol.*, II, 2, q. 7 (Borgnet, 32, pp. 132–33).

38. Hugo Ripelin, *Compendium theol. verit.*, II, 24.

39. St. Thomas Aquinas, *S.c.g.*, II, 81.

40. See Litt, op. cit., p. 198.

41. St. Bonaventure, *II Sent.*, 17, 2, q. 1.

42. St. Thomas Aquinas, *S. th.*, I, 91, 1 ad 2: "Impossibile est aliquid de quinta essentia vel de corpore caelesti dividi, vel elementis permisceri, propter caelestis corporis impassibilitatem. Unde non venit in compositionem mixtorum corporum, nisi secundum suae virtutis effectum."

43. Ibid., I, 118, 2 in c.

44. St. Thomas Aquinas, *II Sent.*, 2, q. 2, a. 3 in c. See Litt, op. cit., p. 198.

45. St. Thomas Aquinas, *S.c.g.*, II, 89.

46. William of St. Thierry reproaches William of Conches with allowing men to be born not from God, but from nature, from spirits and stars. See William of St. Thierry, *De erroribus Guglielmi de Conches*, PL 189, 340. of M. D. Chenu, *La Théologie au XIIe siècle* (Paris, 1957).

47. St. Thomas Aquinas, *Quodlib.*, III, a. 6; *S. Th.*, I, q. 90, a. 3, and q. 64, a. 3; *De Pot.*, q. 3, a. 1, 4.

48. See for example, St. Thomas Aquinas, *Compendium theologiae*, I, 186–187.

49. Ibid., I, 192; *S. Th.*, I, 73, 1 c.
Albert the Great, *Lib. I ethicorum*, tr. 1, c. 6 (Borgnet, 7, 15).

50. Albert the Great, *De resurrectione*, tract. II, q. 10, a. 3. *Opera omnia*, vol. 26, ed. W. Kübel (Aschendorff, 1958), p. 292. St. Thomas Aquinas, *Summa theol.*, I, II, q. 82, a. 1. (Whether or not original sin is a habit.) "In this way it is that original sin is a habit. For it is a disordered disposition growing from the dissolution of that harmony in which original justice consisted".

51. Albert the Great, *III Sent.*, 22, a. 8 (Borgnet, 28, p. 395).

52. St. Bonaventure, *Brevil.*, IV, 6, no. 22.

53. Ibid., IV, no. 7.

54. *Summa theol.*, III, 12, 1 ad 1. ". . . when he saw the heavenly bodies he could understand their power and the effects they have on things here below, although these did not, in fact, fall within his sense experience."

55. Commentarium in III, 12, 1 ad 1.

56. St. Bonaventure, *Brevil.*, IV, 9. nos. 2 and 4; also III *Sent.*, 20, q. 5. On Aquinas, see J. Wright, *The Order of the Universe in the Theology of St. Thomas Aquinas* (Rome, 1957), p. 178: " [Christ] is primarily concerned with repairing the disorder of original sin, since this evil is more universal and deprives the whole race of its ordination to God."

57. Thomas of Celano, II *Vita B. Francisci*, Chap. 125. See A. Mens, *Oorsprong en betekenis van de Nederlandse Begijnen en Begardenbeweging* (Antwerp, 1947), pp. 106–11, and *L'Ombre italienne et l'ombre brabançonne* (Paris, 1967), pp. 55–60.

58. B. Geyer, "Die Siebenzahl der Sakramente in ihrer historischen Entwicklung," in *Theologie und Glaube* 20 (1918): 325 ff.; H. de Lubac, *Exégèse médiévale*, vol. 4 (Paris, 1964), p. 22; J. Dournes, "Bijdrage tot het ontcijferen van het sakramentele zevental," in *Concilium* (Dogmatiek) 4 (1968): 68–85. According to Paolo Scarpi, there were still some theologians at the Council of Trent who attempted to justify the number of sacraments by appealing to the fact that there were seven planets, seven days of creation, seven plagues of Egypt, etc., referring to the earlier example of the scholastic theologians. *Histoire du Concile de Trente*, Vol. 2, (Amsterdam,: Welstein & Smith, 1751), p. 419.

59. Albert the Great, II *Sent.*, 26, a. 1 (Borgnet, 27, p. 444); J. Auer, *Die Entwicklung der Gnadenlehre in der Hochscholastik*, vol. 1, *Das Wesen der Gnade* (Freiburg im Breisgau, 1942), pp. 115–16; H. Doms, *Die Gnadenlehre des seligen Albertus Magnus* (Breslau, 1919).

60. See Litt, op. cit., pp. 6, 185–88.

61. Albert the Great, *Summa theol.*, II, XI, q. 53. (Borgnet, 32, p. 569). St. Bonaventure, II *Sent.*, 14, 1, a. 3, q. 1.

62. St. Thomas Aquinas, *S.c.g.*, III, 150. "That this same assistance is called grace."

63. (How human affairs may be referred to higher causes): "For acts of choice and will are under the immediate governance of God: human knowledge pertaining to the intellect is directed by God through angelic intermediaries. While things pertaining to the body, whether internal or external, and adapted to man's use, are governed by means of the angels and heavenly bodies." Ibid., III, 91. "No particular agent can in every case anticipate the action of the first universal agent: because every action of a particular agent originates from a universal agent: thus here below every movement is anticipated by the heavenly movement. . . . Hereby we refute the errors of the Pelagians. . . ." Ibid., III, 149.

"Order in spiritual beings is more perfect than in corporeal things. Now in corporeal things every movement is caused by the first movement. Therefore in spiritual things every movement of the will must be caused by the first will, which is God's" (Ibid., III, 149). *The "Summa contra Gentiles" of Saint Thomas Aquinas*, literally translated by the English Dominican Fathers from the latest Leonine edition (London: Burns Oates & Washbourne, 1928).

64. A. Landgraf, "Die Lehre der Frühscholastik von Episkopat als Ordo," in *Scholastik* 26 (1955): 496–519. See also J. Crehan, "The Seven Orders of Christ," in *Theological Studies* 19 (1958): 81–93.

65. St. Bonaventure, *Brevil*, VI, 13, no. 5.

66. The expression is repeatedly to be found in St. Bonaventure, especially in his *Collationes in Hexaëmeron*. See H. Berresheim, *Christus als Haupt der Kirche nach dem h. Bonaventura: ein Beitrag zur Theologie der Kirche* (Bonn, 1939).

67. St. Bonaventure, *Brevil*, VI, 12, no. 5. Guardini, op. cit., p. 163.

68. These terms were frequently used by Bonaventure. See, for example, *Brevil.*, VI, 13. Albert the Great rejected as inappropriate the expression "supercelestial hierarchy," which was used to describe the Trinity.

69. St. Bonaventure, *Coll. in Hexaëm.*, IV, 1, no. 20 (ed. Delorme, p. 229).

70. See, for example, Boniface VIII, *Unam Sanctam* (1302). On the notorious comparison between the sun and the moon as applied to the relation between the pope and the emperor, see C. Hageneder, "Das Sonne-Mond Gleichnis bei Innozenz III," in *Mitteilungen des Instituts für Oesterreichische Geschichtsforschung* 65 (1957): 340–68; H. Till-

mann, *Papst Innozenz III,* Bonner historische Forschungen 3, (Bonn, 1954): 266–67; F. Kempf, *Papstum und Kaisertum bei Innozenz III,* Miscellania historia pontificiae 19 (Rome, 1954): pp. 284–85; Robert E. McNally, "The History of the Medieval Papacy: a Survey of Research, 1954–59," in *Theological Studies* 21 (1960): 92–132, esp. pp. 124–30.

71. St. Bonaventure, *Coll. in Hexaëm.,* IV, 4, 20–23 (Delorme, p. 256).

72. Ibid., 4, 24, (Delorme, p. 257)

73. Ibid., 25 (Delorme, p. 258).

74. Ibid., 1, 25 (Delorme, p. 231).

75. Ibid., 1, 22 (Delorme, p. 230).

76. James of Vitry, *Historia orientalis et occidentalis,* lib. II, 34, ed. Fr. Moschus (Douai, 1597), p. 357.

77. Raymond Lull (1235–1315), for example, divides knighthood into seven spheres, on the analogy of the seven planets; *Libre del ordre de cavayleria.* Incipit: Per significanca de les VII planetes. (See Glorieux, op. cit., II, p. 147). Francis A. Yates, "The Art of Raymond Lull: an Approach to It through Lull's Theory of the Elements," in *Journal of the Warburg and Courtauld Institutes* 17 (1954): 115–73.

—It was a popular belief in the Middle Ages that the oil with which the kings of France were anointed was brought from heaven by an angel. See Richard A. Jackson, "The *Traité du Sacre* of Jean Golein," in *Proceedings of the American Philosophical Society* 113 (1969): 309.

78. See, for example, Thomas Aquinas, *De regimine principum* (ca. 1260), I, 1.

H. Ripelin, *Compendium theol. verit.,* VI, 36. Dante too considers the cosmic order as exemplifying the order that ought to prevail in society (*De monarchia,* I, 7).

79. *Epistola S. Ignatii de virtute oboedientiae* (1553).

80. The medieval conception of obedience must be seen in this perspective.

81. *Contra Faustum,* XXVII. *PL* 42, 418.

82. St. Thomas Aquinas, *Summa theol.,* I, q. 103, a, 3.

83. St. Thomas Aquinas, *Compendium theol.,* I, 170.

84. "And since man has both intelligence, and sense, and bodily powers, these things are dependent on one another, according to the disposition of divine providence, *in likeness to the order to be observed in the universe.* For bodily power is subject to the powers of sense and intellect, as carrying out their commands; and the sensitive power is subject to the intellective, and is controlled by its rule." *Summa contra gentiles,* III, 81.

85. M. D. Chenu, *La Théologie au XIIe siècle* (Paris, 1957), p. 36, n. 2, and *S. Thomas d'Aquin* (Paris, 1959), p. 108. Cf. J. Maritain, *De Bergson à Thomas d'Aquin* (Paris, 1947), p.. 72.

86. See St. Thomas Aquinas, IV *Sent.,* 33, q. 1. a. 1 ad 4. See also W. T. Stace, *Religion and the Modern Mind* (London, 1958), pp. 25–44 (the world as a moral order).

87. St. Thomas Aquinas, *Summa theol.,* I, 44, 3.

88. Ibid., Ia, IIae, 19, 10 c; 39, 2 ad 3; 104, 3.

See also F. Meuthen, *Kirche und Heilgeschichte bei Gerhoh von Reichersberg* (Leyden, 1949), esp. p. 29 ff: "Ethos und Ordo"; F. R. Wagner, "Der Begriff des Guten und Bosen nach Thomas von Aquin und Bonaventura," *in Jahrbuch f. Phil. u. spekul. Theol.* 27 (1913): 55–81, 138–58, 306–43; Maurits de Wachter, *Le péché actuel selon Saint Bonaventure* (Paris, 1967).

89. *De planctu naturae.* M. D. Chenu summarizes this as follows: "In *De planctu naturae,* Alan of Lille extends his doctrine of nature to the universe. . . man's moral life is an instance of the life of the world; the universe of freedom presupposes the universe of nature." *La Théologie au XIIe siècle* (Paris, 1957), p. 36.

90. St. Bonaventure, *Coll. in Hexaëm,* 1, 4, no. 14.

91. Ibid, 1, 3, nos. 14–19.

92. Neither in its cosmological nor in its ethical significance can the concept of order be considered as a biblical category. For it was under the influence of Greek philosophy and not of Scripture that medieval theologians made this concept the criterion of good and evil. In his work on the moral theology of the New Testament, Spicq makes no mention of the concept of order, except when discussing the Church (reference is made to Col. 2:5.). See C. Spicq, *Théologie morale du Nouveau Testament*, Etudes bibliques, 1 (Paris, 1965): 151

93. Alexander of Hales, *Summa theol.*, II, I, 2, q. 3, c. 5, solutio; St. Bonaventure, *Brevil.*, VII, 4, nos. 2 and 7; St. Thomas Aquinas, *Comp. theol.*, 171, and II *Sent.*, 11, 2, 6, ad 3. Many believed that the world was created in 4004 B. C. and that it would come to an end in 4004 A. D. Apart from creating a perfect symmetry, this view was also in keeping with St. Paul's statement that Christ had come in the middle of time. According to Dante, however, the world began in 5200 B. C. and would end in A. D. 1800.

94. St. Bonaventure, *Brevil.*, VII, 4, no. 2; IV *Sent.*, d. 47 and d. 48.

95. *Brevil.*, VII, 7, no. 4.

96. Ibid.

97. Albert the Great, *Summa de creaturis*, IV, q. 52 (Borgnet, 34, p. 589).

98. See Lynn Thorndike, op. cit.; Fritz Saxl, *Catalogue of Astrological and Mythological Illuminated Manuscripts in the Latin Middle Ages, III, Manuscripts in English Libraries*, ed. H. Bober (London, 1953), and "The Revival of Late Antique Astrology" and "The Belief in Stars in the Twelfth Century," in *Lectures*, vol. 1 (London: 1957), pp. 73–84, 85–95; Lewis, op. cit., pp. 198–215.

99. On this, see Charles E. Trinkaus, *In our Image and likeness: Humanity and Divinity in Italian Humanist Thought* (University of Chicago Press, 1970), esp. vol. 2, pp. 505–26. Also E. Garin, *Giovanni Pico della Mirandola* (Florence, 1937; Engelbert Monnerjahn, *Giovanni Pico della Mirandola: ein Beitrag zur philosophischen Theologie des italienischen Humanismus* Wiesbaden, 1960); Giovanni di Napoli, *Giovanni Pico della Mirandola e la problematica dottrinale del suo Tempo* (Rome, 1965).

Part Two / Introduction

1. E. J. Dijksterhuis, *De mechanisering van het wereldbeeld* (Amsterdam, 1950), p. 538. Translated as *The Mechanisation of the World Picture* (Oxford: Clarendon Press, 1961).

2. Paul Hazard, *La Crise de la conscience européenne, 1680–1715* (Paris, 1935). Translated as *The European Mind, 1680–1715* (Harmondsworth: Penguin, 1964).

3. Hazard, op. cit., preface.

4. Alexandre Koyré, *From the Closed World to the Infinite Universe* (Baltimore, 1957), pp. 1–3.

5. Friedrich Nietzsche, *Gesammelte Werke*, ed. Musarion, XV, p. 440.

Chapter Four

1. See especially, Alexandre Koyré, *Etudes galiléennes* (Paris, 1940). John Mepham, trans. *Galileo Studies* (Brighton, UK: The Harvester Press, 1978). Alexandre Koyré, *La Révolution astronomique: Copernic, Kepler, Borelli* (Paris, 1961); Thomas S. Kuhn, *The Copernican Revolution* (Cambridge, Mass.: Harvard University Press, 1957); E. A. Burtt, *The Metaphysical Foundations of Modern Physical Science*, rev. ed (Atlantic Highlands, NJ: The

Humanities Press, 1952); E. J. Dijksterhuis, *De merchanisering van het wereldbeeld* (Amsterdam, 1950). Translated as *The Mechanisation of the World Picture* (Oxford: Clarendon Press, 1961).

2. On this, see A. Koyré, *La Révolution astronomique*, p. 74, n. 3.

3. For criticism of the Aristotelian world picture in the fourteenth century, see A. Maier, *Die Vorlaufer Galileis in 14. Jahrhundert* (Rome, 1949), and Gordon Leff, "Gregory of Rimini: Tradition and Innovation," in *Fourteenth Century Thought* (Manchester: Manchester University Press, 1961), pp. 120–54.

4. See especially Chap. 11 and 12, Bk. 2, of *De docta ignorantia*, and the text preserved in codex 211, discovered by F. J. Clemens in 1847 and edited by R. Klibansky as an appendix to E. Hoffmann, *Das Universum des Nikolaus von Cues*, Cusanus-Studien I, Sitzungsberichte der Heidelberger Akademie der Wissenschaften, Phil-hist. Kl. 1929–30, 3, Abhandlung (Heidelberg, 1930), p. 44 ff. E. Vansteenberghe *Le Cardinal Nicolas de Cues*, Paris, 1941; H. Bett, *Nicholas of Cusa* (London, 1932); H. Blumenberg, "Kosmos und System: aus der Genesis der kopernikanischen Welt", in *Studium Generale* 10 (1957): 61 ff.; H. G. Senger, *Die Philosophie des Nikolaus von Kues vor dem Jahre 1440*, in *Beitrage zur Geschichte der Philosophie und Theologie des Mittelalters*, neue Folge, 3 (Münster, 1971).

5. Nicholas of Cusa adopted the expression from *Liber XXVI Philosophorum*, ed. Clemens Baeumker, in *Beitrage zur Geschichte der Philosophie und Theologie des Mittelalters* 25 (Münster, 1928): 207–14, where God is defined as "a sphere whose centre is everywhere and circumference is nowhere." See Dietrich Mahnke, *Unendliche Sphaere und Allmittelpunkt* (Halle, 1937); Marjorie H. Nicolson, *The Breaking of the Circle* (Evanston, IL: Northwestern Univ. Press, 1950); Georges Poulet, *Les Métamorphoses du cercle* (Paris, 1961), esp. pp. II–XXI.

6. F. W. Watson, *The "Zodiacus Vitae" of Marcellus Palingenius Stellatus: an Old School Book* (London 1908); F. R. Johnson, *Astronomical Thought in Renaissance England* (Baltimore, 1937), p. 145 ff.; A. O. Lovejoy, *The Great Chain of Being* (Cambridge, Mass.: Harvard University Press, 1936), pp. 115–17; A. Koyré, *From the Closed World to the Infinite Universe* (Baltimore, 1957), pp. 24–27.

7. In his commentary on Aristotle, *Livre du ciel et du monde* (1377); this work has been edited and translated with notes and an introduction by A. D. Menut and A. J. Denomy, (Madison, WI: The University of Wisconsin Press, 1968); see also A. C. Crombie, *Medieval and Early Modern Science*, vol. 2 (New York: Anchor Books, 1959), pp. 75–83.

8. A. O. Lovejoy, *The Great Chain of Being* (Cambridge, Mass.: Harvard Univ. Press, 1966), p. 102: "In the spatial sense the medieval world was literally diabolocentric." See H. Tuzet, *Le Cosmos et l'imagination* (Paris, 1965), pp. 25–27.

9. *The Divine Comedy: Hell*, Trans. Geoffrey l. Bickersteith (Oxford: Basil Blackwell, 1955), Canto 34, V. 20 ff. Cf. Canto 11, vv. 64–66.

10. Arthur Koestler, *The Sleepwalkers* (London, 1959), pp. 119–219; A. Koyré, *La Révolution astronomique: Copernic, Kepler, Borelli* (Paris, 1961); David C. Knight, *Copernicus, Titan of Modern Astronomy* (New York, 1965); Edward Grant, "Late Medieval Thought: Copernicus and the Scientific Revolution," in *Journal of the History of Ideas* 23 (1962): 197–220; Angus Armitage, *Copernicus, the Founder of Modern Astronomy* (New York, 1965); Alexandre Kirkenmajer, "Copernic comme philosophe," in *Le Soleil à la Renaissance: sciences et mythes*, (Brussels and Paris, 1965), pp. 7–17.

11. Its full title is *De hypothesibus motuum caelestium a se constitutis Commentariolus*. Since the publications of A. Birkenmayer, the origin of this text has been dated as 1512. See A. Koyré, *La Révolution astronomique*, pp. 86–87, n. 31. E. Rosen, *Three Copernican Treatises* (New York, 1939).

12. Leonardo da Vinci had already expressed the view that the sun does not move. "El sol non si muove," *Quaderni d'anatomia*, v., 25.[r] See Vassili P. Zoubov, "Le Soleil dans l'oeuvre scientifique de Léonard de Vinci," in *Le Soleil à la Renaissance: sciences et mythes* (Brussels and Paris, 1965), pp. 179–98.

13. A. Koyré, *La Révolution astronomique*, pp. 36–44.

14. For a more detailed account, see John Dillenberger, *Protestant Thought and Natural Science* (New York, 1960), pp. 41–49.

15. Among the most significant of Tycho Brahe's observations was his discovery in 1572 of a new star in the constellation of Cassiopeia. J. L. E. Dreyer, *Tycho Brahe* (New York, 1963).

16. On Kepler, see A. Koyré, *La Révolution astronomique*, pp. 119–456; Koestler, op. cit., pp. 225–422; Max Caspar, *Johannes Kepler* (Stuttgart, 1948).

17. See A. Koyré, *La Révolution astronomique*, pp. 135–44.

18. *Astronomia nova Aitiologetos seu physica caelestis tradita commentariis de motibus stellae Martis* (1609) had been completed two years earlier in 1607.

19. Letter dated 30 October 1607, *Gesammelte Werke* ed. W. von Dyck and Max Caspar (Munich, 1938), 16: 71.

20. See M. H. Nicolson, *The Breaking of the Circle* (New York, 1949).

21. See A. Koyré, *La Révolution astronomique*, p. 288.

22. Koestler, op. cit., pp. 339–40.

23. Published Linz, 1619. See W. Foerster, *Kepler und die Harmonie der Spharen* (1872), included in *Foerster's Wissenschaftliche Vorträge*, vol. 1 (Berlin, 1867), p. 30. Cf. L. Gunther, *Kepler und die Theologie* (Giessen, 1915); D. P. Walker "Kepler's Celestial Music," in *Journal of the Warburg Institute* 30 (1967): 228–50.

24. 1619 edition, p. 243. Another musical interpretation of the cosmos is to be found in Robert Fludd, *Utriusque cosmi majoris scilicet et minoris metaphysica, physica atque technica historia* (Oppenheim, 1617). See Peter J. Ammann, "The Musical Theory and Philosophy of Robert Fludd," in *Journal of the Warburg Institute* 30 (1987): 198–227; Katharine Brownell Collier, *Cosmogonies of Our Fathers* (New York, 1969), pp. 25–32.

25. Bibliography on Galileo was compiled by Carli-Favaro, *Bibliographia Galileiana* (1564–1895), and Boffito (1896–1940), and was then brought up to date by Ernan McMullin (1940–64). See *Galileo, Man of Science*, ed. Ernan McMullin (New York and London: Basic Books, 1967). Among the recent works: Pio Paschini, *Vita ed opere di Galileo Galilei* (Rome, 1965); Giorgio de Santillana, *The Crime of Galileo* (Chicago, 1955); Ludovico Geymonat, *Galileo Galilei* (Milan, 1957); the English translation of this work includes valuable notes by Stillmann Drake (New York, 1965); James Brodrick, *Galileo* (New York, 1965); Maurice Clavelin, *Philosophie naturelle de Galilée* (Paris, 1968).

26. Galileo in a letter to Kepler dated 19 August 1610, in J. Langford, *Galileo, Science and the Church* (New York, 1966), p. 20.

27. Acording to A. Koyré, it was the authority of Aristotle, more than that of the Bible, that caused great opposition to Galileo. *La Révolution astronomique*, p. 75, n. 6.

28. On the invention of the telescope, see Vasco Ronchi, *Galileo e il suo cannocchiale* (Turin, 1964). Cf. Geymonat, op. cit., with notes by Stillmann Drake, pp. 232–34.

29. Kepler had already written on this subject in his *Dioptrica* (1611).

30. See *Galileo's Complete Works*, ed. Antonio Favaro, vol. 19, p. 348.

31. This point is much disputed. See Geymonat op. cit., pp. 88–89, and the discussion between Stillmann Drake and Giorgio de Santillana, pp. 205–25. Also Paschini, op. cit., p. 524 ff.

32. George J. Gray, *A Bibliography of the Works of Sir Isaac Newton* (London, 1966; facsimile of 2d rev. ed., 1907); Frank E. Manuel, *A Portrait of Isaac Newton* (Cambridge

Mass.: Harvard Univ. Press, 1968); Louis Trenchard More, *Isaac Newton* (New York and London, 1934);

Pierre Brunet, *L'Introduction des théories de Newton en France au XVIIe siècle avant 1738* (Paris, 1931);

Friedrich Dessauer, *Weltfahrt der Erkenntnis: Leben und Werk Isaac Newtons* (Zurich, 1945). *Newton's Philosophy of Nature: Selections from His Writings*, 3d ed., ed. H. S. Thayer, introd. by John Herman Randall Jr. (New York: Hafner, 1955); Alexandre Koyré, *Newtonian Studies* (Cambridge Mass., 1965).

33. See F. X. De Feller, *Dictionnaire historique ou histoire abrégée.*, vol. 6 (Liège, 1816), p. 608.

34. *La Mécanique céleste* (1798–1825).

35. Opinions differ as to Laplace's religious views. G. Sarton believes he was a good Catholic, while Jean Pelsener considers him rather as a materialist. According to René Taton, however, Laplace's religious views were very much subject to change and strongly influenced by the political situation of the moment. See *Isis* 33 (1941): 309–12; 36 (1946): 158–60; 40 (1949): 351.

36. A. Schierbeek, *Opkomst en bloei der evolutieleer* (Haarlem, 1961).

In 1748 a peculiar work appeared that presented a theory of the origin and evolution of the earth, the origin of life from the sea and its further development up to and including man. There were several editions of this work, even though it met with vehement opposition. See Benoit de Maillet, *Telliamed: or Conversations between an Indian Philosopher and a French Missionary on the Diminution of the Sea*, trans. Albert v. Carozzi (Urbana, Ill.: University of Illinois Press, 1968). See P. Hazard, *La Pensée européene au XVIII siècle*, 1 (Paris, 1946): 163–64.

37. *Gesammelte Schriften*, ed. Kön Preuss, Akademie der Wissenschaften, vol. 8, p. 54. A similar view is expressed in Kant's *Critique of Judgement.*

38. See especially J. N. Findlay, *Hegel: A Re-examination* (London, 1958), p. 272.

39. A. Schierbeek, *Goethe als Natuuronderzoeker* (Amsterdam, 1944).

40. Darwin himself alludes to this in the conclusion to *On the Origin of Species* (London: Murray, 1859). "Thus from the war of nature, from famine and death, the most exalted object we are capable of conceiving, namely the production of the higher animals, directly follows. There is grandeur in the view of life with its several powers, having been originally breathed into a few forms or into one; and that, whilst this planet has gone cycling on according to the fixed law of gravity, from so simple a beginning endless forms most beautiful and most wonderful have been, and are being, evolved."

Chapter Five

1. "Error circa creaturas redundat in falsam de Deo scientiam." *Summa contra gentiles*, II, 3.

2. For example, Harry Prosch, *The Genesis of Twentieth Century Philosophy* (New York, 1964). The history of mankind can be divided into only two periods: the prescientific and the scientific. For the Renaissance and the Reformation are "mere internal displacements within the system of medieval Christendom." H. Butterfield, *The Origins of Modern Science* (London, 1962), Preface.

3. Lucien Febvre, *Le problème de l'incroyance au XVIe siècle: la religion de Rabelais* (Paris, 1942); Mikhail Bakhtin, *Rabelais and His World* (London, 1968) Michel Beaujour, *Le Jeu de Rabelais* (Paris, 1969).

4. Donald M. Frame, *Montaigne's Discovery of Man: The Humanization of a Humanist* (New York, 1955); Hugo Friedrich, *Montaigne* (Bern, 1949); J. Moreau, *Montaigne, l'homme et l'oeuvre* (Paris, 1939); Maturin Dréano, *La Religion de Montaigne* (Paris, 1969).

5. On the influence of medieval cosmology on the political thought of Jean Bodin,

see J. W. Allen, *A History of Political Thought in the Sixteenth Century* (London, 1951). Of particular importance is Bodin's *Universale naturae theatrum* (1596).

6. John Webster borrowed the material for his *Duchess of Malfi* from Painter's *Palace of Pleasure* (1576), where a similar fatalistic view is to be found. Cf. Johnstone Parr, *Tamburlaine's Malady* (Kingsport, Tenn, 1953).

7. E. M. Tillyard, *The Elizabethan World Picture* (New York and London, 1943). See also Paul H. Kocher, *Science and Religion in Elizabethan England* (San Marino, Calif., 1953).

8. "Recent research has shown that the educated Elizabethan had plenty of textbooks in the vernacular instructing him in the Copernican astronomy; yet he was loth to upset the old order by applying his knowledge. . . . The greatness of the Elizabethan age was that it contained so much new without bursting the noble form of the old order." Tillyard, op. cit., p. 8.

See also James Winny, ed., *The Frame of Order: An Outline of Elizabethan Belief Taken from the Treatises of the late Sixteenth Century* (London, 1957), This is an anthology in which the cosmological background of the culture of the age is clearly expressed.

9. See especially Richard S. Westfall, *Science and Religion in Seventeenth-Century England* (New Haven: Yale University Press, 1958). This book contains an excellent bibliographical survey, pp. 221–28); P. Barrière, *La vie intellectuelle en France du 16e siècle à l'époque contemporaine* (Paris, 1961); Paul Hazard, *La crise de la conscience européenne* (Paris, 1934). Translated as *The European Mind, 1680–1715* (Oxford: Clarendon Press, 1964). Basil Wiley, *Seventeenth Century Background* (London, 1934); Dorothy Stinson, *The Gradual Acceptance of the Copernican Theory* (New York, 1917); Samuel L. Bethell, *The Cultural Revolution of the Seventeenth Century* (New York, 1951).

10. Patricia Reif, "The Textbook Tradition in Natural Philosophy, 1600–1650," in *Journal of the History of Ideas* 30 (1969): 17–32.

See also William T. Costello, *The Scholastic Curriculum at Early Seventeenth-Century Cambridge* (Cambridge, Mass: Harvard Univ. Press, 1958). In Richard Foster Jones, *Ancients and Moderns: A Study of the battle of the Books* (St. Louis, 1936), we find a number of typical criticisms that were leveled at the university education of the day.

11. John Donne, *Anatomy of the World* (1611), Nonesuch Press, p. 202; cited by A. Koyré in *From the Closed World to the Infinite Universe* (Baltimore, 1957), p. 29; Victor Harris, *All Coherence Gone* (Chicago, 1949); Charles M. Coffin, *John Donne and the New Philosophy* (New York, 1937); Michael F. Maloney, *John Donne: His Flight from Medievalism* (Urbana, Ill.: The University of Illinois Press, 1944).

12. *Pascal's Pensées*, Lafuma 2d ed., trans. Martin Turnell (London: Harvill Press, 1962), no. 340. Cf. also the following note: "Write against those who probe too deeply into the sciences. Descartes." No. 92.

13. Brunschvicg, in his edition of Pascal's *Pensées*, quotes the words of Charron: "La vraye science et la vraye estude de l'homme, c'est l'homme." Nos. 144 and 146 of Brunschvicg edition.

14. *Pascal's Pensees*, Lafuma 2d ed., no. 390; Brunschvicg no. 72.

15. Ibid., no. 390; Brunschvicg no. 27.

16. *Pensées*, Brunschvicg no. 693. See the commentary on this text in René Grousset, *Bilan el l'histoire* (Paris, 1946), pp. 301–6; also Voltaire, *Lettres philosophiques*, 25: 6.

17. *Pensées*, Brunschvicg no. 348; Lafuma 2d ed. no. 217, trans. Martin Turnell.

18. *Pensées*, Brunschvicg no. 206.

19. H. Gouhier, *Les Grands avenues de la pensée philosophique en France depuis Descartes* (Louvain and Paris, 1966), p. 46.

20. *Pensées*, Brunschvicg no. 77. See Brunschvicg's note to this text.

21. See for example, P. Pourat, *La Spiritualité chrétienne*, vol. 2, *Le Moyen-Age*, Paris, 1928, pp. 162-67.

22. Emile Namer, *Bruno* (Paris, 1966), p. 8.
"The Copernican system does not constitute one idea among so many others but is rather the nucleus of all Bruno's ideas." A. Nowicki, *Il Pluralismo metodologico e i modelli lulliani di Giordano Bruno*, Académie polonaise des sciences 27 (Rome, 1925): 11. See also Paul-Henri Michel, *La Cosmologie de Giordano Bruno*, Histoire de la pensée, Ecole pratique des hautes ètudes, Sorbonne, vol. 9 (Paris, 1962); Emile Namer, *La Pensée de Giordano Bruno et sa signification dans la nouvelle image du mond*, Les cours de Sorbonne, Centre de Documentation Universitaire (Paris, 1958-59), and *Les Aspects de Dieu dans la philosophie de Giordano Bruno* (Paris, 1930); A. Corsano, *Il Pensiero di Giordano Bruno nel suo svolgimento storico* (Florence, 1940); A. Guzzo, *Giordano Bruno nel quarto centenario (Turin, 1948)*.

23. See F. R. Johnson, *Astronomical Thought in Renaissance England* (Baltimore, 1937), pp. 165–67; A. O. Lovejoy, *The Great Chain of Being* (Cambridge, Mass., 1966), p. 116; A. Koyré, *From the Closed World to the Infinite Universe* (Baltimore, 1957), pp. 35–39.

24. *Del infinito, universo e mondi; dialoghi metafisici*, ed. Gentile (Bari, 1907), p. 318.

25. Frederick Copleston, *A History of Philosophy*, vol. 3, *Late Medieval and Renaissance Philosophy*, Chap. 16 (New York: Image Books, 1963, p. 69).

26. *Ethics*, I, prop. 15.

27. Ibid., prop. 25.

28. Ibid., II, prop. 10, note 2.

29. *Letter* 2. Letter to Henry Oldenburg, Sept. 1661.

30. *Ethics* I, prop. 11, note. See Martial Gueroult, *Spinoza, vol. 1, Dieu*, Ethique I, (Paris, 1968); E. Lasbax, *La Hiérarchie dans l'univers de Spinoza* (Paris, 1926); Harry A. Wolfson, *The Philosophy of Spinoza* (Cambridge, Mass.,: Harvard Univ. Press, 1948); Alexandre Matheron, *Individu et communauté chez Spinoza* (Paris, 1969).

31. We see "that men do all things for an end, namely, for that which is useful to them and which they seek. Thus it comes to pass that they only look for a knowledge of the final causes of events, and when these are learned, they are content, as having no cause for further doubt." Owing to this procedure, the truth may have been concealed from the human race "if mathematics had not furnished another standard of verity in considering solely the essence and properties of figures without regard to their final causes." *Ethics*, I, Appendix. *The Chief Works of Benedict de Spinoza*, trans. R. H. M. Elwes (London: Bell, 1887), 2:75 ff. All other quotations from Spinoza are to be found in Copleston, op. cit., vol. 4, Descartes to Leibniz.

32. Ibid.

33. Frederick L. Nussbaum, *The Triumph of Science and Reason* (New York, 1962), p. 186; Paul Hazard, *La crise de la conscience européenne, 1680–1715* (Paris, 1935), *The European Mind, 1680–1715* (Oxford: Clarendon Press, 1964), and *La Pensée européenne au XVIIIe siècle* (Paris, 1946), translated as *European Thought in the Eighteenth Century* (London: Hollis & Carter, 1954); Richard S. Westfall, *Science and Religion in Seventeenth-Century England* (New Haven: Yale Univ. Press, 1958); B. Wiley, *Seventeenth-Century Background* (London, 1950); Lester G. Crocker, *An Age of Crisis: Man and World in Eighteenth-Century French Thought* (Baltimore: Johns Hopkins Press, 1969). Robert Niklaus, "The Age of Enlightenment," in *The Age of Enlightenment: Studies Presented to Theodore Besterman* (Edinburgh and London, 1967), pp. 395–412 (bibliographical survey). Peter Gay, *The Enlightenment: An Interpretation*, 2 vols. (New York and London: Norton Library, 1966–77).

34. See Herbert H. Odom, "The Estrangement of Celestial Mechanics and Religion," in *Journal of the History of Ideas* 27 (1966): 533–48.

35. This is clearly expressed, for example, in Voltaire's *Epître à Uranie*, vv. 91–96:
Entends, Dieu que j'implore, entends du haut des cieux
Une voix plaintive et sincère

Mon incredulité ne doit pas te déplaire,
Mon coeur est ouvert à tes yeux;
On te fait un tyran, en toi je cherche un Père.
Je ne suis pas chrétien, mais c'est pour t'aimer mieux.

36. Frank E. Manuel, *The Eighteenth Century Confronts the Gods* (Cambridge, Mass.: Harvard Univ. Press, 1959).

37. As, for example, in J. Abbadie, *Traité de la verité de la religion chrétienne*, a popular handbook of religious education in the eighteenth century, and similarly, the *Catechismus graeco-latinus* (1686), which was used in many Jesuit schools. See René Pomeau, *La Religion de Voltaire* (Paris, 1956), p. 49 ff., esp. p. 112; Ira O. Wade, *The Intellectual Development of Voltaire* (Princeton, N. J., 1964).

38. H. Metzger, "Attraction universelle et Religion naturelle chez quelques commentateurs anglais de Newton, " in *Actualités scientifiques et industrielles*, no. 621 (Paris: drei Lieferungen, 1938).

39. See A. Manuel, *Isaac Newton, Historian (Cambridge, MA: 1963; also H. McLachan, Sir Isaac Newton's Theological Manuscripts* (Liverpool: Liverpool Univ. Press, 1950); H. McLachan, *The Religious Opinions of Milton, Locke and Newton* (Manchester, 1941); E. W. Strong, "Newton and God" in *Journal of the History of Ideas* 13 (1952):147–67; David Kubrin, "Newton and the Cyclical Cosmos: Providence and the Mechanical Philosophy" in *Journal of the History of Ideas* 28 (1967):2325–46; W./A. Austin, "Isaac Newton on Science and Religion" in *Journal of the History of Ideas* 31 (1970):521–42.

40. Part I, chap. 1.

41. Voltaire, Eléments de philosophie de Newton, Part I, chap. 1 (Oeuvres complètes, edition 1785) vol. 31, p. 26.

42. "The entire philosophy of Newton necessarily leads to the knowledge of a supreme being, who has created everything and arranged all things freely." Ibid.

43. "In a word, I do not know if there is a more impressive metaphysical proof and one which speaks more forcibly to man than this wonderful order that governs the world; and was there ever a more beautiful argument than the verse: 'caeli enarrant gloriam Dei' (the heavens proclaim the glory of God)? So you see that Newton does not adduce anything else at the end of his *Opticks* or his *Principia.*" Ibid., p. 29.

44. "In a system which admits the existence of God, there are only difficulties to overcome, while in all other systems there are absurdities to be devoured." Ibid., p. 32.

45. See Paul Hazard, *La Crise de la conscience européenne* (Paris, 1935), p. 262. Translated as *The European Mind, 1680–1715* (Harmondsworth: Penguin, 1964).

46. See in this connection Lester G. Crocker, *An Age of Crisis: Man and World in Eighteenth-Century French Thought* (Baltimore, 1959), pp. 36–70.

47. *Theodicy* (1710).

48. The word *optimism* first appears in a discussion on Leibniz in *Mémoires de Trévoux*, Feb. 1737, p. 207. See Theodore Besterman, "Voltaire et le désastre de Lisbonne: ou, la mort de l'optimisme," in *Studies on Voltaire and the Eighteenth Century* 2 (1956), 12, n. 2.

49. B. Rohrer, *Das Erdbeben von Lissabon in der französischen Literatur des achtzehnten Jahrhunderts* (Heidelberg, 1933);
G. Gastinel, "Le Désastre de Lisbonne," in *Revue du dix-huitième Siècle* 1, (1913) 396–409; Kant dealt with this in one of his early writings, *Geschichte und Naturbeschreibung der merkwürdigsten Vorfälle des Erdbebens welches an dem Ende des 1755sten Jahres einen grossen Theil der Erde erschüttert hat* (Königsberg, 1756). Thomas D. Kendrick, *The Lisbon Earthquake* (London, 1956).

50. See Theodore Besterman, "Voltaire et le désastre de Lisbonne: ou, la mort de l'optimisme," in *Studies on Voltaire and the Eightenth Century* 2 (1956), 7–24.

Paul Hazard, "Le Problème du mal dans la conscience européenne du XVIIIe siècle," in *The Romantic Review* 32 (1941), 147–70.

51. Leibnitz ne m'apprend point par quels noeuds invisibles,
Dans le mieux ordonné des univers possibles,
Un désordre éternel, un chaos de malheurs,
Mêle à nos vains plaisirs de réelles douleurs,
Ni pourquoi l'innocent, ainsi que le coupable,
Subit également ce mal inévitable.
The poem ends with the lines:
Un jour tout sera bien, voilà notre éspérance,
Tout est bien aujourd'hui, voilà l'illusion.

"Leibniz does not tell me by what visible twists an eternal disorder, a chaos of misfortunes, mingles real sorrows with our vain pleasures in the best arranged of possible universes, nor why the innocent and the guilty suffer alike this inevitable evil." *"One day all will be good*, that is our hope, *All is good today*, that is the illusion." T. Besterman, *Voltaire*, pp. 354–55. It seems that Voltaire later put a question mark after the line "One day all will be good, that is our hope." See G. R. Havens, "Voltaire's pessimistic revision of the conclusion of his *Poème sur le désastre de Lisbonne,"* in *Modern Language Notes* 44 (1929): 492. Also Theodore Besterman, "Voltaire et le désastre de Lisbonne: ou, la mort de l'optimisme," in *Studies on Voltaire and the Eighteenth Century* 2 (1956): 19.

52. "Le procès est jugé et la cause est perdue." *La Pensée européenne au XVIIIe siècle* 2: 67. And yet, as Carl Becker points out, Voltaire was not really a pessimist: "Inspite of *Candide* and all the rest of it, Voltaire was an optimist, although not a naive one. He was the defender of causes, and not of lost causes either—a crusader pledged to recover the holy places of the true faith, the religion of humanity. Voltaire, skeptic,—strange misconception! On the contrary, a man of faith, an apostle who fought the good fight, tireless to the end, writing seventy volumes to convey the truth that was to make us free." *The Heavenly City of the Eighteenth-Century Philosophers* (New Haven and London, 1965), pp. 36–37.

Milton P. Foster, ed., *Voltaire's Candide and the Critics* (Belmont, Calif., 1962).

53. F. Mauthner, *Der Atheismus und seine Geschichte im Abendlände* (Berlin, 1912).

54. See, for example, J. Proust, *Diderot et l'Encyclopédie* (Paris, 1963); P. Grosclaude, *L'Encyclopédie* (Paris, 1951); P. Mesnard, *Le Cas Diderot* (Paris, 1952); A. Vartanian, *Diderot and Descartes* (Princeton, 1953; Carl L. Becker, *The Heavenly City of the Eighteenth-Century Philosophers* (New Haven and London, 1932); Arthur M. Wilson, *Diderot* (New York and London: Oxford Univ. Press, 1972).

55. P. Hazard, *La Pensée européenne au XVIIIe siècle* (Paris, 1946), vol. 1, pp. 98–123. Translated as *European Thought in the Eighteenth Century* (London: Hollis and Carter, 1954).

56. R. Pintard, *Le libertinage erudit dans la première moitié du XVIIe siècle* (Paris, 1943), and "Modernisme, humanisme, libertinage: petite suite sur le cas Gassendi," in *Rev. d'histoire littéraire de la France* 48 (1949): 1–51. "Gassendi et le spiritualisme, ou Gassendi "etait-il un libertin?" in *Actes du Congrès du Tricentenaire de Pierre Gassendi* (Digne, 1955), pp. 97–133; A. Cresson, *Le problème moral et les philosophes* (Paris, 1933); Pierre Burriere, *La vie intellectuelle en France du 16e siècle à l'époque contemporaine,* L'Evolution de l'Humanité, 96 (Paris, 1961), p. 200 ff.

57. See A. Koyré, *From the Closed World to Infinite Universe* (Baltimore, 1957), pp. 236–72; Samuel Clarke, *A Collection of Papers Which Passed between the Late Learned*

Mr. Leibniz and Dr. Clarke, in the Years 1715 and 1716, Relating to the Principles of Natural Philosophy and Religion (London, 1717).

58. P. Hazard, *La pensée européenne au XVIIIe siècle* (Paris, 1946), vol. 2, pp. 85–106. Translated as *European Thought in the Eighteenth Century* (London: Hollis and Carter, 1954). L. G. Crocker has shown how the various theories that were developed in this field during the Enlightenment finally resulted in a complete moral nihilism. *Nature and Culture: Ethical Thought in the French Enlightenment* (Baltimore, 1963).

59. R. Lenoble, *Histoire de l'idée de nature* (Paris, 1969), pp. 217–384. Jean Ehrard, *L'Idée de nature en France dans la première moitié du XVIIIe siècle* (Paris, 1963).

60. See Pierre Naville, *D'Holbach et la philosophie scientifique au XVIIIe siècle* (Paris, 1967), p. 364.

61. Ibid., pp. 295–310, 361–69. Diderot wrote: "Look closely and you will see that the word 'freedom' is quite meaningless; that there are not free beings nor can there be any." Letter to Laudois, *Correspondance générale*, ed. Assezat, 19, pp. 435–36.

62. H. A. Ogiermann, *Hegel's Gottesbeweise* (Rome, 1948); R. Vancourt, *La Pensée religieuse de Hegel* (Paris, 1965); Franz Grégoire, *Etudes hégeliennes: les points capitaux du système* (Louvain and Paris, 1958).

"Hegel gives a very small part of his writings to cosmological questions—a curious fact when we consider their great theoretical interest, and still greater practical importance. When he passes out of the realm of pure thought, he generally confines himself to explaining, by the aid of the dialectic, the reasons for the existence of particular facts, which, on empirical grounds are known to exist, or, in some cases, wrongly supposed to exist." John McTaggart, *Studies in Hegelian Cosmology* (Cambridge: At the University Press, 1901), p. 2. And yet one of Hegel's earliest writings was devoted to astronomy, a science that continued to fascinate him: *Dissertatio philosophica de orbitis planetarum* (1801). See Walter Kaufmann, *Hegel: a Reinterpretation* (Garden City, N. Y., 1966), pars. 15, 57.

63. *Encyclopädie*, II, par. 341, 2, p. 487 (Jubiläumsausgabe).

64. See especially *Die Vernunft in der Geschichte* (Hamburg: Hoffmeister, 1955). Translated as *Reason in History*, trans. Robert S. Hartman (Indianapolis and New York: Bobbs-Merrill, 1953).

65. See Hans Schmidt, *Verheissung and Schrecken der Freiheit: von der Krise der antik-abendländischen Weltverständnisses dargestellt im Blick auf Hegels Erfahrung der Geschichte* (Stuttgurt and Berlin, 1964), p. 296. "What is rational is actual and what is actual is rational." Hegel, *Encyclopedia*, par. 6.

66. *System der Philosophie*, par. 249. Ibid., par. 339, 9, p. 466.

"Hegel repudiates any doctrine of the actual historical evolution of living forms in time. . . . Hegel maintains this doctrine even in the face of the geological record, which was fairly well established in his time. He holds that the organic forms found in geological strata never really lived: they are merely paintings or sculptures of the living, imitations and anticipations of organic forms but produced by forces that were inorganic (*Naturphilos.*, p. 480, ed. Glockner). It seems plain that Hegel is here holding a doctrine as much at variance with his own principles as it is out of harmony with the facts. Possibly it is his cautious, genuinely empirical spirit which made him hesitate to launch forth in far-reaching evolutionary speculations, like those of some of his contemporaries. Had the Darwinian and later data been available, he would almost certainly have acknowledged the historical trends in Nature that he admits in the realm of Spirit: if any philosopher is a philosopher of evolution, that philosopher is Hegel. As it is, he sees in the notion of evolution merely a convenient schema of emanation, in which the scale of Nature is read downward from higher to lower, and the lower forms are held to have degenerated from the higher." J. N. Findlay, *Hegel: A Re-examination* (London and New York, 1958), p. 272.

Chapter Six

1. *De perfectionibus moribusque divinis libri XIV* (Antwerp: ex Officina Plantiniana, 1620).

2. Ibid., nos. 46–27

3. Ibid., no. 48.

4. *De providentia numinus et animi immortalitate libri duo adversus atheos et politicos.*

5. Ibid., no. 18.

6. Ibid.

7. Ibid., ratio quarta, no. 32.

8. Ibid., ratio nona, no. 113.

9. See the analysis of C. Ramnoux, "Héliocentrisme et christianisme: sur un texte du Cardinal de Bérulle," in *Le Soleil à la Renaissance* (Brussels and Paris, 1965), pp. 449–61.

10. *Discours de l'Estat et des Grandeurs de Jésus*, 3, 1. See Henri Gouhier, *La Vocation de Malebranche* (Paris, 1926), p. 47.

11. See Henri Gouhier, *La Pensée religieuse de Descartes* (Paris, 1924), p. 57 ff.

12. See Eric Voegelin, *Order and History*, vol. 1, *Israel and Revelation* (Louisiana State University Press, 1956). Preface and Introduction.

13. Letter dated 18 December 1629 (Adam Tannery, I, pp. 85–86). Malebranche also complained about this. *Recherche de la vérité*, II, 2, Chap. 5, p. 212.

14. See Etienne Gilson, *Héloise et Abelard: Etude sur le moyen age et l'humanisme* (Paris, 1938), p. 187; L. Bouyer, *Autour d'Erasme* (Paris, 1955), pp. 139–77; *Erasmi Epistolae*, ed. P. S. & Mrs. Allen, III, 858, p. 375.

15. A. Koyré, *La Révolution astronomique* (Paris, 1961), p. 75, n. 6.

16. See William T. Costello, *The Scholastic Curriculum at Early Seventeenth-Century Cambridge* (Cambridge Mass.: Harvard University Press, 1958), p. 9.

17. On Pierre Gassendi's well-known text, *Exercitationes paradoxicae adversus Aristoteleos libri septem* (1624), see Bernard Rochot, "La Vraie philosophie de Gassendi," in *Actes du Congrès du Tricentenaire de Pierre Gassendi* (1955), pp. 230–34, and also Pierre Gassendi, *Dissertations en forme de paradoxes contre les Aristotéliciens*, Bks I and II, edited with translation and notes by Bernard Rochot, Bibliothèque des textes philosophiques (Paris, 1959).

18. In Molière's *Le Bourgeois gentilhomme*, it is the philosophy teacher who gives instruction in astronomy.

19. O. Loretz, *Galilei und der Irrtum der Inquisition* (Kevelaar, 1966); Jerome Langford, *Galileo, Science and the Church* (New York, 1966).

20. See Geymonat, op. cit.

21. See further in this chapter.

22. Georges Monchamp, *Galilée en Belgique* (Brussels, 1892), p. 122.

23. What Etienne Gilson wrote with regard to the sixteenth century is perhaps even more true of the seventeenth century: "One can say that the Thomistic school of the sixteenth century completely failed in its mission to the extent that it was opposed to the Renaissance, instead of assimilating it and taking spiritual direction from it, as Saint Thomas did from the philosophical movement of the thirteenth century. Not only did Thomism have in its principles the means of doing this but it was its very object to do so, and also . . . one can ask why a man like Cajetan failed in this respect. It is perhaps

because, with the reign of commentators succeeding that of the author, the Thomists lost the conquering spirit of Saint Thomas." "La Tradition française et la chrétienté," in *Vigile* 4 (1931), 1, p. 74, cited by M. D. Chenu, *La Parole de Dieu*, vol. 1, *La Foi dans l'intelligence* (Paris, 1964), p. 135.

24. *Dict. Théol. Cath.*, VI, col. 1090;

Georges Gusdorf, *La Révolution Galiléenne*, Les sciences humaines et la pensée occidentale, III (Paris, 1969), vol. 1, pp. 121–34 (Chap. 5, Les Suites de l'affaire Galilée).

25. This situation does not seem to have changed. Much the same feeling is evident in the public's reaction to plays like Brecht's *Galileo* and Barrie Stavis's *Lamp at Midnight*.

26. F. Dessauer, *Der Fall Galilei und wir* (Linz, 1943), Chap. 7.

27. Trinkaus, op. cit., esp. pp. 530–51. Also H. Busson, *Les Sources et le développement du rationalisme dans la littérature française* (Paris, 1922), and *La Pensée religieuse de Charron à Pascal* (Paris, 1933); Julien-Eymard D'Angers, *Pascal et ses devanciers* (Paris, 1954).

28. M. Grabmann, *Geschichte der Katholische Theologie seit dem Ausgang der Väterzeit* (Freiburg im Breisgau, 1933), pp. 192–207. See also Henri Gouhier, "La Crise de la théologie au temps de Descartes," in *Rev. de theol. et de philos*, 3 série 4 (1954): 19–54.

29. "Ouverts aux idées du siècle, influencés par elles, ils s'en tiennent néanmoins dans leurs écrits à une orthodoxie étroite, figée, traditionelle, qui exclut de parti toute démarche qui les obligerait à s'interroger de nouveau; il ne fallait pas dépasser les Saints Pères, ni Aristote. . . . Devant les problèmes théologiques qui remplissent d'angoisse la conscience chrétienne, ils répondent froidement: quand on a la foi, on ne cherche pas à comprendre!" Alred R. Dessautels, *Les Mémoires de Trévoux et le mouvement des idées au XVIIIe siècle (1701–1734)* Rome, 1956, p. 10.

30. A clear description of his world picture is to be found in his *Tractatus de Meteoris*, I, 2: "Tota haec universi machina ex elementari et caelesti mundo consistit." *Cursus phil. thom.*, *Philosophia naturalis*, vol. 2; and his *Cursus theologicus*, passim. See Litt, op. cit., pp. 12–14.

31. *Clypeus theol. thom.* I, 1, disp. 1, a, 2, digressio brevis.

32. Ibid., II, 7, disp. prooemialis, a. 2.

33. Ibid., disp. 16, a. 3, par. 1.

34. Ibid., par. 2.

Cf. Antonius Goudin, *Philosophia juxta inconcussa tutissimaque Divi Thomae dogmata*, 4, q. 3, a. 3.

35. *Clypeus theol. thom.*, tract. de Angelis, diss. 8, a. 3.

36. Ibid., a. 2, par. 1: "Just as the lower angels which have less universal forms are guided by the higher angels, so all bodily things are governed with the assistance of the angels." Billuart still regarded the empyrean as the abode of the angels.

37. For example, Diego Alvarez (d. 1635), Jean Nicolai (d. 1663), Antoine Reginald (d. 1676), Vincent Contenson (d. 1674), Vincent Buron (d. 1674), Antoine Massoulie (d. 1706), Noel Alexandre (d. 1724), Hyacinthe Serry (d. 1738), and Cardinal Vinc. Ludovicus Gotti (d. 1742).

38. *Dogmata theologica*, ed. Vivès, (Paris, 1865), vol. I, 1. 8.

39. Ibid., I, 1, 8, c. 3, no. 2.

40. Ibid., no. 3.

41. Ibid., c. 10, no. 13.

42. Ibid., c. 4, no. 13.

43. Ibid.

44. Ibid., no. 4.

45. *De sex primorum mundi*, Bk. I, esp. Chaps. 2, 10, 11, 12,

46. F. Cayré, *Patrologie et histoire de la théologie*, vol. 3 (Paris, 1944), p. 144.

47. See Owen Chadwick, , *From Bossuet to Newman: The Idea of Doctrinal Development* (Cambridge: At the Univ. Press, 1957).

48. *Histoire des variations des Eglises protestantes* (1688).

49. Letter to a disciple of Malebranche dated 21 May 1687: "I notice there is a great struggle against the Church on the way under the name of Cartesian philosophy."

50. *Oeuvres complètes de Bossuet*, ed. F. Lachat, (Paris, 1966), vol. II, pp. 164, 233.

51. *Discours sur l'histoire universelle (1681): la politique tirée des propres paroles de l'Ecriture* (1709), esp. Bks. 3–5.

52. Libert Froidmont, *Saturnalitiae coenae* (Louvain, 1616).

53. See Georges Monchamp, *Galilée en Belgique* (Brussels, 1892) pp. 34–52; P. Stévart, *Copernic et Galilée devant l'université de Louvain* (Liège, 1891).

54. Monchamp, op. cit., pp. 182–322, and *Histoire du Cartésianisme en Belgique* (Brussels, 1886). See also P. Féret, "L'Aristotélisme et le Cartésianisme dans l'Université de Paris au XVIIIe siècle," in *Annales de philosophie chrétienne* (April, 1903), pp. 5–25.

55. Robert Lenoble, *Mersenne ou la naissance du méchanisme* (Paris, 1943), p. 14: "It is in fact an entire epoch that abandons theology for science, and Mersenne is unwittingly involved in this movement. A fault develops in his own work between a lagging theology and an advancing science: the line is visible, but it is still a line; it will be more than half of a century before the crack is heard in this crisis of European consciousness."

56. An excellent description of this sociological phenomenon is to be found in Thomas S. Kuhn, *The Structure of Scientific Revolution,*(Chicago: Chicago University Press, 1962). See also Ewert Cousins, "Models and the Future of Theology," in *Continuum* 7 (1969): 78–92.

57. E. Gilson, *Etudes sur la rôle de la pensée médiévale dans la formation du système Cartésien* (Paris, 1930), and *Index scolastico cartésien* (Paris, 1913).

58. H. Gouhier, *La Pensée religieuse de Descartes* (Paris, 1923). Desmond J. Fitzgerald, "Descartes, Defender of the Faith," in *Thought* 34 (1959): 387–404.

59. Letter to Mersenne, Amsterdam, 10 May 1632.

60. Letter to Mersenne, Deventer, November 1633. see also *Discourse on Method*, 5 and 6.

61. Letter to Mersenne, Amsterdam, February 1634.

62. Letter to Mersenne, Amsterdam, April 1634.

63. The first edition appeared in Amsterdam in 1644, and the French translation, which Descartes corrected, appeared in Paris in 1647.

64. See E. A. Burtt, *The Metaphysical Foundations of Modern Science* (Garden City, N. Y.: Doubleday Anchor Books, 1954; 1st ed. 1924, rev. 1932), pp. 105–21.

65. "The God of a philosopher and his world are correlated. Now Descartes' God, in contradistinction to most previous Gods, is not symbolized by the things He created. He does not express Himself in them. There is no analogy between God and the world; no *imagines et vestigia Dei in mundo*; the only exception is our own soul, that is, a pure mind, a being, a substance of which all essence consists in thought, a mind endowed with an intelligence able to grasp the idea of God, that is, of the infinite (which is even innate to it), and with will, that is, with infinite freedom." A. Koyré, *From the Closed World to the Infinite Universe* (Baltimore, 1968), p. 100.

66. H. Gouhier, *La Philosophie de Malebranche et son expérience religieuse* (Paris, 1948); Martiabel Guéroult, *Malebranche* (Paris, 1955).

67. " 'We know by faith that sin has upset the order of nature,'—Continually haunted by the idea of order and always anxious about implacable regularity, Malebranche wishes for a perfect symmetry between the natural and the supernatural order." J. Wehrlé, *Dictionnaire de théologie catholique*, S. V. "Malebranche" (col. 1778).

68. "There are those who think there is no order which is by its nature immutable and necessary, and that the order or wisdom of God according to which he made all things, although the first of creatures, is itself a creature, made by God's free will and not at all produced by the necessity of its being. But the opinion shakes the very foundations of morality by removing the order and the eternal laws on which their immutability depends, and destroys the whole fabric of the Christian religion." *Recherche de la vérité*, XIIIe éclaircissement.

69. See John Martin Creed and John Sandwith Boys Smith, eds., *Religious Thought in the Eighteenth Century* (Cambridge: At the University Press, 1934).

70. For example, J. Abbadie, *Traité de la vérité de la religion chrétienne* (Rotterdam, 1705). See R. Pomeau, *La Religion de Voltaire* (Paris, 1950), p. 5 ff.

71. See P. Hazard, *La Pensée européenne au XVIIIe siècle* (Paris, 1946), p. 116 ff. Translated as *European Thought in the Eighteenth Century* (London: Hollis and Carter, 1954). See also note 37 of previous chapter.

72. "God is good, nothing is more obvious. But goodness in man is love of his fellow-creatures and the goodness of God is love of order; for it is by order that he sustains all that exists, binding each part to the whole." J. J. Rousseau, *Profession de foi d'un vicaire savoyard*, I, 10. See Voltaire, *Eléments de philosophie de Newton*, I, 1, *Oeuvres complètes* (1785), vol. I, p. 29); R. Hooykaas, *The Principle of Uniformity in Geology, Biology and Theology.* (Leiden, 1963)

73. "This insistence on faith, to the detriment of reason, is to be found throughout the extracts of *Mémoires de Trévoux*. And so the reviewers are impatient with those who wish to go too deeply into things and who look for rational explanations. . . . Reference is constantly made to the great qualities every Christian must possess: faith and submission to authority." Desautels, op. cit., pp. 174–75.

74. F. Hocedez, *Histoire de la théologie au XIXe siècle*, vol. 1, *Décandance et reveil de la théologie* (Brussels and Paris, 1948), pp. 104–23; vol. 2, *Epanouissement de la théologie* (Brussels and Paris, 1952), pp. 69–110; J. Bellamy, *La Théologie catholique au XIXe siècle* (Paris, 1904).

75. "I cannot imagine . . . why Darwinism should be considered inconsistent with Catholic doctrine." (Document A. 18. 21 at the Birmingham Oratory.) "There is as much want of simplicity in the idea of distinct species as in that of the creation of trees in full growth, or rocks with fossils in them. I mean that it is as strange that monkeys should be so like men, with no *historical* connection between them, as that there should be no course of facts by which fossil bones got into rocks. The one idea stands to the other as fluxions to differentials . . . I will either go the whole hog, or dispensing with time and history altogether, hold, not only the theory of distinct species but that also of the creation of fossil-bearing rocks." *Sundries*, p. 83.

76. *L'Évolution restreinte aux espèces organiques* (Paris, 1981). (See *Civilta cattolica*, series 18, 5 (1899) p. 48 ff. H. Jans, "Een vergeefs pleidooi voor de evolutie: M. D.. Leroy," in *Streven* 18 (1965) 2, p. 762ff.

77. *Dogma und Evolution*, 1899.

78. *Le Darwinisme au point de vue de l'orthodoxie catholique*, vol. 1, *L'Origine des espèces*, Coll. Lovanium (Brussels, 1921).

79. "Le Transformisme et la discussion libre," in *Revue des questions scientifiques de Bruxelles*, 20 April, 1889). See Comte Bégouen, *Quelques souvenirs sur le mouvement des idées transformistes dans les milieux catholiques* (Paris, 1945).

80. *Coll. Lac.*, V, p. 292.

81. As, for example, Cardinal E. Ruffini, C. Boyer, J. Rabeneck, I. F. Sagüés, M. Daffara, C. Baisi.—K. Rahner, "Abstammung des Menschen." in *Lex. f. Theol. u. Kirche*, 1, 81 ff.

82. Bégouen, op. cit., pp. 37–39.

83. *Acta Apost. Sedis* 46 (1954): 25.
G. Rambaldi, *Decreti della Chiesa su l'evoluzione* (Chieri, 1953); Zoltan Alszeghi, "Development in the Doctrinal Formulation of the Church Concerning the Theory of Evolution," in *Concilium* 26 (1967): 25.

84. *De Deo Creante praelectiones scholastico—dogmaticae* (Rome: Ex typographia polyglotta, 1880.)

85. Ibid., p. vii.

86. Ibid., p. 166.

87. Ibid., pp. 405–27.

88. Ibid., p. 354.

89. *Summa contra gentiles,* III, 22. Cited by Mazella, op. cit., p. 125.

90. "Methodus et principia, quibus Doctores scholastici theologiam excoluerunt, temporum nostrorum necessitatibus scientiarumque progressui minime congruunt." Mazella, op. cit., p. vii, syllabus no. 13.

91. See, for example, the series of articles by Guido Mattiussi, "L'Evoluzione è possibile?" in *Scuola cattolica* 2 (1898): 44–54; 1 (1899): 116–31, 305–16, 504–15; 2 (1899): 98–111.

92. *La Teoria dell' evoluzione secundo la scienza e la fede* (Rome, 1948). p. 1.

93. *Acta Apost. Sedis* 33 (1941): 506 ff.

94. M. Flick, "L'Origine del corpo del primo uomo alla luce della filosofia cristiana e della teologia," in *Gregorianum* 29 (1948): 392–416.

95. *Acta Apost. Sedis* 50 (1958): 5–24.

96. Ibid., p. 12.

97. Ibid., p. 11.

98. Ibid., p. 17.

99. Ibid., p. 19.

100. Ibid., p. 20.

101. Ibid., p. 22.

102. Ibid.

103. Ibid., p. 13.

104. "For each sin involves a disturbance of the universal order." Paul VI, *Indulgentiarum doctrina, in Acta Apost. Sedis* 59 (1967): 7.
The argumentation in *Humanae Vitae, in Acta Apost. Sedis* 60 (1968): 481–503, appeals to an order willed by God and is only valid within a medieval frame of reference.
Traces of the medieval way of thinking are thus to be found in documents of the Church until well into the twentieth century. A clear example of this is the letter of Pius X to the French bishops 25 August 1910, in which he condemns *Le Sillon. Acta Apost. Sedis* 2 (1910): 607–33.

Part Three Introduction

1. d'Alembert, "Essai sur les éléments de Philosophie," *Oeuvres complètes,* vol. 1, pp. 121–23; See Robert Niklaus, "The Age of Enlightenment," in *The Age of Enlightenment: Studies Presented to Theodore Besterman* (Edinburgh and London, 1967), pp. 395–412.

2. That is not to say that the data of faith and the cultural situation in which these are communicated can be considered as two separate entities. For a more nuanced analysis of their relation, see E. Schillebeeckx, "Naar een katoliek gebruik van de hermeneutiek," in *Geloof bij kenterend getij: Peilingen in een sekularizerend Kristendom,* ed. by H. van der Linde and H. A. M. Fiolet (Roermond-Maaseik, 1966), p. 78.

270 / The Theologian and His Universe

3. As, for example, Etienne Gilson, *Les Tribulations de Sophie* (Paris, 1968). One of the chapters is entitled "Lamentations parmi les ruines."

Chapter Seven

1. M. Heidegger, *Holzwege* (Frankfurt, 1950), pp. 69–114. (Die Zeit des Weltbildes.)
2. Walter Biemel, "Reflections à propos des recherches husserliennes de la Lebenswelt," in *Tijdschrift voor filosofie* 33 (1971): 659–683.
3. Joseph J. Kockelmans, *The World in Science and Philosophy* (Horizons in Philosophy) (Milwaukee, 1969).
4. Karl Jaspers and Rudolf Bultmann, *Die Frage der Entmythologisierung* (Munich, 1954); see also Karl Jaspers, "Wahrheit und Wissenschaft," in Karl Jaspers and Adolf Portmann, *Naturwissenschaft und Humanismus* (Munich, 1969).
5. Thomas S. Kuhn, *The Structure of Scientific Revolutions*, 2d ed., International Encyclopedia of Unified Science, vols. 1 and 2; *Foundations of the Unity of Science*, vol. 2, no. 2 (University of Chicago Press, 1970).
6. See Michael Polanyi, "Science and Reality," in *The British Journal for the Philosophy of Science* 18 (1968): 177–96; Edward Mackinnon, *Truth and Expression* (New York, 1971), pp. 71–128.
7. See Milton K. Munitz, "On the Use of *Universe* in Cosmology," in *The Monist* 48 (1964): 185–94.
8. Herman Roelants, "De filosofie en het wereldbeeld van de wetenschap," in *Uitzicht van onze wereld* (Bruges, 1964).
9. *Science et synthèse*, Idées NRF, no. 137 (Paris, 1967), p. 75.
10. These are the findings of a team of scholars led by Cyril Ponnamperuna of the NASA Ames Research Centre, Mountain View., Calif.
11. "The chances that such evolutionary development would lead to humanoids may be regarded as not significantly greater than zero." John C. Eccles, *Facing Reality* (New York, 1970), p. 99.
12. See E. A. Milne, *Modern Cosmology and the Christian Idea of God* (Oxford, 1952), p. 151; Harlow Shapley, *Of Stars and Men* (London: Beacon Press, 1958);
Su-Shu Huang, "Life outside the Solar System," in *Scientific American* (1960), pp. 55–63;
Michael Ovenden, *Life in the Universe* (New York, 1971).
13. C. F. von Weizsäcker, *Die Geschichte der Natur* (Gottingen, 1964). See also H. Siedentopf, *Gesetze und Geschichte des Weltalls* (1961); W. Doring, "Naturwissenschaft und historische Weltbetrachtung," in *Universitas* 14 (1959): 971–80.
14. "History itself is an actual part of natural history." Karl Marx, "Nationalökonomie und Philosophie," in *Jugendschriften*, ed. S. Landshut (Stuttgart: Kröner's Taschenausgabe, no. 209, 1964), p. 245.
15. On the various meanings of the words *evolution, evolutionism, transformism,* see André Lalande, *Vocabulaire technique et critique de la Philosophie*, 10th ed. (Paris, 1968).
16. F. C. Bertiau, "The Science of Cosmogony: Its Basic Principles and Problems," in *International Philosophical Quarterly*, vol. 3, pp. 80–93; Jacques Merleau-Ponty, *Cosmologie du XXe siècle*, Bibliothèque des idées (Paris, 1965), p. 432 ff.; George Gamow, *The Creation of the Universe*, rev. ed., Bantam Pathfinders SP118 (New York, 1965); E. Schatzmann, *L'Origine et l'évolution des mondes* (Paris, 1957); John D. North, *The Measure of the Universe. A history of modern Cosmology* (New York and London: Oxford University Press, 1965).
17. See A. Vibert Douglas, "Forty minutes with Einstein," in *Journal of the Royal Astronomical Society of Canada* 50 (1954) 3, p. 99. The same view was held by A. C. B.

Lovell, *The Individual and the Universe* (New York, 1958), p. 108: "My present attitude to the scientific aspects of the problem is therefore neutral in the sense that I do not believe that there yet exist any observational data in favour of any particular contemporary cosmology. See Jacques Merleau-Ponty, "Les Hypothèses en cosmologie," in *Revue internationale de philosophie* 24 (1971): 32–43.

18. Ronald W. Clark, *Einstein. The Life and Times* (New York and Cleveland, 1971), p. 621.

19. In addition to the works already cited, see G. C. McVittie, *Fact and Theory in Cosmology* (London, 1961).

20. See R. H. Dicke, "Gravitation and the Universe," in *The New Universe* (New York, 1968), pp. 117–27.

21. A survey of the research being carried out in this field is to be found in the report of the symposium held in Moscow in 1957 at the initiative of the International Union of Biochemistry and edited by Oparin, Pasynski, Braunstein, and Pavloskaia: *The Origin of Life on Earth* (Moscow, 1959). An abridged edition also appeared under the title *Aspects of the Origin of Life* (1960).—See also M. G. Rutten, *The Geological Aspects of the Origin of Life on Earth* (Amsterdam and New York, 1962); Manfred Eigen, "Self-organization of Matter and the Evolution of Biological Macromolecules," in *Die Naturwissenschaften* 58 (1971): 465–523.

22. Sir Julian Huxley, *Evolution. The Modern Synthesis* (London, 1942), and *Evolution in Action* (London, 1953); Theodosius Dobzhansky, *Evolution, Genetics and Man* (New York, 1955); George Galord Simpson, *The Meaning of Evolution* (New Haven: Yale University Press, 1949); S. A. Barnett, ed., *A Century of Darwin* (London, 1958); T. A. Goudge, *The Ascent of Life: A Philosophical Study of the Theory of Evolution* (London, 1961); Lucien Cuénot and Andrée Tétry, *L'Évolution biologique* (Paris, 1951); Paul Ostoya, *Les Théories de l'évolution* (Paris, 1951); *De evolutieleer na honderd jaar. Een reeks voordrachten gehouden ter gelegenheid van de Universiteitsdag op 21 maart 1959, te Utrecht,* (Haarlem, 1959); etc. . . . Arthur Koestler and J. R. Smythies, eds., *Beyond Reductionism: New Perspectives in the Life Sciences* (New York, 1969). See especially articles by L. von Bertalanffy and C. H. Waddington.

23. Dijksterhuis is clearly aware of the fact that the expression "mechanisation of the world picture" can easily give rise to misunderstanding. What it means, however, is simply that the motion of the heavenly bodies must be explained only by that branch of applied mathematics we know as mechanics. See H. de Vos, *Beknopte geschiedenis van her begrip natuur* (Groningen, 1970), p. 45.

24. See Errol E. Harris, *The Foundations of Metaphysics in Science* (London, 1965). ". . . the macrocosm is a self-contained self-complete system impregnated by a principle of order that expresses and specifies itself in innumerable different ways, giving rise, within the totality, to various new individual physical entities." (p. 155).

25. For a fuller treatment, see Harris, op. cit., pp. 279–84 (Chap. 14, "The Philosophy of Process and Organism").

26. Max Planck, *Autobiography and Other Papers*, trans. Frank Gaynor (New York, 1949), p. 181: ". . . natural science exhibits a rational world order to which nature and mankind are subject, but a world order the inner essence of which is and remains unknowable to us, since only our sense data (which can never be completely excluded) supply evidence for it."

27. J. Monod, *Le Hasard et la nécessité* (Paris, 1970); F. Jacob, *La Logique du vivant: une histoire del'hérédité* (Paris, 1970).

28. G. N. A. Vessey, *Body and Mind: Readings in Philosophy* (London, 1864), p. 12. See also Keith Campbell, *Body and Mind* (London, 1970); this work contains an excellent bibliography. Also P. K. Feyerabend, "Materialism and the Mind-Body Problem," in *Review of Metaphysics* 17 (1963): 49ff.

29. John C. Eccles, *Facing Reality: Philosophical Adventures by a Brain Scientist* (New York, 1970): "There is no evidence whatsoever for the statement often made that, at an adequate level of complexity, computers also would achieve self-consciousness" (p. 4). C. H. Waddington, *The Nature of Life* (London, 1961): ". . . self-awareness is a phenomenon of a kind for which it seems impossible to see how any explanation in terms of observable phenomena could ever be provided" (p. 120). "Awareness can never be constructed theoretically out of our present fundamental scientific concepts, since these contain no element which has any similarity in kind with self-consciousness" (p. 121). J. B. S. Haldane, *The Inequality of Man* (London, 1932). See also Harris, op. cit., pp. 287–309.

Stanley L. Jaki, *Brain, Mind and Computers* (New York, 1969); Raymond Ruyer, *Paradoxes de la conscience et limites de l'automatisme* (Paris, 1966); A. R. Lacey, "Men and Robots," in *Philosophical Quarterly* 10 (1969): 61–72; A. M. Turing, "Computing Machinery and Intelligence," in *Mind* 59 (1950): 433–60; Eccles, op. cit., pp. 2–4, 171–72, 188.

30. Julian Huxley believes that the fact of mind and its evolution still remains a mystery for natural science. The study of this phenomenon, says Huxley, has scarcely begun. See *Science et synthese*, Idees NRF, no. 137 (Paris, 1967), pp. 67–83.

31. See Anna Teresa Tymieniecka, *Why is there Something Rather than Nothing? Prolegomena to the Phenomenology of Cosmic Creation* (Assen, 1966), pp. 77–91.

32. Clark, op. cit., pp. 157, 159, 323, 338, 341–43, 345, 348, 405, 417, 434, 546, 609. Einstein preferred to use the expression "principle of supercausality," while others proposed the term "super controlled chance."
Heisenberg's uncertainty principle or indeterminacy principle states that it is impossible, even in theory, to measure exactly and simultaneously both the position and the velocity of an object. This is owing to the intimate connection in nature between particles and waves in the realm of subatomic particles.

33. "Even if we consider the world, not in terms of intrinsic relations but, as modern statistics does, in terms of occurring facts and their frequency, the statistical laws in which these arbitrary facts are expressed obviously appeal to a superior order." Tymieniecka, op. cit., p. 83 ff.

34. Part 2, Chap. 21. See Alfred Schutz, *Collected Papers*, pt. 1 (The Hague, 1964), p. 297 ff.

35. James, op. cit., p. 293.

36. "The subjective reality of the world hangs on the thin thread of conversation." Peter Berger, *The Sacred Canopy* (New York: Doubleday, 1969) p. 17.

37. Peter Berger and Thomas Luckmann have given fuller treatment of this. See *The Social Construction of Reality* (New York, 1967); also Alfred Schutz, *Der Aufbau der sozialen Welt* (Vienna, 1960), and *Collected Papers* (The Hague, 1964–67).

38. This point was stressed by M. Merleau-Ponty:
"Everything I know of the world, even by science, I know from my own point of view or from the experience of the world without which the symbols of science would mean nothing. The whole universe of science is constructed on the world of lived experience, and if we wish to consider science itself, giving an accurate evaluation of its meaning and scope, we must first recall this experience of the world of which it is the secondary expression." *Phénoménologie de la perception* (Paris, 1945), pp. 11–111.

39. Cited in Buytendijk's introduction to Eugene Minkowski, *Het menselijk aspekt van de Kosmos* (Utrecht, 1967), p. viii.

40. See A. Dondeyne, "L'Historicité dans la philosophie contemporaine," in *Revue de philosophie de Louvain* 54 (1956): 456–77.

41. From Einstein's contribution to *Living Philosophies: A series of Intimate Credos* (New York, 1931), p. 6.

42. ". . . In this materialistic age of ours the serious scientific workers are the only profoundly religious people. . . . His religious feeling [of the true scientist] takes the form of a rapturous amazement at the harmony of natural law, which reveals an intelligence of such superiority that, compared with it, all the systematic thinking and acting of human beings is an utterly insignificant reflexion." *The World As I see It* (New York, 1934), pp. 266–67.

43. Eccles, op. cit., pp. viii, 6, 101, and 189.

Chapter Eight

1. See Joan E. Jarque, *Bibliographie générale des oeuvres et articles sur Pierre Teilhard de Chardin* (Freiburg, CH, 1970. To this should be added F. Bravo, *La Vision de l'histoire chez Teilhard de Chardin* (Paris, 1970); Philip Hefner, *The Promise of Teilhard* (Philadelphia, 1970); P. Schellenbaum, *Christ dans l'énérgetique Teilhardienne* (Paris, 1971); Claude Cuénot, *Ce que Teilhard a vraiment dit* (Paris, 1972).

J. S. Oosthuizen, *Van Plotinus naar Theilhard de Chardin: Een studie over de metamorfose van de westerse werkelijkheidsbeeld*, proefschrift Univ. Amsterdam (Amsterdam: Rodopi, 1974).

2. N. M. Wildiers, "Teilhard de Chardin et la théologie catholique," in Attila Szekeres, ed., *Le Christ cosmique de Teilhard de Chardin* (Paris, 1969), pp. 151–74.

3. See, for example, *The Phenomenon of Man* (London: Collins; and New York: Harper & Row, 1959). *Man's Place in Nature* (London: Collins; and New York: Harper & Row, 1966).

4. *Oeuvres,* vol. 10, p. 126.

5. See R. Hooykaas, *The Principle of Uniformity in Geology, Biology and Theology* (Leyden, 1963) p. xii.

6. Ibid., pp. 145–62. See also Bravo, op. cit., pp. 238–43.

7. "In the specific instance of the present Essay, I think it important to point out that two basic assumptions go hand in hand to support and govern every development of the theme. The first is the primacy accorded to the psychic and to thought in the stuff of the universe, and the second is the 'biological' value attributed to the social fact around us.

"The pre-eminent significance of man in nature, and the organic nature of mankind; these are two assumptions that one may start by trying to reject, but without accepting them I do not see how it is possible to give a full and coherent account of the phenomenon of man." *The Phenomenon of Man* (London: Collins, 1959), p. 30.

8. See *Comment je crois* (Paris, 1969), pp. 124–29.

9. Similarly, when radio waves were discovered after the Second World War, it was initially thought that these were peculiar to the Milky Way. It was later shown that the transmission of radio waves had to be considered as an inherent property of nebulae. See Bernard Lovell, *The New Universe* (New York, 1968), p. 20.

10. John C. Eccles also believes that man cannot be considered as an epiphenomenon: "My philosophical position is diametrically opposite to those who relegate conscious experience to the meaningless role of an epiphenomenon" (op. cit., p. 1). For Jacques Monod, on the other hand, man, like all living things, is merely the result of chance and should not really have existed. *Science Year, The World Book Science Annual* (1971), p. 384.

11. G. G. Simpson is surely right when he affirms that "The fossil record shows very clearly that there is no central line leading steadily, in a goal-directed way, from a protozoan to man. Instead, there has been continual and extremely intricate branching,

and whatever course we follow through the branches, there are repeated changes both in the rate and in the direction of evolution. Man is the end of one ultimate twig. . . ." *This view of Life: The World of an Evolutionist* (New York, 1964).

12. "After having been regarded for many years as a scientifically subsidiary or an-amalous element of the universe, mankind will in the end be recognised as a funda-mental phenomenon—the supreme phenomenon of nature: that in which, in a unique complexity of material and moral factors, one of the principal acts of universal evolution is not only experienced but lived by us." *Science and Christ*, p. 97.

13. "There is of course an entrenched materialist orthodoxy, both philosophical and scientific, that rises to defend its dogmas with a self-righteousness scarcely equalled in the ancient days of religious dogmatism." Eccles, op. cit., p. 151.

14. See Eccles, op. cit., p. 91.

15. Ibid., p. 142.

16. See, for example, *The Phenomenon of Man*, p. 104.

17. Ibid., pp. 108–9.

18. "Man emerged from a general groping of the world." Ibid., p. 189.
"Evolution proceeds by the preferential use of strokes of chance." *Oeuvres*, 7, p. 303.

19. See, for instance *Science and Christ*, p. 38 *Oeuvres*, 9, p. 66.

20. Offensive though it may be, this is the only correct expression to characterize Teilhard's project.

21. As, for example, Langdon Gilkey, *Naming the Whirlwind: The Renewal of God-Lan-guage* (Indianapolis and New York, 1969), p. 187.

22. "Deprived of the Cosmos and of history man finds himself thrown back upon the unique relation with God. Whether this be negative or positive, existentialism—Christian or atheistic—is the result of a crisis that has deprived man of the natural and the historical order, leaving him naked and alone in the face of a mysterious destiny." Raymond Aron, *Dimensions de la conscience historique* (Paris, 1961), pp. 28–29.

23. See especially Christopher Mooney, *Teilhard de Chardin and the Mystery of Christ* (New York, 1964).

24. "Le principe christique"; the focal point of Teilhard's work is his Christ-cosmic conception of the world. See especially *Le Christique* (1955; also in *Oeuvres*, 10).

25. See A. Hulsbosch, *De Schepping Gods: Schepping, zonde en verlossing in het evolution-istische wereldbeeld* (Roermond and Masseik, 1963).

26. Carl E. Braaten rightly points out that while the first two questions are much discussed in philosophy, the third question is mostly left unanswered. See Martin E. Marty and Dean G. Peerman, eds., *New Theology*, no. 5 (New York and London, 1968), pp. 90–91.

27. *Contra Faustum*, XXVII. *PL* 42, 418.

28. "The only universe capable of containing the human person is an irreversibly 'personalising' universe." *The Phenomenon of Man* (London: Collins, 1959), p. 290.

29. "In the final analysis (or rather in the final synthesis) one can say that ultimately the person is for the whole and not the whole for the human person. But it is because at the final moment the whole itself has become Person." *Oeuvres*, 7, p. 58.

30. "Responsive to the acquisitions of modern thought Christianity finally reflects on the fact that its three fundamental 'personalistic' mysteries are in reality but three aspects of the same process (Christogenesis): its motor principle (Creation), its unifying mechanism (the Incarnation) and its elevatory force (Redemption): all of which hurls us into complete evolution." *Oeuvres*, 10, p. 183.

31. ". . . I looked, and I discovered, as in a state of ecstasy, that I was immersed in God by the whole of nature." *Ecrits du temps de la guerre*, p. 49.

32. "... the Incarnation is an act co-extensive with the duration of the World." *Science and Christ*, p. 64 (*Oeuvres*, 9, p. 92).

Chapter Nine

1. C. G. Jung, *Psychologie und Religion* (Zurich and Leipzig, 1949), p. 16.
2. George A. Lindbeck, *The Future of Catholic Theology* (Philadelphia, 1969), pp. 9–25 ("Vision of a World Renewed").
3. *Wachtend op God* (Utrecht, 1967).
4. *Twentieth-Century Religious Thought* (London, 1963).
5. *Orientatie: nieuwe Wegen in de Theologie* (Baarn, 1971); Voortgezette Orientatie: nieuwe wegen in de Theologie (Baarn, 1971).
6. *Aggiornamento: de Doorbraak van een nieuwe katholieke Theologie* (Baarn, 1968); "Keurmeester van moderne Theologie," in *Tijdschrift voor Theologie* 12 (1972): 445–60.
7. "Thus, the human race has passed from a rather static concept of reality to a more dynamic, evolutionary one. In consequence, there has arisen a new series of problems, a series as important as can be, calling for new efforts of analysis and synthesis." *The Pastoral Constitution on the Church in the Modern World* (Art. 5).
8. H. Rondet, "Le Problème de la nature pure en la théologie du XVIe siècle," in *Recherches des sciences religieuses* 35 (1948): 481–522; P. Smulders, "De oorsprong van de teorie der zuivere natuur," in *Bijdragen* 10 (1949): 105–27.
9. See Ben van Onna, "The State of Paradise and Evolution," in *Concilium* 26 (1967): 137–46.
10. Leszek Kolalowski, "Jesus Christus—Prophet und Reformator," in *Geist und Ungeist christlicher Traditionen* (Stuttgart, 1971), pp. 21–43.
11. W. K. Grossouw, "De vrijheid van de christen volgens Paulus," in *Tijdschrift voor Theologie* 9 (1969): 269–82.
12. See J. B. Metz, Jürgen Moltmann and Willi Oelmuller, *Kirche im Process der Aufklarung* (Munich and Mainz, 1970).
13. See Ernst Käsemann, *Jesus Means Freedom* (Philadelphia, 1970), translation of *Der Ruf der Freiheit* (Tübingen, 1968); J. B. Metz, "Kirchliche Autorität im Anspruch der Freiheitsgeschichte," in Metz, Moltmann and Oelmuller, op. cit., pp. 53–90.
See also J. Sperna Weiland, *Voortgezette Orientatie* (Baarn, 1971), pp. 95–96; J. Moltmann, "Die Revolution der Freiheit," in *Perspektiven der Theologie* (Munich and Mainz, 1968. *Religion, Revolution and the Future* (New York, 1969), pp. 3–18,
On freedom as characteristic of Christ's personality, see Paul M. Van Buren, *The Secular Meaning of the Gospel* (New York, 1965 [1963]), pp. 121–24, and G. Bornkamm, *Jesus von Nazareth* (Stuttgart, 1956).
Hegel considered the concept of freedom as an essential characteristic of Christianity. See Introduction to Berlin edition of *Geschichte der Philosophie* (1820); *Hegel's History of Philosophy*, trans. E. S. Haldane, 3 vols. (London, 1892). The freedom that Christ brought into the world was called by Hegel "the principle of absolute freedom in God." See Wolfhart Pannenberg, *Gottesgedanke und menschliche Freiheit* (Göttingen, 1972), pp. 78–113. C. von Korvin-Kransinski, *Makrokosmos und Mikrokosmos in religions geschichtlicher Sicht* (Dusseldorf, 1960).
14. See, for example, Ernst Benz, *Evolution and Christian Hope: Man's Concept of the Future from the Early Fathers to Teilhard de Chardin* (Garden City, N. Y.), 1966; German ed. 1965; Martin E. Marty and Dean G. Peerman, eds., *New Theology*, no. 5 (New York and London, 1968); Frederick Herzog, ed., *The Future of Hope: Theology as Eschatology*

(New York, 1970); Carl E. Braaten, *The Future of God: The Revolutionary Dynamics of Hope* (New York 1969); Karl Rahner, "Zur Theologie der Hoffnung," in *Schriften zur Theologie* 8 (Einsiedeln and Zurich, 1967): 561–79;

E. Schillebeeckx, *God, the Future of Man* (New York and London, 1968); Ewert Cousins, ed., *Hope and the Future of Man* (Philadelphia, 1972); Walter H. Capps, *Time Invades the Cathedral: Tensions in the School of Hope* (Philadelphia, 1972).

15. See, for instance, Harvey Cox in *The Future of Hope*, p. 77.

16. Fred L. Polak, *De toekomst in verleden tijd. Cultuur-futuristische verkenningen* (Zeist, 1958), p. 13.

17. Ibid.

18. Ernst Käsemann, *Exegetische Versuche und Besinnungen*, vol. 2 (Göttingen, 1968), p. 100. Cf. J. Möltmann, "Theology as Eschatology," in *The Future of Hope*, op. cit., pp. 6–9.

19. Jürgen Moltmann, "Die Kategorie Novum in der Christliche Theologie," in *Perspektiven der Theologie, Gesammelte Aufsätze* (Munich and Mainz, 1968), pp. 174–88.

20. See J. Moltmann, "Theologische Kritik der politischen Religion," in *Kirche im Process der Aufklärung*, op. cit., p. 11.

21. *Tijdschrift voor Theologie* 12 (1972): 145–243. This issue is devoted to political theology and contains a useful bibliography.

22. ". . . political theology is not the same as politics based on theology. Nor does it mean a factual political program developed from Christian faith. There are no specific Christian solutions to the problem of this world for which a 'political theology' would have to develop a theoretical framework." Dorothy Solle, "The Role of Political Theology in Relation to the Liberation of Men," in James M. Robinson, ed., *Religion and the Humanizing of Man* (Plenary addresses at the International Congress of Learned Societies in the Field of Religion), Los Angeles, 1972, pp. 137–134.

23. See T. Rendtorff and H. E. Todt, eds., *Theologie der Revolutie* (Bern, 1968); Richard Shaull, *Uitdaging aan kerk en maatschappij* (Bern, 1972); Jürgen Moltmann, *Religion, Revolution and the Future* (New York, 1969).

24. Ernst Bloch, *Im Christentum steckt die Revolte* (Zurich, 1971).

25. Douglas Browning, ed., *Philosophers of Process* (New York, 1965); Delwin Brown, Ralph E. James Jr., and Gene Reeves, eds., *Process Philosophy and Christian Thought* (Indianapolis and New York, 1971); Ewert H. Cousins, ed., *Process Theology* (New York, 1971).

26. See in this connection Schubert M. Ogden, *The Reality of God and Other Essays* (New York, 1966), p. 56 also in Cousins, op. cit., pp. 119–34; and Charles Hartshorne, *The Development of Process Philosophy*, in Cousins, op. cit., pp. 47–64.

27. Hartshorne, op. cit., p. 53.

28. Hartshorne uses the terms *surrelative* and *surrelativism;* see *The Divine Reality: A Social Conception of God* (Yale University Press, 1964), pp. vii, 21, 76, 88, 90, 99.

29. C. Hartshorne, *Man's Vision of God and the Logic of Theism* (Hamden, Conn.: 1964), p. 3.

30. Bernard M. Loomer, "Whitehead's Method of Empirical Analysis," in Cousins, op. cit., p. 80.

31. Hartshorne prefers to speak of God's "dipolarity."

32. *Process and Reality: An Essay in Cosmology* (New York, 1969 [1929]), p. 413.

INDEX OF NAMES

279

The Author

MAX WILDIERS was born in Antwerp, Belgium. Since receiving his doctorate in theology from the Gregorian University in Rome, his particular field of interest has been the relation between theology and the natural sciences. He has taught at the universities of Leuven (Louvain) and San Francisco as well as at various other centers of higher education. His publications include *An Introduction to Teilhard de Chardin* (New York: Harper & Row). For the present work, *The Theologian and his Universe,* which originally appeared in Dutch and has already been translated into German and Polish, the author has been awarded the triennial Belgian National Prize.